The Seals:
A Panoramic View of the First Half of The Seven Year Tribulation

FIRST PRINTING

Billy Crone

Cover Design:
Chris Taylor

To Tom Roseberry and Sandy Hall.

Both of you have been a wonderful source of encouragement to me,
and without your help and expertise,
over the many book projects we've co-labored in,
I would not have been able to share God's truth,
in such a professional and practical way.

Thank you Tom, not only for our original conversation
in the parking lot of Sunrise which began our friendship,
but thank you as well for being the first person to speak up on my behalf,
at a time when it was so desperately needed.

Thank you Sandy for responding to that original radio interview,
for it has proven to be God's divine appointment that led you to Sunrise,
to become a much needed blessing for the Church family,
and a personal blessing to my own family as well.

For these things and many more, I praise the
goodness and profound wisdom
of God Almighty
for both of you.
I love you both.

Contents

Preface...*vii*

PART 1:   **The Introduction to the Seals**

1. *After the Rapture*... 11
2. *The Blessing of the Seals*.................................25
3. *The Prelude to the Seals*.................................35
4. *The Timing of the Seals*................................. 47

PART 2:   **The Breaking of the Seals**

5. *The Breaking of the Antichrist Seal*......................59
6. *The Breaking of the War Seal*............................115
7. *The Breaking of the Famine Seal*......................... 137
8. *The Breaking of the Death Seal*........................... 175
9. *The Breaking of the Martyrdom Seal*....................... 227
10. *The Breaking of the Doomsday Seal*.........................281

PART 3:   **The Final Warning of the Seals**

11. *The Breaking of the Final Seal*.................................367

How to Receive Jesus Christ.............. 391
Notes...393

Preface

Even though I have been teaching Bible prophecy and expounding on prophecy related issues for many years now, two things struck me like a ton of bricks as I wrote this book. First, I was blown away by the profoundly repetitive nature that God was drilling into our heads in Revelation Chapter 6 alone of how *His wrath* will be being poured out during *the entire* Seven Year Tribulation. I say that because there are certain entities who try to piece up God's wrath during this prophetic time frame. They say His wrath is only poured out in the final quarter, or even in just the second half. They then further compound their fatal error by saying these horrible events recorded for us in the first half or three-quarters is not attributed to God's wrath at all, but rather it's supposed to be due to man or even or satan's wrath if you can believe that. This is not only ludicrous and blasphemous, but there is no way one can arrive at this faulty conclusion if you deal honestly with the verbiage of the original text and the events outlined for us in God's Word concerning the Seal Judgments that make up the first half.

Secondly, I was surprised with an outpouring of sorrow. Never before had I gone down so deep in a study on these passages. I knew the events of the Seal Judgments, the first half of the Seven Year Tribulation were bad, but for some reason we Christians have a tendency to think that the first half is not as bad as it really is. We tend to downplay it and focus more on the second half, which is definitely worse than the first half. This is precisely why it's called The Great Tribulation. However, once I began to peel back the layers of what the Bible was saying in regards to the first half, the Seal Judgments, I couldn't stop thinking how horrific these events were as well. In fact, there were several times I was literally weeping as I was writing. Then I was flooded with the realization that this is still only the halfway point of the Seven Year Tribulation, the worst is yet to come. Cleary God was sending home a message that's been in His Word the whole time, "You don't want to be in *any part* of the Seven Year Tribulation, first or second half. It's *all* His wrath through and through and it's only through the love and mercy of His Son Jesus Christ that one can escape these horrible wrathful events to come. One last piece of advice. When you are through reading this book then will you please *READ YOUR BIBLE*? I mean that in the nicest possible way. Enjoy, and I'm looking forward to seeing you someday!

Billy Crone
Las Vegas, Nevada
2018

Part I

The Introduction to the Seals

Chapter One

After the Rapture

The first call comes into an emergency call center, "911, what is your emergency?" A mom is hysterically screaming: "HELP PLEASE, HELP, my little boy just disappeared." The 911 dispatcher replies, "Ma'am, what do you mean? Has someone taken him?" "No, I was holding him in my arms and he's just gone. Help, please help."

"Flight 418, this is Delta Tower. Please confirm your plans to descend. Flight 418 please check in, OVER." Nervous silence fills the tower's control room. Turning to her supervisor the air traffic controller gasps, "Sir, Flight 418 is not responding."

Nervous travelers begin to shout, "What's going on? We are passing our destination." (But the cockpit is empty, and the flight crew has disappeared.)

A husband and wife are heading home from a ballgame, following a car on highway 39, when the car they are following suddenly veers off the road. The husband jumps out and rushes to the car, only to discover the car is empty. A nurse runs out of a hospital nursery screaming, "ALL THE BABIES ARE GONE!"

A twenty-one-year-old girl is dancing the night away at her favorite nightclub. Just a few hours earlier, she had cussed out her parents and told them to never preach to her again. She quickly dials her parents' phone frantically, only to hear it ring and ring. She hangs up and dials their cell phones, only to get voice mail. Her heart races as she recalls her dad's warning, "Honey, please turn to Jesus…He is coming soon."

A man pulling his car into his favorite restaurant flips off another driver as the car races by and crashes into the building. Angry but shocked, he jumps out to see what just happened. As he opens the door, nobody is there. A terrified panicking woman rushes out of the restaurant screaming, "Where is my baby? Someone, help! Anybody! Where is my baby?"

The man's heart begins to race as he immediately dials his home phone…no answer. He jumps in his car and drives frantically, turning onto the interstate. Cars are piled up everywhere. He illegally backs up the off-ramp and, almost simultaneously, a 757 airplane crashes in the distance. His mind is besieged with fear. Racing to his house he finds no one home. He shouts for his wife. He runs into the living room and there sits a Bible and her clothes—she is GONE!

A husband and father, puts a shotgun to his mouth, tears rolling as he looks at a family picture and his kids' clothes on the floor. He knows what has happened and cries out his last words before pulling the trigger, "Why didn't I listen?" "911, what is your emergency?" "911, what is your emergency?" Report after report of loss and chaos continue to pour in.

BREAKING NEWS...CNM... Lead anchor Andrew Cooper reporting: "Suddenly, without warning, seemingly thousands, if not millions, of people have disappeared. Meanwhile, 911 emergency response systems are crashing due to the overload of calls. A roving reporter stands by with a word from White House correspondents.

This just in, a one-hundred-car pile-up on a Los Angeles freeway...wait, another report...New York subway systems are reporting a major subway crash. The president and the first lady are getting ready to speak to the nation. The word is that they are currently on a conference call with world leaders, and as again, Andrew, this is not only a national crisis, but reports are coming in literally from around the world. The reports keep coming. Thousands of people have just died in one of the worst airplane crashes in history. A 757 airliner just crashed into downtown Chicago and exploded, blowing up five apartment complexes."

Barbara Walters addresses her audience explaining: "We all are at such loss...we, with the millions of you viewers share in your sorrow and shock. We are saddened with such grief as we have been unable to contact Elizabeth and it appears her husband and children have vanished as well.

All the while...fellow cast members are seen in the background hugging and consoling one another.... deep wails and groans come from the audience... 'What do we do...please tell us...what do we do?'" Fights break out in an effort to be heard. Barbara asks for calm, but to no avail.

Outside the studio the streets are perilous hazards as people walk like zombies, having not slept for hours. Many mothers and fathers are seen screaming out names of children.... "Jody!" shouts one delirious woman. "JODY, please Jody...OH GOD where is my daughter?"

Thousands stand in the streets as huge TV monitors in NY City show Oprah coming on live with a New Age author/teacher. Oprah begins, "I am not going to pretend to have any answers, but my mentor is here to answer questions that I am sure many of you have.

Below on the screen, scrolls a list of thousands of the missing with a toll free number for family members to call."

One man sits in front of his TV surfing, hoping to find any answers. He stumbles across a well-known Christian network and is stunned to see a famous minister addressing his international viewing audience. "Ladies and gentlemen, in my deepest horror I stand before you...I am so humbled and ashamed. For years I have preached a message that didn't line up with this book... (holds up the Bible) but right now with everything in me I beg you all to forgive me and LISTEN! What has taken place is an event the Bible foretold that I never dreamed would occur in my lifetime."

BREAKING: A MESSAGE FROM THE PRESIDENT OF THE UNITED STATES OF AMERICA

"Today...I myself, the House and Senate in complete agreement, have decided to declare a state of martial law. Due to the extreme traveling conditions and the desperation of so many, we are setting 9 PM as curfew. At the current time I have dispatched our national guard with the assistance of homeland security officials to collect all weaponry. Any resistance will lead to instantaneous arrest. There will be no trial, you will be held indefinitely."

As the President speaks, one of his staff brings him an urgent message. The President becomes ashen as he turns back to address the nation. "Ladies and gentlemen, it appears our enemies are seizing upon this time as an opportunity. I have just been informed that nuclear weapons in Pakistan, Iran and Russia have been deployed in our direction...I will be with you directly with further instructions."

Instantly national warning sirens begin to blare. Wails and screams are heard. Gun shots blaze as numerous people shoot towards others and many shoots themselves.

"ESPN SPORTS CENTER coming to you live from what was supposed to be home of this year's SUPER BOWL. Numerous NFL players are along beside me here to tell what their views, especially one of the Arizona Cardinals who lost in the first round of the playoffs, are saying. Here is one of their offensive linemen. Thanks for joining us. Please share what's on your heart." "Ya know, our former quarterback Kurt Warner had warned us all that there would come a day when this type of event would happen."

ESPN analyst: "What are you referring to?"

Cardinal player: "Kurt said it was like a catching away or some sorta rapture or something. I mean almost daily he would tell us about Jesus and, dude, we admired him and respected him, but it wasn't for me or many of my teammates, but I wish I would have listened to him now."

Billy O'Reilly clip: "Tonight on Bill O'Reilly, join us as Glenn Beck shares why we are still here. But first here's a memo.

Just 24 hours ago, thousands, literally millions of people just simply vanished from the face of the earth and no one seems to have the answer. But Talking Points is here to set the record straight. It has been hidden for years what really happened in Roswell NM, and as of yesterday it has come to haunt us. It's Talking Points' view that a type of selective elimination has taken place for purposes of which we are not yet aware. But I assure you, I and my staff will go to great lengths to find the answer.

Coming up Next will be my interview with Glenn Beck as he discusses how he predicted a similar event but is still here." Breaking to commercial. "Are you in deep sorrow, seeking answers and someone to talk to ...please call now 1-888-talk 2 the missing through John Edwards."

O'Reilly: "We are here with Glenn Beck. Sir, you had stated over the last few months that you believe the whole world as we know it would change in the blink of an eye, yet you are one of the ones still here. What say you?"

Glenn: "Bill, with all shame and humility I say that I was deceived. As you know, Bill, I had a major bout with alcohol, and to overcome it I turned to religion, and religion is what I got. Unfortunately, I realize now that it is a relationship with Jesus Christ. As you know, Bill, there is a stunning similarity to all the victims, or should I say the fortunate ones. They all were professing born-again Christians."

O'Reilly interrupts: "Oh come on, Glenn, you don't buy into that far right ideology. If you can prove that I will buy you a steak dinner." Beck breaking down begins to sob. "Bill, with all that is in me, YES I BELIEVE THAT. You are crazy enough to believe that some aliens have come. I am choosing to believe what the Bible has said. Bill, out of no disrespect... your famous university, you so gleefully trumpet...started as a school of ministry, you know? Please, Bill...please, America...hear me and join with me in turning your heart to Jesus NOW!"

Day Care Traumatized: "Coming Live from Webrainwash Kids Day Care, this is Molly Madison with KORO NEWS, Atlanta. As you can hear, hundreds of parents are protesting this day care center. Many have been here all night. Pleas of desperation for answers are coming (wails in the background continue). I have with me one parent who has a plea, this is Cindy Jo. Mam, what would you like to say?"

Holding up a picture of her missing child and her voice breaking she sobs, "Please...anyone, if you have seen this child...my child...please call...PLEEAASE"

News lady: "Thanks, Cindy...and yes, please, if anybody watching this has any answers please call our studio. Joining me now is day care worker Sabrina to tell her story. Sabrina, thanks for your time. Please share with us what happened here yesterday."

Sabrina: "Yesterday during our sing along hour the kids were singing He's Got the Whole World in His hands when instantly they all vanished...I MEAN RIGHT BEFORE MY EYES THEY JUST VANISHED! I feel so hurt for all the parents, but I PROMISE YOU...this daycare did nothing wrong! My little boy is gone, too, and I am in complete shock as to what to do."

BREAKING NEWS President Barak Obama: "As I had warned, nuclear missiles have been fired and I am sad to report that just moments ago, although our defense systems were able to destroy four of the seven warheads, 3 nuclear weapons penetrated our defenses and I have just received word that the cities of Los Angeles and Kansas City, and the whole southern half of Florida have been destroyed. As part of our MAD agreement (mutually assured destruction) we have responded in kind to all three nations.

Secretary of State...Hillary Clinton is en route to an emergency meeting of the UN. Vice President Biden is in hiding and I myself will be in security session with our military generals. Our heart goes out to all the victims and their families. I assure you we will be taking all necessary steps to bring calm and peace to this most devastating hour.

At this moment I ask all citizens to convene at local stations being set up by our national guard to verify citizenship with an emergency ID that is already in place. I realize there will be long lines and hours of inconvenience but in this extreme moment of uncertainty all security measures must be taken."

Just a short while later ...Geraldo Rivera, FOX NEWS, flying in a nuclear-safe news helicopter, surveys the damage in Kansas City and screams into the microphone: "MR. O'REILLY, THIS IS THE MOST DEVASTATING SIGHT I HAVE EVER WITNESSED! Not even in my worst dreams, Bill...complete annihilation. Everything, and I mean everything that is still standing, is on fire."

Bill interjects: "Geraldo, any sign of life?"

Geraldo: "NO, BILL ...NO!!! IT'S GONE...KANSAS CITY IS GONE ALONG WITH EVERYBODY WHO LIVED HERE!"

Privately Katie Couric sits in her prep room staring off in the distance, recalling her interview with Alaska Governor Sarah Palin. In haunting detail, she recalls the joy and peace in Palin's life and the instant awareness that the Palin family is now missing. Katie knows in her heart that, despite years of her rebellion towards God, she has known all along what she heard years ago in Vacation Bible School....that, yes indeed, the BIBLE was and IS the WORD OF GOD. In moments she must go and face the nation. "Do I betray my profession, or do I betray my newfound faith? No, it's a must...I must tell the world the TRUTH! Jesus has come back for His Bride."

"This is Wolf Blitzer, CNN, reporting from the White House Lawn. Moments ago, we were told that an apparent suicide attempt just took place by a top staffer, this just coming moments after an earlier report that both her daughters have been reported missing.

Insiders are saying our President has reacted furiously to all attempts to bring any sympathetic gestures. We will be back shortly with further details!"

Cuts to a commercial.... GOLD LINE FOR TIMES LIKE THESE...

"This is CNN's Wolf Blitzer back with you live from the White House where just a short time ago it was confirmed by a top Presidential aide that the First Lady is receiving medical attention after a failed suicide attempt. White House staff has informed us that the President is just moments away from addressing the nation concerning the welfare of his own family and this nation. While we wait let's send it back to you, Anderson."

"Anderson Cooper here at CNN headquarters bringing you up to speed. Again, in the last 48 hours we have seen our world turned upside down...recapping, first the instantaneous disappearance of millions of global citizens and, as if that wasn't bad enough, it catapulted one disaster after another....as of one hour ago there have been over 20 plane crashes reported across the globe with the loss of life totaling in the hundreds of thousands. Interstates and highways are littered with abandoned cars that will take weeks to clear. Amtrak is reporting they too are at least a week away from being up and running.

And as reported, 3 nuclear bombs have hit our nation's cities destroying Los Angeles, California, Kansas City, Missouri, and the southern half of the state of Florida. And just 4 hours ago following the MAD response of the USA, Iran,

Russia and Pakistan have all been hit with a nuclear attack and we are still awaiting word on its effects. As we all know it will be catastrophic!!! Wall Street as well as all global markets have been put on hold, and the markets have been stayed as there is no way to calculate the extreme consequences this will have on the worldwide markets."

BREAKING NEWS ALERT, President Obama: "Ladies and Gentlemen, citizens of the USA and the world, I stand before you a broken man. Normal protocol in more certain times would allow for myself to keep all personal issues relating to the welfare of my young precious daughters in the utmost of secrecy. But I and my wife, like all of you have suffered loss at this most distressful time. After discovering that one of our most trusted friends, like hundreds of thousands of you and your children and family members, is missing; that revelation was more than my wife could bear and as it has been reported in the last 12 hours my wife made a vain attempt to end her life. Thankfully that attempt failed, and she is with her physician and her mother recovering. Our spiritual mentor, Reverend Wright, is by her side as well.

And as such I have taken the liberty to speak with him privately, leading up to this address. I have also spoken with several other spiritual advisors, and we have conferred that the reckless attempts of many to suggest that somehow this was an event relegated to a select group of people in this multi-cultural world are both narrow minded and prejudicial, and at a time such as this I will neither tolerate nor standby as, in the position and authority I have. I find it paramount to take this opportunity to silence all voices of hate and bigotry. So, effective immediately, during this time of declared Martial Law, I am instituting a moratorium of any mention of what is being called The Rapture. It will be equal to hate speech, and the prosecution of such crimes will be severe and swift.

Next, addressing the grievous attacks by our known enemies and our swift and aggressive retaliation: Again let me say how much I sympathize with all of you suffering this atrocity...but let it be known all around the world that we have successfully struck back with such fervor that not only are those nations' leaders now extending their deepest regret and urgent requests for face to face meetings but the whole world has asked for an emergency conference to be held right here at the UN headquarters. Prime Minister Putin has recommended that I take the lead of ushering in a very strong unified response globally in reacting to the devastating loss of all those missing and those who have died due to such events. Over the next days and hours, I will be asking all of you, as well as, all of the citizens of the world to remain calm, to observe our curfew, and to stay tuned for further instructions. I have the utmost confidence in the goodness of the people of the world, and in no short order, I believe with the right spirit and will, we all can come to a place of change that will take us to new heights and put this god forsaken time behind us. Until next time…Peace and Farewell."

In a small country farmhouse, a man hugs his wife as she sobs for her children. They had always sent their kids to church services but never went themselves. They know their children are safe…they know they are with Jesus, but they also know what's ahead. The husband's heart begins to fail as his mind torments him with the sermons he heard that warned of THE GREAT TRIBULATION.

So many things will change…"[1]

The depiction just presented is not only an eye opening, shocking experience to say the least, but it's merely a tiny piece of the traumatic jaw dropping reality that awaits those who reject Jesus Christ as their Lord and Savior today. This is their future. And lest you think this is just an emotional embellishment and/or that we're over-dramatizing this reenactment for personal effect, you need to realize it's based on actual events that the Bible says are coming one day to our planet. And might I add, very soon.

Following the Rapture of the Church which, by the way, could happen at any moment, the Bible says that all unbelievers on the planet will be ushered into a period of time called the 7-year tribulation, which is literally the worst time in the history of mankind. I didn't say that, Jesus did.

Matthew 24:21-22 "For then there will be great distress, unequaled from the beginning of the world until now – and never to be equaled again. If those days had not been cut short, no one would survive, but for the sake of the elect those days will be shortened."

The 7-year Tribulation will be so bad Jesus says, that if God didn't keep it to just 7 years no one would be left alive! Obviously, it's a time-frame you want to escape, which can only be avoided by getting saved now through Jesus Christ and Him alone. And for those of you wondering why this Tribulation period is kept to exactly 7 years, let's revisit that question from our previous study, *The Rapture: Don't Be Deceived*. The answer is found in the Book of Daniel.

Daniel 9:20-27 "While I was speaking and praying, confessing my sin and the sin of my people Israel and making my request to the LORD my God for his holy hill – while I was still in prayer, Gabriel, the man I had seen in the earlier vision, came to me in swift flight about the time of the evening sacrifice. He instructed me and said to me, 'Daniel, I have now come to give you insight and understanding. As soon as you began to pray, an answer was given, which I have come to tell you, for you are highly esteemed. Therefore, consider the message and understand the vision: Seventy 'sevens' are decreed for your people and your holy city to finish transgression, to put an end to sin, to atone for wickedness, to bring in everlasting righteousness, to seal up vision and prophecy and to anoint the most holy. Know and understand this: From the issuing of the decree to restore and rebuild Jerusalem until the Anointed One, the ruler, comes, there will be seven 'sevens,' and sixty-two 'sevens.' It will be rebuilt with streets and a trench, but in times of trouble. After the sixty-two 'sevens,' the Anointed One will be cut off and will have nothing. The people of the ruler who will come will destroy the city and the sanctuary. The end will come like a flood: War will continue until the end, and desolations have been decreed. He will confirm a covenant with many for one 'seven.' In the middle of the 'seven' he will put an end to sacrifice and offering. And on a wing of the temple he will set up an abomination that causes desolation, until the end that is decreed is poured out on him.'"

If you've ever wondered why it's specifically a "7" year Tribulation and not 94 or 135 or even a 2-year Tribulation, here it is. This is where it all began. The 7-year Tribulation is the final "seven" of "Seventy sevens" also known as the 70th week prophecy of the Book of Daniel. (KJV translates "sevens" as "week" as in "seven" days in a week) There will be a "total" of 70 sevens until God basically wraps up history and fulfills the rest of His promises that He made to the Jewish people. However, after 62 sevens and 7 sevens for a total of 69 sevens have passed, after the decree that goes out to restore and rebuild Jerusalem from Daniel's time, the Anointed One or the Messiah will be "cut off." That's exactly what we see with Jesus' Triumphal entry into Jerusalem. History records for us the date when King Artexerxes issued that commandment to rebuild Jerusalem in 445 B.C. So, if you take the 69 sevens or years mentioned above that need to transpire before the Messiah is cut off, and times that by 7 for each year, you get a total of 483 years. To calculate the exact number of days, you need to take the 483 years and times it by 360 (because the Jewish calendar only had 360 days for each year) and you get a grand total of 173,880 days. So, what happened 173,880 days after the decree to rebuild Jerusalem? Well that just happens to be the exact date Jesus made His Triumphal entry into Jerusalem where He was rejected or cut off from His people! That's not by chance! And neither is the "event" that is presented in the next verse.

Daniel 9:27 "He will confirm a covenant with many for one 'seven.' In the middle of the 'seven' he will put an end to sacrifice and offering. And on a wing of the temple he will set up an abomination that causes desolation, until the end that is decreed is poured out on him."

So here we see the Last Days Antichrist will make a covenant with the people of Israel which is the very event that triggers or starts the final "seven" or "week" of the 70th week prophecy, i.e. the 7-year Tribulation. Then halfway into that final seven, the "middle of the seven", the Antichrist goes up into the Jewish Temple and declares himself to be god, which is called the abomination of desolation.

First of all, we know this final "seven" is still future because the Jewish people had their Temple destroyed in 70 A.D., and thus in order for this passage to be fulfilled, there needs to be another rebuilt Jewish Temple which obviously hasn't happened yet. However, they are making plans for it right now as we speak, but it's not fully into existence yet. But once this final week commences after the Rapture of the Church, all hell breaks loose on this planet as God's focus goes back on the Jewish people to consummate the "final week." And again, that's one-time frame you don't want to be a part of, as this researcher admits:

"Every dimension of our culture, every dimension of our society is escalating on the down slide, being devastated by depravity, more and more given over to lust and pride and self-indulgence, immorality and rejection of God and Christ and the truth of Scripture. And thus, man is sentenced, his whole world is sentenced to divine wrath. Man will drink the cup of wrath to the fullest.

Jeremiah the prophet looked at the coming period of God's judgment in reference to Israel and what they would have to face when he wrote, 'Alas, for that day is great, there is none like it, and it is the time of Jacob's trouble,' Isaiah, on the other hand, looked also at the final wrath and saw it not so much from the perspective of the Jews, but in chapter 34 of Isaiah he looked at it with reference to the Gentiles.

In verse 1, 'Draw near, O nations, to hear and listen; O peoples, let the earth and all it contains hear and the world and all that springs from it, he's engulfing all of humanity, for the Lord's indignation is against all the nations and His wrath against all their armies. He has utterly destroyed them, He has given them over to slaughter so their slain will be thrown out, their corpses will give off their stench, the mountains will be drenched with their blood and all the host of heaven will wear away and the sky will be rolled up like a scroll.

All their hosts will also wither away as a leaf withers from the vine, or as one withers from a fig tree, for my sword is satiated in heaven. Behold it shall descend for judgment upon Edom and upon the people whom I have devoted to destruction. The sword of the Lord is filled with blood, it is sated with fat with the blood of lambs and goats, with the fat of the kidneys of rams For the Lord has a sacrifice in Bozrah and a great slaughter in the land of Edom there will come a final day of judgment.'

For the Jews it will be the time of Jacob's trouble, and for the Gentiles it will be the slaughter of the world."[2]

But what of the Church? Again, the Church escapes this time of God's wrath at the Rapture of the Church prior to this final week of Daniel's 70th week prophecy, the 7-year Tribulation. Such clear evidence of this truth includes the following:

- The Jewish People and the Unbelieving Gentiles are the Audience of the 7-year Tribulation.
- The Church is not mentioned even once during the events of the 7-year Tribulation.
- The Church is promised not to experience God's wrath being poured out in the 7-year Tribulation.
- The Church is specifically promised to be kept from the 7-year Tribulation.
- The Church is seen up in heaven during the 7-year Tribulation.
- The Church comes back with Jesus at His Second Coming at the end of the 7-year Tribulation.[3]

For an exhaustive and detailed discussion of this Biblical truth of the Church being absent from the earth during the final week of Daniel's 70th week prophecy, the 7-year Tribulation, again, please check out our previous study, *The Rapture: Don't Be Deceived*. Now, with that said, I do believe, however, that there will be a lot of "church-goers" who find themselves left behind and thrust into this horrible 7-year Tribulation along with the Jewish people and the other unbelieving Gentiles. Why? Because going to a church service doesn't save you. Getting dunked or sprinkled with water doesn't save you. Trying to be a good person doesn't save you because we can never be good enough. All "religious people" who have bought into the lie of thinking that salvation is made complete in their own works, they too, like the Jewish people and the unbelieving Gentiles, are headed for a rude awakening, as this person remarks:

"Well then, after the Church has gone, what is going to take place in the world? We are in heaven already; the Rapture having taken place. Let us suppose that last night, while things were going on in the ordinary way, suddenly there was a heartening shout heard from the glory. Every redeemed one responded to the trumpet of God. In a moment the graves were opened, and in every place where the believing dead were resting, the bodies were raised, and the living saints were changed. We found ourselves caught away.

We entered with Him into the Father's house and gathered around the throne and fell down to worship. We will say that we have had twenty-four hours in heaven. At first our hearts would just be too full of Christ to think of anything else. (O sinner, you wouldn't be there. It is saved people I am talking about.)

But He, Himself, stirs us at last to think of what He is about to do. We say to ourselves, 'What is going to happen next in that world we have left behind?' We look down to that poor scene where we lived yesterday. Look at the streets of the great cities. We can see the headlines, 'A great number of people have disappeared!' There is a rush to get the newspapers to find out all about this strange event. Throngs are crowding the popular churches to hear the preachers give their explanation of the great disappearance of so many people.

I believe there will be lots of church-going for a little while after the Rapture of God's people; those left behind will be crowding into the churches as never before. I think I see the Rev. Mr. Smooth-things standing in his pulpit, with pale, wan face. He looks at scores of parishioners he hasn't seen for many years and thinks to himself, 'Now, I have to explain to these people. I have been telling them for twenty years that this talk of the Coming of Christ is false.'

People who believed in the Coming of Christ were looked on as idiotic ranters who didn't know what they were talking about. I think I hear mutterings down in the congregation: 'We trusted our souls to you. You had been to the colleges, seminaries, and universities, and read a whole library of books. We believed you when you told us the old idea of salvation by the blood of Christ was all worn out and that we could save ourselves by culture. We believed you when you said Christ's Coming was only a fantastic notion. Now explain this to us.'

Another cries, 'What about my grandmother? She believed in her Bible to the end. She was reading just the other day.' In an hour when ye think not, the Son of man cometh. 'Now Grandmother is gone, and I am here. Now, Pastor, explain all this.'

Oh, there are going to be some wonderful meetings after the Lord has come! There is that world seething with corruption, men's hearts failing them for fear. Christian statesmen will have gone; Christian business men and people of all ranks who knew Christ will have disappeared. Cities and communities will be in turmoil. What are they going to do? Let's look at the Book and see."[4]

So yes, let us look at the Book, the Bible, and see what is about to happen to the planet after the Rapture of the Church. What horrible events will explode onto the scene and give credence to the warnings from Jesus. You don't want to be there; get saved now. Why? Because it will be the worst time in the history of mankind.

Chapter Two

The Blessing of the Seals

What we are about to embark upon in Revelation Chapter 6 is an exciting sneak peek and completely accurate account of the future events that are coming upon mankind and all of planet earth. And, might I add, much sooner than most people would want to believe. It's not a pretty future; frankly, it's shocking to the core, or as Jesus says, it's the worst time in the history of mankind. Yet, this is what is contained within the Book of Revelation. It is the real-life future account of what is about to be thrust upon any and all who are left behind after the Rapture of the Church. One researcher puts it this way:

"Early Edition was a popular television program in the early 1990's that featured a young man who regularly received the next day's newspaper a day ahead of time. Because he always knew the future, the man's task in each episode was to save people from a tragedy or problem he had read about in tomorrow's newspaper.

So, if he knew a building was going to burn, he tried to keep people from entering into it. Or if someone was going to be hurt by an act of violence, or in an accident, he tried to prevent the encounter from taking place. Most of us would like to have the knowledge that this man did. Yet, we fail to realize that the Book of Revelation is an 'early edition' of future events."[1]

Therefore, you'd think that this truth would make headline news around the world, that is, that we actually have a book on the planet, the Bible, and the

Book of Revelation, that gives us a 100% accurate account of what lies ahead for the future of all mankind. No more searching, wondering, hoping, groping. This Book is it. You don't need to go anywhere else. It will always steer you right, it is never wrong, just stick with it and enjoy seeing the future 100% accurately all the time, every time. However, the unfortunate irony is, the Book of Revelation, let alone the Bible, seems to be the least read of books today. Not because people don't want to know that future, they do, desperately so. It's just that they are sadly turning to faulty and unreliable sources, like secular psychics or so-called mediums, instead of the Holy Scripture. Yet one look at their track record, versus the Bible that never gets anything it records wrong, reveals how psychics are one of the last places you would want to go to, to ascertain future events:

What Psychics Missed Concerning World Events in Just One Year

- Hurricane Sandy and the immense destruction in New York and New Jersey.
- Largest earthquakes being 8.2 and 8.6 in Indonesia (only two ≥ 8 magnitude, in April).
- Largest death toll from earthquakes being 306 in Iran (6.3-6.4 mag in August) and 139 in Guatemala and Mexico (7.4 mag in November).
- Palestinian successful bid to become a UN "Non-member observer state."
- Greatly escalating crisis in Syria.
- Julian Assange and being given asylum by Ecuador but trapped in the UK.
- Pussy Riot fall-out in Russia.
- Facebook IPO debacle.
- Aurora, CO theater shooting. Newtown, CT school shooting – the worst US school shooting in decades.
- Death of Whitney Houston, Gore Vidal, Ravi Shankar, Phyllis Diller, Dick Clark, Ernest Borgnine, Andy Griffith.
- Death of Neal Armstrong, Sally Ride, Patrick Moore, Ray Bradbury.
- Death of Gen. Norman Schwarzkopf, Rodney King.
- The Italian cruise ship Costa Concordia running aground, killing 15 people.
- CIA director David Petraeus' affair and resignation.
- Discovery/announcement of the Higgs Boson.
- Successful landing of Curiosity on Mars.
- Any scores/medals/rankings at the Olympics.
- And the most important event of the year, the end of an era: Twinkies went bankrupt.

Yet in spite of this, people believe that [insert whatever term you want to use – 'psychics,' 'astrologers,' 'intuitives,' etc.] can tell the future or advise them in tough decisions. They can't. At least not any better than a random person off the street, and they're much more likely to give you an answer that's too vague to be of any use. And yet, despite being unable to find estimates on how much people spend annually on their 'services,' I was able to find one that says people spend over $300 million annually just on calls to the 'psychic' hotlines. Meanwhile, you go to some of these peoples' websites and they charge huge sums of money -- $50 a reading, $99.99 for a minimum of 15 minutes, or $350 for an hour, $600 for a reading with a 2-month-long waiting list…the amounts are huge. And people pay it.[2]

It's sad when you look at the facts concerning so-called psychics and mediums, isn't it? Yet in spite of this horrible track record concerning the prediction of future events, unlike the Bible that gets it right 100% of the time, our world is still enthralled with these faulty prophets of the future, as these sobering statistics likewise reveal:

- Approximate annual earnings of men who have consulted a psychic: $40,000/$95,000 a year.
- Approximate annual earnings of women who have consulted a psychic: $20,000/$100,000 a year.
- Men average age: Between 27 and 54.
- Women average age: Between 21 and 60.
- How much money women are willing to spend on a psychic/medium: Up to $5,000.
- How much money men are willing to spend on a psychic/medium: Up to $2,000.
- Percentage of men who ask their psychic to "put a spell or a curse" on somebody: 3%.
- Percentage of women who ask their psychic to "put a spell or a curse" on somebody: 51%.
- Percentage of men who admit having contacted a psychic: 39%.
- Percentage of women who admit having contacted a psychic: 69%.
- Percentage of men who would recommend consulting a psychic: 28%.
- Percentage of women who would recommend consulting a psychic: 68%.
- Percentage of divorced women who have consulted a psychic: Between 57% and 63%.

- Percentage of divorced men who have consulted a psychic: Between 21% and 29%.
- Percentage of women who would consult a psychic on sentimental matters: 85%.
- Percentage of men who would consult a psychic on sentimental matters: 11%.
- Percentage of women who would consult a psychic on career/professions matters: 35%.
- Percentage of women who would consult a psychic more than once: 53%.
- Percentage of men who would consult a psychic more than once: 11%.
- Approx. number of women in the United States who have spent more than $5000 for psychic reading in 2011-2012: 375,000.
- Approx. number of men in the United States who have spent more than $5000 for psychic reading in 2011-2012: 5,000.
- Approx. number of women in the United States who have spent more than $10,000 for psychic reading in 2011-2012: 275,000.
- Approx. number of men in the United States who have spent more than $10,000 for psychic reading in 2011-2012: 300.
- Approximate annual earning of a very successful psychic/medium in the United States: Over $5,000,000.
- Percentage of psychics/mediums who would not give you a refund: 97%.
- Approx. $ amount earned by psychics/mediums who have scammed clients in 2011-2012: $200,000,000.[3]

Wow! Talk about a total rip off! These hucksters are not only handing out faulty information, but they're obviously simultaneously draining people's finances as they are becoming millionaires themselves. Why? All because people *want to know the future*. Now, if that wasn't bad enough, the very same report also indicated that so-called "members of the clergy" had also consulted a psychic/medium and jointly conducted so-called "exorcisms," and these same "clergy" or "priests" even went on to say that they consider *themselves* to be a psychic or medium! Furthermore, if you can believe it, this report even shared how 99.99% of these psychics actually claim to believe in God! Yet they, and the people who seek out their faulty advice on the future, are clearly not listening to the One and Only *real* God Who forbids this activity:

Deuteronomy 18:9-14 "When you enter the land the LORD your God is giving you, do not learn to imitate the detestable ways of the nations there. Let no one be found among you who sacrifices his son or daughter in the fire, who practices divination or sorcery, interprets omens, engages in witchcraft, or casts spells, or who is a medium or spiritist or who consults the dead. Anyone who does these things is detestable to the LORD and because of these detestable practices the LORD your God will drive out those nations before you. You must be blameless before the LORD your God. The nations you will dispossess listen to those who practice sorcery or divination. But as for you, the LORD your God has not permitted you to do so."

Why? Because it's a demonic practice that opens up the door to demonic deception and God doesn't want you deceived! He wants you to *know* the future, that's why He has accurately recorded it for us in the Bible. The truth about future events can only be found in His Book, the Bible, not demonic psychics or mediums!

The other problem people have with knowing future events, is not only going to unfortunate faulty sources outside the Bible, but it's also in having a faulty attitude towards the future events contained in the Bible, that is the Book of Revelation. Believe it or not, there is a trend in the Church today where Bible prophecy and the Book of Revelation especially is not only on the downside of teaching and preaching from the pulpit, but many people in the "Church" are now calling the Book of Revelation a book of "doom and gloom," and thus they say it *shouldn't* be taught from the pulpit or even read by the individual Christian. The problem is that's not what the Bible says!

Revelation 1:1-3 "The revelation of Jesus Christ, which God gave Him to show His servants what must soon take place. He made it known by sending his angel to his servant John, who testifies to everything he saw – that is, the Word of God and the testimony of Jesus Christ. Blessed is the one who reads the words of this prophecy and blessed are those who hear it and take to heart what is written in it, because the time is near."

As you can see, contrary to the "doom and gloom" skeptics, God says, not once, not twice, but you will experience a *triple-fold blessing* if you study Bible prophecy. He didn't mince words. Right out of the gate He made it clear how people will be blessed if they read, hear, and take to heart, this prophetic message concerning Jesus Christ in the Last Days, that He's coming back in the future, which is what the Book of Revelation is all about. This is not even counting the fourth promise of a blessing at the back of the Book of Revelation in Chapter 22, so it's really four:

Revelation 22:7 "Behold, I am coming soon! Blessed is he who keeps the words of the prophecy in this book."

I think it's pretty clear in the Bible that if you want to be blessed by God in your walk with God, what do you need to be studying? Bible prophecy, right? Yet, why is it then that many people, even in the Church, would say it's *not* a blessing to study Bible Prophecy, when God clearly says that it is? Why do they say these same oft repeated remarks of, "Don't make me read this! Don't make me hear this week after week after week! Don't make me take this to heart! This is freaking me out! Stop! This is 'doom and gloom!" Why would they do that, when the Bible clearly says that studying Bible prophecy, that is, future events, is a source of blessing?

Personally, I think one reason is due to a *spiritual factor*, that is, spiritual warfare! Put yourself in the enemy's shoes. The devil is not dumb! He knows what he's doing! If he is about "that close" so to speak to pulling off the antichrist's kingdom, then it's common sense; what's the last book you want people in? The Bible, and specifically Bible Prophecy, especially the Book of Revelation, because that's where you find out in intimate detail all his plans and what he's up to! The Bible is the only Book on the planet that exposes what satan and the antichrist and the false prophet will be doing in the Last Days! It's all right there for anyone to read, so the enemy of our souls keeps us out of it by spreading this lie in the Church today, that it's bad to study Bible prophecy, that it's scary, it'll split your church, it's "Doom and Gloom!" The result? The Church is left *clueless* as to what he's up to in the Last Days, even though they are the only ones on the planet who have the only Book on the planet, the Bible, that exposes his dastardly plans for the future in great detail!

The second reason I believe this false message of "doom and gloom" concerning the study of Bible prophecy has spread in the Church is the *ironic factor*, that is, little do the Churches and Pastors who refuse to teach on Bible Prophecy realize that they are actually fulfilling Bible Prophecy. In fact, this behavior is one of the biggest signs that we're in the Last Days!

2 Timothy 4:3-4 "For the time will come when men will not put up with sound doctrine. Instead, to suit their own desires, they will gather around them a great number of teachers to say what their itching ears want to hear. They will turn their ears away from the truth and turn aside to myths."

Here we see how the Apostle Paul tells young Pastor Timothy that in the future, when you are getting close to the Last Days, a time will come when "people in the Church will not put up with sound doctrine." In other words, they're not going to like hearing the Bible. "Instead, to suit their own desires, they will gather around themselves a great number of teachers to say what their itching ears want to hear *and* turn aside to myths." What's interesting is that the Greek word there for "itching" is "knetho" which means, "to desire only that which is pleasant," and "myths" there in the Greek is "muthos" which literally means, "stories made up." So according to the Bible, how do you know you're living in the Last Days? When you see in the Church the only things you get from the pulpit, by and large, are "pleasant things" and a bunch of stories made up! I just described to you about 90% of the American Church! This is why many Churches, Pastors, Bible study leaders/teachers won't preach on Prophecy! The irony is, they are actually fulfilling prophecy...in a bad way! *Yet they don't know it because they refuse to study the very thing that warns them against it!*

My question though, as a Shepherd myself, is "How in the world can you be a faithful Shepherd if you skip nearly one-third of the Bible that deals directly or indirectly with Bible Prophecy? Are you saying it's not a blessing to the sheep when God so blatantly says to the contrary that it is? Are you smarter than Him? Do you know more than Him? Why would you, a Shepherd who professes to love the sheep, want to keep the sheep from a blessing? Is that being a loving Shepherd? Is that showing genuine concern for them? Besides, as a Shepherd, we're supposed to teach the flock the whole counsel of God, not just some of it! And who makes you the arbitrator and what gives you the right to decide which portions of the Bible are "good" versus "bad" for God's people when God says it's all good, it's all from Him, especially Bible Prophecy!

The facts are, Bible prophecy is some of the best news we could ever hear as Christians, and it is the much-needed antidote to deal with the perilous days we live in where evil abounds. The Book of Revelation is not "doom and gloom." Rather, it reminds me that I'm going to heaven, a place beyond my wildest dreams, I'm going to the millennium where my greatest adventure waits, and best of all, I'm going to see My King, face to face, who loves me and Who won for me an amazing life for all eternity. What a blessing that news is, and it's all obtained when you read, hear, and take to heart the prophetic events that are 100% accurately recorded for us only in the Bible. The more I study them, the more I am reminded that in Jesus Christ, as a Christian, I am a winner, not a loser, I am blessed beyond measure! What a future is in store for me! In fact, nobody has a brighter, more secure future than God's people! Why would I not want to read about that? As a Shepherd why would I not want to tell the sheep that? Bible prophecy is the most *relevant* and *exciting* topic we could be studying today as the Church, gaining all kinds of blessings as this researcher agrees:

"Now we have arrived at Revelation 6. Revelation 6-18 deals with a seven-year period called 'The Tribulation' (Matt.24:21; Rev.7:14). This section makes up almost two-thirds of the book of Revelation. This should cause us to stop and ask, 'Is Revelation relevant? If so, why should we spend time studying the tribulation period when we believe that we will be Raptured prior to this time?'"

Studying the Tribulation Serves Several Important Purposes

(1) All Scripture is important and worthy of our careful study and application to our lives (2 Timothy 3:16-17)

(2) We learn a great deal about the nature of man, God, and satan.

(3) As we see the signs of the coming Tribulation developing before our eyes, it fills us with hope and expectation that the Lord's coming is near.

(4) Though we won't live through the Tribulation if we know the Savior, the Lord Jesus loves to take His own people into His confidence and tell them what is going to happen, even if it doesn't directly affect their own lives.

(5) The Tribulation should scare the living daylights out of us. God's holiness, as expressed through His justice and wrath, should overwhelm us. It should spark a newfound appreciation for His love and grace.

The Names of the Tribulation

- The indignation (Isa.26:20; 34:2)
- A day of (God's) vengeance (Isa.34:8; 63:1-6)
- Jacob's trouble or distress (Jer.30:7)
- Daniel's 70th week (Dan.9:24-27)
- A time of trouble or distress (Dan.12:1)
- The end time (Dan.12:9)
- The day of the Lord (Joel 1:15; 2:1; 1 Thess.5:2)
- Tribulation and the Great Tribulation (Matt.24:9;24,29; Mark 13:19,24; Rev.7:14)
- The hour of testing…to test those who dwell on the earth (Rev.3:10)
- The great day of their (i.e., the Father and the Lamb) wrath (Rev.6:17)
- Hour of His judgment (Rev.14:7)

The Nature of the Tribulation

- It is a time of unprecedented trouble (Joel 2:2; Zeph.1:14-18; Matt.24:21)
- It is a time of God's wrath or indignation and the vindication of God's holiness (Zeph.1:15,18: Rev.6:17; 1 Thess.1:10; Rev.14:7,10; 19:2) God's wrath against man's sin and rebellion will be withheld no longer.
- It is a day of utter darkness, gloom and extreme cloudiness (Joel 2:2; Zeph.1:15)
- It is a day of destruction and global catastrophes (Joel 1:15; 2:3; 1 Thess.5:3; Rev.6-19)
- It is a day of extreme lawlessness, sin and demonic activity (Rev.9:20-21; 2 Thess.2:12)
- It is a day of extreme deception and delusion (2 Thess.2:9-12; Rev.9:1f; 13:2-3,11-18; Dan.8:24f) This deception is caused by a number of factors:

  (a) The removal of the Spirit indwelt church with its restraining influence (2 Thess.2:6-8)

  (b) The increase of demonic activity (2 Thess.2:8-10)

  (c) The blinding judgment of God (2 Thess.2:11-12)

- It is a time of death (Rev.6:3-11; 9:15,18; 11:13) Large portions of the populations of the earth will be wiped out suddenly, both human and animal.
- It is a time of utter negative volition, cold indifference, and rebellion against God even though the world will know it is under the wrath of God (Rev.6:14-17; 9:20; 11:10,18)
- It is a time of internationalism religiously (Rev.17), politically (Rev.13,17), economically (Rev.18), and militarily (Joel 3:2,9-14; Rev.17)
- It is a time of extreme Anti-Semitism (Rev.12; Matt.24:9,13f)
- It is a time of unprecedented apostasy and blasphemy against God (Rev.11:1f; 13:1f; 2 Thess.2:3f)
- It is a time of the martyrdom of believers, both Jew and Gentile (Rev.6:9; 7:14f)
- It is a time of global and universal war, human and angelic (Rev.6:2-4; 16:14; 19:14f; Joel 3:2,9f; Rev.12:7)

(6) The Tribulation should also sober us. It should lead us to take our lives more seriously and to live them according to eternal values. As a result, we will not put so much attachment upon the things of this earth, once we see what will

become of them. We will also live more thoughtfully for eternity, finding our source and satisfaction in God.

(7) The Tribulation should compel us to go out into our world as ambassadors for Jesus Christ, delivering people from the wrath to come. Believe me when I say that no human being will want to go through this time. If all of these terrifying events don't cause us to tell others about Jesus Christ, what will?"[4]

Sounds to me like there are *a lot of blessings* in there that I don't want to miss out on! In fact, I've often wondered why the Church today seems to be so anemic. Where's the power gone? How about the passion? Why are souls not being saved like we hear in stories of yesteryear? Why are we no longer making much of a difference to the moral decay and spiritual darkness surrounding us? Where's our salt? Where's our light? Why and how have we become so worldly minded and seem so lost ourselves? Maybe it's because we've been tricked into *losing out* on the very thing that staves off all these detrimental factors. Maybe we're not studying the blessing from God, Bible prophecy. It's a vital, powerful, and relevant blessing to the Body of Christ. I didn't say that, God did.

The facts are, one of the fastest ways to get that salt and light and passion back for the lost while removing the power-draining worldliness that surrounds us, is to simply get back to reading, hearing, and taking to heart Bible prophecy. It tells us the good news that we are not saved for this world, but the world to come. We are not losers, but winners. Our future is brighter and more secure than anyone else on the whole planet. Things are looking up, not down! So, if you want to fire yourself or the Church up again, then let's get back to studying Bible prophecy. That journey begins in the next Chapter!

Chapter Three

The Prelude to the Seals

Believe it or not, the discussion of the Seal Judgments does not begin in Revelation Chapter 6. Chapter 6 is the breaking of the seals, but the events surrounding the opening of the seals actually begin in Revelation Chapters 4 and 5. This is a very important distinction to make because it answers some highly important questions that some people seem to get confused over concerning the events that take place on the earth after the seals are opened up, as well as who is left behind on earth to face Daniel's 70th week, the 7-year Tribulation.

And the **first question** that gets answered with the context of the opening of the seals in Revelation Chapters 4 and 5 is the **Location of the Church**. As was previously mentioned, the Church escapes Daniel's 70th week, the 7-year Tribulation, via the Rapture of the Church which takes place prior to the opening of the seals. This event is verified when you take a look at Revelation Chapter 4 which contextually leads into Revelation Chapter 5 where you see the beginning of the events surrounding the opening of the seals. These events take place in heaven, the very throne room of God, and wonder of wonders, just who happens to *already be there in heaven*? The Church! You see this contextually in a couple of different ways.

First of all, it just so happens that the word "Church" is mentioned repeatedly in Revelation Chapters 1-3, but it is never mentioned as being on the earth in Revelation Chapters 6-18, the chapters that deal with the 7-year Tribulation period. Is this by chance? I think not. The word "Church" is absent because the Church is absent! They left at the Rapture prior to the 7-year Tribulation.

Second, the very next thing *we do see* following Revelation Chapter 3, the last mentioning of the Church on earth until they return with Jesus at His Second Coming at the end of the 7-year Tribulation, is the Church being mentioned *in heaven* in Revelation Chapters 4-5. They are seen as the 24 Elders surrounding the very throne of God.

Revelation 4:4 "Surrounding the throne were twenty-four other thrones and seated on them were *twenty-four elders*. They were dressed in white and had crowns of gold on their heads."

Revelation 4:10-11 "The *twenty-four elders* fall down before Him who sits on the throne and worship Him who lives for ever and ever. They lay their crowns before the throne and say: 'You are worthy, our Lord and God, to receive glory and honor and power, for You created all things, and by Your will they were created and have their being.'"

They are also mentioned in Revelation Chapters 5, 7, 11, and 14 and *in all occurrences*, they are clearly located *in heaven*. For proof of these 24 Elders clearly being one and the same as the Church, one only needs to look at the contextual evidence. Observe such things as:

- The Timing of the 24 Elders.
- The Location of the 24 Elders.
- The Crowns of the 24 Elders.
- The Title of the 24 Elders.
- The Number of the 24 Elders.
- The Position of the 24 Elders.
- The Distinction of the 24 Elders.
- The Redemption of the 24 Elders.
- The Clothing of the 24 Elders.[1]

All of these indicators clearly present the 24 Elders as being the Church in heaven, not Israel, the angels, or any other fanciful theory that some people have come up with. Biblical context demands it to be the Church. Again, for an exhaustive, detailed discussion of the identity of the 24 Elders, please see our previous study, *The Rapture: Don't Be Deceived*.

But as you can see, Revelation Chapters 4-5, the Chapters that deal with the events surrounding the opening of the seals, actually reveal the location of the Church. They are no longer on earth, but they're in heaven as the 24 Elders, surrounding the actual throne room of God. Therefore, since the Church is already enjoying and worshipping Jesus in heaven as the 24 Elders, excited that the seals are *about* to be opened, there's no way you can place them within the horrible events of the 7-year Tribulation that begin *after* the opening of the seals. The Church is *already* seen in heaven *before* the 7-year Tribulation begins with the opening of the seals.

The **second question** that gets answered with the context of the opening of the seals in Revelation Chapters 4 and 5 is the **Originator of the Wrath**. According to these chapters the wrath that is to be poured out on the planet during the 7-year Tribulation, Daniel's 70th week, is not coming from man and it's certainly not coming from satan as some would say. Rather, it's coming from God Himself and it's literally a time when He, the Creator of the Universe, is "going to war" with our wicked and rebellious planet. One man puts it this way:

"One of the most breathtaking passages on the Second Coming is Revelation 5. This looks at the Second Coming from Heaven's vantage point. Here we meet the conqueror of the world as He is about to come to take over the universe, to redeem it, to destroy the wicked and to establish and bless His people.

The scene as Chapter 5 opens is the same as Chapter 4. The scene is Heaven and in the center of the scene is the throne of God; God on His throne being worshiped and shining forth in all His glory. Chapter 4 and Chapter 5 of Revelation anticipate the 7-year Tribulation that breaks forth in Chapter 6. Chapter 6 to 19 is the record of the exploding judgment of God in the world, His judgment poured out on the earth.

But what you have in 4 and 5 is a glimpse into Heaven as the divine war machine begins to move, the end of which will be the establishment of the glorious Kingdom of Jesus Christ in His great return as described in Revelation Chapter 19.

There was this whole matter of overcoming sin, overcoming satan, overcoming demons, overcoming death, overcoming hell that had to take place. As Jesus moved toward the cross, in John 12:31 He said, 'Now judgment is upon this world, now the ruler of this world shall be cast out.' He knew when He went to the cross that He was starting what He would finish some day in the future. I'm going into combat with satan and I will win."[2]

And that all begins here in Revelation Chapter 5. The scene is being set for God's wrath to be poured out on the planet. He is going to war with the planet and its ungodly inhabitants. God is the originator of all this. The ultimate consummation of the full victory of Christ on the cross is now being put into play. All of heaven, including the Church as the 24 Elders, is excited and bursting out in praise over this climactic event. And it all begins with the opening of the seals.

Now, here's the problem. Even though this is absolutely clear in the context surrounding the events regarding the opening of the seals in Revelation Chapter 5, that God is the originator of this wrath to come, and that the Church is in heaven celebrating this event, some people will still make two fatal errors. One, they say that the Church is still on earth and two, that this wrath is not really all God's wrath.

Let's deal with the **first fatal error** that the **Church is on Earth** during this time of God's wrath. For the life of me, I don't know how people can make this erroneous statement when the Bible clearly reveals that the Church is not appointed unto God's wrath, period. I didn't say that, He did.

Romans 5:8-11 "But God demonstrates His own love for us in this: While we were still sinners, Christ died for us. Since we have now been justified by His blood, how much more shall we be saved from God's wrath through Him! For if, when we were God's enemies, we were reconciled to Him through the death of His Son, how much more, having been reconciled, shall we be saved through His life! Not only is this so, but we also rejoice in God through our Lord Jesus Christ, through whom we have now received reconciliation."

1 Thessalonians 1:10 "And to wait for His Son from heaven, whom He raised from the dead – Jesus, who rescues us from the coming wrath."

1 Thessalonians 5:9-11 "For God did not appoint us to suffer wrath but to receive salvation through our Lord Jesus Christ. He died for us so that, whether we are awake or asleep, we may live together with Him. Therefore encourage one another and build each other up, just as in fact you are doing."

So, as you can see, the Bible clearly and emphatically declares that the Church is *saved from, rescued from,* and *not appointed unto* God's wrath which includes His wrath being poured out during the 7-year Tribulation, which begins with the opening of the seals. So how can you say that the Church will be on earth during this time when God pours out His wrath? Answer? They can't! This is why they are already seen in heaven as the 24 Elders who are praising God along with the rest of heaven over these events.

Revelation 5:11-12 "Then I looked and heard the voice of many angels, numbering thousands upon thousands, and ten thousand times ten thousand. They encircled the throne and the living creatures and the elders. In a loud voice they sang: 'Worthy is the Lamb, who was slain, to receive power and wealth and wisdom and strength and honor and glory and praise!'"

Now let's turn to the **second fatal error** that people make with Revelation Chapter 5, the events surrounding the opening of the seals, and that is that this **Wrath is not all from God**. Believe it or not, there are those who will still try to dance around this Biblical truth that the Church will never experience God's wrath in the 7-year Tribulation by saying that not all of the 7-year Tribulation is God's wrath. That's how they still try to "squeeze" the Church into this time-frame, God's wrath in the 7-year Tribulation, to seemingly not create a contradiction in Scripture with the above texts that say the Church is not appointed into God's wrath. What they do is, they say that only part of the 7-year Tribulation is God's wrath. But once again, that's not what the Bible says. Once the first seal opens up at the beginning of the 7-year Tribulation, God's wrath continues non-stop for the next 7 years.

Revelation 6:16-17 "They called to the mountains and the rocks, 'Fall on us and hide us from the face of him who sits on the throne and from the wrath of the Lamb! For the great day of their wrath has come, and who can stand?"

NOTE: Even though the word "wrath" is not found in Revelation until 6:16-17, the famine, sword, pestilence, and wild beasts in the first four seal judgments are often associated with God's wrath in other places in the Bible. See (Jer. 14:12; 15:2; 24:10; 29:17; Ezek. 5:12, 17; 14:21). Also, the verb "has come" doesn't even mean the "wrath" started just then. It's in the Greek aorist tense which speaks of a past event. This means the "wrath" has already been going on and these people in this text are just now acknowledging it.

Revelation 11:18 "The nations were angry; and Your *wrath* has come."

Revelation 14:10 "He, too, will drink of the wine of God's fury, which has been poured full strength into the cup of His *wrath*."

Revelation 14:19 "The angel swung his sickle on the earth, gathered its grapes and threw them into the great winepress of God's *wrath*."

Revelation 15:1 "I saw in heaven another great and marvelous sign: seven angels with the seven last plagues – last, because with them God's *wrath* is completed."

Revelation 15:7 "Then one of the four living creatures gave to the seven angels seven golden bowls filled with the *wrath* of God, who lives for ever and ever."

Revelation 16:1 "Then I heard a loud voice from the temple saying to the seven angels, 'Go, pour out the seven bowls of God's *wrath* on the earth.'"

Revelation 16:19 "The great city split into three parts, and the cities of the nations collapsed. God remembered Babylon the Great and gave her the cup filled with the wine of the fury of His *wrath*."[3]

So, as you can see, the Bible emphatically declares that God's *wrath* is going to be poured out during the *entire* 7-year Tribulation, not some of it, as some would have you and I believe. Again, this is why the Church is seen already in heaven removed from the *entire* 7-year Tribulation. We have to be! Why? Because we are *saved from, rescued from,* and *not appointed unto* God's wrath which includes His wrath being poured out during the 7-year Tribulation, which begins with the opening of the first seal. Once that first seal opens up, God's wrath is coming forth for the next 7 years non-stop and thus the Church cannot be there. How do we know? Because the first seal is the first judgment of many to come in a unified sealed scroll that contains all of God's wrath as He initiates His plan to take the planet back. Let's take a look at that scroll in Revelation Chapter 5.

Revelation 5:7 "He (Jesus) came and took the scroll from the right hand of Him (God the Father) Who sat on the throne."

This scroll contains *all the wrathful events* that God will pour out on the planet during the 7-year tribulation. Once it's opened up, *all* the wrathful events come gushing forth, *all* from God, non-stop for the next 7 years. It's *all* coming from God's Hand, from God's throne, from God's direction, as this researcher admits:

"In Revelation Chapter 5, John is caught up into this vision and says, 'I saw.' The Almighty has, in this vision, extended His arm, and is holding something on the palm of His hand. It's a document. It's a scroll. It's made of papyrus or parchment or animal skin, as ancient scrolls were.

Now this particular scroll that John sees in the vision is written inside and on the back, and then rolled up and sealed with seven seals rolled a little bit and sealed, rolled a little more and sealed, rolled a little more and sealed, rolled a little more and sealed. Now this gives us a clue as to what it is. Roman wills were sealed seven times.

This is God's last will and testament. This is God holding out the title deed to the universe. This was typical of a contract in the ancient world. They would write the details of the contract on the inside and then would write a summary of the contract on the outside so that one would know what it was all about.

Here is an official, legal document. It is the title deed, really, to the universe. And God has the ownership and He is passing it to His heir, to His rightful heir to take possession of what is His. The details of the inside unfold from Chapter 6 on. So, this scroll describes the process by which possession of the universe is to be retaken by God through His rightful heir, back from the usurper who took it when paradise was lost in the garden.

The scroll then, is the full account of how the rightful heir will take back what is His through severe wrath and judgment. It is the scroll of doom. It is the scroll of terror. It is the scroll of judgment. The final monumental act in the Heavenly scene is the great culminating act in human history. This is what precipitates all the judgments that precede the Second Coming described in Chapters 6 to 19.

The goal of redemption is about to be reached. Paradise is to be regained. The ungodly are to be destroyed. Christ is coming back. Satan will be conquered, demons and the devil cast into the lake of fire, and only the righteous will prevail. The Son of Man starts all that, inaugurates all that, initiates all of that, pulls the trigger on all of that, sets it in motion when He reaches over and takes the scroll out of the hand of God.

He takes back the universe step by step, seal by seal by seal. The seventh seal is broken and describes seven trumpet blasts. The seventh trumpet is blown and describes a series of seven bowls. And then Jesus comes at the end of that great unleashing of judgment to establish His Kingdom. But it is all set-in motion in this one act, the taking of the scroll.

It's little wonder that everything in Heaven broke loose in praise. The end could be seen in sight. All Heaven bursts forth. All that God promised is about to take place. All that we've prayed for is about to happen."[4]

So, here's the point. How can you say that only some of the wrathful events contained within this single unified scroll are from God, while the rest are supposed to be from man or satan? Who gives you the right to split up God's wrath contained within this single unified scroll? It's sealed! It can't be split up! It's a self-contained legal scroll from God! It's the title deed to the universe in the hand of God, coming from God, all about God, belonging to God, instituted from God, started by God, unleashed by God in the very throne room of God, being passed on to the Son of God, containing all *His wrath* to be poured in the 7-year Tribulation as *He* takes the planet back, not man or satan! What gives you the right to split it up and attribute any of it to man or satan? Once that scroll is opened up *by Jesus*, there's no stopping *His* wrath! There's no piecing it up! It's all from God, all about God, through and through, gushing forth for the next 7 years! To say this is coming from man or satan is not only contextually ludicrous, it's blasphemous! Why? Because the whole context of Revelation Chapter 5 is all about heaven giving God glory and praise for taking the scroll and opening it up. Judgment Day has come! Evil will be vanquished, satan will finally be bound. All heaven shouts for joy at what God is about to do. See for yourself.

Revelation 5:8-14 "And when He had taken it, the four living creatures and the twenty-four elders fell down before the Lamb. Each one had a harp and they were holding golden bowls full of incense, which are the prayers of the saints. And they sang a new song: 'You are worthy to take the scroll and to open its seals, because You were slain, and with your blood you purchased men for God from every tribe and language and people and nation. You have made them to be a kingdom and priests to serve our God, and they will reign on the earth.' Then I looked and heard the voice of many angels, numbering thousands upon thousands, and ten thousand times ten thousand. They encircled the throne and the living creatures and the elders. In a loud voice they sang: 'Worthy is the Lamb, who was slain, to receive power and wealth and wisdom and strength and honor and glory and praise!' Then I heard every creature in heaven and on earth and under the earth and on the sea, and all that is in them, singing: 'To Him who sits on the throne and to the Lamb be praise and honor and glory and power, for ever and ever!' The four living creatures said, 'Amen,' and the elders fell down and worshiped."

And yet, some would have us believe that this praise and worship and glory and honor directed to God for pouring out His wrath during the 7-year Tribulation, taking the planet back with the opening of the scroll, should actually be going to man or even satan? With all due respect, I'll stand off to the side as the lightning bolt gets you! Giving man or satan the praise and glory and honor that is only due to God is blasphemous! Only the Lamb, only God, is worthy of this distinction, as this man shares:

"The question is asked in Revelation Chapter 5, 'Who is worthy to open the scroll and to break its seals?' Neither man nor angel stir. The saints in Heaven don't stir. The holy angels don't stir. Who has the right to take the universe back? Who has the power to take it back? Who has that privilege to overthrow the intruder, the interloper, satan, the prince of the power of the air, the ruler of this world, the prince of darkness?

Michael was there. He didn't say anything even though he is a super angel who had contended with satan over the body of Moses, as Jude tells us. Gabriel was there, as glorious an angel as he was, given the privilege of enunciation as to the birth of John the Baptist to Zacharias and Elizabeth, and then, of course, to Mary, and even to Joseph, most likely. Gabriel was there, but he doesn't speak.

And then there were 10,000 times 10,000 angels who were there and they didn't say anything. And thousands of thousands, and the four living creatures were there, those very unique cherubs that surrounded the throne of God, and they didn't say anything.

The spirit of Abraham was there, and Isaac, and Jacob, and Joseph, Elijah, Elisha, Moses. Job was there. Ezekiel was there. Daniel was there. They didn't say anything. Peter was there. James was there. Even when John was writing this, they were dead.

No one to open it; no one to look and examine its contents. No one who had the legal right, no one who had the authority, no one who had the power to execute it effectively...except the Lamb.

The Lamb of God, who takes away the sin of the world, is the lion of Judah who will usurp back from the usurper, the universe. Here is the picture of Christ. And He moves to the conflict. 'He came and took it out of the right hand of Him who sat on the throne.'"[5]

Man is not worthy of this honor. Satan is certainly not worthy of this honor. Only the Lamb is worthy to open the scroll, to take it and open it and unleash all of God's wrath to be poured out during the 7-year Tribulation. In fact, it can't be man or satan because the very purpose of the scroll is to take back the universe. Is satan going to defeat himself? Can man fix the planet? No! Only the Lamb was worthy to get the job done and that's good news! This is not a time for tears, this is a time of glory, and praise, and honor, and worship to be given *to the Lamb,* not man or satan. And that's what Revelation Chapter 5 is all about. Why? Because only Jesus can do what He's about to do. Only He is worthy to give us the ultimate victory, and it all begins with the opening of the seals, as this researcher points out:

"John's reaction is really amazing. In Revelation Chapter 5 verse 4 he says, 'I began to weep greatly because no one was found worthy to open the book or look into it.'

W.A. Criswell writes: 'These represent the tears of all God's people through all the centuries. Those tears of the Apostle John are the tears of Adam and Eve driven out of the Garden of Eden as they bowed over the first grave, as they watered the dust of the ground with their tears over the silent, still form of their son Abel. Those are the tears of the children of Israel in bondage as they cried unto God in their affliction and slavery. They are the tears of God's elect through the centuries as they cried unto heaven. They are the sobs and the tears that have been wrung from the heart and soul of God's people as they looked on their silent dead, as they stand beside their open graves, as they experience the trials and sufferings of life, heartaches and disappointments indescribable. Such is the curse that sin has laid on God's beautiful creation, and this is the damnation of the hand of him who holds it, that usurper, that interloper, that intruder, that alien, that stranger, that dragon, that serpent, that satan-devil.'

But John's weeping was not fitting. He shouldn't have wept because of what was about to happen. In Luke 7, Verse 11 we see Jesus: 'Now as He approached the gate of the city, behold a dead man was being carried out, the only son of his mother and she was a widow. And a sizeable crowd from the city was with her.

And when the Lord saw her He felt compassion for her and He said to her, `Do not weep, stop sobbing; it's inappropriate.' Why was it inappropriate? It was inappropriate because of what Jesus was about to do. 'And He came up and touched the coffin and He said, `Young man, I say to you, arise.' And the dead man sat up and began to speak. And Jesus gave him back to his mother.' Jesus was saying your tears are inappropriate because of what I am about to do.

And so, it is with John's tears here in Revelation Chapter 5 because of what Jesus Christ was about to do. All we can do is praise Him for what He is. The whole created universe is now on the brink of its anticipated glory. Endless blessing, endless honor, endless praise, endless glory, endless worship to God, to Christ. The whole universe chimes in. What a moment.

They're all so ecstatic because it's going to happen. The curse is reversed. And the Kingdom comes, and God will reign. The stage is set."[6]

And so now let's turn to that stage that has been set for us, when God pours out His wrath upon this wicked and rebellious planet for 7 years non-stop, the time when He sets in motion the taking back of the planet with His Son Jesus's Triumphal Return ruling and reigning over all the earth with His Beautiful Bride the Church. It all begins in Revelation Chapter six, and the breaking of the seals.

Chapter Four

The Timing of the Seals

In order to get a fuller understanding behind the purpose and meaning of the Seal Judgments, one also needs to nail down the *timing* of the Seal Judgments. As we shall soon see, they occur over the first 3½ years of the 7-year Tribulation, Daniel's 70th week. This timing of the Seals is confirmed when one also looks at the parallel passages in the Bible that also cover these Judgments. Of course, I am referring to Matthew 24 or what's also known as the Olivet Discourse, and Daniel Chapter 9. This parallel between Revelation 6, the Seal Judgments, Matthew 24 and Luke 21 can be demonstrated by the following chart:

Matthew 24/Luke 21 & Revelation 6

Signs of His Coming		**First Six Seals**
24:4-5:	False Christs	6:1-2: White Horse (Antichrist)
24:6-7:	War	6:3-4: Red Horse (Global War)
24:7:	Famine	6:5-6: Black Horse (Global Famine)
Luke 21:11:	Pestilence	6:7-8: Pale Horse (Global Death)
24:9-13:	Martyrdom	6:9-11: 5th Seal Altar of Souls (Global Martyrdom)

Luke 21:11: Signs in the Sky

6:12-17 6th Seal
(Signs in the Sky)[1]

What's so important about this comparison chart of Matthew 24 and Luke 21 to Revelation 6 is not only the fact that it gives us even more details about this prophetic time-frame so as to obtain a fuller understanding, but it also reiterates the *timing* of these judgements and to *whom* these judgments are referring. Both are dealing with the *first half* of the 7-year Tribulation and both are referring to *Israel* and the *unbelieving Gentiles,* not the Church. The Church will *never* be placed under God's *wrath,* let alone be a part of the horrible event called *The Day of the Lord,* as this researcher admits:

"Since it is the Lamb Who unleashes the events about to transpire, we are not surprised by the close correlation between the sequence of events here and those which Jesus, the Lamb of God, taught would come in the Synoptic Gospels. They include:

1. False Messiahs: Matt. 24:5, 11; Mark 13:6; Luke 21:8; Rev. 6:2.
2. Wars: Matt. 24:6-7; Mark 13:7; Luke 21:9; Rev. 6:4.
3. Famines: Matt. 24:7; Mark 13:8; Luke 21:10; Rev. 6:5-6, 8.
4. Pestilences: Luke 21:11; Rev. 6:8.
5. Persecution: Matt. 24:9; Mark 13:9-13; Luke 21:12-17; Rev. 6:9-11.
6. Earthquakes: Matt. 24:7; Mark 13:8; Luke 21:11; Rev. 6:12.
7. Cosmic Phenomena: Matt. 24:29; Mark 13:24-25; Luke 21:11; Rev. 6:12-14.

As the Lamb opens the seals, a sequence of events is initiated which is closely parallel to Matthew 24 (also Mark 13 and Luke 21). Here we can see that the "birth pangs" or "beginning of sorrows" of Matthew 24 equate with the first four seals of Revelation 6, which are placed during the first half of the 70th week of Daniel.

Since the Bible says that the Day of the Lord will also include "the beginning of birth pangs," we can therefore conclude that the broad Day of the Lord (the time when God pours out His divine wrath, anger, and destruction) will also encompass the first four seals of Revelation 6."[2]

This means the Church cannot be a part of this time-frame. Why? Because the Bible declares and fully reassures us that the Church will be removed at the Rapture of the Church *prior* to the Day of the Lord, long before it ever begins. This is the wonderful truth that we see the Apostle Paul comforting the Thessalonian believers with.

2 Thessalonians 2:1-5 "Concerning the coming of our Lord Jesus Christ and our being gathered to him, we ask you, brothers, not to become easily unsettled or alarmed by some prophecy, report or letter supposed to have come from us, saying that the Day of the Lord has already come. Don't let anyone deceive you in any way, for that day will not come until the rebellion occurs and the man of lawlessness is revealed, the man doomed to destruction. He will oppose and will exalt himself over everything that is called God or is worshiped, so that he sets himself up in God's temple, proclaiming himself to be God. Don't you remember that when I was with you I used to tell you these things?"

So here we see the Apostle Paul *comforting* and *reassuring* the Thessalonian Church from a misconception going around at that time by some false teachers saying that these Christians missed the Rapture because the Day of the Lord had already come. But Paul says, "No! No! No! No!" Christians are *not* going to be around during that time frame and he's very emphatic about it. Why? Because the Bible says the Day of the Lord is all about God's judgment and bringing people low. It's a time when He pours out His wrath, and anger, and desolation, and vengeance, and destruction, and it's terrible. It's a time of gloominess, darkness, distress, and trouble, and refers to the cataclysmic final judgment of God upon the wicked, not the Church. And since the Day of the Lord is also associated with the "birth pangs" of Matthew 24 and Revelation 6, events that take place *during the first half* of the 7-year Tribulation, the Church cannot be there.

Besides, if the Thessalonians thought that the Rapture came *after* the 7-year Tribulation started, and then received a letter from Paul saying that the Day of the Lord had already started which occurs during the 7-year Tribulation, then would they not have been excited beyond words? Of course! They would have been hopeful that the Rapture was at the door because the 7-year Tribulation had already begun! They wouldn't have been troubled or fearful. They would have been excited! Yet that's precisely the point. The Apostle Paul is writing to alleviate their fears and troubled hearts concerning this fake letter that said the Day of the Lord had already begun and thus they were in the 7-year Tribulation. This lie is what freaked them out because they knew the Rapture occurred before this horrible time frame. This is also why Paul says comfort or encourage one another with these words. You're not going to be there, Church. Calm down. The Rapture occurs before all that!

That's why Paul also says, "Don't be deceived" and you should know better! "Don't you remember I already told you this?" In essence, "Why are you falling for this? You know you can't be there! I already went over this with you guys. Christians are nowhere around in the 7-year Tribulation! First or second half! We left at the Rapture, prior to the 7-year Tribulation!" So, he says, "Don't freak out and listen to these false teachers!" The timing of these events prove that the Church cannot be included in that time-frame. (Note: For an even more detailed discussion concerning the Church's absence from the Day of the Lord, see our previous study, *The Rapture: Don't Be Deceived*.)

Yet even more proof can be seen that the Church not only escapes the Day of the Lord and God's wrath in the 7-year Tribulation, but that that time period has nothing to do with the Church period, by observing the context and audience of Matthew 24, Revelation 6, as well as Daniel 9. In Matthew 24, the Chapter starts out with the Apostles asking Jesus what are the signs of His coming.

Matthew 24:3 "As Jesus was sitting on the Mount of Olives, the disciples came to Him privately. 'Tell us,' they said, 'when will this happen, and what will be the sign of Your coming and of the end of the age?'"

This "coming" that is being referred to is not the Rapture but the Second Coming of Jesus, which occurs at the end of the 7-year Tribulation. This is why the events that follow in Matthew 24, the "signs" of His Second Coming, are all signs that take place *during* the 7-year Tribulation leading up to His Return at the end. They start off with the first half (false christs, war, famine, death, martyrdom, signs in the sky), then move all the way to the end of the second half with Jesus' Second Coming. This lines up perfectly with the timing of Revelation Chapter 6. They are one and the same events dealing with the same time frame, the first half of the 7-year Tribulation (false christs or the antichrist, war, famine, death, martyrdom, signs in the sky). The dividing line between the first half and second half of the 7-year Tribulation is marked off for us in Daniel 9 with the event called the abomination of desolation.

Daniel 9:27 "*He* will confirm a covenant with many for *one 'seven.' In the middle of the 'seven'* he will put an end to sacrifice and offering. And on a wing of the temple he will set up an abomination that causes desolation, until the end that is decreed is poured out on him."

As we've already seen, he the Antichrist will make a covenant with the people of Israel, which is the very event that triggers or *starts* the final "seven" or "week" of Daniel's 70th week prophecy, the 7-year Tribulation. This is paralleled in Revelation 6 with the *breaking of the first seal*, the Antichrist Seal.

Revelation 6:1-2 "I watched as the Lamb opened the first of the seven seals. Then I heard one of the four living creatures say in a voice like thunder, 'Come!' I looked, and there before me was a white horse! Its rider held a bow, and he was given a crown, and he rode out as a conqueror bent on conquest."

The "confirming of the covenant" and the "breaking of the first seal" both occur at the same time, the beginning point of the 7-year Tribulation, the final "seven" of Daniel's 70th week prophecy. Then halfway into that final seven, the "middle of the seven" as Daniel says, the Antichrist goes up into the Jewish Temple and declares himself to be god, which is called the abomination of desolation. The Apostle Paul also mentions this "halfway-point abomination marker" in 2 Thessalonians Chapter 2.

2 Thessalonians 2:4 "He will oppose and will exalt himself over everything that is called God or is worshiped, so that he sets himself up in God's temple, proclaiming himself to be God."

This is why Matthew 24 perfectly aligns with Revelation 6. The first half of Matthew 24 is dealing with the events of the first half of the 7-year Tribulation, just as Revelation 6 and the seal judgments are also dealing with the events of the first half of the 7-year Tribulation. The *timing* is impeccable.

Therefore, since both passages are dealing with events that take place *during* the 7-year Tribulation, then we can know confidently that *neither of them* can be referring to the Church. Why? Because, as we saw earlier, the Church is *saved from*, *rescued from*, and *not appointed unto* God's wrath which includes His wrath being poured out during the *entire* 7-year Tribulation. This comforting truth is further reiterated when one takes a look at the context of Matthew 24. We know contextually that Matthew 24 cannot be referring to the Church period, first half or second half, because Jesus starts the chapter off by saying that the Jewish Temple will be torn down to the ground and destroyed, which did happen in 70 AD. But then a few verses later He says a rebuilt Jewish Temple comes back into existence with Jewish people apparently worshipping at it again.

Matthew 24:15 "So when you see standing in the *holy place* 'the abomination that causes desolation,' spoken of through the prophet Daniel – let the reader understand - …"

As Jesus states, this "abomination of desolation" in the "holy place" or "temple" is mentioned in the Book of Daniel whereas, we just saw, the Antichrist goes up into that Temple and declares himself to be god halfway into the 7-year Tribulation. The point is this. The Jewish Temple being destroyed or rebuilt has no significance for the Church. Jesus says the Church doesn't need a manmade Temple because we have become the Temple of God by the indwelling Holy Spirit.

1 Corinthians 3:16 "Don't you know that you *yourselves are God's temple* and that God's Spirit lives in you?"

So, the Church is only concerned about "being" God's temple, not a "destroyed" or "rebuilt" Jewish Temple. However, a manmade Jewish Temple being destroyed and rebuilt is a very significant issue for the Jewish people to whom this Chapter is addressed.

Furthermore, Jesus also tells the people during that time frame to "flee to the mountains."

Matthew 24:16 "Then let *those who are in Judea flee to the mountains*."

Notice He says, "those in Judea." Where's that? Israel. This is not the Church nor can it be the Church. Think about it. Only a small minute fraction of the Church, i.e. Christians, live in Israel. If this were referring to the Church, it would make this command to flee absolutely meaningless. Secondly, the command to flee is "to the mountains." Most scholars believe the place referred to here is the ancient rock city of Petra. Question: "Can the whole Church fit into Petra?" I think not. However, the remnant of the Jewish People can. Next, we see Jesus mentioning that those people of that time are apparently "keeping the Sabbath Day."

Matthew 24:20 "Pray that your flight will not take place in winter or on the *Sabbath*."

Question: "Does the Church observe a traditional Jewish Saturday Sabbath?" No. But the Jewish people do, even to this day! We Christians not only worship on Sunday in honor of the Resurrection of Jesus Christ, but we are never given the command to worship on the Jewish Sabbath day. Why? Because we have the Lord of the Sabbath Himself, Jesus Christ. We have the "reality" not the "shadow." That's why the Bible says this when referring to the Church and the Jewish Sabbath:

Colossians 2:16-17 "Therefore do not let anyone judge you by what you eat or drink, or with regard to a religious festival, a New Moon celebration or a Sabbath day. These are a shadow of the things that were to come; the reality, however, is found in Christ."

Technically, we are free to worship Jesus any day we want as New Testament Christians. However, traditionally we usually come together "the first day of the week" (Sunday) in honor of the Resurrection of Jesus.

Acts 20:7 "On the first day of the week we came together to break bread."

Therefore, the point is this. How could Jesus be talking about the Church in Matthew 24 when He says these people need to "pray that their flight doesn't take place on the Sabbath" if the Church doesn't worship on the Sabbath? Could it be He's referring to the Jewish people who still do to this day worship on the Sabbath? I think so.

In addition, this would also mean that the following often misquoted passages of Scripture in Matthew 24, that some would say is referring to the Rapture of the Church, cannot be referring to the Church as well. The whole Chapter of Matthew 24 is referring to Israel, not the Church.

Matthew 24:31 "And He will send his angels with a loud trumpet call, and they will gather His elect from the four winds, from one end of the heavens to the other."

Matthew 24:40-41 "Two men will be in the field; one will be taken and the other left. Two women will be grinding with a hand mill; one will be taken and the other left."

Unfortunately, many people will misquote these passages as Rapture passages when they are not. As has already been demonstrated contextually, Matthew 24 has nothing to do with the Church, but rather Israel. Therefore, whatever is happening in these passages is happening to Israel. And wonder of wonders, it is! The angels coming and gathering the "elect," with one person being taken while another is left, is simply talking about the angel harvest at the *end* of the 7-year Tribulation where the "elect" or Israel and any "believing" Gentiles who have not died during the 7-year Tribulation are "gathered" to enter the Millennial Kingdom. The "others" are the unbelieving unredeemed who are "taken" and cast into hell. Obviously, they are not going to be a part of the Millennial Kingdom at the end of the 7-year Tribulation. We see this angel "harvest" mentioned again in Revelation 14, Matthew 13 with the "pulling" of the Wheat and Tares, and in the "separation" of the "sheep and goats" in Matthew 25.

Therefore, since the events mentioned in Matthew 24 are clearly not speaking about the Church, but rather the whole Chapter is referring to Israel, then neither can Revelation Chapter 6 be speaking about or be directed to the Church, because it exactly parallels the first half of Mathew 24. Again, this is why these two passages perfectly align. The *audiences* are the same and the *timing* is the same. Both deal with the first half of the 7-year Tribulation, the Seal Judgments, and the Church is nowhere around. They left at the Rapture, prior to the beginning of these horrible events of Daniel Chapter 9 where we saw the "mid-point" event of these 7 years, dealing with the Church. How do we know?

- The Church is never mentioned once in Daniel Chapter 9.

- The Church wasn't even in existence until 570 years after the Book of Daniel was written.

- The Old Testament writers, including Daniel, had no knowledge of the Church. The New Testament declares that it was a "mystery" to them.

- The Book of Daniel was written by a Jewish man with a Jewish name, for a Jewish people, for a Jewish time, not the Church.

- This time is also referred to in the Bible as Jacob's trouble, not the Church's trouble. It's not "Paul's Doom" or "Peter's Demise" or even "Ananias' Agony." It's Jacob's trouble, referring to the Jewish people. (Note: For an even more detailed discussion of the audience of Matthew 24 and Daniel Chapter 9 see our previous study, *The Rapture: Don't Be Deceived.*)

Therefore, as you can see, contextually, in all three passages, Revelation 6, Matthew 24, and Daniel 9, they are dealing with the time when God's wrath will be poured out upon the rebellious House of Israel and the rebellious Gentiles on earth, not the Church, His Beloved Bride, who is safely tucked away in heaven. It is the beginning of the end for the rejecters of Jesus, as the Church is separated from the planet, like these men share:

"The sixth chapter of Revelation is the great watershed, the great divide, of the Book of Revelation. Here is a division that is all-important.

Traveling on Highway 66 across northern New Mexico, you go through Albuquerque, then Gallup, to Winslow, Arizona, and up to Flagstaff. Somewhere in that area there is a place called the Continental Divide. I am told that you could drop a chip in a stream which is flowing on the west side of the divide, and it would end up in the Pacific Ocean, or you could put a chip in a stream on the east side of the divide, and it would eventually end up in the Atlantic Ocean by way of the Gulf of Mexico. This is a very important division which separates those two chips so that they find themselves worlds apart. We have such a great divide at Chapter 6 of the Book of Revelation.

In Revelation Chapter 4 we found ourselves transferred to heaven. John was caught up to heaven, and we went right up with him and began to see things in heaven. However, we did not see anything labeled the Church, because the Church was the name given to it down here on the earth. But we did see the twenty-four elders. The elders had to get there some way – they were caught up, and they represent the Church which will be at this time in heaven with Christ.

From here on in the Book of Revelation, the Church is no longer mentioned on the earth at all. There is an invitation at the end of the book which comes from the Church, but that refers to this day in which we live. The Church will be delivered from this period of judgment. Why? Is it because they are such nice, sweet, Sunday school children? Oh, no. They are sinners, but they are saved by the grace of God. Only those who reject the grace of God go into the 7-year Tribulation period. What happens on the earth when the Church leaves? The 7-year Tribulation takes place and that is the subject of chapters 6–18.

The seals encompass the entire period of the 7-year Tribulation (Rev. 3:10), culminating with the return of Christ. The seventh seal contains the seven trumpet judgments (Rev. 8:1-11:19), and the seventh trumpet (Rev. 11:15) contains the seven bowl judgments (Rev. 16:1-21). The seven seals thus contain all the judgments to the end when Jesus Christ returns.

The 7-year Tribulation is triggered from heaven. Jesus Christ directs the entire operation. This is the reason that Psalm 2:9 says, 'Thou shalt break them with a rod of iron...' Many will say that they don't like all this. Do you have a better suggestion as to how He should put down the rebellion on this earth? If you do, would you pass it on to the Lord Jesus? How do you think He should put it down?

Suppose He came like He did more than nineteen hundred years ago. Do you think they are ready in Moscow, in the Kremlin, to turn authority over to Him? How about in any other country? How about in our country? I'm telling you, they are not about to turn it over to Him in Washington, D.C. Neither of our political parties is interested in putting Jesus Christ on the throne. They have some very unworthy men on both sides who would like to be on the throne.

My friend, may I say to you that Jesus alone is the One who is worthy. And how is He going to come to power? Exactly as the second psalm says: 'Thou shalt break them with a rod of iron...' We are going to see that taking place from now on in the Book of Revelation – this is judgment on the earth."[3]

And so now let us turn our attention to this *breaking of the planet* from Jesus, a time when the Church is safely guarded up in heaven, and the rejecting world begins to feel His rod of wrath. It all begins now in Revelation Chapter six.

Part II

The Breaking of the Seals

Chapter Five

The Breaking of the Antichrist Seal

The **first thing** we see in the breaking of the planet is the **Opener of the First Seal**.

Revelation 6:1 "I watched as the Lamb opened the first of the seven seals."

The phrase, "I watched," is also translated as "Now I saw," or "Then I saw," and it draws our attention right out of the gates to a *shift* that is taking place. The Church or the Twenty-four Elders are safe up in heaven following the Rapture of the Church (Revelation Chapter 4). All of heaven has just finished giving God glory, honor, and praise for the Lamb, Jesus, being worthy to open the scroll, the title deed to the earth, to reverse the curse (Revelation Chapter 5), *but now* the judgment of the planet begins (Revelation Chapter 6). What is to follow are the "future" events that "will take place later" as was mentioned in Revelation Chapter 1.

Revelation 1:19 "Write, therefore, what you have seen, what is now and *what will take place later*."

- Chapter 1 – The Unveiling of Jesus Christ (what you have seen)
- Chapter 2-3 – The Church on Earth (what is now)
- Chapter 4 – The Church in Heaven (what will take place later)
- Chapter 5 – The Lamb & the Scroll (what will take place later)
- Chapter 6 – The Lamb Opens the Scroll (what will take place later)

Revelation Chapter 1 also tells us the identity of the One Whom the Book of Revelation is all about and why it is was written.

Revelation 1:1a "The revelation of Jesus Christ, which God gave him to show his servants what must soon take place."

The word "revelation" is "apokalupsis" in the Greek and it means, "a disclosure or an unveiling." It is "revelation" (singular), not "revelations" (plural). Thus, this whole Book of Revelation is a "single" albeit huge "unveiling" of Jesus Christ, the resurrected real Jesus Christ, not some namby pamby twisted version of Jesus that is unfortunately so often presented by the ungodly world or worldly Church. This Book is an "unveiling" of the risen Lord who came the first time mild, meek merciful, to procure the forgiveness of our sins, but *now* what is about to be "disclosed" is that He is coming back again, this time as the Lion of the tribe of Judah, to dish out His wrath against sin, as this man shares:

"Here in Revelation there is an explosion of detail about the return of Jesus Christ. The word is apokalupsis, from which we get the word apocalypse, that means literally, to take the cover off, to uncover, to unveil, to reveal. That word is used eighteen times in the New Testament. And when it is used of a person, it always indicates that he becomes visible. And so what you have here is truth becoming clearly visible.

Now many people assume that this book hides things. People read this book and are absolutely confused by it. People read it and assume that it is some kind of mysterious, strange, exotic, unsolvable riddle, some puzzle that man could never understand. They assume it is vague or obscure or complex or incomprehensible and confusing. But this book is not the hiding, this book is the revelation; important to note that. It is not the covering, it is the uncovering.

And what does it reveal? What does it uncover? It reveals warnings to the Church about its besetting sins. It reveals instruction to the Church about the need for holiness. It reveals the amazing power and glorious overcoming strength of Christ and the Christian over sin and satan. It reveals the ultimate triumph of believers who are killed for the cause of Christ. It reveals the glory of worship. It reveals the end of human history. It reveals the final political setup of the world. It reveals the triumph of God's saving purpose.

It reveals the career of antichrist and the final battle of Armageddon and the alignment of the nations of the world. It reveals the need to fight the forces of evil patiently. It reveals the glories of Christ's kingdom on earth and in the new heaven and the new earth. It reveals the triumph ultimately of God's saving purposes, no matter what satan endeavors to do. It reveals the victory of Christ over all powers, human and demonic. It reveals the final end of satan and the final end of sin.

It is the opposite of a puzzle, it is the opposite of a mystery, it is not a covering, it is not a hiding; it is an unveiling. It is the apocalypse, the unveiling, the disclosure of details heretofore hidden from human view, the history of the end of the universe, and how it will take place and what will come after that.

It is the revelation of Jesus Christ. It is the unveiling of the glory of Christ in His second coming, as He takes back the earth from the usurper, satan, and establishes His kingdom, both the kingdom in this world and the kingdom in the world to come. It is Christ who is unveiled. It is Christ who is manifest. It is Christ who is uncovered. It is Christ presented in glory, Christ presented in majesty."[1]

And that is what we see here in Revelation Chapter 6. The "unveiling" of Christ now in charge of unleashing His judgment upon wicked and sinful and unrepentant planet earth. This is what John "now sees," this is what he "watches," the *Lamb opened the first of the seven seals."*

We also *now see* yet another reminder of just Who is responsible for these judgments about to be poured out upon planet earth during the 7-year Tribulation. Once again, it is *the Lamb*. He is in charge. He is instituting this, not man or satan. The wrath that is to be poured out is coming from Him. It is a carry-over from what John *sees* starting back in Chapters 4-5. There we saw the throne room of God with the Lamb of God taking the scroll, and *now* John sees the Lamb opening the first seal. This will begin a chain of events, all ordered of God, coming from God, at the Hand of God, starting with the *first of the seven seals* moving all the way to the end of the 7-year Tribulation with the Return of Jesus Christ at His Second Coming. The message is loud and clear what John *sees*, it is none other than the *Lamb,* Jesus Christ Himself, who institutes the proceedings. As one-person states:

"The Lord Jesus breaks the seals, and the four horses ride forth. He is directing everything now. As we were told at the beginning, this is the Revelation, the

unveiling, of Jesus Christ. He is no longer walking among the lampstands, for they have all been removed from this earth. He is no longer the High Priest, standing as intercessor, but He is now the executor of God's will upon the earth as He opens the seals of the book. All the judgments of the 7-year Tribulation usher forth from the seals out of which come the trumpets, and the bowls."[2]

In fact, it gets even more apparent that it is *the Lamb* Who is in charge of these proceedings, all the way to the very end, when one looks at the rest of the context of Revelation Chapter 6. In each seal, God is emphatically declaring and reminding us just where and from whom all these judgements are coming:

Revelation 6:1a "I watched as the *Lamb* opened the first of the seven seals."

Revelation 6:3 "When the *Lamb* opened the second seal, I heard the second living creature say, 'Come!'"

Revelation 6:5 "When the *Lamb* opened the third seal, I heard the third living creature say, 'Come!'"

Revelation 6:7 "When the *Lamb* opened the fourth seal, I heard the voice of the fourth living creature say, 'Come!'"

Revelation 6:9 "When *He* opened the fifth seal, I saw under the altar the souls of those who had been slain because of the Word of God and the testimony they had maintained."

Revelation 6:12 "I watched as *He* opened the sixth seal. There was a great earthquake. The sun turned black like sackcloth made of goat hair, the whole moon turned blood red."

Revelation 8:1 "When *He* opened the seventh seal, there was silence in heaven for about half an hour."

Who is in charge of these judgements from the very outset? It is repeatedly reiterated in the beginning of each seal. It is *the Lamb*, He, God, who is doing all this. Therefore, how anyone can say these events are the supposed wrath of man or satan, is not only unbelievable, it's downright unbiblical. God is "screaming out" from the text that *He is in charge*, no one else! Why? Because the *purpose* of the 7-year Tribulation is to fulfill *the purposes of God*, not man or satan:

The Purposes of the Tribulation

1. To discipline Israel for her stubborn rejection of Christ and bring the nation to faith in Christ (Zech.12:10; Matt.23:37-39). This prepares her for restoration and regathering for the Millennium (Jer.30:1-17; Ezek.20:33-38).

2. To judge the Gentile nations for their wickedness and rejection of Jesus Christ (Zeph.1:15,17,18; Joel 3:12-14; Rev..6:16-17). The Tribulation will also be used to bring many Gentiles to faith in Christ (Matt.24:14; Rev.7:9; 13:10).

3. To reveal the true character and agenda of satan. The Tribulation will permit satan's program to come to its logical conclusion resulting in God's judgment. It will demonstrate that satan is the cause of war, murder, and deception, and that he deserves God's judgment (Isa.14:12-17; Ezek.28:12-19; Matt.25:41; Rev.12:7-12; 20:1-3).

4. To demonstrate that God is holy (Rev.4:8; 6:10), righteous (Rev.15:3-4), just (Rom.3:26; 1 Pet.3:18), patient (2 Pet.3:9), and still on the throne (Rev.4:1-11).[3]

No, man is not in charge here, *the Lamb*, God, Jesus, *He* is! His purpose for the very 7-year Tribulation is now being *opened* with *the first of the seven seals*. It is a complete utter fulfilment of His desires and will for the planet. It's His title deed, it's His right, and it's His doing. It is completely His doing through and through, as is seen in the even the number of seals. It was the *first of the seven seals*. Why are there seven? Why not 2, or 97, or even 16? One researcher surmises an answer:

"The Lamb broke one of the seven seals to remind you that seven is a number of completion. That's why there are seven seals, seven trumpets, and seven bowls because that completes the judgment. When all of them are complete, the universe is Christ's, the Kingdom has come, and the Millennium is here.

All of these events also occur in a period called the 7-year Tribulation which is a week, the seventieth week of Daniel, a period of seven years.

Jesus divided it into two parts, the birth pangs, the first half, and the Great Tribulation, the second half, separated by the abomination of desolation which is when the Antichrist desecrates the temple in Jerusalem and heats up the persecution and tries to destroy Israel and set himself up as God to be worshipped by the whole world."[4]

Again, man or satan is *not* in charge here. This is what John sees. It is *the Lamb*, God, Jesus, *He* is in charge! These judgements that are to follow *the Lamb opened the first of the seven seals* are completely coming from *Him*, God, to completely fulfill His purposes for this wicked and rebellious planet for the next 7 years. The judgement is *now* set in motion, the action to *break the planet* and take it back has begun:

"Now the action of the Book of the Revelation begins here in chapter 6. This is the act of our God, our kinsman Redeemer, in whose hands God Almighty has placed the authority of this universe [Dan.7:13-14; Matt.28:18]. This is the act of that great sovereign Lord who takes back out of the hand of the usurper and the interloper and the intruder and the stranger and the alien.

This is the act by which, in the judicial proceedings of God, our Lord and Savior takes back out of the hands of satan our rightful inheritance [John 12:31; Rev.12:7-10]. This is the casting out of the dynasties of evil; this is the forever casting away of the powers of darkness, and this is the bringing in of light and life and liberty and everlasting righteousness [1 Cor.1:28; 15:54].

Now those seven seals [Rev.5:1] encompass all of the story of God, from the Rapture [Rev.4:1] until the return [Rev.19:11-21]. These seven seals include the whole proceedings of the Almighty after God's people are taken out of the earth [1 Cor.15:51-57; 1 Thess.4:14-17] and until they come back with their reigning Lord, given the possession of God's inheritance [Rev.19:14; 20:4].

The seventh seal is the seven trumpets [Rev.8:1-2], and the seventh trumpet is the seven-golden bowls, of the seven vials, of the wrath and plagues of Almighty God [Rev.11:15,16]. And when they are finished – when the seventh seal and the seventh trumpet and the seventh bowl, when these are finished, then is finished the judgment of God upon sin and upon iniquity [Rev.15:1].

Then is the cleansing of this earth [Rev.19:1-3]. Then is the binding of satan [Rev.20:1-2]. Then is the establishment of the millennial kingdom in which God's children shall reign with Him in this earth [Rev.20:4]."[5]

The **second thing** we see in the breaking of the planet is the **Ordering of the First Seal**.

Revelation 6:1b "Then I heard one of the four living creatures say in a voice like thunder, 'Come!'"

As if it wasn't reiterated enough so far in the first half of the first verse alone just Who is in charge of these judgements that are about to be unleashed on planet earth and where they are coming from, now John *sees* another reminder that God, *the Lamb* is the One causing these wrathful events to come forth. First, Jesus from the throne room of God *opens* the *first of the seven seals;* now *one of the four living creatures* from the throne room of God gives an *order* to begin the pouring out of judgments contained within *the first of the seven seals.* Scripturally, the *living creatures* are angelic beings under God's command, God's direction, and exist to fulfill God's purposes. The word "angel" in the Greek is "aggelos", and it simply means "a messenger, an envoy, one who is sent." Thus, these *living creatures* and the *one* seen here are simply God's holy angelic Cheribum surrounding His throne, ready to do His will, as this man shares:

"Now here we see four living beings that are both in and around the throne, in the center or in the middle of the throne and around it. It gives the sense of an inner circle moving through and around the throne very close to the presence of God. They're in it and they're around it all at the same time in motion, surrounding God and moving.

Ezekiel describes them very vividly in Ezekiel Chapter 1. They are called the four living creatures from the Greek verb zao, to live. They are living ones, not really animals. They shouldn't probably be called beasts or creatures; that would be a different word, theria, but they are living ones, living beings.

Ezekiel saw these four living creatures with all of these various faces and manifestations. And he saw the spirit of those living creatures in some kind of wheels that were moving, and those wheels seemed to be bright and flashing, and it was all in motion. This was the original light show, believe me. This was supernatural lasers flashing and refracting through the prisms of these very beings.

Now who are these living creatures? These incredibly beautiful and glorious beings who were so utterly indescribable? Don't try to take everything in Ezekiel Chapter 1 and comprehend it; it is just a grandiose description of the indescribable. But we know who they are. Chapter 10 of Ezekiel and verse 15: 'Then the cherubim rose up, they are the living beings that I saw by the river Chebar.'

Cherubim are angels that's the plural of cherub. Cherubim are angels frequently referred to in the Old Testament in connection with God's divine power. For example, in Psalm 80 verse 1, Psalm 99 verse 1, and elsewhere we find the cherubim associated with the power of God.

We also can note that they appear to be concerned about the holiness of God. They then are in God's presence and they are guarding His holiness. And they are there for the purpose of expressing His power when He bids them to do that.

Now you know, in the inner sanctuary, the Holy of Holies, the cherubim were spread out over the Mercy Seat in the Ark of the Covenant. And there they are, the symbols guarding the holiness of God, the symbols representing the power of God as He acts against sin. And so, they were very special angels...involved in judgment...ready to do His bidding.[6]

And that again takes us back to the whole *purpose* of the 7-year Tribulation. God is dishing out His wrath that has been stored up against all the ungodliness and unrepentant sin and wickedness that's been going on in front of Him on planet earth. And lest you doubt that these *living creatures* or cherubim are actually fulfilling God's will concerning His judgment upon sin during the 7-year tribulation, it just so happens we see them giving the orders for the beginning of God's judgments at the *beginning* of the 7-year Tribulation, as well as completing His judgments at the *end* of the 7-year Tribulation:

Revelation 6:1 "I watched as the Lamb opened the first of the seven seals. Then I heard one of the four *living creatures* say in a voice like thunder, 'Come!'"

Revelation 15:7 "Then one of the four *living creatures* gave to the seven angels seven golden bowls filled with the wrath of God, who lives for ever and ever."

As you can see from the Bible, *from beginning to end*, Jesus the Lamb, is in charge of the judgments during the 7-year Tribulation. This is made clear by His special envoy of holy Cheribum angels, or *living creatures* surrounding His throne, ready and waiting to do His will concerning His judgement of sin, giving the *orders* for the judgments to commence in the 7-year Tribulation. Again, how anyone can say these events have anything to do with man or satan's will is beyond me, not to mention what the Scripture is clearly teaching us. Again, God is in charge of these events through and through.

And lest there be any doubt as well that what is about to come forth from the very throne room of God is a foreboding, horrible, ominous, and terrible judgment against sinful humanity for the next seven years, one of the *living creatures* reveals this doom and gloom message in two different ways.

The **first way** we see God's judgment upon sin is with **The Living Creature's Voice**.

Revelation 6:1b "Then I heard one of the four living creatures say in a voice like thunder, 'Come!'"

Notice the *living creature* makes this announcement not with a pleasant whisper, a jovial tone, or even a celebratory exaltation, but rather he uses *a voice like thunder*. Thunder is the Greek word "bronte" and it simply means, "thunder and/or peals of thunder." It is the same word that is used to describe the largest and most terrifying of all dinosaurs in the English language, the "Brontosaurus," or "bronte" (thunder) "saurus" (lizard). You don't want to see this terrible "thunder lizard" coming your way. You would be "deeply impressed" by it. And neither do you want to be around when this Cheribum makes this "thunderous, terrible" announcement from the very throne room of God. The world is about to become "deeply impressed" by His judgment.

In the Bible, *thunder* implies and signifies that something bad is coming. Something ominous is on its way, like a coming storm, only it's the coming storm of God's judgment nearly arriving. It is terrifying, yet majestic, signaling God's judgment is at hand. In fact, *thunder* in and of itself is a scary thing. It immediately grabs your attention. No matter what you're doing or where you are, the sound of thunder jolts you to your core, especially if it's unexpected. It makes you jump out of your shoes. Man, or beast know all too well the terrors of *thunder*. When I lived in western New York for a period of time, my two miniature dachshunds would literally crawl up into a ball around my head at night, (yes, they slept with me) shaking like a leaf, when the thunderstorms would light up the night sky, and they would continue to shake and shiver until the *thunder* subsided. It is a terrifying noise that one cannot forget, man or beast. It immobilizes you, and this is how *the voice of the living creature* sounded, *like thunder*.

Furthermore, *thunder* is used as a deliberate backdrop in scary movies. Hollywood uses it to carefully set the emotional stage of the audience to send a clear message that something ominous and terrifying is about to arrive, or even that some horrific and life-threatening situation is about to be encountered that one should do their best to avoid. So, in essence, the message here is clear from God. The *living creature with a voice like thunder* tells us that God's *horror show* is about to start playing on planet earth, and all the unredeemed need to tremble, shiver, and shake at this foreboding announcement. Therefore, it is no surprise that we see its usage throughout the Book of Revelation concerning the other judgments of God during the 7-year Tribulation:

Revelation 4:5 "From the throne came flashes of *lightning*, rumblings and peals of thunder. Before the throne, seven lamps were blazing. These are the seven spirits of God."

Revelation 6:1 "I watched as the Lamb opened the first of the seven seals. Then I heard one of the four living creatures say in a voice like *thunder*, 'Come!'"

Revelation 8:5 "Then the angel took the censer, filled it with fire from the altar, and hurled it on the earth; and there came peals of *thunder*, rumblings, flashes of lightning and an earthquake."

Revelation 10:3-4 "And he gave a loud shout like the roar of a lion. When he shouted, the voices of the seven *thunders* spoke. And when the seven *thunders* spoke, I was about to write; but I heard a voice from heaven say, 'Seal up what the seven *thunders* have said and do not write it down.'"

Revelation 11:19 "Then God's temple in heaven was opened, and within His temple was seen the ark of His covenant. And there came flashes of lightning, rumblings, peals of *thunder*, an earthquake and a great hailstorm."

Revelation 14:2 "And I heard a sound from heaven like the roar of rushing waters and like a loud peal of *thunder*. The sound I heard was like that of harpists playing their harps."

Revelation 16:18 "Then there came flashes of lightning, rumblings, peals of *thunder* and a severe earthquake. No earthquake like it has ever occurred since man has been on earth, so tremendous was the quake."

Revelation 19:6 "Then I heard what sounded like a great multitude, like the roar of rushing waters and like loud peals of *thunder*, shouting: 'Hallelujah! For our Lord God Almighty reigns.'"

Furthermore, *thunder* is also used in this same foreboding manner to speak of God's judgment in the Old Testament as well:

- Sent as a plague upon the Egyptians.
  Exodus 9:23-24

- The Philistines, in battle with the people of Israel.
  1 Samuel 7:10

- Sent as a judgment.
  Isaiah 29:6

- On Mount Sinai.
  Exodus 19:16; Psalms 77:18; Hebrews 12:18,19

- A sign of divine anger.
  1 Samuel 12:17,18

- A manifestation of divine power.
  Job 26:14; Psalms 77:18[7]

Therefore, the message God, the Lamb, is sending through this living creature becomes crystal clear: He, God, *the Lamb* is in charge of these ominous, horrible, terrifying, earth-shattering and shaking judgements. It is He Who is about to unleash these frightful events upon the whole planet, not man or satan. In fact, to further drive the Biblical point home, *thunder* is often associated with the very *voice of God Himself*, as this person shares:

"In the Bible, God's voice is often depicted as thunder, or, alternately, when thunder occurs, it is God speaking. We're told that thunder, when it is God's voice, presages judgment. We remember the people at Mt Sinai were scared out of their wits upon hearing the thunder, and begged Moses to ask that God not

speak aloud again (Ex.20:19).

We recall Revelation 10:1-4 and the mystery of the Seven Thunders. 'And I saw another angel come down from heaven clothed with a cloud: and a rainbow was upon his head, and his face was as it were the sun, and his feet as pillars of fire. And he had in his hand a little book open: and he set his right foot upon the sea, and his left foot on the earth. And he cried with a loud voice, as when a lion roars: and when he cried, seven thunders uttered their voices. And when the seven thunders had uttered their voices, I was about to write: and I heard a voice from heaven saying to me, seal up those things which the seven thunders uttered, and do not write them.'

Thunder, when it is not a God-controlled weather phenomenon, is a direct representation of God's power. Even adults startle when a particularly loud boom of thunder claps above them. The booming noises could be interpreted as God's instrument to invoke awe and righteous fear into those who do not yet fear The Lord.

The throne of God is surrounded by thunder. 'From the throne came flashes of lightning, rumblings and peals of thunder. Before the throne, seven lamps were blazing. These are the seven spirits of God.' (Revelation 4:5).

When Jesus spoke to Paul on the road to Damascus, those who were with Paul heard thunder. God said to Job, 'Hast thou an arm like God? Or canst thou thunder with a voice like Him?' (Job 40:9). The Bible shows us time and time again that sometimes when God speaks, it sounds like thunder, or a boom.

Not every thunderclap is God speaking. Sometimes it is simply one of the forces of nature controlled by God. Sometimes it is His voice as heard by flawed and un-glorified man. Other times – as recorded in the Bible from past to future – it is an expression of His divine wrath."[8]

Again, not man or satan, this wrath that is to be poured out upon sinful wicked humanity on planet earth, for the next seven years, is coming from the very throne room of God Himself. He, *the Lamb opened the first of the seven seals* whereupon His very special messenger angel, the *living creature*, makes this *thunderous* truth known to all loud and clear. There is no escaping the correct and obvious conclusion; the wrath of the Lamb has come, and all of earth should shudder in great fear. One man encapsulates it this way:

"We've seen the throne, we know who's on it, we know who's before it, in and around it, we know what's coming from it and we know what's being directed at it. This is a true visit to heaven. And may I suggest to you the proper response?

It doesn't tell us what happened to John here, but back in Chapter 1, the first time he had a vision it says in verse 17, 'I fell at His feet as a dead man.' That is very reminiscent of the experience of Isaiah, because back in Isaiah Chapter 6 when Isaiah had his vision of heaven he had a similar response. Isaiah 6 verse 6, 'Then I said, Woe is me, I am destroyed for I am a man of unclean lips and I live among a people of unclean lips.'

When John had his first vision, he went into a coma out of sheer fright; panic set in because he knew that if he saw God in His throne, holy God, holy, holy, holy God, that God saw him, and God saw his sin and it frightened him into a paralysis. Isaiah had the same response. Woe is me, I am damned, I am ruined. I have seen God and God has seen me. And if God has seen me, I am done. Ezekiel, 'When I saw it,' he says, 'I fell on my face.'

It's the right response. They all had it, same response...fell over in absolute fear. You can't just take a trip to heaven like this and walk away. You've got to realize this is holy God that you have seen. And it ought to shake all of us to the core to realize that He sees us and sees our sin and our iniquity. He is infinitely holy. The holy angels are there, surrounding Him. His holiness blazes forth in judgment. And that should put fear in all of us.

Let me tell you something, folks. The world is full of people who, when confronted by the holiness of God, will be consumed. The first time they take a visit to the throne room, they will be consumed because when they get there it's going to be called the Great White Throne. And all of the ungodly of all of the ages are going to come to that throne and be cast into the lake of fire which burns with fire and brimstone forever."[9]

The **second way** we see God's judgment upon sin is with **The Living Creature's Command**.

Revelation 6:1b "Then I heard one of the four living creatures say in a voice like thunder, 'Come!'"

Now that the ominous *tone* has been set by the *living creature* that God, *the Lamb*, is in control of these judgments and He is the One *ordering* them upon sinful humanity, we see a *command* given by the *living creature* that reiterates this truth as well. The *living creature* does not say please, or will you, or mother may I, or would you consider doing such and such for me, and he certainly doesn't say, let me check in with man or satan first. No! An *order* is given by God's messenger to *come*! *Come* and do what? To begin the judgment from God for the next seven years upon sinful humanity and planet earth. It all starts here. It all starts now. This is not a request, this is not a discussion. It is an *order* from God given via His holy angelic Cheribum the *living creature* who exists to do His will.

Come is the Greek word "erchomai" and it means, "to arise, come forth, to show oneself." Thus, God is giving the *command* via his angel with a *commanding* voice to, "*Come*, proceed, show yourself, arise and be the first of My tools of judgment upon planet earth for the next seven years." The *living creature* is not speaking to the Apostle John, but rather, contextually, in the very next verse, verse 2, we see clearly that it is being directed to the first horse rider, the white horse rider, the first of the four horsemen of the apocalypse. When this *command* is given, to *come*, the white horse rider immediately appears. Thus, this *command* to *come* is *the very command* that *begins* the *very seven-year Tribulation*.

God then adds further emphasis that this is also referring to a foreboding event by the punctuation. Notice the *command* to *come* contains an exclamation point. This white horse rider is to *come!* This is not a whisper by the *living creature*. This is not a casual statement, and neither is it open for discussion. There are no pleasantries here. The *order* is given from on high and the white horse rider is to *come!* God Who is holy, holy, holy, now gives a strong commanding *order* via His Holy Cheribum for His holy and righteous judgment to begin to fall upon sinful and wicked humanity. There is no turning back now. The prophesied 7-year Tribulation, Daniel's long-awaited 70th week is to finally begin. No more waiting, no more wondering, it is here! The order for mankind's darkest hour, as stated elsewhere by Jesus *the Lamb*, is now breathed forth. The *order* from God will not be changed, it will not be stopped, and no man or devil can thwart what He the Holy One is now unleashing. The time has come, for not one, not two, not three, but seven years of non-stop wrath from God to be poured out on this wicked and deluded planet. It will finally be utterly judged *now*! All the wrath God has been storing up throughout the ages is now going to gush forth. The beginning of the end has begun with one simple yet profound authoritative *command* from God's Holy Cheribum, *the living creature*. He says, *Come!*

In fact, the *command* to *come* not only contains an exclamation point for emphasis, but it is also written in the Greek imperative which clearly speaks of a command being given "involving the imposition of one's will upon another." Who's will? God *the Lamb's* will! This is His direction, His judgment, His doing, through and through. Again, for people to state this *order*, let alone the horrible chain of events to follow, is coming from man or satan, is ludicrous to the highest degree when one deals openly and honestly with the Biblical text. It is *the Lamb* Who is in charge here, He is the One Who is sovereignly judging this world, as these researchers also state:

"The first four seals seem to belong together (6:1-8).

(1) They are introduced by one of the four living creatures (6:1, 3, 5, 7).
(2) Each seal is preceded with a call to "Come."
(3) Each seal contains the image of a horse and rider (6:2, 4, 5, 8).
(4) In each of the seals there is a progression of meaning given for each of the four seals: conquering, making war, famine, and death.
(5) Each of these seals is opened by the Lamb, Jesus Christ.
(6) Each seal is given its authority by Christ ("and to him was granted..."). John sees the whole process of judgment under the control of God.

The conqueror has only what Almighty God allows him to have. God is completely sovereign, so His people do not need to be dismayed.

None of the horrendous judgments about to take place transpire until the Lamb opens a seal. Human history records a litany of wars, natural disasters, famines, and the like, but what is about to come forth upon the earth is completely unique.

What has transpired up to now is the routine manifestation of human selfishness, sin, and the fallen world in which man lives. But with the opening of the seals by the Lamb, divinely-initiated judgments begin which are historically unique in a number of aspects:

*1. **Severity** – The judgments are more severe than any previously experienced in history. This coming day is unique so there is 'none like it' (Jer.30:7; Dan.12:1; Mtt.24:21; Mark 13:19; Rev.3:10).*

2. ***Wrath of the Lamb*** - *Unlike previous times when God the Father has manifested His wrath upon nations, this is the time of the 'wrath of the Lamb' (Rev. 6:16). It is the Son, the Lamb of God, Who's wrath is being manifested.*

3. ***The Final Flowering of Sin*** – *Humanism and satanism will be at their apex on a global scale. The ascent of man, as humanists view human history, will have reached its apex – which is in reality its lowest point since the ascent is really a descent. At this time, there will be a full flowering of sin unique in all history for its depravity and extent.*

4. ***Ushering in God's Kingdom on Earth*** – *The wrath of the Lamb which comes forth is not merely a disconnected judgment of sin. It is part and parcel of the sweeping away of the systems of man to make way for the promised Messianic Kingdom on earth – the only kingdom which will never pass away.*

The cherubim are the administrative agents of God toward this earth, and this is the Lord God Almighty casting out of the powers and principalities of darkness. And when the cherubim say, 'Come,' it is addressed to one of the agencies by which the denouement of this time in history comes to its final consummation." [10]

And as we shall now see, that "agency" is none other than the antichrist himself and the false utopia he fools mankind into accepting. They think his message and abilities are the greatest thing since sliced bread, but in reality, they learn all too late, it's the end!

The **third thing** we see in the breaking of the planet is the **Object of the First Seal**.

So, having observed these two very important factors in the first verse of Revelation Chapter 6 of Who is in charge here and Who is the One dishing out these judgments, let us now begin to dive in verse by verse throughout the rest of this Chapter and exhaust the information contained within these Seal Judgments that are clearly coming from God. As we shall soon see, this first act is the breaking of the Antichrist Seal. *He* is the *object* of discussion. Thus, God's first judgment upon planet earth for the next seven years is to send a false leader, with a false peace, promoting a false utopia.

Revelation 6:2 "I looked, and there before me was a white horse! Its rider held a bow, and he was given a crown, and he rode out as a conqueror bent on conquest."

Matthew 24:4-5 "Jesus answered: 'Watch out that no one deceives you. For many will come in My name, claiming, 'I am the Christ,' and will deceive many.'"

Daniel 9:27 "He will confirm a covenant with many for one 'seven.' In the middle of the 'seven' he will put an end to sacrifice and offering. And on a wing of the temple he will set up an abomination that causes desolation, until the end that is decreed is poured out on him."

As was stated in the prior chapter dealing with the *timing* of the seals, Revelation 6, Matthew 24, and Daniel 9 are prophetically dealing with the same time-frame, the beginning of the 7-year Tribulation. Therefore, by observing all three of these passages, we shall be able to glean the most detailed information concerning the *object* of this first seal, that is, the antichrist. We know it is the antichrist simply by observing the context of Daniel 9:27 where the *he* who makes a covenant with *the many* is speaking of the antichrist making a peace treaty with Israel, which is very clear in Daniel Chapter 9 and other Chapters of Daniel as well. The word "covenant" there is the Hebrew word "beriyth" which means, "a treaty, a covenant, an alliance of friendship, or pledge." And in Daniel Chapter 11 we see that after this "covenant" is made with the Jewish people, *the many*, that the antichrist will turn his back on the agreement and desecrate the newly rebuilt Jewish temple and commit the abomination of desolation:

Daniel 11:30-31 "Then *he* will turn back and vent his fury against the holy covenant. *He* will return and show favor to those who forsake the holy covenant. His armed forces will rise up to desecrate the temple fortress and will abolish the daily sacrifice. Then they will set up the abomination that causes desolation."

The Apostle Paul also confirms the identity of the one who commits this abomination of desolation as none other than the antichrist himself.

2 Thessalonians 2:4 "*He* will oppose and will exalt himself over everything that is called God or is worshiped, so that he sets himself up in God's temple, proclaiming himself to be God."

Then Jesus informs the Jewish people that after the antichrist commits this horrible act of abomination halfway into the 7-year Tribulation, they must flee for their lives because the antichrist will now hunt down all resisters including the Jewish people, the very ones *he* made the covenant with:

Matthew 24:15-20 "So when you see standing in the holy place 'the abomination that causes desolation,' spoken of through the prophet Daniel – let the reader understand – then let those who are in Judea flee to the mountains. Let no one on the roof of his house go down to take anything out of the house. Let no one in the field go back to get his cloak. How dreadful it will be in those days for pregnant women and nursing mothers! Pray that your flight will not take place in winter or on the Sabbath."

So, as you can see, we are dealing with one and the same person here. All these passages are clearly speaking about the antichrist. It is *he* that confirms the covenant or treaty with Israel that starts the very seven-year Tribulation in Daniel 9. Therefore, since Revelation 6 and the opening of the first seal is also dealing with the beginning of the seven-year Tribulation, like Daniel 9:27, the white horse rider *must also* be speaking of the same *object*, the antichrist. Furthermore, his identity is likewise confirmed by Daniel, Paul, and Jesus who also state how *he* will break this *covenant* he made at the *beginning* of the 7-year Tribulation by committing the horrible act of the abomination of desolation, declaring himself to be God in the rebuilt Jewish temple, *halfway* into the 7-year Tribulation. The *object* spoken of here is clearly the Last Days antichrist through and through as these researchers share:

"In the Olivet Discourse, Jesus predicted that a number of individuals will mislead many people (cf. Matt. 24:5, 24; Mark 13:6; Luke 21:8). This has led some interpreters to conclude that a personification of ungodly activity is what the rider represents in this verse. The most probable view is that this is a prophecy of Antichrist, who will make a covenant with Israel, but only as a pretense for destroying the Jews (cf. Dan. 9:27; 1 Thess. 5:3). The horseman is either Antichrist, or a trend or movement of which he is the chief example."

As Christ is God's Man, so satan has his man; and his man will ultimately and finally appear [Matthew 24:5; Revelation 6]. When God's people are taken away [1 Corinthians 15:51-57; 1 Thessalonians 4:14-17; Revelation 4:1] and the days of that terrible tribulation begin, the first thing that shall happen is: in the restlessness and in the revolution and in the prospect of a catastrophic war, there will appear this great, final dictator, this great, final world tyrant [Matthew 24:5].

And he will bring peace and he will bring every promise of affluence and prosperity. And the nations of the world and the peoples of the earth shall flock after him. 'This is our Fuhrer, this is our Il Duce, this is our great leader, this is the savior and the hope of the world.' And he comes riding a white horse, conquering and to conquer [Revelation 6:2]; the entire military and economic and political resources of the world are at his disposal and in his hands.

Now, when you do that, when you make that identification, you will find that it will fit every prophecy in the Bible precisely. For example: in the second Thessalonian letter, and the second chapter, God says, after this falling away, after this apostasy, and after God's people are taken away, 'The man of sin will be revealed' first [2 Thessalonians 2:3]. That's the first thing that happens, the coming across of the stage of history of this white horseman [Revelation 6:2].

The first thing: 'That man of sin will be revealed, the son of damnation, who opposeth and exalteth himself above all that is called God. [2 Thessalonians 2:3-4] the mystery of iniquity already works; only He that now preventeth prevents until He be taken out of the way' [2 Thessalonians 2:7].

God's Holy Spirit in God's people is here in this earth and as long as we're here, that great denouement will not come to pass, satan's masterpiece cannot be revealed, the Tribulation cannot come. The fire and the flame and the fury cannot fall upon Sodom until Lot be taken hence, said the angel; 'I can do nothing until thou become hence.' [Genesis 19:22].

First, God's people have to be taken out. But the minute Lot, even though he was a compromised Christian vexing his soul with the filthy conversation of Sodom [2 Peter 2:7], even though he was a compromised Christian, yet he was God's man; he was a saved somebody. And the angel said, 'I can do nothing until ye become hence.' [Genesis 19:22]. And after Lot was taken away, the fire and the flames fell, the brimstone and the judgment of God [Genesis 22:24-25].

So, it is here. There is in this world what prevents this great and final judgment – it's you! It's God's people. But there is coming a day when the Holy Spirit, housed and templed in the hearts of God's people [1 Corinthians 3:16; 6:19], will be taken out of the way. And then the first thing, 'And then shall that wicked one be revealed.' [2 Thessalonians 2:8].

He will appear, satan's masterpiece, 'whom the Lord shall consume with the spirit of His mouth, and shall destroy with the brightness of His parousia, His appearing, His comings: [2 Thessalonians 2:8], in the nineteenth chapter of the Book of the Revelation [Revelation 19:11-20]. I'm just trying to say, to show you, that when you make that identification, it fits the prophecy all the way through. "[11]

And I would wholeheartedly agree. In fact, let us now take a look at even more details given to us in the Scripture as to why the identity of this *object* of the first seal is none other than the antichrist himself, specifically in verse 2 of Revelation Chapter 6.

The **first detail** given about the object of the first seal is **The Horse**.

Revelation 6:2a "I looked, and there before me was a white horse!"

Now, of all things for the antichrist figure to appear on the world scene riding upon, it just happens to be a *horse*. Not a moose, cow, giant turtle, or even an elephant, but a horse, and a *colored* one at that. This naturally gives rise to a couple of questions.

The **first question** about the horse is **Why is it White**?

Revelation 6:2a "I looked, and there before me was a *white* horse!"

Throughout the Bible we see that the color *white* is often used to symbolize righteousness and purity. The following verses are just a few examples of this conclusion in both the Old and New Testament.

WHITE IS SYMBOLIC OF RIGHTEOUSNESS

Daniel 7:9 "As I looked, thrones were set in place, and the Ancient of Days took His seat. His clothing was as *white* as snow; the hair of his head was *white* like wool. His throne was flaming with fire, and its wheels were all ablaze."

Matthew 17:2 "There He was transfigured before them. His face shone like the sun, and His clothes became as *white* as the light."

Mark 9:3 "His clothes became dazzling *white, whiter* than anyone in the world could bleach them."

Revelation 1:14 "His head and hair were *white* like wool, as *white* as snow, and His eyes were like blazing fire."

Revelation 6:11 "Then each of them was given a *white* robe, and they were told to wait a little longer, until the number of their fellow servants and brothers who were to be killed as they had been was completed."

Revelation 19:8 "And to her was granted that she should be arrayed in fine linen, clean and *white*: for the fine linen is the righteousness of saints."

Revelation 20:11 "Then I saw a great *white* throne and Him who was seated on it. Earth and sky fled from His presence, and there was no place for them."

WHITE IS SYMBOLIC OF PURITY

Psalm 51:7 "Cleanse me with hyssop, and I will be clean; wash me, and I will be *whiter* than snow."

Isaiah 1:18 "Come now, let us reason together, says the LORD. Though your sins are like scarlet, they shall be as *white* as snow; though they are red as crimson, they shall be like wool."

Daniel 11:35 "And some of them of understanding shall fall, to try them, and to purge, and to make them *white*, even to the time of the end: because it is yet for a time appointed."

Daniel 12:10 "Many shall be purified, and made *white*, and tried; but the wicked shall do wickedly: and none of the wicked shall understand; but the wise shall understand."

Revelation 3:18 "I counsel you to buy from me gold refined in the fire, so you can become rich; and *white* clothes to wear, so you can cover your shameful nakedness; and salve to put on your eyes, so you can see."

Revelation 7:9,13,15 "After this I looked and there before me was a great multitude that no one could count, from every nation, tribe, people and language, standing before the throne and in front of the Lamb. They were wearing *white* robes and were holding palm branches in their hands. Then one of the elders asked me, 'These in *white* robes – who are they, and where did they come from?' And he said, 'These are they who have come out of the great tribulation; they have washed their robes and made them *white* in the blood of the Lamb.'"

So, as you can see, when the Scripture uses the color *white* to describe something, it is referring to something righteous and/or pure. So, does that mean then that this *white* horse rider, the antichrist, is actually a *righteous* and *pure* figure? Absolutely not! We know he is satanic and dark to the core. Rather what is being implied here is the *he appears* as if he were righteous and pure. It's all part of his devilish ruse that he foists upon gullible sinful mankind, as these researchers agree:

"This one is not righteous or pure. He's fake. He is not like Christ Who is righteous and holy and pure, but he is a counterfeit. This is woven into his very Biblical name.

The term 'antichrist' in the Greek, antichristos, is obviously a combination word. The word anti is familiar to us in English. We use it as 'anti,' and that's what it means. He is anti-Christ. He is against Christ. But it also has the idea of 'in the place of.' He is against Christ and puts himself in the place of Christ. He is a usurper. He is a satanic liar who, coming against Christ, replaces Christ. In Mark 13 three times Jesus calls him pseudo Christos, false Christ.

This verse does not say who rides this 'white horse.' However, it is most likely the coming Antichrist (Dan.9:26-27; 1 Thess.5:3). This rider represents a conquering power that no one can resist (Matt.24:3-6). This person has the semblance of Christ, but he is not Christ (Rev.19:11-19). He comes as a deceiver.

The horse gave an appearance of purity, but that does not necessarily mean the rider was righteous. When men wage war they always pretend to be fighting for righteousness."[12]

And that's exactly what Jesus said elsewhere would happen at the very beginning of the 7-year Tribulation.

Matthew 24:4-5 "Jesus answered: 'Watch out that no one deceives you. For many will come in My name, claiming, 'I am the Christ,' and will deceive many.'"

Unfortunately, the *many* will be just that, the bulk of the planet. They will fall for the antichrist's satanic ruse, appearing to be the world's savior, righteous and pure, when in reality he's satan's man bringing death and destruction.

This conclusion also just happens to fit with the *historical* usage of the color *white*. As we saw, in the Bible, *white* is used to symbolize righteousness and purity, but in history it is used to speak of *victory*. In fact, history records for us that Roman conquerors would make a triumphal procession into Rome after being *victorious* and winning a battle, oftentimes using *white* horses. Let's take a look at the historical practice:

"The Roman triumph (triumphus) was a civil ceremony and religious rite of ancient Rome, held to publicly celebrate and sanctify the success of a military commander who had led Roman forces to victory in the service of the state or, originally and traditionally, one who had successfully completed a foreign war.

Exceptional military achievements merited the highest possible honors, which connected the vir triumphalis ('man of triumph,' later known as a triumphator) to Rome's mythical and semi-mythical past. In effect, the general was close to being 'king for a day,' and possibly close to divinity.

On the day of his triumph, the general wore a crown of laurel and the all-purple, gold-embroidered triumphal toga picta ('painted' toga), regalia that identified him as near-divine or near-kingly, and even was known to paint his face red in honor of Rome's supreme deity, Jupiter, the mighty king of the gods, the god of law, governance, and strength.

He was the star of the show, the god-like victor, and would ride a spectacular tall-sided chariot pulled by four horses in a lavish procession which went through the streets of Rome, under the gaze of his peers and an applauding crowd, to the temple of Capitoline Jupiter. The spoils and captives of his victory led the way; his armies followed behind. Once at the Capitoline temple, he sacrificed two white oxen to Jupiter and laid tokens of his victory at Jupiter's feet, dedicating his victory to the Roman Senate, people, and gods.

Republican morality required that, despite these extraordinary honors, the general conducts himself with dignified humility, as a mortal citizen who triumphed on behalf of Rome's Senate, people, and gods.

By the Late Republican era, triumphs were drawn out and extravagant, in some cases prolonged by several days of public games and entertainments. Triumphal processions were notoriously long and slow; the longest could last for two or three days, and possibly more, and some may have been of greater length than the route itself.

Some ancient and modern sources suggest a fairly standard processional order. First came the captive leaders, allies, and soldiers (and sometimes their families) usually walking in chains; some were destined for execution or further display. Their captured weapons, armor, gold, silver, statuary, and curious or exotic treasures were carted behind them.

Certain episodes of the battle might be represented in the procession via paintings or even enactments involving real captives. If the occasion was marking a naval triumph, there might be a nautical theme going on with ships' beaks and captured equipment. There were musicians, torch-bearers, and flag wavers to add to the pageantry, as well as examples of the exotic flowers and animals from the conquered region. Next came the war-booty with the more gold and silver on display the better.

Then, all on foot, came Rome's senators and magistrates, followed by the general's lictors (magisterial attendants) in their red war-robes, their fasces (a bundle of rods with a projecting ax blade used as an emblem of authority) wreathed in laurel, then the general in his four-horse chariot. A companion, or a public slave, might share the chariot with him or, in some cases, his youngest children. His officers and elder sons rode horseback nearby.

His unarmed soldiers followed in togas and laurel crowns, chanting 'io triumphe!' and singing ribald songs at their general's expense. Somewhere in the procession, two flawless white oxen were led for the sacrifice to Jupiter, garland-decked and with gilded horns. All this was done to the accompaniment of music, clouds of incense, and the strewing of flowers. Tradition required that, for the duration of a triumph, every temple was open. The ceremony was thus, in some sense, shared by the whole community of Roman gods.

Religious dimensions aside, the focus of the triumph was the general himself. The ceremony promoted him – however temporarily – above every mortal Roman. This was an opportunity granted to very few. His sumptuous triumphal chariot was bedecked with charms against the possible envy (invidia) and malice of onlookers. In some accounts, a companion or public slave would remind him from time to time of his own mortality (a memento mori).

Sculpted panels on the arch of Titus (built by Domitian) celebrate Titus' and Vespasian's joint triumph over the Jews after the siege of Jerusalem, with a triumphal procession of captives and treasures seized from the temple of Jerusalem – some of which funded the building of the Colloseum.

Historian Procopius describes the procession's display of the loot seized from the Temple of Jerusalem in 70 A.D. by Roman Emperor Titus, including the Temple Menorah. The treasure had been stored in Rome's Temple of Peace after its display in Titus' own triumphal parade. Another panel shows the funeral and apotheosis of the deified Titus.

The dictator Camillus was awarded four triumphs but was eventually exiled. Later Roman sources point to his triumph of 396 BC as a cause for offense; the chariot was drawn by four white horses, a combination properly reserved for Jupiter and Apollo. The demeanor of a triumphal Republican general would have been closely scrutinized by his aristocratic peers, as well as the symbols which he employed in his triumph; they would be alert for any sign that he might aspire to be more than 'king for a day.'

Augustan ideology insisted that Augustus had saved and restored the Republic, and it celebrated his triumph as a permanent condition, and his military, political, and religious leadership as responsible for an unprecedented era of stability, peace, and prosperity.

During the Renaissance, kings and magnates sought ennobling connections with the classical past. Flavio Biondo's Roma Triumphans (1459) claimed the ancient Roman triumph, as a rightful inheritance of Holy Roman Emperors.

In the Royal Entry of Holy Roman Emperor Charles V into Rome on April 5, 1536, after his conquest of Tunis in 1535, Panvinio described it as a Roman triumph 'over the infidel.' The Emperor followed the traditional ancient route, 'past the ruins of the triumphal arches of the soldier-emperors of Rome,' where 'actors dressed as ancient senators hailed the return of the new Caesar as miles christi,' (a soldier of Christ).

The Emperor appeared as a triumphant Roman Imperator: mounted on a white horse and wearing a purple cape, he embodied the figure of the ancient conqueror. At the head of a procession marching along the ancient Via Triumphalis, Charles had re-established himself as the legitimate successor to the Roman Empire."[13]

So, this is what we see with this first seal and the *white* horse rider. The antichrist will feign righteousness and purity, but just like the Roman conquerors of old, he will be riding forth *victorious* in his *conquest* to *enslave* the world. They think he will usher in a time of global *law*, *governance*, and *strength*, but it is actually the beginning of a long *procession* of evil events leading to global domination and tyranny. Little does the world realize that even though they *crown* him *king for a day*, he does not take this scepter of leadership on behalf of the people, but his ruse is such that he will abuse that given authority and eventually force the world who *crowned* him to literally *worship* him as a *god* for 3½ years. In his *false-divinity*, like the Roman *conquerors* of old he, too, will ransack *Jerusalem* and its *Temple*, and commit this abomination of desolation, mentioned by Daniel, Jesus, and the Apostle Paul. And then he, too, will hunt down and begin exterminating the *Jewish people*. It happened before and, sadly, it will happen once again. Like a giant deceptive satanic net, the world and even the Jewish people have been caught in the trap laid by this false messiah, this fake righteousness and phony purity of the antichrist himself, the rider on the *white* horse. He may appear as a *soldier of Christ*, but he is the satanic counterfeit, the *antichrist*, as these men share:

"Well then, what is this, this white horseman [Revelation 6:2] that precedes the red of carnage and blood, that precedes the black of famine and dearth and want, and the ghastly green of Hades and of Death? [Revelation 6:3-8].

The Lord replies, 'First, take heed that no man deceive you [Matthew 24:4]. For many shall come in My name, saying, I am the great Fuhrer; I am the great Il Duce, I am the great savior, I am the deliverer of the nations, I am the leader of the world, I am the great Stalin, 'steel,' or I am Tojo to bring my nation to victory. There will be deceivers, there will be many deliverers, there will be many self-styled saviors, there will be many' [Matthew 24:5]. That's the first thing the Lord says about this outline of history, 'There will be false Christs.'

Then the next thing He says is, 'And ye shall hear of wars and rumors of wars, nation against nation, and kingdom against kingdom' [Matthew 24:6-7], that red horse of war and blood [Revelation 6:4]. Then He says, 'And there shall be famine' [Matthew 24:7], that black horse [Revelation 6:5-6] 'Our skin' says Jeremiah, 'was black like an oven, because of the terrible famine' [Lamentations 5:10]. And then He says, 'And there shall be pestilences' [Matthew 24:7], that fourth horse of pestilential death [Revelation 6:7-8], following bloodshed and war and carnage and famine.

Well, if I can trust the Lord in what He says [Matthew 24:4-7], and if I can trust the Lord in the Revelation that He gives to the apostle John [Revelation 6:2-8], then I have the identification of those four horsemen. The first one represents the great deceiver, the great and final Antichrist [Revelation 6:2], the great and final false deliverer of whom all others are but adumbrations, portents, prefigurations. They're just sketches, they are just shadows of that final great world dictator that is yet to come.

Following his appearance, as he comes in peace, and as he comes promising victory, and as he comes making treaties, and as he comes and upon him are the eyes of all the nations of the earth, there are these indescribable bloodsheds and murders, the awful, awful want and famine that inevitably goes with war, the terrible pestilential presence of death and the grave; insatiated, swallowing up its illimitable victims.

God says, 'First, there will come on the scene the great deceiver, the great world deliverer, the great world savior [Matthew 24:5], he is satan's masterpiece - satan always is an imitator. Thus, the antichrist is a great imitator, and so he imitates the Lord Christ here.'

This fits the entire evil picture in Revelation. The satanic powers, and especially the antichrist, are seen as perverted imitations, or anti-types of God and Christ. There is, for example, a counterfeit trinity (satan and the two beasts) in Rev. 12 and 13. Then there is the contrast between Israel, the mother of Messiah (Rev 12), and Babylon, the mother of harlots (Rev. 17-18).

This terrible imitation of Christ, this christ of hell, rides through the events of the tribulation period to meet his anti-type, the rider on the white horse in Rev. 19. This second rider on a white horse is the true Ruler and Almighty Judge who will appear at the very end of history."[14]

In other words, *he* meets Jesus the *real Messiah*, the *real Christ*, the *real Savior of the world*, at the end of the 7-year Tribulation at the Battle of Armageddon where *he* along with his evil cohort, the false prophet, will be squashed like little bugs and cast into the Lake of Fire forever and ever where they will be tormented day and night for their deceitful ways.

The **second question** about the horse is **Why is it a Horse**?

Revelation 6:2a "I looked, and there before me was a white *horse*!"

As was stated earlier, of all things for the antichrist figure to appear on the world scene riding upon, it just happens to be a *horse* and a *white* one at that. Not a green moose, purple cow, translucent giant turtle, or even a pink elephant, but a *white horse*. Once again, this naturally gives rise to the question, "Why?" Well, some would say it's in reference to the *horses* mentioned in the Book of Zechariah.

Zechariah 1:8-11 "During the night I had a vision – and there before me was a man riding a red horse! He was standing among the myrtle trees in a ravine. Behind him were red, brown and white horses. I asked, 'What are these, my lord?' The angel who was talking with me answered, 'I will show you what they are.' Then the man standing among the myrtle trees explained, 'They are the ones the LORD has sent to go throughout the earth.' And they reported to the angel of the LORD, who was standing among the myrtle trees, 'We have gone throughout the earth and found the whole world at rest and in peace.'"

Zechariah 6:1-6 "I looked up again – and there before me were four chariots coming out from between two mountains – mountains of bronze! The first chariot had red horses, the second black, the third white, and the fourth dappled – all of them powerful. I asked the angel who was speaking to me, 'What are these, my lord?' The angel answered me, 'These are the four spirits of heaven, going out from standing in the presence of the Lord of the whole world. The one with the black horses is going toward the north country, the one with the white horses toward the west, and the one with the dappled horses toward the south.'"

Now we do see here a similarity in the *colors* of the *horses* mentioned by Zechariah and John in the Book of Revelation, even sprinkled in with a theme of God's judgment being directed from heaven, however, that's about where the similarities in these passages concerning these *horses* stop. First of all, the *order* and the *color* of these *horses* are not exactly the same:

John's Horses Revelation 6	Zechariah's Horses Chapter 1
White	Red
Fiery Red	Another Red
Black	Brown
Pale	White

John's Horses Revelation 6	Zechariah's Horses Chapter 6
White	Red
Fiery Red	Black
Black	White
Pale	Dappled

Furthermore, neither is the *purpose* of these *horses* the same. John's *horses* are agents of God's *wrath* during the first half of the 7-year Tribulation that Jesus said was the *worst time* in the history of mankind. But Zechariah's *horses* go throughout and find, "*the whole world at rest and in peace.*"

More likely then, the reason we see the antichrist figure riding on this white *horse* is not so much it being a direct parallel to the horses mentioned by Zechariah, as some might say, but rather because *horses* in that day, and actually even up until recent times, were literally considered to be the *battle tank* or *war machine* of the day:

"The horse was the most widely used animal throughout the recorded history of warfare. Early mounts could pull a chariot or carry lightly armored skirmishing forces. With the appearance of heavier mounts and the invention of the stirrup, the horse-mounted cavalry became the most prestigious combat arm in Europe for several centuries. A knight's warhorse was trained to bite and kick.

The combination of the horse-mounted warrior armed with a bow made the steppe people's armies the most powerful military force in Asian history. With the appearance of modern ranged weapons and motor vehicles, horse use for military purposes fell into decline. However, horses and mules are still used extensively by various armies today for transport in difficult terrain.

The Hittites became well known throughout the ancient world for their prowess with the chariot. Widespread use of the chariot in warfare across most of Eurasia coincides approximately with the development of the composite bow, known from c. 1600 BC.

The oldest known manual on training horses for chariot warfare was written c. 1350 BC by the Hittite horse master, Kikkuli. An ancient manual on the subject of training riding horses, particularly for the Ancient Greek cavalry is Hippike (On Horsemanship) written about 360 BC by the Greek cavalry officer Xenophon. One of the earliest texts from Asia was that of Kautilya, written about 323 BC.

Many different types and sizes of horse were used in war, depending on the form of warfare. The type used varied with whether the horse was being ridden or driven, and whether they were being used for reconnaissance, cavalry charges, raiding, communication, or supply.

Weight affects speed and endurance, creating a trade-off: armor added protection, but the added weight reduced maximum speed. In other places, multiple types were needed; warriors would travel to battle riding a lighter horse of greater speed and endurance, and then switch to a heavier horse, with greater weight-carrying capacity, when wearing heavy armor in actual combat.

The destrier is the best-known war horse of the medieval era. It carried knights in battles, tournaments, and jousts. It was described by contemporary sources as the Great Horse, due to its significance. The war horse was also seen in hastiludes – martial war games such as the joust, which began in the 11th century both as sport and to provide training for battle. Specialized destriers were bred for the purpose, although the expense of keeping, training, and outfitting them kept the majority of the population from owning one.

A good destrier was expensive. 7th century Salic law gives a price of 12 solidi as weregild, or reparational payment, for a war horse, compared to 3 solidi for a sound mare or 1 solidus for a cow. In later centuries destriers became even more expensive: the average value of each of the horses in a company of 22 knights and squires in the county of Flanders in 1297 compares to the price of seven normal coursers. The price of these destriers varied between 20 and 300 livres parisis (parisian pounds), compared to 5 to 12 livres for a normal courser.

Horses used in close combat may have been taught, or at least permitted, to kick, strike, and even bite, thus becoming weapons themselves for the warriors they carried.

Horse cavalry began to be phased out after World War I in favor of tank warfare, though a few horse cavalry units were still used into World War II, especially as scouts. By the end of World War II, horses were seldom seen in battle, but were still used extensively for the transport of troops and supplies. Today, formal battle-ready horse cavalry units have almost disappeared, though the United States Army Special Forces used horses in battle during the 2001 invasion of Afghanistan.

Horses are still seen in use by organized armed fighters in Third World countries. Many nations still maintain small units of mounted riders for patrol and reconnaissance, and military horse units are also used for ceremonial and educational purposes. Horses are also used for historical reenactment of battles, law enforcement, and in equestrian competitions derived from the riding and training skills once used by the military. "[15]

So, as you can see, *horses* are used throughout history for *battle* purposes, even on up to modern times. This is precisely why we see that the *horses* mentioned throughout Scripture, not just in the Book of Revelation, take on this same "battle" usage and mentality:

Job 39:19-25 "Do you give the *horse* his strength or clothe his neck with a flowing mane? Do you make him leap like a locust, striking terror with his proud snorting? He paws fiercely, rejoicing in his strength, and charges into the fray. He laughs at fear, afraid of nothing; he does not shy away from the sword. The quiver rattles against his side, along with the flashing spear and lance. In frenzied excitement he eats up the ground; he cannot stand still when the trumpet sounds. At the blast of the trumpet he snorts, 'Aha!' He catches the scent of battle from afar, the shout of commanders and the battle cry."

Psalm 76:5-6 "Valiant men lie plundered, they sleep their last sleep; not one of the warriors can lift his hands. At your rebuke, O God of Jacob, both *horse* and chariot lie still."

Proverbs 21:31 "The *horse* is made ready for the day of battle, but victory rests with the LORD."

Revelation 6:2a "I looked, and there before me was a white *horse!*"

Revelation 6:4a "Then another *horse* came out, a fiery red one!"

Revelation 6:5a "I looked, and there before me was a black *horse!*"

Revelation 6:8a "I looked, and there before me was a pale *horse!*"

Again, of all things for the antichrist figure to appear on the world scene riding upon, it just happens to be a *horse*. Not a moose, cow, giant turtle, or even an elephant, but a *horse*. As you can see both Biblically and historically, the horse clearly represents war, battle, fierceness, fearlessness, power, and conquest. It struck fear into the hearts that it came charging upon and oftentimes mowed them down in a bloody slaughter. It was the attack tank of its day. And so, it becomes a very fitting vehicle for this antichrist figure to enter the world scene upon. He is going to war with mankind. He seeks to do battle for the satanic forces. He is fearless and fierce as he is bent on this global conquest.

However, remember, *he* the antichrist is *not* the One in charge. God is! The antichrist, satan, and the false prophet only get to do what God *allows* them to do. Again, this is one of the clear messages in the Book of Revelation. This is Jesus the *Lamb* taking back the planet. Therefore, these war *horses,* including the white one the antichrist rides, are used as acts of God's judgment upon wicked and sinful mankind. They have chosen to reject the True Victor, Jesus, the Lamb of God, and so they will now receive His evil counterfeit, the imposter, the deceiver, the antichrist. They think he's ushering in a victorious global peace with his emergence on a white *horse*, but what they really got was a blackened nightmare, bringing death and destruction, doing battle for the forces of satan. It truly is mankind's darkest hour. As with the *living creatures,* the *horses* in Revelation ride at the command of God. They too exist to serve His purposes, and they ride forth in judgment to inflict His wrath.

The **second detail** given about the object of the First Seal is **The Rider**.

Revelation 6:2 "I looked, and there before me was a white horse! *Its rider* held a bow, and he was given a crown, and he rode out as a conqueror bent on conquest."

This *horse* did not come onto the scene bareback. There is no empty saddle here. It's not alone. It specifically says he has a *rider*. Therefore, this next detail about the object of the First Seal also brings up a couple of questions.

The **first question** about the rider is **Who is it Riding on the Horse**?

Now, we've already established, based upon the timing of this first seal with the inclusion of the parallel passages that go along with it, that the *rider* mentioned here is clearly the antichrist as is also mentioned by Daniel, Jesus, and Paul. However, unfortunately, there are some out there who would say that this *rider* is actually Jesus Christ, or frankly just about anything or everything *but* the antichrist. Yet, a quick look at the factual comparisons between the real Messiah Jesus Christ and the fake phony antichrist, even in the Book of Revelation itself, reveals how this *rider* mentioned here in the first seal could never be Jesus, let alone some of the other faulty theories out there. Rather, it must be the fake Jesus, the antichrist himself. Consider the following observations by various researchers:

"There have been many suggestions concerning who or what this rider represents. These include a Roman emperor, the Parthian invasion of the Roman Empire, Messiah, and the Antichrist. Others have taken him to represent the Word of God, a personification of judgment, the victorious course of the gospel, warfare in general, triumphant militarism, or the personification of ungodly movements."

"Though some have argued that this rider on the white horse is the Lord Jesus, since Jesus is described in 19:11-16 as coming on a white horse to destroy his enemies, but 'this is to play havoc with the whole scheme of John's vision.' The only similarity between this rider on the white horse and Jesus in 19:11-16 is the color of the horse! Everything in this chapter indicates that the rider represents some form of distress or hardship, and not only is Christ already represented in the vision as the one opening the seals, but he certainly would not appear as merely one of the Four Horsemen."

"Who is this? Some say it's Christ. No, it can't be Christ. Why? Because Christ is opening the seal. It can't be Christ, this rider has a stephanos, that's a crown that you win as a prize. Christ wears a diadema for a crown, that's a kingly crown, over in chapter 19 when we see Him. It can't be Christ because Christ

doesn't come at the beginning, He comes at the end. It can't be Christ; He doesn't carry a bow, He carries a sword."

"When the Messiah returns as King of Kings to defeat His foes and establish His kingdom on Earth, He is depicted as riding on a white horse (19:11). This, however, is not the Messiah, because:

(1) The Lamb is the one opening the seal, not the one revealed in the opening of the seal.
(2) It occurs at the beginning rather than at the end of the Final Seven Years.
(3) His weapon is a bow - a worldly weapon; the Lord will destroy His enemies with a "sword" that comes from His mouth (His Word - cf. Ephesians 6:17).
(4) After the Messiah returns at the end of the seven years and defeats His enemies, He will establish peace on Earth, rather than His victory being followed by all the terrible events portrayed in the breaking of the succeeding six seals, especially the martyrdom of His people (6:9-10)."

"Now there are several things to be said about that before such an identification is made. The first thing is this: there is an incongruity about it to start off with. Here is the Lord Christ, the Lamb, Lion of God. He pulls aside the curtain in order that you might see. And then as He pulls aside the curtain as the Lamb of God, in the snap of His finger He changes into the garb of a soldier and He comes riding out in a white horse. The idea of it is sort of incongruous to begin with.

There's another thing about it that is sort of incongruous as you look at it: evidently these four horsemen have a common denominator. There is something common to all four of them. They all four ride in some particular meaning together – the white, the red, the black, and the greenish pale – they all have some kind of a meaning in common.

Now, if the first one is Christ, if the white horse and its rider is the Lord God [Revelation 6:2], then He is associated with the bloodiest and the most pestilential and the most terrifically horrible of all of the associates that mind could imagine.

Now, I can imagine the Lord with Meshach, Shadrach, and Abednego in the fiery furnace; the Lord walked with His three children [Daniel 3:23-26]. I can imagine the Lord Christ with His disciples of His heart; there He is with Peter and James and John [Matthew 17:1-2]. But somehow, I don't fit in the Lord with Ahab and Jezebel, or with Baal and Aphrodite.

Somehow, I don't fit in the Lord with Herod the Great, who killed the babes at Bethlehem [Matthew 2:16], and Herod Antipas, who slew John the Baptist [Matthew 14:1-12], and Herod Agrippa I, who slew James, the brother of John [Acts 12:1-2].

And somehow, I can't quite fit the Lord Christ into the blood of war and carnage and murder in the red horse [Revelation 6:3-4], and the awful raging famine in the black horse [Revelation 6:5-6], and the pestilential death of that pale ghastly green horse [Revelation 6:7-8]. They just don't fit.

All right, another thing to be considered: when the Lord Christ comes, He comes in the nineteenth chapter, in the eleventh verse of the Apocalypse, in its consummation and its denouement and its great, final, crowning victorious day [Revelation 19:11-16].

We look for the Lord from heaven, we look for Him to come with His people, we look for Him to come in triumph and in glory, and He does come. But He comes in the nineteenth chapter of the Book of the Revelation [Revelation 19:11], and He doesn't come here [Revelation 6:2]. It doesn't fit.

Then another thing: when you look at those two; the Man who rides on the white horse, the Lord God our Christ, in the nineteenth chapter of the Book of Revelation, He has on His head a diadema [Revelation 19:12]. That's a Greek word, a diadema, a diadem.

Never in the language is that word used for any other except the crown of a reigning sovereign monarch. And that is the kind of crown that we would expect to grace the brow of the Son of God and our Savior. He comes with a diadem, a diadema, and His weapon is the sword of the Word [Revelation 19:12-15].

This white horseman is not like that at all: his crown is a stephanos, something a man could win down here in this earth, as in a race. And he has in his hand not a sword of the Word of the God, but he has a bow, and that with no shaft and no arrow [Revelation 6:2]."

"This is not the white horse which carries He who is Faithful and True in Revelation 19:11. For it is the Lamb who has just loosed the first seal sending this horseman out. It violates all logic for the same person to be opening the seal and sending himself forth.

Moreover, it would be inappropriate to have an angelic being call forth Christ or his servants. If Christ rides forth here, who is it that remains in heaven to open the remaining seals?

This rider carries a bow whereas Christ's weapon is a sword (Rev. 2:12; 19:15). This rider is alone whereas Christ is followed by the armies in heaven also riding on white horses (Rev. 19:14). Finally, this rider sets forth at the beginning of the Tribulation whereas Christ rides forth at its end."

"The rider cannot be Christ, because Christ is already symbolized by another figure in the scene, namely, the Lamb. The rider on the white horse is part of a group that brings devastating calamities and destruction upon the earth. It seems unlikely that he would bring good when the others bring woe. The picture here is not of the victory of Christ but of the wrath of God.

The Messiah cannot appear before the messianic judgments. A picture of the victorious Christ would be quite out of place in a passage telling of disaster after disaster."

"Thus, the two riders on white horses serve as theological bookends for Revelation. The messiah figure in Revelation 6 is a fraudulent copy of Jesus Christ, the true messiah. When the white horse rider of Revelation 6 goes out to conquer, havoc and death result. When the Messiah on the white horse of chapter 19 goes out to conquer, he ushers in peace and salvation."[16]

So, as you can observe, no, this *rider* is *not* Jesus Christ, let alone a Parthian invasion, the Word of God, a personification of judgment, the victorious course of the gospel, warfare in general, triumphant militarism, or the personification of ungodly movements. Rather, it is clearly mankind's worst nightmare, the antichrist, *riding* upon the world scene as an act of judgement from Almighty God. The world thinks *he* will be galloping in a wonderful time of global unheralded peace, when in reality he comes charging forth under orders, the orders of the *Lamb* unleashing God's wrath, a time of literal hell on earth. It begins here, as this researcher shares:

"One of the most significant and meaningful of all of the prophecies in the Word of God is the prophecy of the seventy weeks in Daniel. It says there that this prince, this Antichrist, this satan's masterpiece, this great, false deceiver, it says that he will come in peace, and he will make his covenant with the people [Daniel 9:27]. He's going to have the great systems of religion in this world back of him and for him.

The Roman church is going to acclaim him, just like it did Il Duce, just like it does any other Fuhrer or dictator by which they think they can strangle the life of a nation and of a people. The Roman church is going to hail this dictator, this coming world tyrant.

And the Jewish people find in him a marvelous surcease from the terrible afflictions that beset them on every hand. And he's going to write a treaty with the Jewish people, and they're going to have their homeland, and they're going to rebuild their temple, and they are going to reinstitute the Mosaic rituals and the sacrifices [Daniel 9:27]. And for a while, he is truly the savior of the world. And the whole unbelieving world acclaims him, this masterpiece of satan [Revelation 13:3].

Then according to the prophecy and according to the Revelation, in the midst of his meteoric rise to power and to conquest, then it is revealed what he really is: he's the fiend of hell. He's the masterpiece of the devil. He is the great Antichrist, the opposer and blasphemer of God [Revelation 13:6]. And in the midst, and in the midst of his career, he turns, and he becomes the enemy of the Jewish nation [Revelation 13:7] and there is a wave of antisemitism like the earth has never known before [Revelation 13:15-17].

And then he turns on the Roman church, and according to the seventeenth chapter of the Book of the Revelation: that leader, that beast, that ruler with the ten horns, he shall hate the whore, and he shall make her desolate and naked, and shall eat her flesh and burn her with fire" [Revelation 17:16]. Oh, what this world dictator does as he moves across the stage of human history!"[17]

The **second question** about the rider is **Why does he have a Bow**?

Revelation 6:2b "I looked, and there before me was a white horse! Its rider *held a bow.*"

Here we see John revealing not only what the *horse* is carrying, but now what the *rider* on the *horse* is *carrying*. A *bow*. Not a lance, a giant sword, a dagger, or even a sledgehammer. Of all things this *rider* is carrying with him, it just happened to be a *bow*. Why? Well, some would say that this *bow* represents the "false peace" that the *rider* the antichrist figure, ushers in at the beginning of the 7-year Tribulation. They arrive at this conclusion due to the fact that the *bow* is mentioned *without arrows* and thus they say it speaks of a bloodless coup or peaceful takeover of the world. In other words, the antichrist *conquers* through diplomacy at first as the false messiah, not through war. The following are common conclusions over this *bow*:

"You say, 'How do you know it represents the false peace?' Well the fact is he has a bow, that's a symbol of a warrior. But if you have a bow you also need something else, what? An arrow, he doesn't have any. The absence of arrows speaks of a bloodless victory. Worldwide peace brought by this covenant maker and his cohorts in a bloodless way."

"You'll notice he has a bow but no arrows which means he has a certain amount of authority, but he conquers without ever shooting anything. It is a conquering without bloodshed."

"The rider on the 'white horse' is a picture of the Antichrist, the final world ruler, as a counterfeit of Christ at his return. (Rev.19:11 2) He carries 'a bow' with no arrows. The Antichrist appears to come in peace but is 'bent on conquest.'"

"The bow is the most common biblical symbol of war. But notice that there is no mention of this conqueror having arrows. Both Daniel and Revelation indicate that the evil prince who is to come will conquer not by brute force but primarily by sinister intrigue – by deceiving the world into following him (Daniel 8:23, 25; Revelation 13:3, 4)."[18]

Now, it very well could be that the mentioning of this *bow* "without arrows" that the antichrist figure has with him on this *horse* represents the "false peace" that he ushers in at the beginning of the 7-year Tribulation. Yet, I do not see this as the *primary* or *only reason* to conclude that this *rider* will *conquer* by peaceful means at first. I say that because if you look at the other Biblical usages of the word *bow* in the Scripture, it can certainly mean *warring intentions* without ever mentioning arrows as well:

THE BOW SYMBOLIC OF MILITARY POWER OR THREAT OF WAR

Psalm 46:9 "He makes wars cease to the ends of the earth; He breaks the *bow* and shatters the spear, He burns the shields with fire."

Jeremiah 51:56 "A destroyer will come against Babylon; her warriors will be captured, and their *bows* will be broken."

Hosea 1:5 "In that day I will break Israel's *bow* in the Valley of Jezreel."

Zechariah 9:13 "I will bend Judah as I bend my *bow* and fill it with Ephraim."

THE BOW SYMBOLIC OF STRENGTH

Job 29:20 "My glory will remain fresh in me, the *bow* ever new in my hand."

Job 30:11 "Now that God has unstrung my *bow* and afflicted me, they throw off restraint in my presence."

Jeremiah 49:35 "This is what the LORD Almighty says: 'See, I will break the *bow* of Elam, the mainstay of their might.'"

THE BOW SYMBOLIC OF CONQUERING

Isaiah 41:2 "Who has stirred up one from the east, calling him in righteousness to his service? He hands nations over to him and subdues kings before him. He turns them to dust with his sword, to windblown chaff with his *bow*."

And this is certainly what the antichrist does during the 7-year Tribulation. He seeks to *conquer* the whole world to the point where he is actually *bent on conquest*. He also comes with great *military power* and *strength* and *threatens war*. All these truths can be rightly concluded with the mere usage of the word *bow* without ever having to mention *arrows*. To put it another way, someone can mention how they are going to ride around my house with a gun, waving it, yet not once mention anything about bullets, and I would still rightly conclude that this was a violent threat. I certainly wouldn't take it as an act of peace. So, it is with the antichrist *riding* with a *bow*. It *could* mean his *false peace* he ushers in, but it could *also mean* other *warring* characteristics that the Bible mentions about him as these men share:

"The Antichrist's very rise to power is a violent one, for, as Daniel 7:8 points out, he will conquer three kings as he is on his way from his status as a 'little horn' to a horn greater than even the great horn Alexander the Great was in his day. Antichrist will eventually head an eleven-nation federation (Rev.17:9-13). But his victory is only temporary, for Christ will appear and put an end to it (17:14; 19:11-20)."

"The bow is also a symbol of war and conquest. The feared Parthians were well known for their archery skills in battle. A 'Parthian shot' still means a final, devastating blow, to which there is no possible answer.

The dreaded Parthians, on Rome's eastern flank, were an undefeated enemy. In a failed invasion, the Roman armies were defeated in A. D. 62 by the Parthian general Vologeses in the Tigris river valley. The disaster must still have been remembered in the days when Revelation was written.

The Churches in the Roman province of Asia (to whom the book was written) must have been quite aware of the Parthians as bowmen riding white horses. Such a horseman could serve as an immediate metaphor of military power and conquest."[19]

Now, with that said, I do believe that this time period *does involve a false global peace* ushered in by the antichrist; not so much because of just the *bow*, but because of other parallel passages that allude to this *peaceful* conclusion:

Daniel 9:27 "*He* (antichrist) will *confirm a covenant* (peace treaty) with many (Israel) for one 'seven' (7-year Tribulation). In the middle of the 'seven' *he* will put an end to sacrifice and offering. And on a wing of the temple *he* will set up an abomination that causes desolation, until the end that is decreed is poured out on him."

Matthew 24:4-5 "Jesus answered: 'Watch out that no one deceives you. For many will come in My Name, claiming, 'I am the Christ (false messiah); and will deceive many."

1 Thessalonians 5:1-3 "Now, brothers, about times and dates we do not need to write to you, for you know very well that the day of the Lord (7-year Tribulation) will come like a thief in the night. While people are saying, '*Peace and safety,*' destruction will come on them suddenly, as labor pains on a pregnant woman, and they will not escape."

Revelation 6:3-4 "When the Lamb opened the second seal, I heard the second living creature say, 'Come!' Then another horse came out, a fiery red one. Its rider was given power to *take peace from the earth* and to make men slay each other. To him was given a large sword."

So here we see that the very event that starts the 7-year Tribulation is when the antichrist makes a *peace treaty* or covenant with Israel and becomes the world's false messiah. Everyone is crying out *peace and safety,* but it doesn't last long. The next rider on the next horse, in the second seal opened by the Lamb of God, gives the orders to *take peace from the earth,* and so in effect it is short-lived at best. So, the *bow* this *rider* carries could in fact represent this false peace, or it could fit his other *warring* characteristics. Either way, we know when this *rider* appears on the scene, *peace* is part of the deception *he* uses to fool the world into receiving *hell on earth,* as these men share:

"Although the Antichrist's reign includes war, it also includes peace. Peace is a buzzword today. Many of the world's greatest thinkers speak of the need of a one-world government – a new world order. The Antichrist will camp on this and make 'peace' his campaign message. Of course, the world will buy in, which will allow him to be enthroned on earth as a 'god' and political leader.

A number of years ago, the newspapers carried a story of a woman in Fayetteville, Arkansas, who named the United Nations as the beneficiary of her $700,000 estate, 'in the fervent hope that this relatively small contribution may be of some effect in bringing about universal peace on earth and good will among men.' Upon reading this account, J. Vernon McGee, the well-known radio preacher, commented, 'That woman poured her money down a rat hole,' because you cannot buy peace with $700,000 or even $700 trillion. Jesus Christ, the Prince of Peace, is the only way to find peace."

"Now first there will be peace. Let's go back to Daniel 9 for a moment. Verse 27 picks it up. 'He will make a firm covenant with the many for one week.' Who's he? He is the prince who is to come of verse 26. He's the Antichrist. He's also called in Daniel 'the little horn,' chapter 7 verse 8. He's called 'the king of fierce countenance,' chapter 8 verse 23. He's called 'the willful king,' or the king who does whatever he wants, chapter 11 verse 36.

The Antichrist is the leading orchestrator of peace. He is a false Christ. He leads all the other false Christs and false Messiahs to bring this world peace. He makes a covenant with Israel. Yes, certainly Israel is a key player and the many certainly focuses on Israel since they are the nation in view here. But it extends beyond Israel. It is a covenant that involves the protection of Israel from all of those who might harm them. So, it is a kind of major peace pact. Who knows how many nations may be involved in it?

That's how the period of Tribulation is going to begin. Peace, global peace. And the Antichrist specifically makes a peace treaty with Israel...a covenant to be their protector, their peacemaker, their deliverer, their Messiah, their Savior. But, in the middle of the week, in the middle of the seven years - that's why we know it's a seven-year period, it's called a week of years - in the middle of the week he will put a stop to sacrificing and grain offering.

You know what's going to happen? That peace treaty with Israel is going to be so comprehensive and so complete that they're going to be back in their sacrificial system. They're going to be back making sacrifices. They're going to be back offering grain offerings. They're going to have their temple. And in the middle of it, he's going to come in and desolate the place, he's going to make it desolate and he's going to try to destroy Israel and conquer the world.

It will all break loose then as Antichrist desecrates the Holy of Holies, sets himself up as God to be worshipped by the whole world, and that leads the world into massive warfare that ultimately ends up in Armageddon."

"How can a person conquer without using deadly force, when this has been the exclusive method of choice for conquerors throughout history? This apparent contradiction has often been rectified by viewing the Antichrist as a great diplomat who will use diplomacy to peacefully bring a willing world into an era of global government.

But is this a realistic view? Revelation 13:7 tells us that 'he was given authority to rule over every tribe and people and language and nation.' Given the global history of nationalism, tribalism, racism, and other animosities among men, it seems beyond comprehension that any man, no matter how charismatic, could conquer the world with mere words.

This gives us the perfect opportunity to apply the golden rule of biblical interpretation: 'When the plain sense of Scripture makes common sense, seek no other sense.' The Bible is clearly telling us that one of the ways believers will be able to identify the Antichrist is by recognizing his ability to conquer the world without using deadly force.

But, again, given what we know about history, is it possible to conquer the world without using deadly force? Right now, it's not. But very soon, it will not only be possible, but absolutely necessary."[20]

The **third question** about the rider is **Why was he given a Crown?**

Revelation 6:2c "I looked, and there before me was a white horse! Its rider held a bow, *and he was given a crown.*"

Here we see the second piece of attire this *rider* on the *horse* is carrying. Not just a *bow* presumably in his hand, but now *he was given a crown* presumably on his head. Why? Well, I think the two aspects concerning this second attire the antichrist appears with reveals the answer. First, of all things to be given to the antichrist, it just happens to be a *crown*. Not a watch, a shiny pair of pants, a jacket, or even a new shirt. Of all things this *rider* is wearing, it just happened to be a *crown*. Why? Well, some would say that this *crown* represents the "authority" that the *rider,* the antichrist, now has over the world. He's the new "world dictator." He's the "victor" who seemingly did what no one else could do up until that point; bring peace to the world, even in the Middle East.

This certainly fits the purpose of the kind of *crown* mentioned here in the Greek. It is not the (royal) "diadema" crowns, plural, worn by the real Messiah Jesus Christ at His Second Coming at the end of the 7-year Tribulation. This is the "stephanos" singular, or (victor) *crown* that the antichrist wears. This shows us that his deceptive *false peace* has been *crowned* victorious over the earth as this researcher agrees:

"He is rewarded with the crown which is a reward, stephanos, rather than a diadema which is a king's crown that belongs only to one who is in the rightful line of the king. Peace is king. And peace is crowned king by the world. He went out conquering and to conquer. He's rung up a long series of triumphs in bringing world peace.

This is the deception that Jesus talked about when He said many would be misled. This is the golden age, this is the utopia that Antichrist helps to establish with his covenant with Israel that Daniel spoke about, peace...misleading, deceptive, false peace...orchestrated worldwide by many false messiahs and led by the Antichrist.

And, of course, once the peace is established, the Antichrist rises to the top. In fact, in 2 Thessalonians 2:9 it says he will come with all power and signs and false wonders and with all the deception of wickedness for those who perish, and God will send a deluding influence so that they might believe what is false.

Why? In order that they may be judged. God's going to delude the world. He's going to let the delusion run. They're all going to fall into the false peace, bow down to this great world ruler who epitomizes it. And it's a trap in which they will be caught and killed.

The world is headed for war, but first it's headed for peace. [21]

    The second answer comes as to why the antichrist appears with a *crown* of all things when one focuses on the fact that the crown was *given* to him. This shows us that his *authority* to take over the world with this *false peace* came from elsewhere. He didn't do this, it was *given* to him. Certainly, we see that the world and its leaders *crown* the antichrist as their new savior. This even fits another tradition in the Roman Triumphal Processions. The *victors* could not have these ceremonies without first getting *permission*:

"In Republican tradition, only the Senate could grant a triumph. A general who wanted a triumph would dispatch his request and report to the Senate. Officially, triumphs were granted for outstanding military merit; the state paid for the ceremony if this and certain other conditions were met.

Most Roman historians rest the outcome on an open Senatorial debate and vote, its legality confirmed by one of the people's assemblies; the senate and people thus controlled the state's coffers and rewarded or curbed its generals.

Some triumphs seem to have been granted outright, with minimal debate. Some were turned down but went ahead anyway, with the general's direct appeal to the people over the senate and a promise of public games at his own expense.

Others were blocked or granted only after interminable wrangling. Senators and generals alike were politicians, and Roman politics was notorious for its rivalries, shifting alliances, back-room dealings, and overt public bribery. "[22]

So, whether it was with the people of the world's full approval, back room dealings, just the ruling elite, or maybe even a combination of all three mixed in with deceptive intrigue, just like it was in the Old Roman Empire, so it is with the Last Days champion in the newly Revived Roman Empire. *He*, the antichrist, will have his triumphal day *given* to him by the world, as this man shares:

"He is sort of democratically crowned here. It doesn't seem that he took it, but it was just given to him, like he's been honored by the world and elevated and given prominence. This peace has been made king by the world, everything is subservient to peace, and since the architect of peace is primarily the Antichrist, everything is subservient to him.

The world crowns peace as king. All over the world peace becomes the issue. That is certainly the mood of the day, isn't it? World peace, global peace, and peace will be crowned king. And peace will be conquering and come to conquer even more, a series of triumphs leading to a golden age of prosperity with the promise that more prosperity and more peace is to come.

All of this, of course, is deceptive and it's a false security. As we saw even in Matthew 24:4 and 5, Jesus said, 'Don't let people deceive you with this; it is a deceptive peace that doesn't last long.' Why? The prophets have always said there is no peace for the wicked. False teachers say peace, peace, but there is no peace. "[23]

So, the world certainly falls for the deception of the antichrist, the false messiah, and actually *gives* him *authority* to usher in this world peace. They *crown* him to do so. However, the Bible also says that satan himself is *also* the one who gives the antichrist his *power*:

Revelation 12:9 "The great *dragon* was hurled down – that ancient serpent called the *devil*, or *satan*, who leads the whole world astray. He was hurled to the earth, and his angels with him."

Revelation 13:2 "And I saw a beast coming out of the sea. He had ten horns and seven heads, with ten crowns on his horns, and on each head a blasphemous name. The beast I saw resembled a leopard but had feet like those of a bear and a mouth like that of a lion. The *dragon gave the beast his power and his throne and great authority.*"

So, the question is, "Who really *gives* the antichrist this *crown*, this *authority* to rule the world with this false deceptive peace? Is it the people of the world, the ruling elite, or is it satan?" Actually, it's *neither*. Yes, the world, from man's perspective, really does *give* the antichrist this *crown of authority* to literally rule them. And yes, the whole thing really is a devilish ploy from satan himself duping them into *giving* this *authority* to his man, the actual antichrist, in the first place. Which, by the way is yet another reason why this *white horse rider* could never be Jesus:

"His authority to rule is given to him by satan (Revelation 13:4). This is another indication that this conqueror is not Jesus. The true Messiah has no need to be given the authority to rule the world, which He, as God the Son, created (John 1:1-3).

The 'crown' the antichrist wears is actually a wreath (Greek: stephanos), as worn by Greek or Roman conquerors – not the same as the 'crowns' (Greek: diadema) that will be worn by the King of Kings when He returns with the armies of Heaven to restore His kingdom on Earth (19:12, 14, 16)."[24]

Yet, never forget that the Bible is clear, satan only gets to do what *God gives him permission to do*. We see this profound yet obvious truth in the Old Testament.

Job 1:6,8-12 "One day the angels came to *present themselves* before the LORD, and satan also came with them. Then the LORD said to satan, 'Have you considered my servant Job? There is no one on earth like him; he is blameless and upright, a man who fears God and shuns evil.' 'Does Job fear God for nothing?' satan replied. 'Have you not put a hedge around him and his household and everything he has? You have blessed the work of his hands, so that his flocks and herds are spread throughout the land. But stretch out your hand and strike everything he has, and he will surely curse you to your face.' *The LORD said to satan,* 'Very well, then, everything he has is in your hands, but on the man, himself *do not lay a finger.*'"

Job 2:3-6 "Then the LORD said to satan, 'Have you considered my servant Job? There is no one on earth like him; he is blameless and upright, a man who fears God and shuns evil. And he still maintains his integrity, though you incited me against him to ruin him without any reason.' 'Skin for skin!' satan replied. 'A man will give all he has for his own life. But stretch out your hand and strike his flesh and bones, and he will surely curse you to your face.' *The LORD said to satan, 'Very well, then, he is in your hands; but you must spare his life.'*

As you can see, satan not only had to *present* himself before God's throne to get *permission* to do anything against Job, but he couldn't even sneeze if you will without God's permission. He couldn't even touch Job unless God allowed it. God is clearly in control, not satan! We see the same truth in the New Testament when satan had to also *ask permission* to go after the Apostle Peter:

Luke 22:31 "Simon, Simon, satan has *asked* to sift you as wheat."

In other words, satan couldn't do squat against the Apostle Peter unless God *gave him permission*. Once again, satan is not the one in charge here or at any time. Jesus, the Lamb, God is. In fact, the Bible goes on to say that God is the One Who even gives earthly rulers the authority to rule:

Romans 13:1-2 "Everyone must submit himself to the governing authorities, for there is no authority except that which *God has established*. The authorities that exist have been *established by God*. Consequently, he who rebels against the authority is rebelling against what *God has instituted*, and those who do so will bring judgment on themselves."

And that's really the issue that's going on here in our text with the antichrist being *given* a *crown*. The world has rebelled against God's established authority, the One and Only true Messiah Jesus Christ, and instead accepted the false messiah the antichrist. So now all they've accomplished is to invite God's judgment upon themselves during the 7-year tribulation. He, God, is the One in charge of them all. This is what we see throughout the Book of Revelation, not just here in the beginning of Chapter 6. God is in charge of all these judgments. Here's just a small sampling in Chapter 9:

Revelation 9:1 "The fifth angel sounded his trumpet, and I saw a star that had fallen from the sky to the earth. The star was *given* the key to the shaft of the Abyss."

Revelation 9:3 "And out of the smoke locusts came down upon the earth and were *given* power like that of scorpions of the earth."

Revelation 9:4 "They were *told* not to harm the grass of the earth or any plant or tree, but only those people who did not have the seal of God on their foreheads."

Revelation 9:5 "They were not *given* power to kill them, but only to torture them for five months. And the agony they suffered was like that of the sting of a scorpion when it strikes a man."

Over and over again, the Bible is clear, especially in the Book of Revelation, that God is the one in control and He is the One who *gives* authority. Not the antichrist, not the false prophet, not even satan himself are loose cannons on deck getting to do whatever they want. Rather, they only get to do what God Almighty *gives them permission* to do. And as an act of His divine wrath being poured out upon wicked, sinful, rebellious mankind for trying to usurp His *authority*, He now *gives the authority* for them to fall for this Last Days delusion of false peace. They rejected the One and Only True Messiah Jesus Christ and so now they are *given permission* to *crown* the Last Days false messiah over them. And so, it is, just like the choosing of Barabbas over Jesus in His first coming, so the world will once again choose a *criminal* over *Christ* prior to His Second Coming. Thus God, as an act of judgment, will *give them permission* to *crown* their new earthly king as the new messiah, only to discover, soon enough, they just made the greatest mistake of their lives, as these men share:

"John sees a white horse with a rider who has a bow and a victor's crown (not a royal crown) that was given to him, meaning he was permitted by God to have his victories. All events in the apocalyptic section of the book are initiated from the throne described in chapter 4 and must be understood in that light. Though indirect, all that transpires under the seals is in implementation of the 'book of doom' through the agency of the Lamb introduced in chapter 5."

"Although the rider likely believes he has gained his own crown for himself, it is only his by permission. Everything which proceeds from the opening of the seals is subject to the permission of the one seated on the throne and the Lamb. The sovereignty of God is heavily emphasized throughout the book of Revelation – there is nothing which transpires that God Himself does not grant authority for.

This is seen in the frequently-found phrase "was given" which denotes the granting of permission to an agent from another, namely God (Rev. 6:2, 4, 8, 11; 7:2; 8:3; 9:1, 3, 5; 11:1; 13:5, 7, 14-15; 16:8; 19:8; 20:4).

- *The first horseman is granted his crown (Rev. 6:2)*

- *The second horseman is given to take peace with a great sword (Rev. 6:4)*

- *Death and Hades, who ride with the third horsemen are given authority to kill a fourth part of the earth (Rev. 6:8)*

- *The four angels are given the power to hurt the earth and sea (Rev. 8:3)*

- *The star from heaven is given the key to loosen the demonic locusts from the abyss (Rev. 9:1)*

- *Who were themselves given power to torment men (Rev. 9:5)*

- *The beast is given authority to continue for forty-two months (Rev. 13:5)*

- *And to make war against the saints and overcome them (Dan. 7:25; Rev. 13:7)*

- *The fourth bowl is given the ability to scorch men (Rev. 16:8).*

All of these horrific and terrible realities – the very manifestation and flowering of sin of which God is no author – are harnessed for His purposes. The troubling and yet comforting reality is that there is no creature which ultimately does not serve God's purpose, either willingly or unwillingly.

Troubling, because in the inscrutable purpose of God such evil is allowed to continue. Comforting, because everything we suffer is subject to God's approval and purpose (Job 2:6; Rom. 8:28).

How irresistible the grasp of Omnipotence on the powers and forces of evil. They are effectually bridled till the plans of God are ripe and ready for action. Once the reality of God's sovereignty is understood, the bondage of satan is seen for what it is. For satan has less freedom in rebellion against God than he once had in obedient service of the Master."[25]

The **fourth question** about the rider is **Why does he ride out to Conquer?**

Revelation 6:2d "I looked, and there before me was a white horse! Its rider held a bow, and he was given a crown, *and he rode out as a conqueror bent on conquest.*"

Now we see the final aspect given to us by the Apostle John concerning this first seal and its *white horse rider.* We've observed the *rider's* articles with the *bow* and *crown*, but now we see his *motive* for appearing and carrying these articles in the first place. The message is clear. He *rides out* not for the good of humanity, the needs of the poor or downtrodden, over even the highest benefit of all mankind, but rather *he rode out as a conqueror bent on conquest.* That's it! That cat's out of the bag. His true colors are now known for all to see, even from the very beginning of the 7-year Tribulation. Like the Parthians of old, the antichrist will accomplish the seemingly impossible:

"A Roman army had had actually to surrender to Vologeses, the king of the Parthians. It was seldom in history that such shame and ignominy had come to the arms of Rome. Now the Parthians rode on white horses and they were the most famous bowmen in the world. The bowmen of the Parthians were the terror of the world, and even the conquerors of unconquerable Rome."[26]

So, it is with this great Last Days bowman, this great warrior deceiver. The antichrist pulls off the seemingly impossible. Surely it can't be done! Surely no one could ever vanquish Rome, let alone the whole world! Yet that's precisely what the antichrist does. He *rides forth* to *conquer* the whole world. His reign, his time of *terror* is coming. It is such a sad turn of events. The world thinks they are getting great peace, unheralded peace, peace unthinkable, global peace and a fantastic global ruler, but they are soon to discover that it's really hell's man who unleashes a literal hell on earth. They fall for his lies. They fall for his deceptive promises of peace. Yet, there's no excuse. The world is still fully accountable for their decision to *crown* this beast as their global king. All they had to do is read the Bible and see they were warned repeatedly, over and over again, century after century, as these men share:

"Like Antiochus Epiphanes before him, he would 'come in peaceably, and seize the kingdom by intrigue and after the league is made with him he shall act deceitfully' (Dan. 11:21-23). And in the latter time of their kingdom, when the

transgressors have reached their fullness, a king shall arise, having fierce features, who understands sinister schemes. His power shall be mighty, but not by his own power; he shall destroy fearfully and shall prosper and thrive; he shall destroy the mighty, and also the holy people.

Through his cunning He shall cause deceit to prosper under his rule; and he shall exalt himself in his heart. He shall destroy many in their prosperity. He shall even rise against the Prince of princes; but he shall be broken without human means. And the vision of the evenings and mornings which was told is true; therefore, seal up the vision, for it refers to many days in the future. (Dan. 8:23; Revelation 6:2)

There is no question among expositors that Antiochus is in view in this prophecy. What was prophesied was fulfilled literally through him. However, the prophecy looks beyond Antiochus to a future person (the Antichrist) of whom Antiochus is only a foreshadowing. This coming one is said to 'stand against the Prince of princes' (Dan. 8:25), the Lord Jesus Christ.

Thus, the prophecy must go beyond Antiochus and look forward to the coming of one whose ministry will parallel that of Antiochus. From Antiochus certain facts can be learned about the forthcoming desecrator:

(1) He will achieve great power by subduing others (Dan. 8:24).
(2) He will rise to power by promising false security (Dan. 8:25).
(3) He will be intelligent and persuasive (Dan. 8:23).
(4) He will be controlled by another (Dan. 8:24), that is, satan.
(5) He will be an adversary of Israel and subjugate Israel to his authority (Dan. 8:24-25).
(6) He will rise up in opposition to the Prince of princes, the Lord Jesus Christ (Dan. 8:25).
(7) His rule will be terminated by divine judgment (Dan. 8:25).

So, it may be concluded that there is a dual reference in this striking prophecy. It reveals Israel's history under the Seleucids and particularly under Antiochus during the time of Greek domination, but it also looks forward to Israel's experiences under Antichrist, whom Antiochus foreshadows. So, before the terrors of the Tribulation break loose and lead to the battle of Armageddon there will come a period of world peace. But it will be a deceptive peace, as the world is lulled into a false sense of security followed by war, famine, and death. The world's desperate desire for international peace will serve as the bait for the satanic trap. That longing for security and safety will play into the hands of Antichrist, satan's ruler, who will convince the world that he can provide them."

"This is no pretty picture. But God is the Lord of truth, and He writes here things as they are, as they will be. It is for the cheap and worldly optimist to speak words of 'Peace, peace; when there is no peace' [Jeremiah 8:11], and to paint rosy pictures of human nature and of the destiny of nations, when God says, 'It will end in a flood; war and desolations are determined to the end' [Daniel 9:26], so God says.

However, man may say it, however the false leader may deceive a nation, God says this is the future. And He unveils it to us in His honesty, that we might prepare ourselves, and save our souls, and deliver our people."[27]

Yet mankind doesn't listen, they don't prepare themselves and save their very souls through the One and Only True Messiah Jesus Christ. Instead they reject God's truth, they reject His warnings, mock the Bible, and receive the prophesied coming future antichrist, thus sealing their fate. There is no excuse.

But then the antichrist goes a step further. He not only takes over the whole world after his deceptive lie of false peace, and the world falls for it even though they should've known better, but he then demands that the whole world worship him after his deceptive lie of being *crowned* to serve humanity. Just like in the Roman Triumphal Processions, he forsakes the constant reminder that he is just a mere mortal:

"Star of the show, the god-like victor would ride a spectacular tall-sided chariot pulled by four horses. He wore a laurel crown and carried a laurel branch in his right hand. In his left hand, he carried an ivory scepter with an eagle at the top, symbolic of the triumph.

He was accompanied by a slave whose job was to hold above his head a gold crown and continuously whisper in his ear that, amongst all this adoration, he should remember that he was only a mortal and not actually a god. For this reason, he would repeat respice or 'look behind.'"[28]

But the antichrist doesn't look behind, he only looks ahead to *conquer*. In fact, he is so *bent* on world *conquest* that he not only demands total control of the whole planet, but then he even violates Roman protocol and demands the whole world to worship him as a god. Not a mere mortal, but a god. This *crowning* has gone to his head. He swells with satanic pride. Oh, he feigns for the first half of the 7-year Tribulation that he is in compliance with the custom whispered into his ear to remember that he is a mere mortal *given* this authority to serve man, but halfway into the 7-year Tribulation, he will show his true colors by committing the abomination of desolation in the rebuilt Jewish temple declaring himself god. In one fell swoop he ignores the whisper, and shouts to one and all, "Worship me! I am god!"

Yet, even here, the One and Only true God demonstrates that He is still the One Who is in total control. There is Only One God and One God Alone, God Almighty and He demonstrates that He alone has the ultimate power and authority over the planet by using the antichrist for His purposes. Again, God is not the author of this satanic behavior, but He *allows* it to fulfill His *divine purposes*. He's in control, as this researcher demonstrates:

"The antichrist will particularly deceive Israel, whose people have for so long desired peace, and he 'will make a firm covenant with the many [Israel] for one week' (Dan. 9:27). Antichrist's peace pact and protection of Israel will not last, however: 'in the middle of the week [the Seventieth Week of Daniel's prophecy; the Tribulation] he will put a stop to sacrifice and grain offering; and on the wing of abominations will come one who makes desolate, even until a complete destruction, one that is decreed, is poured out on the one who makes desolate' (Dan. 9:27).

The false peace that Antichrist brings will come to an abrupt halt at the midpoint of the Tribulation when he desecrates the temple in Jerusalem, betrays the Jewish people, and launches deadly attacks on them (Matthew 24:4-10).

Like Antiochus before him, the Antichrist plays a special role in relation to Israel during the events to come: God will have specific purposes for bringing Antichrist on the world scene.

One purpose will be the punishment of Israel. . .[the] desolation of Israel by the Antichrist will be part of God's judgment of the nation because it rejected its Messiah in His first coming [John 5:43]

A second purpose will be the repentance of Israel. . . God will bring the Antichrist on the world scene to play a major role in shattering [Israel's] rebellion [Dan. 12:7]

A third purpose will be the judgment of the world. . . God will judge the world by giving it the kind of ruler it deserves.

A fourth purpose will be the exposure of the world's unbelief. God will bring the Antichrist on the world scene and permit him to make his claim to be God to demonstrate mankind's unbelief.

A fifth purpose will be the instigation of the final showdown between Christ and Satan's forces and the defeat of those forces."[29]

If there's one thing clear in the Bible, it's that God doesn't lose, ever! Jesus *will* win! Satan *will* be defeated. God *will* have the last word! He is in full control at all times, not satan, not the antichrist, and not the false prophet. All three will be defeated and judged for their audacious crimes against God, yet God *allows* them to seemingly control the world as an act of His judgment upon the world for their own rebellion towards Him. God *allows* the world to believe this deceptive lie. Thus, the deceiver of the nations, this antichrist, this fake phony messiah who appears to come in peace bringing peace for all, really is *hell bent* on enslaving mankind under his satanic rule and for all the world to worship him. It starts here. It starts now. Basically, what Jesus rejected, this man, satan's man, the antichrist accepts:

Matthew 4:8 "Again, the devil took Him to a very high mountain and showed Him all the kingdoms of the world and their splendor. 'All this I will give you,' he said, 'if you will bow down and worship me.'"

The satanic trap was set, the antichrist, unlike Jesus Christ, takes the bait, and now *rides out* to claim his reward. He wants it and he wants it now. No dilly-dallying around here. No procrastination. No idle chatter. He is *bent* on getting his devilish prize. He is on a *conquest* to get his hands on *the kingdoms of this world* and he is not messing around. This is exactly what the Greek says concerning this phrase, '*a conqueror bent on conquest.*" It's actually the Greek words, "exerchomai nikao nikao." "Exerchomai" means, "to go or come forth," and "nikao" means, "to carry off the victory, to come off victorious, to overcome, to prevail." "Nikao" is not only mentioned once, but twice in a row. This is obvious for emphasis in the Greek. It tells us that the antichrist doesn't just "come forth victorious," rather he literally, "came forth victorious and he is going to carry off this victory to its ultimate conclusion if it's the last thing he's going to do. He is *bent* on it. He *will* prevail. He *will* overcome. He *will* get his prize!

He is *doubly* sure about it! That's why some translations say he went "conquering and to conquer." Nobody is going to stop this deceptive figure from acquiring his satanic reward for making a deal with the devil. He *will* get total control over *the kingdoms of this world*. He *will* demand worship as a god. The charge starts *now*! Get out of his way! If you get in the way of his satanic reward, you too will be slaughtered in his wake. The *conquest* and the *conquering* of the world has begun. In a satanic lust, the antichrist *rides forth* as a *conqueror bent on conquest*. It is the beginning of the end for mankind, as this man shares:

"We are moving today in the direction of a world dictator. More and more is this true. All the nations of the world are disturbed. Lawlessness abounds, and governments are not able to control as they should. This is all preparing the way for the coming of one who is going to rule.

Antichrist does not appear as a villain. After all, satan's angels are angels of light. He is not going to have horns or cloven feet. Rather, he is going to be the most attractive man the world has ever seen. They will elect him, and the world will acclaim him because he has come in his own name. But when he takes over, it sure is going to be bad for the world.

By forcing on mankind more and more lethal weapons and at the same time making the whole world more and more interdependent economically, technology has brought mankind to such a degree of distress that we are ripe for deifying any new Caesar who might succeed in giving the world unity and peace.

That will be the platform that Antichrist will come in on – world unity and peace. I think that if anybody appeared on the scene now and offered the world that, the world wouldn't ask whether he came from heaven or hell. I don't think they would care, because they want peace at any price, and we have spent billions of dollars trying to obtain it.

G. K. Chesterton observed in his day: 'One of the paradoxes of this age is that it is the age of Pacifism, but not the age of Peace.' There is a great deal of talking about peace. We have given away billions of dollars throughout the world, and we do not have peace. The Ford Foundation, one of the world's wealthiest private organizations, has announced that their money eventually will be used to work for world peace and better government, living and education conditions – yet the world gets worse all the time.

When Antichrist comes to power, he is going to talk peace, and the world will think that it is entering the Millennium when it is actually entering the Tribulation. The Tribulation comes in like a lamb, but it goes out like a lion. A promise of peace is the big lie the world is going to believe. [30]

Chapter Six

The Breaking of the War Seal

The **fourth thing** we see in the breaking of the planet is the **Ordering of the Second Seal**.

Revelation 6:3 "When *the Lamb* opened the second seal, I heard the second *living creature* say, 'Come!'"

Once again, God is sending a clear message as to Who is the One responsible for releasing this next wave of wrath upon planet earth. It is not the hand of man, nor is it the wiles of the devil. It is the *Lamb* who is opening the *second seal* and it is His *living creature* who exists to do His will that is giving the order to, "*Come!*" Notice the exclamation point again. This is not a casual tone. This is not a whisper. This is not a suggestion. This is a loud abrupt command from God's holy messenger surrounding His holy throne to immediately unleash this next wave of planet-wide judgment. The inescapable conclusion from the text is that Almighty God is the originator of this next event from on high.

Furthermore, neither is there any hesitation here from God's throne room. As soon as the first seal and its rider accomplish their deceptive ruse upon planet earth, with a false peace and false utopia takeover, *immediately* here comes the next rider, the *second seal*, the next wave of judgment. There is no time to rest and enjoy this false peace, no time to relish in it, no time to bask in it and take it all in and exhale a huge sigh of relief. Not at all! Planet earth is on a horrible wrathful journey that will last for seven years non-stop. Basically, this shows us how this false peace and false utopia of the antichrist is short-lived. It should not come as a surprise for only the Prince of Peace Jesus Christ can usher in a true and lasting peace upon the planet, and He will do just that in the Millennial Kingdom for 1,000 years. But this fake pseudo christ, the antichrist, can hardly even sustain this false peace for even a brief period. What a failure, unlike the real One and Only Christ.

Now, will this false peace last for one year, six months, or even less? We don't know for sure. The text doesn't tell us. However, we do know logically that it has to be much shorter than 3½ years which makes up the first half of the 7-year Tribulation in which the Seal judgments occur. This is only the *second seal*, which ends the false peace. Therefore, logically, the first seal false peace cannot last very long at all. All the seals have to be compressed within the *first part* of the first half (3½ years) of the 7-year Tribulation. Either way, just like all his other satanic lies this one, too, this message of false peace from the antichrist that was used to bait the whole world into submitting to him, comes crashing down in a mere moment by the hand of God. *The Lamb* opens the *second seal*, the *living creature* shouts *"Come!"* and *immediately* this false global peace comes to a screeching halt. Again, this is very reminiscent of the deceptive peace that the Apostle Paul said the unbelieving world would be crying out for, but then would have it all removed from them in a mere moment:

1 Thessalonians 5:1-3 "Now, brothers, about times and dates we do not need to write to you, for you know very well that the day of the Lord (7-year Tribulation) will come like a thief in the night. While people are saying, '*Peace and safety,*' *destruction will come on them suddenly*, as labor pains on a pregnant woman, and they will not escape."

In the *second seal*, the false utopia has come crashing down. The global party is over. The confetti lay dormant. Sudden destruction has burst upon the planet with one simple command from God, *"Come!"* The antichrist's false promises are shown to be illusory, just like the emperor's new clothes. No real fabric to it, just another coat of lies. It never had any real substance, it never could last, because it was all fake in the first place. There was nothing there the whole time, yet the people of the world still fell for the illusion of peace. They wanted to *see* it so much that they couldn't *peer through* the deception that it really was. Yet, in one fell swoop, with the *second seal*, God removes the antichrist's clothes to reveal the naked truth, the nothingness of it all.

Now, as sad as that is, not only will we see horrific war and utter global destruction from here on out in the rest of the 7-year Tribulation, but believe it or not, the people of the planet will still be clinging to this false message of peace from the antichrist instead of receiving the true and lasting peace from the only One Who can give it, that is, Jesus Christ. In fact, Jesus clearly warned about this deception during the 7-year Tribulation:

Matthew 24:4-5,10-11,23-25 "Jesus answered: 'Watch out that no one deceives you. For many will come in My Name, claiming, 'I am the Christ' and will deceive many. At that time many will turn away from the faith and will betray and hate each other, and many false prophets will appear and deceive many people. At that time if anyone says to you, 'Look, here is the Christ!' or, 'There he is!' do not believe it. For false Christs and false prophets will appear and perform great signs and miracles to deceive even the elect – if that were possible. See, I have told you ahead of time."

Jesus simply warns repeatedly, ahead of time, that there will be false prophets and false teachers duping and deceiving the whole planet *during the entire 7-year Tribulation*, from beginning to end. So, it is here, even in the beginning portion of the 7-year Tribulation, with the *second seal*, that we see these false prophets already at work deceiving the inhabitants of the earth into yet another satanic trap of false peace and false safety, thus sealing their utter doom. One researcher puts it this way:

"The day of the Lord will be darkness and not light. It will be judgment and not mercy. It will be wrath and not blessing. The day of the Lord will bring a disruption of the physical order, a cosmic catastrophe caused by God Himself, as He overrules the natural process. Under the fury of divine judgment on the day of the Lord, the whole earth will be devastated and will become like a turbulent sea or like the rising and falling of the Nile River which overflows its banks for miles, drowning and submerging everything in its wake. The sun will go out at noon and cover the whole world in darkness. Supernatural fire will come to destroy the sea and the land. The prophetic view of the day of the Lord is indeed frightening, frightening.

The Apostle Paul talks about this day, because it has implications for his readers. When we understand the fear of the Lord, that should put something into our lives that might not otherwise be there in terms of motivation and responsibility. Paul has a message to give to these believers about living in the light of God's devastating, final and eternal judgment on the ungodly.

First, he gave a marvelous insight into the Rapture. That's a different event. The Rapture is the catching away of the Church. That's not something to fear; that's something to comfort. In fact, he says, 'Comfort one another with these words.' The Rapture is a blessed event. It's a wonderful event. It's a hopeful event. It's a joyous event. It's the time of our glorification. It's the time of our reward. It's the time when we become like Jesus Christ. It's the time when we enter into His wonderful, eternal presence in the Father's house, in the room that He's been preparing for us ever since He left.

But from that wonderful event, that hopeful event, Paul moves to that horrible event called the day of the Lord. The final cataclysmic judgment by God on the wicked. It refers to the time of the culmination of God's fury and wrath in final climactic judgment. The prophets spoke of it. The writers of the New Testament speak of it. And always, it refers to the unleashing of God's final fury on sinners on the earth. In all discussions of the day of the Lord there's a sense of nearness, of expectation, an element of surprise. It will be sudden, unwelcomed, harmful, and unexpected.

Unbelievably, absolutely incomprehensibly, the people in the world at that time are going to have an inexplicable response on the surface. 'While they are saying, 'Peace and safety,' then destruction will come.' Stop at that point. You say, "What? They're saying what?" They're saying, "Peace and safety." In spite of the fact that even before the mid-point of the seven-year Tribulation there will be evidences listed in the first five seals of Revelation that will show that we're moving toward the end, the response of people is peace and safety.

What does that mean? 'Everything will be fine. We're headed for a time of peace. We're headed for a time of safety.' You say, 'That's absolutely ludicrous. That's absolutely ridiculous. Who in the world would ever come up with that kind of a response?' Pretty simple, if you think about it. They're being convinced by a special group. A special group of people are working real hard to convince them that peace and safety is coming. They're called false prophets.

Peace and safety, peace and safety. Everything is going to be fine; we're moving toward a wonderful time; all this is going to be over. This is the beginning of, I can hear it now, this is the beginning of the new age; the old one is falling apart. It's all disintegrating, and all of the Christians who have been Raptured were the problem. We got rid of them and the whole thing is now being reshuffled, and we're going to come in to the dawning of a new age.

Listen, believe it, folks, in the latter times before the final holocaust of the day of
.the Lord, the world will literally be crawling with demonically inspired false
prophets lying about what is going on. And that is why they'll be saying peace
and safety, peace and safety. The Lord says the prophets are prophesying
falsehood in My name. I have neither sent them, nor commanded them, nor
spoken to them. They are prophesying to you a false vision, divination, futility
and the deception of their own minds.

Why, an unimaginable thought, will the world believe false prophets who say this
is just the dawning of a wonderful new time of peace? I'll tell you why, because
those false prophets will do great what? Signs and wonders, great signs and
wonders. Whatever capability hell has to put on a show, it will put it on then. And
even with all that's happening, the witless world will buy the satanic lies, and go
like sheep to a slaughter, even though they've been warned, and warned, and
warned, and warned.

If you know and love the Lord Jesus Christ, the future you look for is all
glorious. If you don't know Him, the future you look forward to is all terrifying. It
is no insignificant thing that the whole world has its eyes on the Middle
East. That's where all the consummation of God's history will take place. It
could be in this generation; it could be soon. We must be ready. If you know
Christ, you'll be taken before it hits. If you don't, you'll be destroyed when it
comes."[1]

The trap is set by the antichrist, it is maintained by lying false prophets
and, unfortunately, the lost and dying world falls for it all the way to the end of
the 7-year Tribulation. Even though the whole planet is crumbling all around
them and the short-lived false peace and false utopia party atmosphere is long
gone, this deceitful message of false peace is still clung to by the inhabitants of
the earth in one final death grip. All because, just like Jesus forewarned, in that
day many false prophets would come in My Name and deceive *many*. The world
wanted this lying illusory peace more than the truth, and thus the lying satanic
bags of dead man's bones were more than happy to dupe them into their ultimate
doom. How sad it is that the world not only rejects Jesus' offer of eternal
salvation, but here we see they even reject his warning of false prophets that
would come promoting this false peace and false safety and lead them to their
eternal destruction. Speaking of which, we will now see the specifics of this
planetary-wide horrific destruction in the very next verse, the *object* of this
destruction, *the second seal rider*.

The **fifth thing** we see in the breaking of the planet is the **Object of the Second Seal**.

Once again, we are reminded in the *second seal*, just like in the first seal, and frankly, all of the seals, that Almighty God is the One Who is in charge here and He is the One Who is responsible for dishing out all these judgments upon planet earth. So now let us turn our attention to the *object* of this next wave of judgments coming from God, the *second seal,* and as we shall soon see it is simply the breaking of the War Seal. *War* is the *object* of discussion. Thus, God's second judgment upon planet earth for the next seven years is a global war to counteract and expose the emptiness of the antichrist's false peace and false utopia.

Revelation 6:3-4 "When the Lamb opened the second seal, I heard the second living creature say, 'Come!' Then another horse came out, a fiery red one. Its rider was given power to take peace from the earth and to make men slay each other. To him was given a large sword."

Matthew 24:6-7a "You will hear of wars and rumors of wars but see to it that you are not alarmed. Such things must happen, but the end is still to come. Nation will rise against nation, and kingdom against kingdom."

Once again, as we saw in the chapter dealing with the *timing* of the seals, Revelation 6 and Matthew 24 are prophetically dealing with the same time-frame, the beginning of the 7-year Tribulation. Therefore, by observing both of these passages, we shall be able to acquire even more detailed information concerning the *object* of this first seal, that is, a *global war*. Now, we know this *second seal* judgement is dealing with *war* due to the obvious above stated facts. We see the activities of war, *men slay each other*, the weapons of war, *a large sword*, and the verbiage of war, *wars and rumors of wars*. Furthermore, we also see that both passages are speaking of a *global* war because both texts are clearly *global* in context. Peace is taken from *planet earth,* and *nations* will rise against *nations* and *kingdoms* against *kingdoms*. Thus, this global war counteracts the short-lived global false peace from the antichrist and produces an earth-shattering wake-up call. In fact, when you take a look at other passages dealing with the antichrist, you clearly see that this global war that begins here will actually continue on until the very end of the 7-year Tribulation, as this researcher points out:

"Here the story gets ugly and stays that way until Christ establishes His Kingdom. Daniel 8 says regarding Antichrist, 'He will destroy to an extraordinary degree, he will destroy mighty men and the holy people.' Now you remember, he is the one who orchestrated a peace treaty with Israel. He made a covenant with them. He probably will be the instrument of world peace, but when war starts to break out all over everywhere, to contain his power and to maintain his authority, he's going to have to turn to war.

He slaughters many, including Jews and Gentile believers. He may not initiate the wars, he may be attempting to resolve them toward the midpoint, then he does his foul deed of abomination and that is part of, only part of, the holocaust that he creates.

Then, 'The king of the south will collide with him.' Now we don't know who the king of the south is but if you go south from the land of Israel you're in Egypt. And it would not be too hard to believe that Egypt would come against the Antichrist since he has now established his throne in Israel, in Jerusalem. That's where he set himself up as God to be worshiped by the whole world. Probably the king of the south is not identified only as Egypt because it's the whole of the south, the whole Muslim world of Egypt, Libya, Ethiopia, Africa, the alliance that comes against him comes from that part of the world. An African army of some kind moves against the Antichrist who is not only ruling the world but has set his throne as God in the city of Jerusalem.

Also, you will note, the 'king of the north' will storm against him, chariots and horsemen and many ships and, of course, the modern equivalent of all of that. Here comes the king of the north. Who is that? Well some believe it is the massive nation of Russia. There's every reason to think it might be because it talks about it being in the north and that is north. It is also reasonable to assume that it could be another Arab conspiracy.

So here is Antichrist, he's trying to control war all over the place. He abominates in the temple, he sets that up. We move into the second half, war is still going on all over the globe. And now the world is turning on him. The king of the south comes, the king of the north comes. Then the antichrist goes on to conquer other countries, overflow, pass through them. He holds the Middle East in his hands, all of its resources. He is the sovereign invincible god in his own mind, he consumes the harlot church, the false religion that is remaining in the world, according to Revelation 17. He has a partner called the False Prophet who calls the whole world to worship him. There is an unending, blood-letting going on. Then, 'Rumors from the east and the north will disturb him, and he will go forth with great wrath and to destroy many.' The rumors from the east could be the army of 200 million in the book of Revelation that moves, coming from the east. And he moves with great wrath to destroy and annihilate many. He's a powerful, powerful force. And yet he will come to his end, he'll meet his match.

He thinks he's conquered the world...as the kids today say...Not! Wrong. It isn't going to happen because the Lord is going to come. So, wars start in the beginning and they stretch through. War keeps escalating until Christ comes back to conquer him."[2]

What a divine wake-up call! The exact polar opposite of what you thought you were getting from this slick deceptive world leader. Global peace turns into global war, and from this point forward, it never stops until the One and Only True Prince of Peace, Jesus Christ, comes back to defeat this big liar at the end of the 7-year Tribulation. You thought you were about to experience unending peace and prosperity, but you really got global war and horrible slaughter. In fact, this is truly what this *second seal* is all about. Not just a global war, but a gruesome horrible *slaughter*. It is the most gruesome bloody mess the world has ever seen, and the planet will become bathed in it. Let us now look at the proof of this horrible global slaughter that is coming to the planet in the details of the *second seal*.

The **first detail** given about the object of the second seal is **The Red Horse**.

Revelation 6:4a "Then another horse came out, *a fiery red one.*"

As was noted in the *first seal*, of all things for these riders of God's apocalyptic judgment to appear on the world scene riding upon, it just happens to be a *horse*. Not a moose, cow, giant turtle, or even an elephant, but a horse, and a *colored* one at that. This naturally gives rise to a couple of questions. Now, we already saw that the *horse* was basically the *battle tank* or *war machine* of the day. Thus, each of these riders come barreling onto the world scene, directed from the very throne room of God, like charging tanks onto a battle scene ready to go to war against humanity on behalf of the Almighty. Yet, the obvious difference with this *second seal* rider is his *color*. In the original Greek he comes out on a "purrhos" or literally *fiery red one*. So once again, this naturally gives rise to the question, "Why is it this particular color? Why is it *red*, literally *fiery red?*" Well I believe the answer is revealed when one takes a look at the Biblical use and symbolism of the color of red, as well as the secular and historical use of the color red:

THE BIBLICAL USAGE OF THE COLOR RED

Death & Destruction

Exodus 15:4 "Pharaoh's chariots and his army he has hurled into the sea. The best of Pharaoh's officers are drowned in the *Red* Sea."

Purification

Numbers 19:2 "This is a requirement of the law that the LORD has commanded: Tell the Israelites to bring you a *red* heifer without defect or blemish and that has never been under a yoke."

Blood

2 Kings 3:22 "When they got up early in the morning, the sun was shining on the water. To the Moabites across the way, the water looked *red* – like blood."

Sorrow

Job 16:16 "My face is *red* with weeping; dark shadows ring my eyes."

Intoxicating Drink

Proverbs 23:31 "Do not gaze at wine when it is *red*, when it sparkles in the cup, when it goes down smoothly!"

Sin

Isaiah 1:18 "'Come now, let us reason together,' says the LORD. 'Though your sins are like scarlet, they shall be as white as snow; though they are *red* as crimson, they shall be like wool."

Battle Gear

Nahum 2:3 "The shields of the soldiers are *red*; the warriors are clad in scarlet. The metal on the chariots flashes on the day they are made ready; the spears of juniper are brandished."

Approaching Storm

Matthew 16:3 "And in the morning, 'Today it will be stormy, for the sky is *red* and overcast.' You know how to interpret the appearance of the sky, but you cannot interpret the signs of the times."

Approaching Army

Revelation 9:17 "The horses and riders I saw in my vision looked like this: Their breastplates were *fiery red*, dark blue, and yellow as sulfur. The heads of the horses resembled the heads of lions, and out of their mouths came fire, smoke and sulfur."

Defeated devil

Revelation 12:3 "Then another sign appeared in heaven: an enormous *red* dragon with seven heads and ten horns and seven crowns on its heads."

Thus, as you can see, the Biblical use of the color *red* paints quite the ominous scene. Death and destruction is coming with this *red horse rider*. A bloody battle is approaching, a storm that brings sorrow. The planet will be purified from man's sinful deeds because they listened to the intoxicating lies of a defeated satan. God's battle-geared army is coming to set things straight. Others state that red is the color of war, violence, or warfare. It is often associated with murder, blood, wrath, or anger, as in the sayings, "seeing red," or "being caught red-handed," meaning that the individual was caught with the blood of murder still on his hands. Red is also used to warn people, get their attention, scare them and/or signal outright danger.[3] Again, this is not a good sign for planet earth! A bloody, violent, murderous judgment is coming upon it! In fact, the obvious war-like meaning behind this red horse is even more apparent when one takes a look at the ancient Roman usage of the color red:

"Red was used to color the skin of gladiators. Red was also the color associated with army; Roman soldiers wore red tunics, and officers wore a cloak called a paludamentum which, depending upon the quality of the dye, could be crimson, scarlet or purple. In Roman mythology red is associated with the god of war, Mars. The vexilloid (flag-like object) of the Roman Empire had a red background with the letters SPQR in gold. A Roman general receiving a triumph had his entire body painted red in honor of his achievement." [4]

So, it is that the *true colors* of the antichrist's deception reveals itself. He promises the world a false peace and phony prosperity riding triumphantly on his white horse, yet no sooner than the world lets out a global sigh of relief, the fiery red war paint on his body unveils his bloody, murderous, motives. As the red horse rider appears from God, the planet is jolted out of their false sense of security as it slowly begins to dawn on them, they've been duped. They're not getting the so-called peace they were promised, rather they are about to be bathed in a bloody slaughter, the exact polar opposite of what they were expecting. In essence, the reward these people get for rejecting Jesus Christ, and instead listening to the intoxicating lies of the antichrist and all the other false prophets of peace and safety, is a global slaughter, as these researchers state:

"As the Lamb opened the second seal a red horse appeared. Its rider brought anarchy and bloody warfare! 'When they shall say, Peace and safety; then sudden destruction cometh upon them' (1 Thessalonians 5:3). The first effort in the world we have left behind will be to bring in universal peace apart from Christ. But it will end in universal, bloody warfare, greater far than has ever been known."

"Rather than resulting in 'peace on Earth,' as during the coming reign of the Messiah, the reign of Anti-messiah will result in widespread violence, bloodshed, and war."

"Now this force that is coming, you'll notice, is red as opposed to white. And red like fire and red like blood speaks of the holocaust, of war. War in its most frightening and devastating form. We know it's war because it says he takes peace from the earth, men slay each other, and a great sword was given to him.

We also know it's war because it parallels what Jesus said about war and rumors of war and nations rising against nation. God then sends as a judgment on the short-lived peace, the false peace, immediate war. You will notice then it also says, 'A red horse went out and to him who sat on it, it was granted...' By whom? By God. Please remember this because it's a very important point. All of these things that are happening are happening at the command of God.

Some people will try to tell you that this is not the wrath of God because they will say we want to make sure that we are delivered from the wrath of God as Christians, but we also want Christians to go through the Tribulation, so we can't call this the wrath of God. And it has been called a number of things, sometimes the wrath of men, sometimes the wrath of satan.

There's only one thing you could call it Biblically and that is the wrath of God. It comes from the throne in the little scroll in the hand of God and is executed by the Lord Jesus Christ Himself. It is God's unfolding wrath, it is God who has granted this red horse, the authority and the power to move and bring war. It was God who allowed the false peace, it is God who starts the wars. God allows it.

As we read in Matthew 24, they're going to involve nations all over the earth, nation will rise against nation, kingdom will rise against kingdom. I don't know how it happens but just when everybody's sort of breathing in the air of euphoria, war is going to start to break out and it's going to escalate all over everyplace."[5]

Just imagine all the jaws dropping and all the face palming going on all across the planet at this time. What a deception, what a letdown, what an anguish. Such a reverse of emotions! But as we shall soon see, there is not much time for the inhabitants of the earth to stagger in their remorse due to their unfortunate decision to listen to the antichrist instead of Jesus Christ. They will now be literally running for their very lives as a massive global slaughter breaks out upon them. This is the judgment the *second seal rider* brings. And just as his color implies, this will not just be a bloody global war coming upon them, but a *fiery* red one, one the likes of which the world has never seen or will ever see again.

The **second detail** given about the object of the second seal is **The Rider**.

Revelation 6:4 "Then another horse came out, a fiery red one. Its *rider* was given power to take peace from the earth and to make men slay each other. To him was given a large sword."

The *second seal horse* also contains a *rider* and it, too, like the first seal horse, did not come onto the scene bareback. The saddle here is likewise not empty, nor is this horse alone. Both horses have riders upon them and the *rider* of this one, the *fiery red one*, clearly reveals several horrible and shocking details concerning the fiery trial that is now coming to the planet. When one simply asks the appropriate questions concerning this next detail about the object of the *second seal*, the *rider*, the gruesomeness of what is about to occur comes galloping into focus.

The **first question** about the rider is **Why was He Given Power to Remove Peace**?

Revelation 6:4a "Then another horse came out, a fiery red one. Its rider was given power to *take peace from the earth*."

As was already stated, what is about to occur is the exact polar opposite of what the inhabitants of planet earth thought they were going to receive. Instead of global and lasting peace, they get instant global war. Why? Because they rejected Jesus Christ, and instead trusted and placed their hopes in the false promises of false peace, false utopia, from the antichrist. Therefore, Almighty God *takes it away*, all of it. Now notice it's not just a section of the world that has its peace removed, nor just a city, or even one single country. No. Peace is *taken from the earth*. The whole planet will not have any peace at all! All of it, all sense of peace completely and utterly taken away by God. Think of what this means. Imagine the atmosphere and existence on planet earth at this time. Peace is defined as, "a state of tranquility, harmony between individuals; safety, and security." The opposite of peace is "rage, havoc, discord, and war." This will now be the status of the planet *all the time* as an act of judgment from God for rejecting the One and Only True Messiah Jesus Christ. Where there was once a general accord, friendship, love, reconciliation, truce, unity, armistice, cessation, neutrality, order, and pacification around the world, there is now, from this point forward, a general global disagreement, hatred, discord, violence, agitation, worry, anxiety, disharmony, distress, frustration, fighting, and war. Any and all sense of peacefulness on the whole planet is *taken* away by God. Snap! It's gone! In fact, the word "taken" there in the Greek means, "to seize, to lay hold of, to carry away and remove." Thus, God now "takes a hold of" the general peace that He gives to mankind, and then "seizes" the false peace and false utopia of the antichrist, and together He "removes" them both and "carries them away" never to return until the Prince of Peace Jesus Christ comes back at the end of the 7-

year Tribulation to set up the Millennial Kingdom. In an instant, peace is gone, all of it, every last bit of it. One minute it was there, taken for granted, the very next second it instantly disappeared.

Now, that's shocking enough. But what's even more alarming is what was *given* in peace's absence. It is the very opposite of peace, that of war, division, hatred. It wasn't just that peace was removed, but that it was replaced with something, the very thing that is the very enemy of peace, all peace stands against, that is war, violence, and bloodshed. In short, God gives the order and in one fell swoop, from one moment to the next, man's utopia turns into mankind's greatest nightmare. God *gives power* to this *second seal rider* to thrust this horrible reality upon the whole *earth,* and the shock and awe response will be overwhelmingly indescribable. You can hear them cry, "What happened? How can this be? We didn't see this coming? It all changed in a flash! Why? Why? Why?" Oh, the agony, the despair, the regret, the weeping, the gnashing of teeth. They didn't just have peace taken away, they received everything opposite in its place. We've seen throughout history war, division, and hatred in various places at various times, but this text is telling us that this will now be the everyday living and existence for the whole *earth. All peace is gone*! How horrific it must be to experience this! It never stops. There is no respite. It's now just one continual existence of war, hatred, discord, fighting, slaughter, and violence. No rest from it. Everyday people wake up, that is if they're still alive, and it's just more of the same. More global disagreement, more global hatred, more global discord, more global violence, more global war. Every minute that passes just increases their level of never-ending global worry, anxiety, and distress. Yet, it shouldn't come as too much of a surprise. God not only warned this would happen, but many political pied pipers have come upon the world scene doing the same thing, promising false peace when the planet is actually on the verge of war, as this man shares:

"The first horseman could not be Christ, because when He brings peace to this earth, it is going to be permanent. This is a short-lived peace. Immediately after the white horse went forth, here comes the red horse of war on the earth. The peace which the rider on the white horse brought to the earth was temporary and counterfeit. The Antichrist presents himself as a ruler who brings peace to the world, but he cannot guarantee it, for God says, 'There is no peace, saith my God, to the wicked' (Isa. 57:21). And that passage of Scripture certainly has been fulfilled.

Isn't peace exactly what every candidate for office in our country has promised? Certainly, that has been true in my lifetime. I never shall forget the candidate who said that our boys would never again go across the ocean to fight. What baloney that was! We were promised peace, and every candidate since then has promised peace. One of them dropped two atom bombs, and immediately afterward we began to talk about peace. Every candidate since then – no exception and regardless of party – has said he was going to bring peace. My friend, we are as far from peace today as we have ever been. Already the clouds are gathering for World War III.

Antichrist will be a phony. He won't bring peace because here goes the fiery red horse of war riding throughout the earth again. And this is going to be a real-world war."[6]

In fact, it gets even worse. The next detail about the *second seal rider* shows us just how macabre things are really going to get on planet earth during this time. People will literally be "butchering" one another! It's a wholesale slaughter of mankind, one to another!

The **second question** about the rider is **Why Does He Make Men Slay Each Other?**

Revelation 6:4b "Then another horse came out, a fiery red one. Its rider was given power to take peace from the earth *and to make men slay each other*."

Here we see the second thing the *rider* on this *fiery red horse was given power* and authority to do by God. He not only was ordered from on high to instantly remove *peace from the earth*, but here comes the polar opposite. He now *makes men slay each other*. Notice it's not disagree with one another, or argue with one another, or even fight with one another. The verbiage is eye-opening. It is *slay* each another. This is one of the most graphic scenes thus far in the Seal Judgments. It is like a horror movie breaking upon planet earth, only it's not a make-believe movie, it's now wicked and rebellious planet earth's gruesome reality. This gruesomeness is further illuminated when one takes a deeper look at the word "slay" that is there. It is the Greek word "sphazo" which literally means, "to slaughter, to butcher, to murder with violence." People don't just die, they aren't just murdered, they are literally butchered violently! That means take all your Freddy Kruegers, take all your Jasons, take all your Chainsaw Massacre horrible shows, and unleash that same sick murderous behavior depicted in those wicked rotten movies and now make it the attitude of everyone on the planet *for real*! What a gruesome, bloody, nightmarish scene! No wonder Jesus said the following words:

Matthew 24:22 "If those days had not been cut short, no one would survive, but for the sake of the elect those days will be shortened."

In other words, if God didn't put a cap on the time of this slaughterous murderous behavior, mankind would chop each other up into little pieces down to the very last man, woman, and child. In fact, the Greek word here "sphazo" is the exact same word used elsewhere in the Book of Revelation to describe the death of Jesus:

Revelation 5:9 "And they sang a new song: 'You are worthy to take the scroll and to open its seals, because You were *slain*, and with Your blood You purchased men for God from every tribe and language and people and nation."

And so, the law of reaping and sowing comes into play here for mankind. They chose not to receive the love and mercy and forgiveness of *the Lamb* who was brutally murdered and slain (sphazo) on their behalf, and instead welcomed and received the lying deceptive false peace of the antichrist. Therefore, they will reap what they sow. Instead of receiving the healing of the "sphazo" of Jesus Christ that could have effectively rescued them from the wrath to come, they will now receive the horrible "sphazo" of mankind and begin to literally butcher, slaughter, and slay one another. It's hard to even put into words how horrible and shocking and sickening this time frame will be.

Furthermore, the text implies that it's not just militaries that *slay each other*. It is *men* slaying each other. The idea is that the planet erupts in a butcherous slaughter on one another. They don't wait for the armies to show up and do the dirty work for them. No. They do it themselves, to their fellow man. Everybody's acting like a horror flick, a serial murderer unleashed, unrestrained, unstoppable, only ceasing when some other serial murderer kills them. The wholesale carnage that is depicted here is unbelievable. It's not just that peace is taken away, it's that the planet begins to chop each other up, literally, individually, as these men share:

"The rider on the blood-red horse has a sword representing a different type of warfare than that of the bow: man wrestling with man, nation with nation.

Internal strife, class wars, civil wars, the breaking up of all established order is illustrated here."

"Although the rider on the white horse appears to conquer by means of negotiation and avoids bloodshed, this does not last. Eventually he shows his true colors as the second rider joins the ride – bringing war and death."

"This will be a time of unprecedented bloodshed which will forever puncture the naive view of humanism that man is inherently good."

"Sometime early in the first three and a half years, in the birth pangs, in the beginning, world peace turns into war. That initiated peace, that counterfeit prosperity comes to a fast end. War is going to break out everywhere. The whole earth is going to lose its peace.

Secondly, violent slaughter begins to take place all over the world. And we don't know the specifics of that except to say just exactly what the Scripture says. There will be a slaughter all over the earth.

By the way, this war runs pretty much through the whole rest of the Tribulation. Certainly, runs past the midpoint and on well into the second half. The slaughter runs on beyond this as well. It starts early, it goes on for a long time."

"The kind of a red horseman that this refers to is not only nation rising against nation and kingdom against kingdom, but it is more nearly the idea, the picture of class fighting class and party fighting party, the kind of a thing you saw over in Algiers, where Frenchmen were murdering Frenchmen. And they do it in the night, and they do it in the day, and they do it at twilight, and at noontime; and everyone lives in the fear of his life, and there's murder and bloodshed everywhere.

The red horseman: the earth bathes in one another's blood, 'That they should kill one another,' Americans killing Americans, Britishers killing Britishers, Frenchmen killing Frenchmen, Germans killing Germans, Russians killing Russians; the whole world in a ferment of blood and revolution [Rev. 6:3-4]."[7]

   Wow! What a bloody scene! Yes, militaries from around the world will be involved, but it's much more intimate than that. People are against people, neighbor against neighbor, family against family, friend against friend, countrymen against countrymen; all people *all over the earth* will start to *slay*, butcher, and murder one another. You don't want to be there!

The **third question** about the rider is **Why was He Given a Large Sword**?

Revelation 6:4c "Then another horse came out, a fiery red one. Its rider was given power to take peace from the earth and to make men slay each other. To him was *given a large sword*."

Now we see John revealing not only what the *rider* on the *fiery red horse* is given power to *do*, but what the *rider* on the *fiery red horse* was given to *carry*. It's only one item but it says it all. A *large sword*. Not a white flag, not a giant wad of cash to distribute to everyone, or even a blanket of comfort to aid the planet. Not even close! Of all things this *rider* was given by God to carry with him, it just happened to be a *large sword*. This sadly fits the scene perfectly. From the antichrist's fake false peace, waving a white flag, promising economic prosperity and comfort to the whole planet, to wholesale slaughter of mankind across the globe, people killing each other depicted by not just a sword, but a *large sword*. This is not talking about a mere casual slaughter, it's shouting forth that it will be a *large* one! It's actually the Greek word "megas machaira" which literally means, "a large knife used for killing animals and cutting up flesh." Of course, the context tells us this "cutting up of flesh" is not on animals but actual humans. Here we see that people will be acting like animals, treating each other like animals, even to the point where they are cutting each other up, filleting them, carving their victims into pieces like a hunter does with his prey. It's such an unspeakable, gross, mutilating scene. How horrible this will be! This is simply wholesale carnage of mankind, one pitted against another on a very *large* scale! Everywhere you go, this is what's going on. Mankind has turned into a butcherous animal, chopping one another to pieces. The whole world has in effect gone mad, as this researcher agrees:

"A great sword is wielded by the second horseman, but it is sent by God: For thus says the LORD God of Israel to me: 'Take this wine cup of fury from My hand, and cause all the nations, to whom I send you, to drink it. And they will drink and stagger and go mad because of the sword that I will send among them. Then I took the cup from the LORD'S hand, and made all the nations drink, to whom the LORD had sent me.' (Jer. 25:15-17)

This is the pattern of God's judgment to nations who reject Him – He makes them mad and turn upon one another. 'I will summon a sword against Gog on all my mountains, declares the Sovereign LORD. Every man's sword will be against his brother.' (Ez. 38:21). While Scripture does not give the details, the advances in modern weaponry suggest a terrible, unimaginable holocaust."[8]

In fact, this unimaginable holocaust is illuminated even more when you compare this *large sword* that was used by the Romans to other weapons they had in their arsenal:

"Now, I want you to look at something here. There is a Greek word for a sword of a soldier when he goes marching to war. That's a rhomphaia, the sword of a soldier as he walks, as he marches into battle, a rhomphaia. But there is another Greek word for a sword: we'd call it a 'dirk,' or a 'knife.' It's a machaira. And the word that is used here is machaira that is, the kind of a weapon that you would hide, you'd conceal beneath your coat. A machaira would be a knife like you would cut the throat of an animal or cut the throat of a man."

"This machaira is the word that is used for the soldier's sword, the one they carried into battle. It also is used often for the assassin's weapon. It depicts war and assassination and rebellion and revolt and massacre, deadly force involving slaughter and death. That is the intent of the megala machaira, the great sword. At this particular time, whatever positive things have been going on in the world come to a screeching halt. Read Jeremiah 25 if you get a chance, from verses 15 on, and you will see something of the unfolding of this horrible war."[9]

This difference in Roman swords and weaponry gives us even more insights to this horrible global slaughter. The *large sword* depicted here is not a giant two-handed sword that can only be wielded by an Arnold Schwarzenegger huge Conan the Barbarian type soldier or person, but it is a precision instrument. Soldiers used it, yes, but so did *assassins*. It was used in war alright, but it was also used as a *concealed weapon* tucked away in one's coat to quickly murder someone when walking by. A sudden jab, slice of the throat, and move on before anyone even notices what happened. This is wholesale carnage no matter where you go on the planet. Not just in the battlefield, but in the highways and byways, in the alleys and street corners, in the house and outside the front yard, at schools and businesses, playgrounds and parties; slaughter is everywhere. No wonder Jeremiah goes on to say the following statement:

Jeremiah 25:27 "Then tell them, 'This is what the LORD Almighty, the God of Israel, says: Drink, get drunk and vomit, and fall to rise no more because of the sword I will send among you.'"

It makes you want to vomit just trying to describe the macabre scene! No place to run, no place to hide. Whether it's the open, visible weaponry of military invasions, or the hidden concealed weapons of the average Joe walking past you on the street, no one can be trusted. One minute they appear to be your friend, the next minute they slit your throat! Family against family, friend, against friend neighbor against neighbor; a *great slaughter* breaks out everywhere! Imagine civil war, literally, on every corner. Nations are now against nations, kingdoms are now against kingdoms. War and strife is everywhere. Murder is rampant. Blood covers the streets, homes, and businesses. Terrorists are having a heyday. Jihadists think they're in heaven. No one will be safe from anyone! A *large sword* has descended upon the planet and there is no escape and no stopping it for the next nearly 7 years until Jesus Christ the Prince of Peace comes back at His Second Coming! All because mankind rejected the love and forgiveness of the One and Only Messiah and instead accepted the lying, evil, deceptive promises of the false messiah. Therefore, God now gives the planet over to what they want and what they deserve. He gives them over to destruction, wrath, and they begin to do things *that ought not to be done,* as this man concludes:

"The rider of this horse removes 'peace from the earth.' Further, he was to cause men to 'slay [lit. slaughter] one another.' The 'great sword' represents authority to slay people. It does not denote international warfare but revolution in which people turn on one another. The result is anarchy, riot, and civil war. In light of the terrorism, bombings, and civil war taking place around the world, we need little imagination to think of what will be happening on an even larger scale.

It has always been so throughout history. From 1496 B.C. to A.D. 1861, the world knew 3,130 years of war and 227 years of peace. In the last 400 years European nations have signed more than 8,000 peace treaties. In the 20th century 8.5 million died in World War I, and 22 million died in World War II. The Vietnam conflict cost the U.S. 58,000 of our young men and maimed another 100,000 for life. What our text tells us is that in the years just prior to the second coming of Christ, God is going to give civilization over to war.

Romans 1:24,26,28 'Therefore God gave them over in the desires of their hearts to impurity, to dishonor their bodies among themselves. For this reason, God gave them over to dishonorable passions. For their women exchanged the natural sexual relations for unnatural ones, and just as they did not see fit to acknowledge God, God gave them over to a depraved mind, to do what should not be done.'"[10]

Mankind should never murder one another, let alone slaughter and butcher each other like animals as this text reveals they will do in the Seal Judgments. Yet so it is, for those who reject Jesus Christ and spurn His gracious merciful offer to be rescued from this horrible timeframe. Salvation or the sword, the choice is yours. And to think we're just getting started. The next horse is coming, and we haven't seen anything yet!

Chapter Seven

The Breaking of the Famine Seal

The **sixth thing** we see in the breaking of the planet is the **Ordering of the Third Seal**.

Revelation 6:5a "When *the Lamb opened the third seal*, I heard the third living creature say, 'Come!'"

I had an instructor in Bible College that always used to say the repeated phrase to us students, "Repetition increases remembrance. Repetition increases remembrance. Repetition increases remembrance. That's right, repetition increases remembrance." He would do this as a way to illustrate the importance and value of repeatedly studying a particular topic and/or truth from the Bible over and over again. If you repeatedly study it, you'll likely never forget it. Why? Because repetition increases remembrance. The more you study it, ingest it, read it, hear it, the more it gets locked into your brain. Advertisers do the same thing when they try to get us to buy their products. They repeatedly bombard us with unending commercials full of repetitious phrases and repeated phone numbers to make sure we never forget where to go and how to get their product now! So, it is here with God. A basic rule in Bible interpretation is, whenever you see something repeated in Scripture, pay attention, God is trying to get a very important message across to you. Now, all of His Word is important, yet if you see something repeated, you better wake up! Don't miss what He's trying to share. For instance, the Bible not only tells us that God is Holy, but it repeatedly states that He is Holy, Holy, Holy.

Isaiah 6:1-5 "In the year that King Uzziah died, I saw the Lord seated on a throne, high and exalted, and the train of his robe filled the temple. Above Him were seraphs, each with six wings: With two wings they covered their faces, with two they covered their feet, and with two they were flying. And they were calling to one another: '*Holy, holy, holy* is the LORD Almighty; the whole earth is full of His glory.' At the sound of their voices the doorposts and thresholds shook, and the temple was filled with smoke. 'Woe to me!' I cried. 'I am ruined! For I am a man of unclean lips, and I live among a people of unclean lips, and my eyes have seen the King, the LORD Almighty.'"

Revelation 4:8-11 "Each of the four living creatures had six wings and was covered with eyes all around, even under his wings. Day and night, they never stop saying: '*Holy, holy, holy* is the Lord God Almighty, who was, and is, and is to come.' Whenever the living creatures give glory, honor and thanks to Him who sits on the throne and who lives for ever and ever, the twenty-four elders fall down before Him who sits on the throne, and worship Him who lives for ever and ever. They lay their crowns before the throne and say: 'You are worthy, our Lord and God, to receive glory and honor and power, for You created all things, and by Your will they were created and have their being.'"

Not once, not twice, but three times in a row we see this attribute of God repeated in Scripture. Why? Because He really wants you to understand and never forget this particular attribute of His. He is Holy. All of His attributes are important, but don't ever forget this one because it ties everything together. So, it is here with the ordering of the *third seal*. Not once, not twice, but now three times in a row we have God trying to drill into our heads a very important message. *The Lamb opened the third seal*. Not satan, not man, not even mother earth, but *the Lamb* is the One Who is responsible for unleashing this next seal as well as *all the other seals*. God is the One Who is in charge of these judgments through and through. Don't ever forget that! This is very important! God is repeating Himself. Why? Because repetition increases remembrance! He doesn't want you to miss this very valuable and important truth. Yes, our Lord Jesus came the first time as the Sacrificial Lamb to be bruised, beaten, and even killed on our behalf. But the second time He will come as *the Wrathful Lamb* Who will this time be the One dishing out the beatings! In fact, later in the seals we see how even the inhabitants of the earth acknowledge this very important truth.

Revelation 6:15-17 "Then the kings of the earth, the princes, the generals, the rich, the mighty, and every slave and every free man hid in caves and among the rocks of the mountains. They called to the mountains and the rocks, 'Fall on us and hide us from the face of Him who sits on the throne and from the *wrath of the Lamb*! For the great day of their wrath has come, and who can stand?'"

So, it is today. You can either acknowledge *now* what God has been trying to tell us here in Revelation 6 for nearly 2,000 years, that Jesus, *the Lamb*, is coming back to pour out His wrath upon planet earth and you better get saved before it's too late. Or, as these people found out here too late, ignore it, scoff at it, mock it, and be forced to admit this truth in the 7-year Tribulation. No wonder God is using this teaching technique called repetition increases remembrance. He's trying to get this very important truth locked into our brains before it's too late. Don't scoff. Don't mock at it. Receive it before it's too late. God is not willing that any should perish but wants all to come to repentance.

2 Peter 3:3-9 "First of all, you must understand that in the last days scoffers will come, scoffing and following their own evil desires. They will say, 'Where is this 'coming' He promised? Ever since our fathers died, everything goes on as it has since the beginning of creation.' But they deliberately forget that long ago by God's word the heavens existed and the earth was formed out of water and by water. By these waters also the world of that time was deluged and destroyed. By the same word the present heavens and earth are reserved for fire, being kept for the day of judgment and destruction of ungodly men. But do not forget this one thing, dear friends: With the Lord a day is like a thousand years, and a thousand years are like a day. The Lord is not slow in keeping His promise, as some understand slowness. He is patient with you, not wanting anyone to perish, but everyone to come to repentance."

The wrath of God is coming. It happened before, it's going to happen again. God is being merciful to us by not only repeating this message to us over and over again, but He's giving us time to respond. Yet, it won't last forever. The day of judgment is coming, and people need to take this message as very serious and get saved through Jesus Christ before it's too late. In fact, to show you just how wonderful and merciful the heart of God really is in giving people a chance to respond in repentance through Jesus Christ before it's too late so as to avoid *the wrath of the Lamb*, let us recall that this phrase we see here in the opening of the *third seal* is not only repeated *three times*, but in *every time* a seal is mentioned! *He, the Lamb*, is the One Who is responsible for this wrath being poured out on the planet for 7-years! Don't ever forget it! Why? Because "Repetition increases remembrance. Repetition increases remembrance.

Repetition increases remembrance. That's right, repetition increases remembrance." The *wrath of the Lamb* is coming, and you better be ready!

The **seventh thing** we see in the breaking of the planet is the **Object of the Third Seal**.

As if a global slaughter of people, militaries and individuals alike, literally chopping each other up into pieces wasn't enough to get your attention, again, the polar opposite of their short-lived fake, false, phony peace, it's about to get even worse. This is what we see in the *object* of this next wave of judgments coming from God, the *third seal,* and as we shall soon see it is simply the breaking of the Famine Seal. *Famine/Starvation* is the *object* of discussion at hand. Thus, God's third judgment upon planet earth is a global famine to further arouse people's attention, to acknowledge Him and His wrath being poured out upon the planet, and to respond appropriately.

Revelation 6:5-6 "When the Lamb opened the third seal, I heard the third living creature say, 'Come!' I looked, and there before me was a black horse! Its rider was holding a pair of scales in his hand. Then I heard what sounded like a voice among the four living creatures, saying, 'A quart of wheat for a day's wages, and three quarts of barley for a day's wages, and do not damage the oil and the wine!'"

Matthew 24:7b "There will be famines...."

Once again, Revelation 6 and Matthew 24 are prophetically dealing with the same time-frame, the beginning portion of the 7-year Tribulation. Therefore, by observing both of these passages, we shall be able to acquire even more detailed information concerning the *object* of this next seal, the *third seal,* that is, a *global famine*. We know this *third seal* judgement is dealing with *famine* and *starvation* conditions, due to stated verbiage in both texts. *Food* on a global basis is being *measured* and doled out. The food that is measured out to the inhabitants of the earth is *barely enough to survive*. These are the *famine* conditions Jesus mentions in the parallel passage of Matthew 24. Thus, this global famine pulls the rug out from underneath wicked and rebellious and even murderous planet earth. They fell for the false peace of the antichrist, then immediately turned around and spent their energy slaying and slaughtering one another. Why, they must be *famished* after all that! Everybody knows that after an intense, long, hard work-out your body naturally craves *food* big time! It needs to be replenished and replenished now! But *now* God will take that away from you. You will not be able to restore yourself. You will not be able to satisfy your craving. As an act of judgement, planet earth's food supply will be totally decimated. At the end of an exhaustive murderous spree, an intense workout of murder which God condemns, people wipe off the sweat of their brow only to discover there's nothing to replenish themselves with. No baked goods, no energy bars, no big burgers at the local restaurant, just the fruit of their wicked deeds. *Famine!* They have simply reaped what they have sown. The *third seal* is opened by *the Lamb* and the Global food supply goes down the tubes. Global War turns into Global Famine. The bottom drops out and people are thrust into a whole new wave of empty despair, as this researcher shares:

"Hunger is the effect of worldwide war. Jesus said this also. Jesus said, following the nation rising against nation and kingdom against kingdom, 'There will be famine,' Matthew 24:7; this too is God's judgment. He's done it before. Haggai 1, Ezekiel 4, God has brought famine before and He'll bring it again.

Haggai 1:10-11 "Therefore, because of you the heavens have withheld their dew and the earth its crops. I called for a drought on the fields and the mountains, on the grain, the new wine, the oil and whatever the ground produces, on men and cattle, and on the labor of your hands."

Ezekiel 4:16-17 "He then said to me: 'Son of man, I will cut off the supply of food in Jerusalem. The people will eat rationed food in anxiety and drink rationed water in despair, for food and water will be scarce. They will be appalled at the sight of each other and will waste away because of their sin."

When there is this kind of war all over the globe, people stop producing, the slaughter is massive, food supplies are destroyed. And you can imagine, war at this level with the kind of weaponry we have today, will be devastating. And as a result, rationing is going to take place because of the scarcity of food.

That's why it says in verse 5 that the rider on the black horse also has a weapon of sorts; it isn't a great sword like the other rider, but it is a pair of scales in his hand. And that is used for measuring. And what it means is that food is going to be rationed, it's going to be measured out, weighing out food, food lines.

We find that very easy to understand, don't we? Some of you may even remember food lines in World War II. Some of you have seen pictures of food lines in

Eastern Europe. You've seen third world countries today where there is rationing of food. Starving people all over everywhere getting in line."[1]

So, it descends here not to just one country, not just one region, not just one city, but to the whole planet. *Famine!* Why? Because the whole planet rejected Jesus Christ, and instead followed the antichrist, and then turned around and went on a global murderous spree of their fellow man. Therefore, God now takes away your ability to catch your breath, replenish yourself, and gather your senses. As soon as the last bead of sweat drops to the ground after finally ceasing from your murderous workout, because of your sin God gives the order to unleash the *object* of the *third seal. Famine!* In the silence, your stomach rumbles, it cries out to be appeased and the word *food* rushes to your brain. You awaken from your bloody nightmare and your body is shouting to you to satisfy your flesh, but now you look around as you slowly come out of your murderous daze only to spy a world full of emptiness. Mother Hubbard eat your heart out! Where there were once restaurants galore, now there is nothing but food lines, everywhere! One minute you could choose between regular, medium, or extra-large, but now there's nothing, literally! Nobody even asks if you'd like fries with that because there are no fries! Everything was destroyed in your blind fury to murder, murder, murder! Now the only option you ever get is, "Would you like a quart of wheat for a day's wages, or three quarts of barley?" So now let us turn our attention to this horrible global choice given to the people of the planet during this time of Global Famine as an act of judgement from God in the details of the *third seal.*

The **first detail** given about the object of the third seal is **The Black Horse**.

Revelation 6:5b "I looked, and there before me was a black horse!"

Once again, we see the chosen *vehicle* and its *color.* That next seal rider charges towards planet earth issuing forth the next wave of Judgment from God. When *the Lamb opens the third seal,* we also see its rider bursting forth upon the world scene riding a *horse,* the *battle tank* or *war machine* of the day, yet this time the color is *black.* This naturally gives rise to a couple of questions.

The **first question** about the horse is **Why is it Black?**
Revelation 6:5b "I looked, and there before me was a *black* horse!"

Throughout the Old and New Testaments, we see that the color *black* is often used to speak of bad times, sorrowful times, mourning, and the effects of famine. Furthermore, if you combine it with the secular and historical uses of the color black, you get an even clearer picture as to why this next wave of judgment from God that's about to be thrust upon mankind in the *third seal,* is yet another dark nightmare descending upon the planet:

Darkness

1 Kings 18:45 "In a little while the sky grew *black* with clouds and wind, and there was a heavy shower. And Ahab rode and went to Jezreel."

Revelation 6:12 "I looked when He broke the sixth seal, and there was a great earthquake; and the sun became *black* as sackcloth made of hair, and the whole moon became like blood."

Doom

Deuteronomy 4:11 "You came near and stood at the foot of the mountain while it blazed with fire to the very heavens, with *black* clouds and deep darkness."

Gloom & Terror

Job 3:5 "Let darkness and *black* gloom claim it; Let a cloud settle on it; Let the *blackness* of the day terrify it."

Judgment

2 Peter 2:17 "These are springs without water and mists driven by a storm, for whom the *black* darkness has been reserved."

Jude 1:13 "Wild waves of the sea, casting up their own shame like foam; wandering stars, for whom the *black* darkness has been reserved forever."

Mourning

Jeremiah 4:28 "For this shall the earth mourn, and the heavens above be *black*: because I have spoken it, I have purposed it, and will not repent, neither will I turn back from it."

Wasting Away

Job 30:26-31 "Yet when I hoped for good, evil came; when I looked for light, then came darkness. The churning inside me never stops; days of suffering confront me. I go about *blackened*, but not by the sun; I stand up in the assembly and cry for help. I have become a brother of jackals, a companion of owls. My skin grows *black* and peels; my body burns with fever. My harp is tuned to mourning, and my flute to the sound of wailing."

Effects of Famine

Lamentations 4:8-9 "Their visage is *blacker* than a coal; they are not known in the streets: their skin cleaveth to their bones; it is withered, it is become like a stick. They that be slain with the sword are better than they that be slain with hunger: for these pine away, stricken through for want of the fruits of the field."

Lamentations 5:10 "Our skin was *black* like an oven because of the terrible famine."

If the inhabitants of the earth thought things were bad so far, it's about to get even darker! Gloom and doom is headed their way! The judgment of God is coming again with a whole new wave of terror that will literal begin wasting them away. A blanket of mourning is about to descend upon the planet of which there is no escape. Now add this shocking revelation to the secular and historic usage of the color black:

"Black is the darkest color resulting from the absence or complete absorption of light. Black is often used to represent darkness; it is the symbolic opposite of white (or brightness).

The word black comes from Ancient Greek 'phlegein' ("to burn, scorch"), the Old English 'blæc' ("black, dark", also, "ink"), and from the Proto-Germanic 'blakkaz' ("burned"). In Latin, the word for black, 'ater' and to darken, 'atere,' were associated with cruelty, brutality and evil. They were the root of the English words 'atrocious' and 'atrocity'.

For the ancient Greeks, black was also the color of the underworld, separated from the world of the living by the river Acheron, whose water was black. Those who had committed the worst sins were sent to Tartarus, the deepest and darkest level. In the center was the palace of Hades, the king of the underworld, where he was seated upon a black ebony throne.

In the Roman Empire, black was the color of death and mourning. In the 2nd century BC Roman magistrates began to wear a dark toga, called a toga pulla, to funeral ceremonies. Later, under the Empire, the family of the deceased also wore dark colors for a long period; then, after a banquet to mark the end of mourning, exchanged the black for a white toga. In Roman poetry, death was called the hora nigra, the black hour.

Black is still used today in various idioms and expressions to speak of dark times.

- *A blacklist is a list of undesirable persons or entities (to be placed on the list is to be "blacklisted").*

- *A black comedy is a form of comedy dealing with morbid and serious topics.*

- *A black mark against a person relates to something bad they have done.*

- *A black mood is a bad one.*

- *A black market is used to denote the trade of illegal goods, or alternatively the illegal trade of otherwise legal items at considerably higher prices.*

- *Black propaganda is the use of known falsehoods, partial truths, or masquerades in propaganda to confuse an opponent.*

- *Blackmail is the act of threatening someone to do something that would hurt them in some way, such as by revealing sensitive information about them, in order to force the threatened party to fulfill certain demands.*

- *The black sheep of the family is the ne'er-do-well.*

- *To blackball someone is to block their entry into a club or some such institution. In the traditional English gentlemen's club, members vote on the admission of a candidate by secretly placing a white or black ball in a hat. If, upon the completion of voting, there was even one black ball amongst the white, the candidate would be denied membership, and he would never know who had "blackballed" him.*

And even today black is still the color traditionally worn at funerals and memorial services. In some traditional societies, for example in Greece and Italy, some widows wear black for the rest of their lives."[2]

So, it will be for planet earth. For the rest of the 7-year tribulation, people will be walking around immersed in an existence of darkness and death. What a horrific picture painted for us here by Almighty God. Of all colors to pick for this next *horse* descending upon the planet, it's *black*. God is sending a very clear message. Dark times, mournful times, undesirable times are coming with this *black horse rider*. The whole planet will become one big funeral service, non-stop, until the end of the 7-year Tribulation. More people will die than at any other time in the history of mankind. Death, decay, corpses, crying mourning, anguish, atrocities, heartache, tears, loss, and unspeakable behavior will be the daily existence of those who remain. The earth is turned into a planet full of Jobs scraping themselves on heaps of rubbish. Why? Because they rejected the light of Jesus Christ, and instead followed the black lies of the antichrist. They have now reaped what they have sown, darkness, dark times, death and destruction, and there is no escape.

The **second detail** given about the object of the third seal is **The Rider**.

Revelation 6:5b-c "I looked, and there before me was a black horse! Its *rider* was holding a pair of scales in his hand."

The *third seal horse* is not alone. Just like the first two, this horse carries a *rider* that ushers in yet another series of horrible judgments from the throne room of God. As the *black horse* is carrying its deadly cargo, so is the *rider*. He too is carrying something. A quick look at these items the *rider* is carrying and the details surrounding them, will bring this dark and ominous time into view. *Famine* is coming, the worst ever in the history of mankind:

The **first question** about the rider is **Why is He Holding a Pair of Scales**?

Revelation 6:5c "Its rider was *holding a pair of scales in his hand.*"

The first thing we see this *black horse rider* carrying, literally *holding*, to release upon planet earth is *a pair of scales*. So, the natural logical question is, "What are the scales for? What do they mean? Of all things for this rider to hold, why scales?" Was he on some sort of diet? Did he just return from a fishing trip and want to weigh his catch? Who goes around holding *a pair of scales*? Well, the answer to that is found in the *context*, as well as the customs and mannerisms of the day when this prophecy was written down for us. First of all, the *context* tells us what these scales are for. It's for the *weighing out* and *distribution of food*. *Wheat* and *barley* will be doled out in specific *limited* portions at *extremely high prices*. This is a clear indicator that this next wave of judgments from God is all about famine conditions and scarcity of food. Furthermore, since the context is *global*, this means this famine is likewise global. The whole planet will now experience this food shortage, this scarcity of even basic food staples. It will be carefully weighed and balanced so as to not lose even one seed of grain lest things get even worse for the inhabitants of earth, as these men share:

"These scales in the hand of the horseman are not the kind used by Weight Watchers, but rather are the kind used to measure out grain. This implies that food will have to be weighed out and rationed with care. As is generally true, scarcity and famine follow war."

"The black horse has a rider with 'a pair of scales in his hand.' A scale would be used to measure and carefully dole out food. It could refer to bread being rationed by weight in a famine, or grain being measured by volume. We see this being done in the Old Testament. God told the Israelites they would suffer famine if they sinned, and they would be forced to 'dole out the bread by weight.'

Leviticus 26:26 "When I cut off your supply of bread, ten women will be able to bake your bread in one oven, and they will dole out the bread by weight. You will eat, but you will not be satisfied."

In the siege of Jerusalem, the people would 'eat rationed food in anxiety and drink rationed water in despair.'

Ezekiel 4:16 "He then said to me: 'Son of man, I will cut off the supply of food in Jerusalem. The people will eat rationed food in anxiety and drink rationed water in despair, for food and water will be scarce. They will be appalled at the sight of each other and will waste away because of their sin.'"[3]

Now, since most of us have never even come close to experiencing true famine conditions, let alone the kind of horrific famine conditions mentioned here coming to the planet during the first half of the 7-year Tribulation, let us *visually* immerse ourselves into what this will look like on a global scale. The following are some pictorial examples of the effects of various smaller famines throughout recent history. Imagine the whole planet looking and living like the following. What does it look like to *waste away*? What if these were your family photos:

The Great Bengal famine that killed 10 million people.

The Great Famine of India in 1877 that killed 5.25 million.

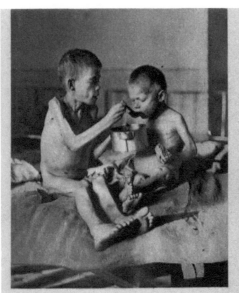

La famine en Russie. III. LES DEUX ÉTAPES DE LA FAIM:
les membres squelettiques, le ventre ballonné (par l'herbe,
la paille, l'écorce d'arbre, les vers, la terre). Ces enfants
ne peuvent plus être sauvés, il est trop tard. Pour les sau-
ver, il eût fallu les nourrir avant ce degré d'épuisement.

Starving Russian children during the Russian Famine of 1921-1922,
which killed an estimated 5 million.

The Siege of Leningrad Famine 1941-1944 that killed 1.5 million.

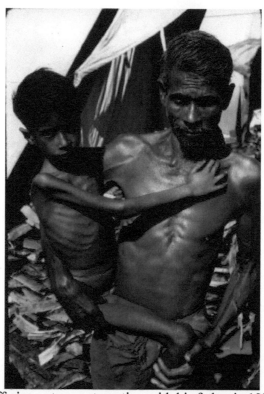

A child suffering extreme starvation with his father in 1972 in India.

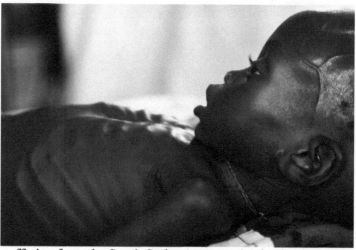

A child suffering from the South Sudan 'man-made' famine in 2016-current.[4]

As gut-wrenching and heart-breaking as those photos really are, now try to imagine what this text is trying to reveal to us. These conditions, these photos, these kind of effects from famine that you just saw will not just be commonplace in one city, nor just affect merely one country or region. But the Great Famine that God will be sending in the *third seal* will affect *the whole world all at the same time*! Everywhere you turn this will be how people look on planet earth! Why? Because they rejected the light of Jesus Christ, and instead followed the dark lies of the antichrist, their *crops* have come in. It's *harvest time*! The *scales* are ready! They will reap what they have sown. Dark, deadly times, full of death and destruction will be *weighed* out!

Furthermore, famines are not only caused by poor farming practices and bad weather. If you look at the historical track record for famines, and even more so in modern history, many of the famines are caused by wars, military conquests, and government oppression. So, it will be in the 7-year Tribulation. The antichrist will go on a satanic conquest and institute the most oppressive government this planet has ever seen. He will then launch forth in a seemingly unending campaign of wars, one after another, leaving not only death and destruction in its wake, but global famine on a massive scale that we can hardly comprehend. The *rider* has gone forth, the *scales* have come out, and wicked and rebellious humanity is about to be *weighed* from Almighty God with another horrific judgment. *Famine*! Lest there be any doubt that God Himself really will unleash this kind of judgment upon mankind, the next details will erase it.

The **third detail** given about the object of the third seal is **The Voice**.

Revelation 6:6a "Then I heard what sounded like *a voice among the four living creatures.*'"

The Church today has been so inundated with so many false views of God from so many false teachers who have flooded the pulpit. These false teachers try to paint for us an idolatrous phony picture of God that they have created themselves. They would have us believe that God is some sort of Cosmic Grandfather in the Sky who would never even hurt a flea. They say He's just your forever Best Buddy in heaven who's there at your every beck and call ready to do your will. As one person stated, "We have turned God into the Divine Prozac!" This is not only an unbiblical and egregious view of God, but that false representation of God is blown away with this *voice* we see mentioned in this text. It is yet another reminder of just Who is responsible for these judgments unleashed upon planet earth. It's not satan. It's not man. *It is God*! *He* is the One Whom the *four living creatures* surround, as this researcher also agrees:

"This is amazing in verse 6, 'I heard as it were a voice in the center of the four living creatures.' You tell me, who is in the center of the four living creatures? Who's in the center? Around whose throne, are they? God's throne...God's throne, so there's no question in my mind but that God is here speaking because these creatures, these four living angels, these four cherubim, are surrounding the throne of God."[5]

How much clearer does it have to get? How many times does the Bible have to tell us just Who the *real God* is before we submit to the truth? How many times do we have to be reminded that *all of these judgments* from the beginning of the 7-year Tribulation to the end of the 7-year Tribulation are coming *from God*, all of them, not from man, and certainly not satan! This is the *voice of God* dishing out these orders! *He* is the ultimate source of all these judgments, make no mistake about it. In fact, even a cursory reading of the Bible, Old and New Testaments, reveals that this is not the first time God has judged His creation, let alone with the specific instrument of famine:

FAMINES IN SCRIPTURE

- In Canaan in Abraham's day (Gen. 12:10)

- In Canaan in Isaac's day (Gen. 26:1)

- In Canaan in Jacob's day (Gen. 41:54-57)

- In Canaan during the judges (Ruth 1:1)

- In Canaan in David's day (2 Sam. 21:1)

- In Canaan in Elijah's day (1 Ki. 17:1)

- In Canaan in Elisha's day (2 Ki. 4:38)

- In Samaria in Elisha's day (2 Ki. 6:25)

- In Canaan in Elisha's day (2 Ki. 8:1)

- In Jerusalem in Zedekiah's day (2 Ki. 25:3; Jer. 14)

- In Canaan in Nehemiah's day (Neh. 5:3)

- In an unknown land (Lk. 15:14)

- In the Roman Empire in Paul's day (Acts 11:28)

Famines were judgments of God. They are mentioned elsewhere in connection with judgments (2 Sam. 24:13; Ps. 105:16; Isa. 51:19; Jer. 14:15; 15:2; 24:10; 27:8; Ezek. 5:12; 12:16) and foretold as a sign of the second coming of Christ (Mt. 24:7; Lk. 21:11).[6]

So much for God being a Cosmic Grandfather in the Sky Who wouldn't hurt a flea! Time to smash that idol once and for all! Not once, not twice, but multiple times in the Bible the *real God* will send forth *famine* as an act of His judgment upon wicked and rebellious mankind, just like we see here in Revelation 6. Only this time, it will be on a *global scale*. God made this planet and mankind. Therefore, He can judge it if He wants to, and He *will* according to *His voice* mentioned here in this text. If you still falsely think, even after all this, that God is your forever Best Buddy in heaven just waiting at your every beck and call ready to do your will, *how wrong you are*, as this researcher admits:

"The fact that the voice announcing the prices comes from the living creatures that are in the middle of and around God's throne (Rev.4:6) suggests that God has something to do with price lists. When we watch prices go up and down, and when we hear the weather reports and crop reports, and when we listen to the latest stock prices and economic indicators, we never think of anything divine connected with them. How wrong we are!"[7]

I would agree. God is in control at all times and He always will be, including when it comes to dishing out this Global Famine on planet earth mentioned here in this *third seal*. In fact, some of the descriptions from the other famines mentioned throughout the Bible reveal just how horrific a judgment these famines from God really are:

Lamentations 4:1-11 "Because of thirst the infant's tongue sticks to the roof of its mouth; the children beg for bread, but no one gives it to them. Those who once ate delicacies are destitute in the streets. Those nurtured in purple now lie on ash heaps. The punishment of my people is greater than that of Sodom, which was overthrown in a moment without a hand turned to help her. Their princes were brighter than snow and whiter than milk, their bodies ruddier than rubies, their appearance like sapphires. But now they are *blacker than soot*; they are not recognized in the streets. Their skin has shriveled on their bones; it has become as dry as a stick. Those killed by the sword are better off than those who die of *famine*; racked with hunger, they waste away for lack of food from the field. With their own hands compassionate women have cooked their own children, who became their food when my people were destroyed. The LORD has given full vent to his wrath; he has poured out his fierce anger. He kindled a fire in Zion that consumed her foundations."

Children begging for bread with no response? Young and old alike destitute in the streets lying in heaps? Their bodies blackened, not even recognizable? Their skin shriveled to the bones racked with hunger? They waste away dry as a stick? Why? Because they too rejected God and instead spent their time sowing another crop, a sinful one. So it is with any other crop-eventually it's harvest time and you will reap what you have sown. An outpouring of God's wrath. As it was with Israel in the past, so it will unfortunately be again for all rebellious mankind in the future. The Bible says they are storing up the fire of God's wrath for the day of destruction.

Romans 2:5-6 "But because of your stubbornness and your unrepentant heart, you are storing up wrath against yourself for the day of God's wrath, when His righteous judgment will be revealed. God 'will give to each person according to what he has done.'"

Laugh and mock and scoff all you want, but I wouldn't recommend it. All you're doing is making things worse. Just like Israel in the Old Testament, so it is with planet earth in the future. The Bible tells us that mankind will once again unfortunately plant another crop of wickedness and rebellion, thinking they'll be just fine when in reality harvest time is about to be poured out upon them! The wrath of God they stored up is now in full bloom! Much to their horror, instead of receiving the so-called peace and prosperity they were promised by the satanic lying antichrist, they will now have reaped the horrific wrath of Almighty God in the form of a global famine, worse than anything the world has ever seen. So, once again, let us try to conceptualize just how horrendous and dreadful this soon coming future time of judgment will be by taking a look at another recent famine. The following is the shocking description of the true events that took place during the Siege of Leningrad in 1941-1944 and the famine that followed. This time we will not look at just a single picture, but the following are the actual events:

"It was beyond horror. They ate cats, sawdust, wallpaper paste...even their own babies. It was Leningrad's agony as the Nazis tried to starve it into submission.

The German siege of Leningrad lasted 900 days from September 1941 to January 1944. During that time...nearly a third of the population at the siege's beginning, starved to death. Roughly one in three. Many of them in the streets. It quells the appetite. Starvation on such a scale makes one feel almost guilty for having enough and to spare.

Few people outside realized what the siege was like. For years afterwards, Stalin kept it dark. Deaths were underestimated. Its party leaders were purged. Then, with the collapse of communism, archives began to open with their police records and siege diaries. It is a stark shocking tale. Two arresting quotations will give you an idea:

Writer Dmitri Likhachev looks back: 'In time of famine people revealed themselves stripped of all trumpery. Some turned out marvelous, incomparable heroes. Others - scoundrels, villains, murderers, cannibals. There were no half measures.'

Note this timetable, kept in a pocket book by Tanya Savicheva: '28 December 1941 - Zhenya died. 25 January 1942 - Granny died. 17 March - Lyoka died. 13 April - Uncle Vasya died. 10 May - Uncle Lyosha died. 13 May at 7.30am - Mama died. The Savichevs are dead, everyone is dead. Only Tanya is left.' Tanya was 12.

We don't know what happened to her, but we do know about Irina Bogdanova, who was eight and was left alone in the family flat when her mother, aunt and grandmother died one by one from dysentery in February 1942. She was found ten days later and handed in to an orphanage where she woke up to realize that the girl sharing her bed was dead. The days Irina spent along with her dead family were a total blank.

The toll of that first winter is staggering. Leningrad was totally unprepared for siege - as Russia was for the German attack. It took only 12 weeks for the German and Finnish armies to cut off the city. Over a million children and dependents were still in the city when the ring closed. In all there were 3.3 million mouths to feed.

Quite soon the bread ration had to be halved. By mid-November manual workers received 250 grams a day, the rest only half of that. But the bread had been adulterated with pine shavings. So, people were existing (or failing to) on 400, even 300 calories.

Pet owners swapped cats in order to avoid eating their own. There wasn't a dog to be seen. Only the zoo preserved its star attractions, like 'Beauty' the hippopotamus, with special rations of hay.

People searched desperately for substitute food. Cottonseed cake (usually burned in ships' boilers), 'macaroni' made from flax seed for cattle, 'meat jelly' produced from boiling bones and calf skins, 'yeast soup' from fermented sawdust, joiners' glue boiled and jellified, toothpaste, cough mixture and cold cream - anything that contained calories. They even licked the dried paste off the wallpaper.

The Black Market flourished openly on street stalls with ever rising prices. A fur coat fetched fewer and fewer kilograms of flour. Meanwhile the Party chiefs and their friends and connections, continued to look well fed to general resentment. The first news that people had died from starvation met with incredulity: 'Not the one I know? In broad daylight? With a Master's Degree?' But before long people were concealing deaths in the family, hiding the bodies so that the deceased's ration card could be used until it expired. Husbands and fathers helped to feed their families posthumously.

It was a very severe winter - temperatures of minus 35 degrees. Trams froze in their tracks. Buildings burned for days - fire services ceased to function. Factories closed, hospitals were overwhelmed, cemetaries could not keep pace. Bodies, shrouded but uncoffined, were dragged through the streets on sleds. At one cemeteries gate a corpse propped upright with a cigarette in its mouth extended a frozen arm and finger as a sign post to the newest mass graves.

Of course, there was a crime wave, mainly of adolescent muggers thieving food and ration cards. One 18-year-old killed his two younger brothers for their cards. Another murdered his granny with an axe and boiled her liver. A 17-year-old stole a corpse from a cemetery and put it through a mincer.

Rumors of cannibalism abounded. Amputated limbs disappeared from hospital theatres. Police records released years later showed that over 2,000 people were arrested for cannibalism; 586 of them were executed for murdering their victims. Most people arrested, however, were women. Mothers smothered very young children to feed their older ones."[8]

Straight out of the Book of Lamentations! The Famine conditions were so bad that even the *women cooked their own children*! It happened to Israel, it happened again to Leningrad, and unfortunately it will happen again in the very near future. Only this time it will occur all across the planet all at the same time! What God, the *voice among the four living creatures,* is telling us is that these kind of horrendous behaviors, unspeakable events, heinous crimes displayed by mankind upon mankind during general famine conditions is simply coming again. Only this time, again, it won't just be happening in Leningrad, in one city in one country at one place, but literally all over the planet all at the same time! Now wonder Jesus said you don't want to be there! It truly is the worst time in the history of mankind!

Matthew 24:21-22 "For then shall be great tribulation, such as was not since the beginning of the world to this time, no, nor ever shall be. And except those days should be shortened, there should *no flesh* be saved: but for the elect's sake those days shall be shortened."

Why don't you want to be in the 7-year Tribulation? It's not just the famine that should scare you, it's the effects of the famine! Unless God shortened the time frame no human *flesh* would survive. What a horrific, shocking, fearful reality. The walking dead is no longer just a make-believe series, it has just become planet earth's reality! If that wasn't enough from the *voice* of God, *surrounded by the four living creatures,* to shock you into getting saved before it's too late, what that *voice* says makes it even clearer.

The **first question** about the voice is **What is it Saying**?

Revelation 6:6b "Saying, 'A quart of wheat for a day's wages, and three quarts of barley for a day's wages, A quart of wheat for a day's wages, and three quarts of barley for a day's wages, and do not damage the oil and the wine!'"

The *voice* mentioned here not only tells us Who is speaking and from where these judgments are being directed, that is God, but now we see what the *voice of God* is saying, "*A quart of wheat for a day's wages, and three quarts of barley for a day's wages, and do not damage the oil and the wine!*" So, the natural question is, "What does God mean by all this? He's talking about certain types of food, specifically grains, that one has to work for, but then He mentions two other food related items that will not be damaged or harmed. What's that all about?" Well, a careful examination of the customs and mannerisms and historical usage of these words and items during the time when this text was written gives us the answer.

First of all, let's start off with the food that is *not* protected, the *wheat* and the *barley*. The *voice of God* not only calls out the two *types* of grain, but He also tells us *how much* of these grains a person can have during this time. It's reduced to either *one quart* of wheat or *three quarts* of barley. Food is reduced down to a *quart* measuring. Not a gallon, not a whole sack full, not fourteen pounds worth, not even a bushel, but specifically and only a *quart*. So again, what's that all about? Of all measures used on the planet, why specifically a *quart*, and why specifically the grains of just *wheat* and *barley*? Well, the English word *quart* is the Greek word "choenix" which spoke of the amount of food a person consumed in a day. As it turns out, *wheat* and *barley* were food staples of the day. *Wheat* was for human consumption, while *barley* was basically animal feed:

"The English word 'quart; translates 'choenix.' A 'choenix' of wheat was the daily ration of one adult. Thus, in the conditions pictured by Revelation 6, the normal income for a working-class family would buy enough food for only one person. The less costly barley would feed three people for one day's wages."

"The measure spoken of here is the Greek measure of capacity of very ancient usage, the choenix. As early as the time of Homer it was indicated as the amount of wage given to a workman for a full day's work (Odyssey XIX: XXVIII). Herodotus also gives this as the measure of wheat consumed by each soldier in the army of Xerxes (VIII: CLXXXVII). Using wheat in this context is speaking of hardship indicating severe famine and rising prices."

"The prices of both 'wheat' (good food) and 'barley' (cheap cattle food) will be very high. A quart of wheat will provide one day's ration for a person, but it will cost a whole day's wages."

"A loaf of wheat bread or three loaves of barley for a day's pay. This is generally regarded as a minimum-sustenance diet. Therefore, this verse foreshadows a time when an entire day's wage will barely yield enough food to survive."

"And in the midst of the throne, the voice of God. And God says, 'A quart of wheat for a denarius, three quarts of barley for a denarius and do not harm the oil and the wine.' God is speaking. Again, it's a reminder that this is a judgment from God.

Now let me tell you what that means. A quart of wheat would sustain one person who had a very moderate appetite for one day. A denarius is one day's wage. So, you would work just to eat the bare minimum, yourself...which would provide nothing for your family. Famine conditions. All your work would only provide food enough for one person.

Then He says, 'Three quarts of barley for a denarius.' You could get more food to feed your family if you'd settle for barley, but barley was animal food...animal food. It would be lining up taking your choice between bread and dog kibble, basically. Low in nutritional value, barley was cheaper, at least a family could eat that. But it would take all their money for three quarts which would feed three people animal food.

Those are famine conditions and that's what war's going to do to the world. Real famine, global famine is coming fast. World peace, world war, world famine and you're not even out of the first three and a half year, of this period."[9]

No kidding! Think of that! You're just getting started! These horrible judgments from God being poured out upon the planet in the 7-year Tribulation are just getting warmed up! Now let's turn to the second aspect of this passage that the *voice of God* is saying, and that is the *requirement* to get this particular type of food, the *wheat* and the *barley*. As was already alluded to, you don't just walk up to your local store or any store, for that matter and casually get your food at your leisure with cash you have lying around. You don't get it for free or even at a bargain basement price, and you certainly don't get whatever you want as much as you want. Rather, God specifically says these people have to *work for it*, the *wheat* and *barley*, and not just one hour or two hours or even a half a day's work. But rather it is *for a day's wages*, in other words, for a full day's worth of work. So how much does that break down to and what price would that put these two types of grain at? Well, as was mentioned above, the Greek word for the English phrase translated there *a day's wages* is the word "denarius." Let's take a look at that historical meaning:

"The Greek historian Herodotus says that a choenix (quart) of corn was a soldier's daily supply of food. A denarius was a day's wage.

Matthew 20:1-2 *"For the kingdom of heaven is like a landowner who went out early in the morning to hire men to work in his vineyard. He agreed to pay them a denarius for the day and sent them into his vineyard."*

Therefore, a working man will be unable to support his family in that day."

"The expression 'a day's wages' is a translation of the Greek word denarius. The denarius was a Roman silver coin equal in value to the daily wage of a working man. The price of the wheat and barley as described in the vision appears to be ten to twelve times their normal cost in ancient times. Revelation describes a condition where basic goods are sold at greatly inflated prices."

"That famine is intended here is evident, for this amount (a denarius) was a workman's average daily wage. Men will work an entire day and barely procure enough to stay alive. Ordinarily, from sixteen to twenty measures were given for a denarius."

"Most scholars take this to be a reference to widespread famine on the earth. They say that the scales symbolize food being weighed out carefully. It is in such short supply that it must be rationed. Even then no one can get very much because it takes a day's wages to earn a single quart of wheat or, because it is cheaper, three quarts of barley.

This would only be enough food for one person for a day. You would work all day long and all you would be able to earn at best would be enough for your own physical needs. There would be nothing for your family or for anyone else.

During the days of the Weimar Republic in Germany after World War I, I remember as a boy hearing accounts of people taking ten thousand German marks bills, loading them into wheelbarrows, and taking them to market to buy a single loaf of bread. That is what runaway inflation does. It makes money worthless.

That in turn becomes an excuse for the rigid controls over buying and selling which we find in Chapter 13 when, under the reign of antichrist, the whole world is subjected to enormously restrictive controls so that 'no one can buy or sell without the mark of the beast,' (Revelation 13:17)."[10]

Well, this sure smells like a set-up to me! No wonder people are tempted to do the unthinkable and receive the mark of the beast later in the 7-year Tribulation. Could it be that all the antichrist has to do at that time is throw out yet another lie stating that these inhabitants of the earth that somehow survived this horrific famine mentioned here in the *third seal,* will never have to suffer those kind of horrific famine conditions again…if…they just receive his "mark" that will allow them to "buy and sell" to their hearts' content. Makes you wonder, doesn't it? You can see the trap being set early on. These unfortunate people wouldn't even realize that they have been set up for, this future lie as well. In fact, this act of compromise wouldn't be too surprising for as we saw in the earlier accounts, famine has a way of bringing out the worst in people. They do some pretty horrible things and compromise any and all standards of human decency, all just for the promises of some form of nourishment. So, it is in the 7-year Tribulation. People will commit another horrible act of compromise, commit another horrible deed, even though God warned them never to do so, or it would seal their doom. They will receive the mark of the beast.

Revelation 14:9-11 "A third angel followed them and said in a loud voice: 'If anyone worships the beast and his image and receives his mark on the forehead or on the hand, he, too, will drink of the wine of God's fury, which has been poured full strength into the cup of His wrath. He will be tormented with burning sulfur in the presence of the holy angels and of the Lamb. And the smoke of their torment rises for ever and ever. There is no rest day or night for those who worship the beast and his image, or for anyone who receives the mark of his name.'"

The Bible is clear, receiving the mark of the beast is the last thing a person would ever want to do during the 7-year Tribulation. It will seal their fate. They may get some temporary relief to eat and "buy and sell," but now, for all eternity, they will be tormented in the Lake of Fire along with the very one who fed them that lie, the antichrist. Yet that's what famines do. They can bring out the worst in people and seduce them into the most horrible acts of compromise. In fact, speaking of historical behavior in famines, even what we see here in our text where people in this future famine, during the first half of the 7-year Tribulation, will have to work *a day's wages* in order to hardly get any food to survive, believe it or not, has already been witnessed as a customary practice during famines in the past. Let's go back to the fairly recent famine in Leningrad and see this *working for food* practice in play:

"From November 1941 to February 1942 the only food available to the citizen was 125 grams of bread per day, of which 50–60% consisted of sawdust and other inedible admixtures. For about two weeks at the beginning of January 1942, even this food was available only for workers and military personnel.

In conditions of extreme temperatures, down to −30 °C (−22 °F), and city transport being out of service, even a distance of a few kilometers to a food distributing kiosk created an insurmountable obstacle for many citizens. Deaths peaked in January–February 1942 at 100,000 per month, mostly from starvation. People often died on the streets, and citizens soon became accustomed to the sight of death.

While reports of cannibalism appeared in the winter of 1941–42, records on the subject were not published until 2004. Indicative of Leningraders' fears at the time, police would often threaten uncooperative suspects with imprisonment in a cell with cannibals.

Dimitri Lazarev, a diarist during the worst moments in the Leningrad siege, recalls his daughter and niece reciting a terrifying nursery rhyme adapted from a pre-war song:

A dystrophic walked along
With a dull look
In a basket he carried a corpse's arse.
I'm having human flesh for lunch,
This piece will do!
Ugh, hungry sorrow!
And for supper, clearly
I'll need a little baby.
I'll take the neighbors',
Steal him out of his cradle.

Cases ranged from a mother smothering her eighteen-month-old to feed her three older children to a plumber killing his wife to feed his sons and nieces.

By December 1942, 2,105 cannibals arrested were divided into two legal categories: corpse-eating (trupoyedstvo) and person-eating (lyudoyedstvo). The latter were usually shot while the former were sent to prison."[11]

Oh my! What a sad, sad, sad state of affairs all the way around. After hearing the previous sickening behavior of mankind in these other relatively recent famines, it makes one want to grieve and give up even trying to describe what these famine conditions will be like during the first half of the 7-year Tribulation. In fact, we know it's going to be *even worse*! The famine mentioned in *the third seal* will not only most assuredly contain these same kind of horrendous elements as you just read in the Leningrad famine, but probably even worse since the restraining influence of the Church will be gone and has been gone ever since the Rapture of the Church prior to the beginning of the 7-year Tribulation. All human decency and Christian morality and compassion will be gone! Furthermore, keep in mind these kinds of famine-induced atrocities will be happening all over the planet all at the same time. It's a *global* famine with the same sort of unspeakable atrocious *global* results! Wow!

Now, as shocking as that is, the *third seal* famine might very well get even worse, especially for the *poor people*. We see this possible revelation by now taking a look at the third aspect of this passage, what the *voice of God* is saying, and that is the specific items that do get *protected*. God now puts a limit on *two other things*. He not only reduces the food supply down to *one quart of wheat* or *three quarts of barley* for *a day's wages*, but now He says, *do not damage the oil and the wine*! So again, why does God call out these two specific items, and why would they be *protected* during a time of famine? How does that play in with His judgment? Well, let's take a look again at the historical usage:

"Wheat, barley, oil, and wine were the staple foods in Palestine and Asia Minor. 'Do not harm' means, 'Do not tamper with', reflecting the strict control over prices that ungodly rulers under Antichrist's leadership will have at this time."

"As the Tribulation grows worse, the rich as well as the poor will suffer, but at this early stage the poor will suffer more than the rich. Probably the wars that the ungodly rulers under Antichrist's leadership begin will reduce the food supply greatly. These rulers will control it strictly with consequent suffering for many people."

"The voice from the midst of the four living creatures is commanding the one on the black horse not to harm the oil and wine. Again, we see the judgments which pour forth are precisely under the control of God.

Another suggestion is that the common commodities are hard to come by, but luxury items will remain available for the upper classes. It suggests that side by side with abject suffering there is abundance and luxury.

One of the great criticisms of the present time is that there is scarcity in the midst of plenty. This is the situation which will be accentuated a thousandfold when the Antichrist begins his reign. It is a social maladjustment.

This famine will be serious enough to make it unique in history up to that time. The world has already seen many limited famines, but never one like this. So, it is wrong to take a major feature such as this prohibition against hurting the oil and the wine and interpret it as a limitation on human hardship. It indicates rather the inequity that will prevail. The poor will have it extremely hard while the wealthy will experience no interruption to their luxurious lifestyle.

Both oil and wine are listed among the commercial wealth of Babylon at the time of her destruction."

Revelation 18:11-13 "The merchants of the earth will weep and mourn over her because no one buys their cargoes any more – cargoes of gold, silver, precious stones and pearls; fine linen, purple, silk and scarlet cloth; every sort of citron wood, and articles of every kind made of ivory, costly wood, bronze, iron and marble; cargoes of cinnamon and spice, of incense, myrrh and frankincense, of *wine* and olive *oil*, of fine flour and wheat; cattle and sheep; horses and carriages; and bodies and souls of men. They will say, 'The fruit you longed for is gone from you. All your riches and splendor have vanished, never to be recovered.' The merchants who sold these things and gained their wealth from her will stand far off, terrified at her torment."

"The denarius, as a Roman coin, in ancient times was a normal day's wage. In New Testament times this coin would purchase eight quarts of wheat, or eight measures (one measure equals about one quart) or 24 quarts of barley. Wheat was the better grain and barley was normally used only for livestock except in times of scarcity.

During the Tribulation, however, one denarius (a full day's wage) will buy only one measure (about one meal) of wheat, or three meals of barley with nothing left. Of course, the larger the family, the worse it will be.

But note the words, 'do not harm the oil and the wine.' These were luxury items which will apparently be unharmed at this point. There will be plenty of luxury items but only the superrich will have them. The average man will spend all he has on the bare essentials. Barnhouse has an interesting comment from his own experience on this.

Just after World War I, I spent a few days in Vienna at the time when misery was very great...There was a shortage of coal and the police had ordered everyone off the streets by nine o'clock. The city was filled with wealthy refugees from Russia and other countries.

Walking along the boulevard one afternoon as the crowds were coming out of the opera which began early to conform with the curfew regulations, I saw men with bare feet in the snow, their skeletons covered with rags, their ribs seen through the holes in the cloths with which they attempted to cover their bodies. From time to time there was blood on the snow from their feet.

Out of the opera came men escorting women with fortunes in jewels upon them. Never have I seen more wonderful displays in any of the capitals of the earth. The beggars blocked the way to the fine limousines that came for the rich. I saw the men striking the beggars with their canes to clear the way for the women.

Poor girls not clad in the gaudy finery of prostitutes, but with poor clothing and in wooden shoes, clattered about clutching at the passerby and offering to sell themselves for a coin which at that moment could be purchased for one five hundredth part of a dollar. Mark well, there was no famine in Vienna. There was scarcity in the midst of plenty, but there was no hurt to the luxuries.

The picture here is scarcity in the midst of plenty. This will be accentuated in the times of the Antichrist, especially in the last half of the Tribulation via his buying and selling policies."

"This is a picture of scarcity of grain during a time when olive oil and wine are abundant. The grain must be measured very carefully, and it is sold at about twelve times its normal price. At the same time, growers are commanded not to

reduce the production of oil and wine, items which most would consider to be luxuries.

It seems that the common folk would spend all their living on grain to fend off starvation and have nothing left over for the finer things, while the rich would continue to live comfortably and make money on the inflated grain prices.

The Third Seal describes scarcity in the midst of prosperity; the rich get richer as the poor get poorer.

Such a situation is not hard to imagine in our fast-paced, greedy world. Amos shows the rich '[selling] the righteous for silver, and the poor for a pair of sandals' (Amos 2:6). Many businessmen have no qualms about taking advantage of a situation, as long as they are guaranteed to make a profit. We should not be surprised when food prices escalate sharply after a mediocre harvest.

God is not capricious; He does nothing without a purpose. He says that He sends these droughts, floods, diseases, insects, and famines to warn us and cause us to return to Him.

Amos 4:6-9 *'I gave you empty stomachs in every city and lack of bread in every town, yet you have not returned to Me, declares the LORD. I also withheld rain from you when the harvest was still three months away. I sent rain on one town but withheld it from another. One field had rain; another had none and dried up. People staggered from town to town for water but did not get enough to drink, yet you have not returned to Me, declares the LORD. Many times, I struck your gardens and vineyards, I struck them with blight and mildew. Locusts devoured your fig and olive trees, yet you have not returned to Me, declares the LORD.' Our God wants us to receive blessings, not curses, but sometimes He must get our attention and point us in the right direction when we go astray. "[12]*

As it was with the horrible inhumane behaviors previously mentioned in past famines along with the customary practices of having to work for food, so it is here in *the third seal* famine. The order given by God for the *oil* and *wine* not to *not be damaged* seems to reveal yet another all too common wicked behavior displayed during famine conditions. The rich can still get access to certain items, and in some cases even richer off of them, while the average person and certainly the poor suffer greater.

Now again, I don't necessarily believe that the *oil* and *wine* are specifically and only talking about "luxury items" since *oil* and *wine* were "staple foods" at the time John wrote this text:

Deuteronomy 7:13 "He will love you and bless you and increase your numbers. He will bless the fruit of your womb, the crops of your land – your *grain*, new *wine* and *oil* – the calves of your herds and the lambs of your flocks in the land that He swore to your forefathers to give you."

Deuteronomy 11:13-15 "So if you faithfully obey the commands I am giving you today – to love the LORD your God and to serve Him with all your heart and with all your soul – then I will send rain on your land in its season, both autumn and spring rains, so that you may gather in your *grain*, new *wine* and *oil*. I will provide grass in the fields for your cattle, and you will eat and be satisfied."

Hosea 2:8 "She has not acknowledged that I was the one who gave her the *grain*, the new *wine* and *oil*, who lavished on her the silver and gold-which they used for Baal."

Haggai 1:10-11 "Therefore, because of you the heavens have withheld their dew and the earth its crops. I called for a drought on the fields and the mountains, on the *grain*, the new *wine*, the *oil* and whatever the ground produces, on men and cattle, and on the labor of your hands."

God not only gives the staples of *grain*, *wine*, and *oil* as a blessing to people for their obedience, but as you can see, He will also take them away when these same people are disobedient to Him and turn to a false god and idol worship. So, it is in the 7-year Tribulation. The inhabitants of the earth have turned away from God to the false god the antichrist and actually worship him as an idol. So, God does what He's done in the past. He brings famine. He withholds their staples, *grain*, *wine*, and *oil*. But again, notice this time He says, *do not damage the oil and the wine*! Why? Why does He exclude these two staple items, again, not necessarily luxury items? Well, again, I think God could very well be revealing yet another dichotomy in this *third seal* famine that has already repeatedly manifested in the past: that of, the rich can get access to more items, even staple items, while the poor receive only the bare minimum.

So, the question is, "How does this square with God's judgment? Isn't that unfair? Do the rich get away with it? Is God punishing only the poor?" Absolutely not! Throughout the Scripture God has a very special place in His heart for the poor. Rather, what we could very well be seeing here is *an even worse judgement upon the abusive rich*. I say that because typically when the poor suffer they have a tendency to look up and get right with God. He becomes more *valuable* to them. By turning to God, they then receive His *riches*. Yet the *rich* on earth don't think they need God. They are smug in their wealth, content with their economic situation, and generally see no need to repent and get right with God. Therefore, *their wealth seals their doom*. It becomes a detriment, a curse, instead of a blessing. In the end, it is the poor who become the richest. This is the all too common trap of the rich that James mentions:

James 2:5-6 "Listen, my dear brothers: has not God chosen those who are poor in the eyes of the world to be rich in faith and to inherit the kingdom He promised those who love Him? But you have insulted the poor. Is it not the rich who are exploiting you? Are they not the ones who are dragging you into court?"

James 5:1-6 "Now listen, you rich people, weep and wail because of the misery that is coming upon you. Your wealth has rotted, and moths have eaten your clothes. Your gold and silver are corroded. Their corrosion will testify against you and eat your flesh like fire. You have hoarded wealth in the last days. Look! The wages you failed to pay the workmen who mowed your fields are crying out against you. The cries of the harvesters have reached the ears of the Lord Almighty. You have lived on earth in luxury and self-indulgence. You have fattened yourselves in the day of slaughter. You have condemned and murdered innocent men, who were not opposing you."

The rich on earth may have it seemingly easier than the rest of us here on earth for a brief time, and even here in the first half of the 7-year Tribulation, but they will not escape suffering, slaughter, and condemnation no matter how much money they have. As it was in the past, so it will be in again the future. Their wealth produced spiritual poverty. It turned into a curse instead of a blessing. It blinded them to see the greatest riches of all, a relationship with God through Jesus Christ. No, God is actually being merciful to the poor here, as this man shares:

"A denarius represented a day's wage. A quart of wheat or three quarts of barley provided barely enough food for a family to subsist on for a day or two. Oil and wine were luxury items, which, in times of famine (which inevitably follow wars), only the wealthy could afford.

Therefore, what the Lord seems to be telling the rider of the black horse is, 'Let the poor suffer, but do not harm the food of the wealthy,' which could, ironically, be a curse on the wealthy because those who are poor and who suffer are much more likely to repent and accept the Lord's salvation than are those who prosper."[13]

No, God is not being mean to the poor. Rather He is blessing them and giving the rich the harvest they have sown, even in the 7-year Tribulation:

Proverbs 14:31 "Anyone who oppresses the poor is insulting God who made them. To help the poor is to honor God."

Proverbs 19:17 "When you help the poor you are lending to the Lord – and He pays wonderful interest on your loan!"

Proverbs 21:13 "He who shuts his ears to the cries of the poor will be ignored in his own time of need."

Proverbs 28:27 "If you give to the poor, your needs will be supplied! But a curse upon those who close their eyes to poverty."

Proverbs 22:9 "Happy is the generous man, the one who feeds the poor."

Yet again, we could very well be seeing another case of reaping what you have sown here in this command from God in *the third seal, do not damage the oil and the wine*! It shows us the unfortunate greedy heart of the wealthy in times of need. They didn't help the poor, they oppressed them. They shut their ears, refused to give help, didn't feed, and held on to their own meager supplies. So, what did their riches earn for them? What kind of interest did they gain for this behavior? A curse! Your temporary wealth has guaranteed a rotten future, as these men share:

"Let me be very frank. During World War II the rich, for the most part, were able to get meat. They were able to get the luxuries of life. A very wealthy man told me that he never missed getting a big T-bone steak anytime that he wanted it. But I can remember getting very tired of eating tongue, which was one thing we didn't have to have blue chips to get and was something that was not rationed.

In this day that is coming, things won't change. The rich are going to get theirs, but the poor won't be able to get theirs. That is the way it has always been.

I feel like saying, 'Ho hum,' when I hear these sincere, egg headed boys talking about how they are going to work out the poverty problem. All that it has accomplished is that it has given a good job to a lot of them, but so far it hasn't filtered down and been a blessing to the poor. It has never helped the poor to lift themselves up with any degree of pride.

Why? Because the only Man who can lift up the poor is Jesus Christ. None of these egg-headed boys is able to do it. I am sorry to have to say that, but somebody needs to speak out against all of this tomfoolery that our government is going through. All that this wasteful spending of money does is to create more bureaucracy and to sap our tax dollars.

This is the sort of thing that is abroad today, but just think what it is going to be like in that future day."

"The price of wheat and barley will be very high. A quart of wheat would provide one meal, but it would cost a denarius, a whole day's wages. The poor would have little money left over for oil, for fuel and health needs, and for wine to drink.

An inescapable outcome of war is starvation. Worldwide inflation destroys the world economy. Worldwide famine causes great shortages and inflation. Panic in the market causes people to stampede the marketplace to sell their stock. A worldwide depression will make people panic over bread-and-butter issues.

We take food in our cupboards for granted. We let the waitress take potential leftovers away. We toss out half-eaten apples. In America, we have forgotten the old 'waste not, want not' homily. We throw enough food in our garbage cans to feed a family of six, for a day, in India. Our dogs have a diet higher in protein than most of the people in the world."[14]

So, the abundant wealth turns into a curse. Whether it's taking the staple foods of life today for granted because we have so much wealth in comparison to other places in the world, or even the hording or profiting of staple foods in the future with your wealth, the outcome is the same. Your future is bleak! You need to "become poor" in order to gain it all:

Matthew 5:3-6 "Blessed are the poor in spirit, for theirs is the kingdom of heaven."

Those who see can admit their spiritual poverty now and see their need to call upon the name of Jesus Christ and ask Him to forgive and save them from their abundant sins, will not only gain a place in the kingdom of heaven, but they will be also be rescued from the wrath of God in the 7-year Tribulation, including this horrific famine mentioned in the third seal. That is the true blessed riches that no one can take away. Therefore, to make sure no one misses this important warning from God in this third seal famine, let's take a look once again at a teaser if you will of what is coming to the planet on a global scale in the very near future, and what people will be experiencing unless they get right with God now through Jesus before it's too late. The following is the account of another recent famine, this time in China. You tell me if you want to be on the planet when these kinds of conditions abound all over the place:

"China's Great Famine that killed up to 45 million people remains a taboo subject in China 50 years on. Author Yang Jisheng is determined to change that with his book, Tombstone. The horror stories penned by the 72-year-old...are so savage and excessive they could almost be taken as the blackest of comedies, the bleakest of farces; the most extreme of satires on fanaticism and tyranny.

A decade after the Communist party took power in 1949, promising to serve the people, the greatest manmade disaster in history stalks an already impoverished land. In an unremarkable city in central Henan province, more than a million people – one in eight – are wiped out by starvation and brutality over three short years.

In one area, officials commandeer more grain than the farmers have actually grown. In barely nine months, more than 12,000 people – a third of the inhabitants – die in a single commune; a tenth of its households are wiped out.

Thirteen children beg officials for food and are dragged deep into the mountains, where they die from exposure and starvation. A teenage orphan kills and eats her four-year-old brother. Forty-four of a village's 45 inhabitants die; the last remaining resident, a woman in her 60s, goes insane.

Others are tortured, beaten or buried alive for declaring realistic harvests, refusing to hand over what little food they have, stealing scraps or simply angering officials.

Page after page – even in the drastically edited English translation, there are 500 of them – his book, Tombstone, piles improbability upon terrible improbability. But Yang did not imagine these scenes. Perhaps no one could. Instead, he devoted 15 years to painstakingly documenting the catastrophe that claimed at least millions of lives across the country, including that of his father.

Yang's monumental account, first published in Hong Kong, is banned in his homeland. He had little idea of what he would find when he started work: 'I didn't think it would be so serious and so brutal and so bloody. I didn't know that there were thousands of cases of cannibalism. I didn't know about farmers who were beaten to death.'

'People died in the family and they didn't bury the person because they could still collect their food rations; they kept the bodies in bed and covered them up and the corpses were eaten by mice. People ate corpses and fought for the bodies.

In Gansu they killed outsiders; people told me strangers passed through and they killed and ate them. And they ate their own children. Terrible. Too terrible.'

For a moment he stops speaking. 'To start with, I felt terribly depressed when I was reading these documents,' he adds. 'But after a while I became numbed – because otherwise I couldn't carry on.'

The book opens with Yang's return from school to find his father dying: "He tried to extend his hand to greet me but couldn't lift it. I was shocked with the realization that 'skin and bones' referred to something so horrible and cruel,' he writes.

His village had become a ghost town, with fields dug bare of shoots and trees stripped of bark. 'I was 18 at the time and I only knew what the Communist party told me. Everyone was fooled,' he says. 'I was very red. I was on a propaganda team.'

Mao warned colleagues a year later. 'When there is not enough to eat, people starve to death. It is better to let half the people die so that others can eat their fill.' Ruthlessness ran through the system.

The death toll is staggering. It is 'equivalent to 450 times the number of people killed by the atomic bomb dropped on Nagasaki.'"[15]

So, it will be in the not too distant future. Once again people will unfortunately fall for the lies of a satanic regime promising a utopian society for all who would submit to their rule. Only this time it won't be from a communist leader, but the actual prophesied antichrist leader. He too, like communism, will promise life and abundance, but will deliver only death and destruction. Sadly, the inhabitants of the earth will fall for it, reject Christ, and even initially be a part of his propaganda machine, like Mr. Yang was with Mao the communist leader. However, true colors always have a way of coming out and so it will be with the antichrist. A bloody red rampage erupts across the planet and *the third seal* nightmare famine follows. The fruit of his lies are now in full bloom. The death toll is staggering. It is much more that even the 450 times the number of people killed in Nagasaki. We go from millions to billions. We will now see that number recorded for us in the next seal. Hold on! It's about to get even worse!

Chapter Eight

The Breaking of the Death Seal

The **eighth thing** we see in the breaking of the planet is the **Ordering of the Fourth Seal**.

Revelation 6:7 "When *the Lamb opened the fourth seal*, I heard the voice of the fourth living creature say, 'Come!'"

In case God's "repetition increases remembrance" technique didn't get your attention and send the message home as to just Who is the One in charge of these judgements coming upon planet earth during the first half of the 7-year Tribulation, here we have yet another reminder. It is *the Lamb* Who *opened the fourth seal*. Once again, God is reiterating that *He is the One* responsible for these judgments through and through, not man, and certainly not satan. It reminds me of the saying, "Being nagged by someone is like slowly being pecked to death by a duck." Only God of course here is not nagging, He's repeatedly informing us of this truth out of mercy over and over again because what is about to come upon the planet is even worse than what we've seen so far for the inhabitants of the earth. In fact, this same blunt message of Who is responsible for these judgments is also reiterated in the very next verse that mentions the specific four types of judgments in *the fourth seal*.

Revelation 6:8b "They were given power over a fourth of the earth to kill by *sword, famine* and *plague*, and by the *wild beasts* of the earth."

These four judgments mentioned here in the future time of the 7-year Tribulation just happen to be the same exact four types of judgments that God has used in the past and they are horrible! Why? Because, unfortunately, just like people today, people then wouldn't listen to God's warnings either!

Jeremiah 14:11-12 "Then the LORD said to me, 'Do not pray for the well-being of this people. Although they fast, I will not listen to their cry; though they offer burnt offerings and grain offerings, I will not accept them. Instead, I will destroy them with the *sword, famine* and *plague*.'"

Jeremiah 15:2-3 "And if they ask you, 'Where shall we go?' tell them, 'This is what the LORD says: 'Those destined for death, to death; those for the *sword*, to the sword; those for *starvation*, to starvation; those for captivity, to captivity.' 'I will send four kinds of destroyers against them,' declares the LORD, 'the *sword* to kill and the *dogs* to drag away and the *birds of the air* and the *beasts of the earth* to devour and destroy.'"

Jeremiah 21:5-7 "I myself will fight against you with an outstretched hand and a mighty arm in anger and fury and great wrath. I will strike down those who live in this city – both men and animals – and they will die of a terrible *plague*. After that, declares the LORD, I will hand over Zedekiah king of Judah, his officials and the people in this city who survive the *plague, sword* and *famine*, to Nebuchadnezzar king of Babylon and to their enemies who seek their lives. He will put them to the *sword*; he will show them no mercy or pity or compassion."

Jeremiah 24:10 "I will send the *sword, famine* and *plague* against them until they are destroyed from the land I gave to them and their fathers."

Jeremiah 29:17-19 "Yes, this is what the LORD Almighty says: 'I will send the *sword, famine* and *plague* against them and I will make them like poor figs that are so bad they cannot be eaten. I will pursue them with the *sword, famine* and *plague* and will make them abhorrent to all the kingdoms of the earth and an object of cursing and horror, of scorn and reproach, among all the nations where I drive them. *For they have not listened to my words*,' declares the LORD, 'words that I sent to them again and again by my servants the prophets.'"

Jeremiah 42:17 "Indeed, all who are determined to go to Egypt to settle there will die by the *sword, famine* and *plague*; not one of them will survive or escape the disaster I will bring on them."

Ezekiel 14:21 "For this is what the Sovereign LORD says: How much worse will it be when I send against Jerusalem my four dreadful judgments – *sword* and *famine* and *wild beasts* and *plague* – to kill its men and their animals!"

A perfect match, four for four. God used these same four instruments as tools of His judgment in the past when people didn't listen to His warnings to turn around before it's too late, and now we see He's going to do it again here in the future. It was horrible beyond belief in the past, *yet* it will be *even worse* in the future. I say that because the Hebrew word there for "worse" in Ezekiel 14 literally means, "how much more bad, deadly, displeasing, distressing, grievous, harmful, miserable, sad, serious, severe, sore, treacherous, troublesome, ugly, unpleasant, and wretched." Therefore, it's obvious, these specific judgments God used in Ezekiel's time did not produce a good time! However, the next time we see God using these four tools of judgment in the future, it will make Ezekiel's time look like chump change. This is because the context tells us that not just Israel, but *the whole planet* will experience these four tools of God's judgment and all their horrible effects. Furthermore, these effects are unbelievably massive because God actually gives us the death toll of these accumulative judgments upon the inhabitants of the earth. No disaster in the history of mankind will be able to compare to what is about to come upon planet earth *when the Lamb opens the fourth seal*. Most of the planet will be annihilated. It will be the deadliest, displeasing, grievous, harmful, miserable, sad, severe, treacherous, troublesome, ugly, unpleasant, wretched time this planet has ever seen! That is what we will see now in the *object* of *the fourth seal*. Mankind's worst nightmare just got worse!

The **ninth thing** we see in the breaking of the planet is the **Object of the Fourth Seal**.

So far, we've seen the horrible fate of those who have been left behind upon planet earth after the Rapture of the Church prior to the 7-year Tribulation. In a relatively short amount of time these inhabitants of the earth have been bombarded with a global deception, a global slaughter, and a global famine. It's their fault, not God's. It was their choice and their doing. They did it to themselves. Just like with Israel in the past, God sent these people His truth again and again and even warned them repeatedly through faithful preachers and Christians telling them to repent and get right with God before it was too late, but they just laughed it off and mocked and scoffed, and so now they're under His judgment. In fact, we will now see the cumulative effects of these judgments from God. This is what we see the *object* of the *fourth seal* is all about, and it is simply the breaking of the Death Seal. *Global Death* is the *object* of this next wave of judgment upon the planet. This is what all their mocking and scoffing earned them.

Revelation 6:7-8 "When the Lamb opened the fourth seal, I heard the voice of the fourth living creature say, 'Come!' I looked, and there before me was a pale horse! Its rider was named Death, and Hades was following close behind him. They were given power over a fourth of the earth to kill by sword, famine and plague, and by the wild beasts of the earth."

Luke 21:11a "There will be great earthquakes, famines and pestilences..."

As we've already seen, Revelation 6, Matthew 24, and now an additional piece from Luke 21 are prophetically dealing with the same time-frame, the beginning portion of the 7-year Tribulation. Therefore, by observing these passages, we can clearly see that what the planet is in store for now is simply *a mass wave of death.* We know this *fourth seal* judgement is dealing with *death,* and a *massive death* on a global scale, simply due to what the texts say. The rider's name was *Death.* His companion was *Hades* or the *grave* and he is literally scooping people up and sending them straight into hell as fast as they *die.* Then we see these events taking place on a global scale because *one fourth of the earth is killed* in the four mentioned ways. *Massive global death* is what this *fourth seal* is all about. In fact, when you take a look at the other times God uses these four specific tools of judgment, *sword, famine, plague,* and *wild beasts,* it is not only His way of letting people know that these judgments are coming from Him, but it's also to make sure that *no one escapes them,* as this researcher points out:

"The fourfold source of judgment hints at its global scope. As has frequently been the case in the past, hunger follows war: the second horseman took peace from the earth and the effects of his ride contribute to the effectiveness of the fourth horseman. Although the third horseman brought great famine – the greatest experienced to that time – the famine now becomes even more severe. The listing of alternative forms of death pictures inescapable judgment. Those who escape death by the sword may die of hunger. Those who survive the hunger are likely to perish from disease (death). Those who survive the first three will be so weak as to be unable to defend themselves from wild beasts which will become emboldened and attack them.

Ezekiel 5:15-17 *"So it shall be a reproach and a taunt, an instruction and an astonishment, unto the nations that are round about thee, when I shall execute judgments on thee in anger and in wrath, and in wrathful rebukes; when I shall send upon them the evil arrows of famine, that are for destruction, which I will send to destroy you: and I will increase the famine upon you, and will break your staff of bread; and I will send upon you famine and evil beasts, and they shall bereave thee; and pestilence and blood shall pass through thee; and I will bring the sword upon thee: I, Jehovah, have spoken it."*

Ezekiel 6:11-12 *"Thus says the Lord GOD: 'Pound your fists and stamp your feet, and say, Alas, for all the evil abominations of the house of Israel! For they shall fall by the sword, by famine, and by pestilence. He who is far off shall die by the pestilence, he who is near shall fall by the sword, and he who remains and is besieged shall die by the famine.' Thus, will I spend My fury upon them."*

From these passages we understand that what seem like intensified natural disturbances (war, hunger, death, attack by beasts) are in fact expressions of God's judgment. Thus, God's wrath is already seen in the fourth seal – well in advance of the sixth and seventh seals.

The picture being drawn is one of no escape. No matter which group or location a man finds himself in, there is a God-ordained judgment which will result in death:

Ezekiel 33:27 *"Thus shalt thou say unto them, 'Thus saith the Lord Jehovah: As I live, surely, they that are in the waste places shall fall by the sword; and him that is in the open field will I give to the beasts to be devoured; and they that are in the strongholds and in the caves shall die of the pestilence.'"*

Amos predicted this character of the day of Jehovah:

Amos 5:18-20 *"Woe unto you that desire the day of Jehovah! Wherefore would ye have the day of Jehovah? It is darkness, and not light. As if a man did flee from a lion, and a bear met him; or went into the house and leaned his hand on the wall, and a serpent bit him. Shall not the day of Jehovah be darkness, and not light? Even very dark, and no brightness in it?"* [1]

Yes, it will be a dark time, the darkest time in the history of mankind. God is sending a clear message to us. *All inhabitants of the earth* are going to experience the horrible effects of *the fourth seal*. There will be no escape. *Global death* is coming! You can try to hide in a bug out shelter or "waste place" but you'll still get it, for the *sword* is coming your way. You can try to live out a normal life "in the open field" but *wild beasts* will devour you. In fact, you can even be one of those people who builds an underground bunker with all the modern luxuries to ensure your safety, but God will simply allow *pestilence* to float right in to take you out. *No one* will escape the effects of this next seal, *the fourth seal* that *the Lamb* opens. God used these same four judgments of *sword, famine, plague*, and *wild beasts* in the past, and He's going to do it again here in the first half of the 7-year Tribulation. If you miss the Rapture of the Church prior to the beginning of the 7year Tribulation, you just entered your worst nightmare. In fact, picture your worst day ever and add to it the words, "bad, deadly, displeasing, distressing, grievous, harmful, miserable, sad, serious, severe, sore, treacherous, troublesome, ugly, unpleasant, and wretched." This is your future without Christ! It's not make believe, it's real, and once you're in it you're not getting out! There's no reversing it! That's why if you're reading this and you're not saved you need to respond now! Don't laugh, don't mock, and don't scoff like the Israelites of long ago who listened to lying prophets telling them everything was going to be fine when it wasn't. It happened back in Jeremiah's day-please don't make the same mistake today.

Jeremiah 14:11-15 "Then the LORD said to me, 'Do not pray for the well-being of this people. Although they fast, I will not listen to their cry; though they offer burnt offerings and grain offerings, I will not accept them. Instead, I will destroy them with the sword, famine and plague.' But I said, 'Ah, Sovereign LORD, the prophets keep telling them, 'You will not see the sword or suffer famine. Indeed, I will give you lasting peace in this place.' Then the LORD said to me, 'The prophets are prophesying lies in My Name. I have not sent them or appointed them or spoken to them. They are prophesying to you false visions, divinations, idolatries and the delusions of their own minds. Therefore, this is what the LORD says about the prophets who are prophesying in My Name: I did not send them, yet they are saying, 'No sword or famine will touch this land.' Those same prophets will perish by sword and famine.'"

Don't listen to the liars out there today or even your own heart that keeps telling you that everything will be just fine, the planet will get better, humanity will improve, you don't need Jesus, Christians are wackos, the Rapture is a scare tactic meant to enslave, etc. etc. These same lying thoughts and prophets will perish as well. Please, I beg you, God may very well be reaching out to you one last time. If you're not saved, get saved now! This planet is about to be judged by God and ravaged by *sword, famine, plague,* and *wild beasts*. It's going to be so bad that in one fell swoop *one fourth* of the planet will be annihilated! This is no game. This is not a joke. There is only *one way* out and only *one time* to escape what is coming to the planet and that time is *now* through *Jesus Christ*! Call upon His Name and ask Him to forgive you of all your sins before it's too late! Don't be left behind! This will be the most deadly, macabre, corpse ridden existence that human history will ever see. That gut-wrenching reality is what we will now see in the details of the *fourth seal*.

The **first detail** given about the object of the fourth seal is **The Pale Horse**.

Revelation 6:8a "I looked, and there before me was a pale horse!"

Once again, we see the chosen *vehicle* and its *color;* that next seal rider makes his charge towards planet earth that will issue forth the next wave of Judgment from Almighty God. When *the Lamb opens the fourth seal*, we see its rider also bursting forth upon the world scene riding a *horse,* the *battle tank* or *war machine* of the day, yet this time the color is pale. It is the Greek word, "chloros" which actually means, 'green, yellowish pale, or ashen." This naturally gives rise to a couple of questions.

The **first question** about the horse is **Why is it Pale**?

Revelation 6:8a "I looked, and there before me was a *pale* horse!"

This color mentioned of the *horse* in the *fourth seal* is such a major contrast to the other three that it can't help but grab your attention, which is precisely what it is meant to do as we shall soon see. For instance, in the *first seal* we saw the rider's horse was *white* which was used to symbolize the fake righteousness and fake purity of the antichrist and his rise to power. The *second seal* horse was *red* that painted an ominous scene of war, destruction, violence, and a bloody global slaughter. The *third seal* featured a *black* horse that depicted mourning, sorrowful times, and the effects of a horrible dark global famine for the planet. But here we see in the *fourth seal* that the rider's horse is an altogether different color. It is "chloros" or literally a "yellowish green pale ashen color." It is used only four times in the New Testament. Once here in Revelation 6 and three other times to speak of "grass."

Mark 6:39 "Then Jesus directed them to have all the people sit down in groups on the *green* grass."

Revelation 8:7 "The first angel sounded his trumpet, and there came hail and fire mixed with blood, and it was hurled down upon the earth. A third of the earth was burned up, a third of the trees were burned up, and all the *green* grass was burned up."

Revelation 9:4 "They were told not to hurt the grass of the earth, nor any *green* thing, nor any tree, but only the men who do not have the seal of God on their foreheads."

As you can see, the other three uses of "chloros" are referring to the "pale green, yellowish green" color of grass and/or similar plant types. It's not just simply green, but it's a *pale yellowish green*. So, the obvious question is, "Why did God choose this strange combination of odd colors? The other horses were the single colors of white, red, and black. Why is this *horse* in *the fourth seal* a combination of colors that produces a pale yellowish green color?" Well, it just so happens to be the color of *a decaying corpse* and that just so happens to perfectly fit the context of what we're about to see, as this researcher points out:

"The Lamb broke the fourth seal, and the fourth living creature called the fourth horseman out. John next saw an ashen horse the color of a human corpse. The Greek term for "ashen" (chloros) is the one from which we get our English word chlorine. It denotes a yellowish-green color as of a human corpse."[2]

This is precisely what we are about to encounter in *the fourth seal*. When Jesus *the Lamb* opens it up, *one fourth* of the planet with be littered with *human corpses*! *Death* will be *everywhere*! In fact, when you take a closer look at this color "chloros" and its obvious ties to a "decaying human corpse," it also gives you the impression that all the people left behind after the Rapture of the Church prior to the 7-year tribulation, have now just entered the irreversible stages of death for humanity. The "pale color" is just the very beginning. All of the stages of death are listed below:

THE STAGES OF DEATH

1. Pallor Mortis
2. Algor Mortis

3. Rigor Mortis
4. Livor Mortis
5. Putrefaction
6. Decomposition
7. Skeletonization

"Pallor mortis (Latin: pallor 'paleness', mortis 'of death'), the first stage of death, is a post-mortem paleness that occurs in those with light/white skin. Pallor mortis occurs almost immediately (within 15–25 minutes) post-mortem; paleness develops so rapidly after death that it has little to no use in determining the time of death, aside from saying that it either happened less than 30 minutes ago or more, which could help if the body were found very soon after death. Pallor mortis results from the cessation of capillary circulation throughout the body. Gravity then causes the blood to sink down into the lower parts of the body, creating livor mortis.

A living person can look deathly pale. This can happen when circumstances make the blood escape from the surface of the skin, as in deep shock. Also, heart failure (insufficientia cordis) can make the face look grey; the person then also has blue lips.

Skin can also look deathly pale as a result of vasoconstriction as part of the body's homeostatic systems in cold conditions, or if the skin is deficient in vitamin D, as seen in people who spend most of the time indoors, away from sunlight."[3]

In fact, we will not only see the planet littered with human corpses, pale in color, in the first stage of death from the *sword, famine, plague,* and *wild beasts,* but eventually we will even see other events mentioned above that also induce the same *pale death color,* that is from *shock, heart failure* and a *lack of sunlight.*

Revelation 6:15-17 "Then the kings of the earth, the princes, the generals, the rich, the mighty, and every slave and every free man hid in caves and among the rocks of the mountains. They called to the mountains and the rocks, '*Fall on us and hide us* from the face of Him who sits on the throne and from the wrath of the Lamb! For the great day of their wrath has come, and *who can stand?*'"

Luke 21:25-26 "There will be signs in the sun, moon and stars. On the earth, nations will be in anguish and perplexity at the roaring and tossing of the sea. *Men will faint from terror*, (literally dying as in having a heart attack caused by fear) apprehensive of what is coming on the world, for the heavenly bodies will be shaken."

Revelation 6:12 "I watched as he opened the sixth seal. There was a great earthquake. *The sun turned black like sackcloth* made of goat hair, the whole moon turned blood red."

Revelation 8:12 "The fourth angel sounded his trumpet, and *a third of the sun was struck*, a third of the moon, and a third of the stars, so that a third of them turned dark. *A third of the day was without light*, and also a third of the night."

All in all, it is abundantly clear that what we see in the color of this *pale horse* in *the fourth seal* when Jesus *the Lamb* opens it up, is a very frightening picture. Here comes the morgue! *Death* descends upon humanity on an unimaginable scale, never before seen. Mankind is now entering *the various stages of death* and it gets worse from here on out. Just like a decaying corpse, it's all downhill from here and the process of decay cannot be reversed. It's too late! The *death chill* has arrived! The first stage of mass death is now sweeping across mankind with the emergence of this *pale horse rider* when *the Lamb opens the fourth seal*. Yet, another mass wave of death will be coming soon in the Trumpet judgments to follow.

Revelation 9:15 "And the four angels who had been kept ready for this very hour and day and month and year were released *to kill a third of mankind*."

The first stage of mass death has arrived here in the *fourth seal* with *a fourth of the earth killed by sword, famine and plague, and by the wild beasts of the earth*. But it's just the beginning of an irreversible procedure of God's wrath being poured out upon the inhabitants of the earth. *Death* has descended upon the planet. Just like the stages of a corpse, it gets even worse as you go and even more putrefying as you advance through the stages of death. *One fourth of the earth* is bad enough, but another *third of mankind will be killed* shortly. All because they rejected Holy Blessed One Jesus Christ for the lying deceitful Antichrist. They chose to dance with the devil and so they have simply reaped what they have sown. As Jesus stated, the devil is a murderer and has been one from the beginning and he's seeing how many people he can take down with him into the Lake of Fire.

John 8:44 "You belong to your father, the devil, and you want to carry out your father's desire. He was a murderer from the beginning, not holding to the truth, for there is no truth in him. When he lies, he speaks his native language, for he is a liar and the father of lies."

Mankind believed the lie from the devil that everything will be just fine, the planet will get better, humanity will improve, you don't need Jesus, Christians are wackos, the Rapture is a scare tactic meant to enslave, etc. etc. and so, sure enough, the true colors of the evil one that they aligned themselves to came forth. The *pale horse rider* is now bringing you your wages! Death, murder, destruction, corpses littered everywhere! Lest there be any doubt that a massive wave of *death* is about to be unleashed on the planet with this *pale horse*, all one needs to do is now look at its *rider*.

The **second detail** given about the object of the fourth seal is **The Rider**.

Revelation 6:8a-b "I looked, and there before me was a pale horse! Its rider was named Death, and Hades was following close behind him."

This *pale horse* did not appear on the world scene bareback or even with an empty saddle. Like the first three, he too has a *rider*. Therefore, this next detail about the object of the Fourth Seal also brings up a couple of questions.

The **first question** about the rider is **Why was He Given a Name**?

Revelation 6:8b "Its rider was *named Death*, and Hades was following close behind him."

As if the message wasn't already loud and clear enough from Almighty God that when *the Lamb opens the fourth seal*, death, decay, and human corpses will be littering *one fourth* of the planet, it gets even more abundantly clear that this is what is coming from the very Throne of God. We see this in the specific *name* that was given to the *rider* of the *pale horse*. He is *named Death*. Not Darryl, not Dan, not even Dennis. But *death*! This is very telling because the previous three *riders* remained nameless. All we know about them is their horse color, what they were carrying, and the effects of their ride upon the planet. *Yet this rider has a name* and what a name it is! Of all names, this *rider* of *the fourth seal* is simply called Death! Why? Because God is making things about as plain as He can. Make no mistake about it, *death* is coming! How blunter can one be! Out of mercy God wants to make sure that no one misses His warning of what is about to be unleashed upon the planet for their rebellion against Him. What is coming is horrible, it's horrific. It is *death itself* coming! Therefore, if you're reading this and you're not saved today, you better get saved now before it's too late, before you get thrust into this wave of death that will sweep across the whole planet. *Death* will ride and there will be no place to hide! What more does God have to do to get your attention? *Death* is not only a powerfully blunt word that everyone on the planet is familiar with, but *death* here in this passage is the Greek word, "thanatos" which is used in the Bible to speak of, "death of the body, the separation of the soul from the body, the penal consequences of sin, the miserable state of the wicked dead in hell." In fact, the classical Greek and Roman usage of "thanatos" give us even more details of this morbid scene and what it is trying to get across to us:

"In Greek mythology, Thanatos was the personification of death. Thanatos was thus regarded as merciless and indiscriminate, hated by – and hateful towards – mortals and gods alike.

In ancient Roman myth and literature, Mors is the personification of death, equivalent to the Greek Thanatos. The Latin noun for 'death', mors, genitive mortis, is of feminine gender. Latin poets are bound by the grammatical gender of the word.

Horace writes of pallida Mors, 'pale Death,' who kicks her way into the hovels of the poor and the towers of kings equally. Seneca, for whom Mors is also pale, describes her 'eager teeth.' Tibullus pictures Mors as black or dark. Mors is often connected to Mars, the Roman god of war."[4]

Stir it all together and the picture that God is painting for us is literally mind blowing and mind numbing morbid. What follows war is always death along with black and dark times. Pallor Mortis, the first stage of death will now be littering the world scene. Mortis is setting in. That which is hated by all, death itself, will now charge after mankind with its own dark hatred for humanity, one and all, young and old alike. It's pale putrid appearance and eager teeth will decimate, destroy, decay, and kill all who fall into its deadly path. In fact, to "kill with death" is a Hebrew idiom that means to die a horrible, miserable death."[5]

Thus this time frame will not be pleasant, nor will it be pretty when death comes and takes people away. It will be the most horrible miserable death! It is *Death* itself, Thanatos, Mors, the personification of death that the *pale horse rider* is unleashing upon the planet at this time. When *the Lamb opens the fourth seal,* woe to any and all who fall prey to its ravenous and unending appetite. Clearly this specific name given to this *rider* speaks of ominous times! You need to respond now! Time is ticking! If you're reading this and you're not saved, get saved quick! I, along with God, am being repetitive for a purpose. This is serious! If you don't ask Jesus to forgive you of your sins right now, you will have chosen to instead receive the penal consequences of your sin in the future. *Death is coming for you*! You will be thrust into the worst time in the history of mankind, the 7-year tribulation. Your rejection of Christ will put you on *death's hit list* and soon your personal number will come up. He will come for you! He will chase you down! *Death itself* will ride after you and you will not escape! You will *die* at his touch whereupon your soul will be separated from your body and you will be cast into hell along with all the other miserable wicked dead who made the same awful mistake. They too rejected Jesus Christ and instead accepted the Antichrist. Please, turn to Jesus now before it's too late! How much more blunt and clear does God have to get before you wake up and heed His warning here in this text. He loves you! Wake up! Don't be left behind! The grave digger is coming, as this man shares:

"So, he sees this pale, green horse, 'And he who sat on it had the name death, and Hades was following with him and authority was given to them over a fourth of the earth to kill with sword and with famine and with pestilence and by the wild beasts of the earth.'

Here is the pale, ashen, green pallor of death, decomposition, a corpse. And fittingly the one who sat on it has the name thanatos, death, ominous. What follows war is famine, what follows famine is...what? Death...death. And what follows death? Hades. That's just another word for the grave. The grave comes, as it were, the grave digger comes with his shovel to collect the bodies that death destroys."[6]

This "grave digging" entity is what we will now turn our eyes towards. Believe it or not, the picture gets even more gruesome. The *rider, Death,* does not ride alone. He has someone with him following him, cleaning up the trail of dead bodies that he leaves strewn behind. Why anyone would want to risk being in this time frame is beyond me!

The **second question** about the rider is **Why Does He Have a Companion**?

Revelation 6:8b-c "Its rider was named Death, and *Hades was following close behind him.*"

Growing up, many of us had that special best friend that would ride "shotgun" with us in the car. They seemed to have a more privileged status than most. Other companions would ride in the back seat of the car, but this best friend would always be there right next to you. So, it is here with *Death's* ride. He too has a "shotgun" companion if you will, and he too has a specific name like *Death*. Only his name was *Hades* and he *was following close behind him,* Death. Now, maybe not in the front seat, but the idea in the text is the same. Wherever *Death* goes, *Hades* is right there with him. They are traveling buddies, traveling companions. When Death goes on a road trip, Hades is always there riding along. So again, the question is, "Why? Of all traveling companions, why does *Death* ride with this entity called *Hades*?" Well, let's first take a look at what is meant by the word *Hades*. Here in the Book of revelation it is the Greek word, "ades" pronounced "hades" which simply means, "the place of the departed dead." It is used ten times in the New Testament and it is the Greek equivalent of the Old Testament Hebrew word "sheol" which meant the same thing, "the abode of the dead." Both words, "hades" and "sheol" simply imply what we would say in the vernacular today, "the grave." Now, let's add to our knowledge of *Hades* its historical usage. It gives you an even creepier picture:

"Hades was the ancient Greek god of the underworld. While Hades' responsibility was in the Underworld, he was allowed to have power on earth as well. However, Hades himself is rarely seen outside his domain.

Hades was considered the enemy to all life and was hated by both the gods and men; sacrifices and prayers did not appease him, so mortals rarely tried. In Greek society, many viewed Hades as the least liked god and many gods even had an aversion towards him, and when people would sacrifice to Hades, it would be if they wanted revenge on an enemy or something terrible to happen to them.

Hades, as the god of the dead, was a fearsome figure to those still living; in no hurry to meet him, they were reluctant to swear oaths in his name, and averted their faces when sacrificing to him. He was depicted so infrequently in artwork, as well as mythology, because the Greeks were so afraid of him since to many, simply to say the word 'Hades' was frightening. Any other individual aspects of his personality are not given, as Greeks refrained from giving him much thought to avoid attracting his attention.

Feared and loathed, Hades embodied the inexorable finality of death. But he was not Death itself – the actual embodiment of Death was Thanatos. Hades cared little about what happened in the Upperworld, as his primary attention was ensuring none of his subjects ever left. "[7]

Wow! Talk about a creepy scene! This traveling duo of *Death* and *Hades* paints a very dark, ominous, and hopeless future. I truly believe God is being very graphic here with His choice of words to deliberately get our attention. This is serious business and this morbid reality is seriously coming to planet earth during the 7-year Tribulation! It's no joke! You don't want to be there! Once *Hades* appears on the scene, it's final! That's it! There is no going back, you cannot escape, and your fate is sealed! In fact, there is *no hesitation* on the part of *Hades*. As fast as these littered pale corpses are strewn across *one fourth of the planet* from *Death*, he is right there scooping them up throwing them straight into hell. As fast as literally, as we will see, billions of people hit the ground, *Hades* is right there chucking them into the grave. *Hades* was not just following *Death*, he *was following close behind* him. The idea is that *Hades* is right there nipping at *Death's* heels. What we have here is a very well-oiled efficient death machine and grave disposal service. You die, you go to hell. You die, you go to hell. You die, you got to hell. There's no hesitation here, no stopping, no passing go, no collecting $200. If an inhabitant of the earth dies in this time frame, the first half of the 7-year Tribulation, they will *immediately* go straight into hell! It's an afterlife assembly line! One minute you're alive, the next moment your dead, and the very next second, zip! *Hades* chucks you into hell. As fast as *Death* takes people out, *Hades* is right there doing his part. What a traveling companion! Other researchers put it this way:

"The rider is Death, and his companion is Hades or the grave – for Hades is the place of the dead. We should here picture death and Hades gathering up the victims of man's civilization – the casualties of war, starvation and plague."

"John next saw an ashen (lit. pale green) horse the color of a human corpse. 'Hades,' which claims unbelieving people's immaterial part at death, followed on his heels. Death claims the material part of the person and Hades the

immaterial part. Perhaps John saw Hades following Death as a man on foot followed a mounted warrior grimly gathering in his victims, or as a hearse followed a horse."

"Death and Hades are here personified. These two are often found together in Scripture, for Hades is the destination of the unsaved upon passing through the gateway of Death. This seems to be their relationship here because Hades followed behind Death – taking in the soul and spirit of those who had first died.

Elsewhere, the appearance of Death with Hades may denote the destination of the material and immaterial parts of man, respectively. For the body molders in the grave (death) while the spirit and soul enter the underworld (Hades).

Thus, 'Death and Hades delivered up the dead who were in them' may refer to the release of the spirit and soul of the unsaved from imprisonment in Hades to be joined with a bodily resurrection from the grave in order to stand before God in judgment (Rev. 20:13+).

Death and Hades either both ride the same horse, or Death is the horseman and Hades follows on foot. In either case, the two are inseparable as Hades takes in all that Death supplies."

"Following on his heels is 'Hades' which is the destination of the souls that do not know Christ as Savior (cf. Luke 16:23). The mention of Hades following with Death leaves no doubt that those who are slain will be unsaved people who will be cast into hell until they stand before the great white throne judgment (Rev. 20:11-15).

As John has already announced (Rev. 1:18), Jesus holds the keys to Death and Hades. As horrible as they are, their power is limited to what Christ permits; they too were 'given' their authority."[8]

And that's the only bright light in the midst of this very dark scene. As horrible and horribly descriptive as this text is, Death littering the planet with pale decaying corpses by the billions, and Hades immediately appearing in his sinister hearse scooping them up and throwing them straight into hell, God reminds us that *even their power*, as dark, frightening, and macabre as it is, is still limited *by Him*. He, God, is in *full control* at all times, even here in this dark time during the 7-year Tribulation. That's what we see in the next question concerning this *rider*.

The **third question** about the rider is **Who Gave Them Their Power?**

Revelation 6:8b-d "Its rider was named Death, and Hades was following close behind him. *They were given power* over a fourth of the earth."

The key word there is "given." *Death* and *Hades* are not only mentioned by name in this text and then seen galloping forth upon the planet chucking people into hell as fast as they die but notice that it *very specifically* says that their ability or *power* was *given* to them. They don't get to do this dark deed when they want to do it. It's not when they are good and ready or decide it's the right time. No! Nothing happens with *Death* and *Hades* until *they were given power*. This clearly tells us that these two deadly gruesome spiritual traveling companions are at somebody else's beck and call. They are on a leash. They are *not* in control. They never were and they never will be. They have to wait until *they were given power* to ride forth. So again, the question is, "Who is the One Who has power over even *Death* and *Hades?*" Well, if the context hasn't already made this abundantly clear enough to you, other passages in the Bible will. It is none other than *God,* our *Lord Jesus Christ,* Who has the power over *Death* and *Hades*!

Revelation 1:12-18 "I turned around to see the voice that was speaking to me. And when I turned I saw seven golden lampstands, and among the lampstands was someone 'like a son of man,' dressed in a robe reaching down to His feet and with a golden sash around His chest. His head and hair were white like wool, as white as snow, and His eyes were like blazing fire. His feet were like bronze glowing in a furnace, and His voice was like the sound of rushing waters. In His right hand He held seven stars, and out of His mouth came a sharp double-edged sword. His face was like the sun shining in all its brilliance. When I saw Him, I fell at His feet as though dead. Then He placed His right hand on me and said: 'Do not be afraid. I am the First and the Last. I am the Living One; I was dead, and behold I am alive for ever and ever! And *I hold the keys of death and Hades.*"

The operative word there is "keys." In the Bible, "keys" symbolize authority. Thus, Jesus is telling us that He is the One Who has the *authority* over *Death and Hades.* He's got the keys! He's in charge! He has the ultimate authority! Therefore, it's obvious and totally clear from the Scripture that He is; the One *giving Death and Hades power over a fourth of the earth*. Once again, the message is clear that God is in full control, as these men share:

"Hades is the right partner for death. You find them teamed up in chapter 20 verse 13, Hades is death's hearse, he can keep up with death's ride, they work together. This is the result of the second and the third seal. But more than that, look at verse 8, 'Authority was given to them,' by whom again? Who gave the authority? God, because this is the unfolding of His title deed and His scroll; it is His judgment."

"The four horsemen bring immense suffering to the human race. John writes: 'They were given power over a fourth of the earth to kill by sword, famine and plague, and by the wild beasts of the earth' (6:8). Once again, we see that power is given to the horsemen. They can cause only the damage God allows. The evils they represent are not caused by God, of course. In His wisdom and patience God acts to fulfil His covenant purpose even in the midst of humanity's evil opposition."[9]

Right from the very beginning of Revelation in Chapter 1 to even here in our text in Revelation Chapter 6, Jesus makes this one truth abundantly clear. *He is in full control of all things*. Be it *all* the judgments in the 7-year Tribulation or even *Death* and *Hades'* macabre ride in the first half of the 7-year Tribulation. So why is God repeating this truth so adamantly? Because people on the planet have a choice to make while there's still time. Either receive His love, mercy, and forgiveness and be rescued from the grip of *Death and Hades,* or reject His gracious offer through Jesus, He Who holds *authority over Death and Hades*, and He will allow them both to ride upon you and send you straight into hell. *It's your choice!*

I see this as part of God's loving tender care towards us as our Heavenly Father. For instance, do you remember as a child when your Mom kept telling you something over and over again, maybe warning you about a certain danger, and we would say something like, "Okay Mom, I get it, I get it! You can stop telling me now." But sure enough, five minutes later she would tell us again. She did this because she loved us and wanted to make sure we were well and safe. So it is here at this stage of our text. I've personally lost count how many times God has already reiterated this truth that He is in full control of all things, including all the judgments in the 7-year Tribulation. Now He tells us here that He's even in charge of *Death* and *Hades* riding forth in *the fourth seal*. But it's all to inform us how much He must love us, mankind, His creation. It's obvious that He's trying to warn us repeatedly like our Mom to make sure we stay well and safe for all eternity and even escape the 7-year Tribulation itself. He doesn't want us to end up in the hands of *Death* and *Hades*! Remember, this is a time sensitive issue. If you wait too long, then *Death* and *Hades* will ride upon you. This *will* be your future. It doesn't have to be. This is the wonderful truth that God is reminding us here in this passage. Jesus *holds the keys of Death and Hades*. Their *power was given to them* by God. But don't delay. By your own procrastination you could miss out on the blessing of being rescued from the grip of *Death* and *Hades* by the One Who holds them in His grip Personally. No wonder God is being very repetitive with this truth. Time is ticking, and your eternal destiny is on the line! If you don't get rescued from *Death* and *Hades* now, it will only get worse!

Revelation 20:11-15 "Then I saw a great white throne and Him Who was seated on it. Earth and sky fled from His presence, and there was no place for them. And I saw the dead, great and small, standing before the throne, and books were opened. Another book was opened, which is the book of life. The dead were judged according to what they had done as recorded in the books. The sea gave up the dead that were in it, and *death and Hades gave up the dead that were in them*, and each person was judged according to what he had done. Then *death and Hades were thrown into the lake of fire*. The lake of fire is the second death. If anyone's name was not found written in the book of life, he was thrown into the lake of fire."

At the very beginning of the Book of Revelation God makes it abundantly clear that Jesus *holds the keys to Death and Hades,* and for any and all who would choose to receive His love, mercy, and forgiveness, He would release them from their dark and gruesome grip. But be assured, if you mock, scoff, delay, and persist in your stubborn rebellion, *Death* with come for you and *Hades* will throw you straight into hell. Then at the end of the Millennial Kingdom, you will be raised from your torment for a mere brief moment only to stand before God's Great White Throne whereupon you will be judged and be thrown from the frying pan into the fire. You will go from hell into the Lake of Fire *along with Death and Hades*! Only Christ can save you from this horrible fate, as these men admit:

"Both Death and Hades will ultimately be thrown into the lake of fire (20:14). That is, they will be destroyed – swallowed up. Only Christ can unlock the dead from the grave and give them eternal life (1:18)."

"The eventual casting of death and Hades into the Lake of Fire (Rev.20:14+) describes the total victory over these unsavory realities brought about by the cross of Jesus (Hos.13:14; 1 Cor.15:21-26, 1 Cor. 15:54-55, 2 Tim.1:10). They denote those destined for the lake – the unsaved dead whose bodies remained in the grave and souls remained in Hades until the Great White Throne Judgment. Jesus has the keys of Death and Hades."[10]

No wonder God is repeatedly driving this point home, that He is the One Who in in charge here at all times, including the judgments during the 7-year Tribulation, including the dark destructive ride of *Death* and *Hades. They were given power over a fourth of the earth.* In other words, their power was given to them by God. Period. This is the good news and the time-sensitive bad news. It's urgent. You must take this seriously. God can spare you from *Death* and *Hades* if *you so choose,* or also by *your own choosing* He will allow them to trample you down in their death ride and cast you into hell. Again, it doesn't have to be this way. It's your choice. This is why God is being so repetitious. He's trying to rescue you from *Death* and *Hades* before it's too late! If only you would receive Jesus Christ as your Lord and Savior *now!* Please turn to Him *immediately* and *don't delay*! You don't know how many reminders He has left for you, if any. Tomorrow may be too late! But if these repetitious reminders didn't get your full attention concerning this *rider* of *the fourth seal* and the dangers that lie ahead for those who procrastinate, hopefully this last and final question concerning the *rider* will.

The **fourth question** about the rider is **What Did They Do with that Power**?

Revelation 6:8b-e "Its rider was named Death, and Hades was following close behind him. They were given power *over a fourth of the earth to kill* by sword, famine and plague, and by the wild beasts of the earth."

So here we see in a nutshell the horrible full scope of *Death* and *Hades'* destructive ride in *the fourth seal. When the Lamb opened the fourth seal*, the effects of these judgements are specifically announced by God. He is making sure that none of us miss the much-needed merciful forewarning of the horrendous events that will transpire during the first half of the 7-year Tribulation. It's not just one country that will be affected by the gruesome ride of *Death* and *Hades*. It's not merely one particular race of people either. It's not even one section of the earth. It's *one fourth of the earth yhat* will be *killed*. Never has there been a loss of life like this on planet earth since the days of Noah's Flood, which by the way, was another time when Almighty God judged the planet, just like He's doing here in the 7-year Tribulation. The human death toll at this time is such a staggering number that it is hard to fully even comprehend. The current population of the planet is around 7.5 billion and so if you do the math, and if this judgement were to occur today, this means that approximately 1.87 billion people will die. Not 1.87 thousand or 1.87 million, but 1.87 *billion*! Not even all the political wars in the last 100 years or so on planet earth can compare to what's going on here. The mass loss of life is shocking:

- Congo Free State - 1886-1908 - 8,000,000 - Control of colonial profit and power base
- Feudal Russia - 1900-1917 - 3,500,000 - Political control
- Turkish Purges - 1900-1923 - 5,000,000 - Ottoman Empire collapse/Political control
- First World War - 1914-1918 - 15,000,000 - Balance of power
- NOTE: The First World War killed more people than all the religious wars in the past. 6,000 men a day died for 1,500 days in World War I.
- Russian Civil War - 1917-1922 - 9,000,000 - Political control
- Soviet Union, Stalin Regime - 1924-1953 – 20-45,000,000 - Political control
- China Nationalist Era - 1928-1937 - 3,000,000 - Political control
- Second World War - 1937/38-1945 - 55,000,000 - Balance of power/Expansionism
- Sino-Japanese War - 1937-1945 - 21,000,000 – Expansionism
- Post-WWII German Expulsions from Eastern Europe - 1945-1948 - 1.8-5,000,000 - Post-war policies. Retributions/Soviet and Eastern European control
- Chinese Civil War - 1945-1949 - 2,500,000 - Political control
- People's Republic of China - 1949-1975 – 40-80,000,000 - Political control
- North Korean Regime - 1948- 1.7-3,000,000 - Political control
- Korean War - 1950-1953 - 2,800,000 - Political control
- Second Indochina War - 1960-1975 - 3-4,000,000 - Political control
- Ethiopia - 1962-1992 - 1,500,000 - Political control
- Khmer Rouge - 1975-1978 - 2,500,000 - Political control

- Afghanistan - 1979-2001 - 1,800,000 - Political control/Soviet expansion
- Kinshasa Congo - 1998- 3,800,000 – Political control &Resources[11]

Even when you add up all the deaths from all these political wars across the planet over the last 100 years or so, and even taking the higher numbers, you will still only arrive at around 270 million people killed. Now, as bad as that is, here in the 7-year Tribulation, in *the fourth seal* judgement from God, we see that nearly *2 billion* people will die. Man's wars can't even begin compare to what God will do when He goes to war with wicked and rebellious mankind as an act of His judgment. In one fell swoop in the first half of the 7-year Tribulation God takes out nearly 7 times the number of people killed in all these wars over the last 100 years. Furthermore, the deaths caused by man's political wars were spread out over a period of around 100 years. But God allows 7 times the deaths, nearly 2 billion people, in just a couple of years. Thus, in an extremely compressed amount of time, one out of every four people on the whole planet will be wiped from existence. This is absolutely unbelievable! No wonder this is labeled appropriately the *Death Seal*. Not a mere neighborhood, not a single city or even just one country, but one out of every four people on the whole planet will be gone forevermore in *the fourth seal*! Keep in mind, this is still just the first half of the 7-year Tribulation, and there are still massive judgements to come from God. He's just getting started, He's just getting warmed up! Again, no wonder He is driving home this point. He's making sure we're forewarned of this earth shattering event, just like the people in the Days of Noah. They too had advanced warning. God is not willing that any should perish, but that all should come to repentance before it's too late. The death toll that is coming to this planet at this time, during the first half of the 7-year Tribulation, all because of man's wicked and rebellious heart, is staggering beyond comprehension, as these researchers also agree:

"'One fourth of the earth' means that Death and Hades have authority, which they apparently will exercise. The magnitude of this catastrophe can hardly be grasped because nothing comparable has happened throughout history. If limited to two continents, which it will probably not be, it will amount to the elimination of people from two of the world's most populous ones."

"God gives these enemies authority to take one-fourth of the world's population. This is more than the population of China and the United States combined. This is the greatest destruction of human life recorded in history. This evidently is the total number that will die as a result of all the catastrophes predicted so far."

*"The population of the earth at the present time (2013) is about seven billion
people. That means that if the events of the fourth seal occurred today, about
1.75 billion people would die. At the present time, there are widespread wars,
famines, diseases, natural catastrophes, and other causes of death on the earth,
but, as is apparent, during the few years of the opening of the seals of Revelation,
the suffering and carnage will increase exponentially and there will be no
mistaking that we are at the 'End of the Age' and the 'beginning of
sorrows' (Matthew 24:3,8)."[12]*

Yes, the key word there is "beginning." This is just the "beginning" of
the "sorrowful" 7-year Tribulation. There is so much more to go, there is so
much more to come in judgments from God, yet even here, the unbelievable
death toll, the loss of life of *one fourth of the earth* causes one to pause and gasp
in unbelief. Imagine if all of China and all of the United States gone forevermore.
Not a soul to be found. Both countries, completely empty, totally devoid of any
people. Now again, we know this death toll won't just occur in two countries, but
this gives you an idea of the staggering loss of life here in *the fourth seal*. Now
you know why Jesus said this would be the worst time in the history of mankind,
and that unless God shortened the time frame, no one would survive. Again, if
you're not saved and you're reading this, you need to get saved now. This is not a
joke. It really is coming. You don't want to be numbered in the nearly 2 billion
casualties on planet earth! Escape now through Jesus Christ before it's too late!
In fact, speaking of the global casualties, God now drives this loving merciful
forewarning home even further. He not only gives us the *number* of casualties,
He even gives their specific *causes*.

The **first cause** of this nearly 2 billion deaths on planet earth in *the
fourth seal* is **The Sword.**

Revelation 6:8b-f "Its rider was named Death, and Hades was following close
behind him. They were given power over a fourth of the earth to kill *by sword...*"

This brings us back to accumulative effects of *the second seal* judgement
from God and the global war, or literally the global slaughter that will be
occurring all across the planet. If you recall, this will not just be a time of
militaries killing other foreign militaries, but literally man against man, people
against people, individuals slaughtering and butchering one another all across the
world. It's a bloody horrific scene. In fact, the sword mentioned here
"rhomphaia" is different than the sword mentioned in the second seal, that of

"machaira." The first sword was more of a "precision cutting instrument" used for cutting up flesh and thus spoke of the fact that people will literally be butchering each other like animals, even to the point where they are cutting each other up, filleting them, and carving their victims into pieces like a hunter does with his prey. However, the "rhomphaia" sword was more of a "large broad sword that was used by the barbaric peoples." This shows us not only the "broad reaching effects," a huge swath of humanity murdered around the world, but that this will be a total bloody "barbaric" nightmare. People across the planet will not only be cutting each other up like animals, but they themselves will be acting like barbaric animals. It's a bloody horrific barbaric broad butchering mess that's going on here beyond your wildest nightmares, and this is the *first cause* of the nearly 2 billion people that will die in the first half of the 7-year Tribulation.

The **second cause** of this nearly 2 billion deaths on planet earth in *the fourth seal* is **Famine**.

Revelation 6:8b-g "Its rider was named Death, and Hades was following close behind him. They were given power over a fourth of the earth to kill by sword, *famine*..."

Here we are brought back to accumulative effects of *the third seal* judgement from God and the global famine that will be occurring on the planet during the first half of the 7-year Tribulation. If you will recall, this was a very black, mournful, grievous time where people will literally be wasting away into nothing but skin and bones. Furthermore, as we saw with historical examples, most likely people could very well be resorting to cannibalism involving even eating of their very own family, even their own children. It's a shocking mind-numbing macabre reality that that planet will be experiencing during this time right after the global slaughter. First, people kill each other, then people eat each other. You definitely don't want to be on the planet during this time. This is the *second cause* of the nearly 2 billion people that will die in the first half of the 7-year Tribulation.

The **third cause** of this nearly 2 billion deaths on planet earth in *the fourth seal* is **Pestilence**.

Revelation 6:8b-h "Its rider was named Death, and Hades was following close behind him. They were given power over a fourth of the earth to kill by sword, famine *and plague*..."

Now we are shown the *third cause* of nearly 2 billion people dying in the first half of the 7-year Tribulation. Unlike the first two, this cause has not been mentioned before, yet it certainly makes sense as to why it, *plague*, follows. In fact, the word "plague" here is actually the Greek word we saw before for "death" that is "thanatos." Most of the time it's translated just that, "death", but on some occasions, as it is here, contextually it is translated as "pestilence" as to the *cause* of death. We certainly see that is an accurate contextual translation from all the previously mentioned Old Testament passages where God uses these four same judgments upon wicked and rebellious people.

Jeremiah 14:11-12 "Then the LORD said to me, 'Do not pray for the well-being of this people. Although they fast, I will not listen to their cry; though they offer burnt offerings and grain offerings, I will not accept them. Instead, I will destroy them with the *sword, famine* and *plague*.'"

Jeremiah 24:10 "I will send the *sword, famine* and *plague* against them until they are destroyed from the land I gave to them and their fathers."

Jeremiah 42:17 "Indeed, all who are determined to go to Egypt to settle there will die by the *sword, famine* and *plague*; not one of them will survive or escape the disaster I will bring on them."

Ezekiel 14:21 "For this is what the Sovereign LORD says: How much worse will it be when I send against Jerusalem my four dreadful judgments – *sword* and *famine* and *wild beasts* and *plague* – to kill its men and their animals!"

Thus, as you can see, it is a perfect match. This is not by chance in the Scripture. God used these exact same four judgments in the past and now He's using them again here in Revelation in the future. What follows the *sword* and *famine* is *plague*. Therefore, the translation of "thanatos" here as "plague" or pestilence or disease is an accurate Biblical translation. Furthermore, we also see that historically and logically *plague*, or pestilence or disease, always seems to follow the ravages of war and famine in any area littered with the death and decay of corpses. In fact, it's another indicator of the severity and hopelessness of the seal judgments. Once these four causes of death are unleashed, there is no escape. You might make it through one or two of them, but there's another one ready to get you, including death by *plague*. It truly is a frightening time, as this man shares:

"This is the last seal which will lose a horse and rider. The first four seals are to be understood as a group, four being indicative of their global effects. Pale is [chlōros] from which we derive chlorophyll, which denotes the green pigments found in plants, properly, 'greenish-yellow,' like young grass or unripe wheat.

Here it denotes 'the color of a person in sickness as contrasted with the appearance of health,' for the name of the rider of the pale horse is death [thanatos]. Thucydides uses it of the appearance of persons stricken with the plague. In Homer, it is used of the paleness of the face from fear, and so as directly descriptive of fear.

But in the present connection, it designates the yellowish green of decay, the pallor of death. It is a pale ashen color that images a face bleached because of terror. It recalls a corpse in the advanced state of corruption."[13]

In fact, speaking of "terror," let us now take a historical look at deaths caused by *plagues* and what makes them such a "terrible" time. Why is God mercifully warning us so many times repeatedly about these frightening judgments? Let's take a look at what others went through historically when *plagues* ravaged the earth:

- **Plague of Athens 430–427 BC**

  The Plague of Athens was a devastating epidemic which hit the city-state of Athens in ancient Greece during the second year of the Peloponnesian War (430 BC), when an Athenian victory still seemed within reach. In the next 3 years, most of the population was infected, and perhaps as many as 75,000 to 100,000 people, 25% of the city's population, died. It is believed to have entered Athens through Piraeus, the city's port and sole source of food and supplies. The city-state of Sparta, and much of the eastern Mediterranean, was also struck by the disease. The plague returned twice more, in 429 BC and in the winter of 427/6 BC. Modern historians disagree on whether the plague was a critical factor in the loss of the war. However, it is generally agreed that the loss of this war may have paved the way for the success of the Macedonians and, ultimately, the Romans. The disease has traditionally been considered an outbreak of the bubonic plague in its many forms, but re-considerations of the reported symptoms and epidemiology have led scholars to advance alternative explanations. These include typhus, smallpox, measles, and toxic shock syndrome.

- **Antonine Plague 165–180 AD**

  The Antonine Plague (also known as the Plague of Galen, who described it), was an ancient pandemic, of either smallpox or measles, brought back to the Roman Empire by troops returning from campaigns in the Near East. The epidemic claimed the lives of two Roman emperors – Lucius Verus, who died in 169, and his co-regent who ruled until 180, Marcus Aurelius Antoninus, whose family name, Antoninus, was given to the epidemic. The disease broke out again nine years later, according to the Roman historian Dio Cassius, and caused up to 2,000 deaths a day at Rome, one quarter of those infected. Total deaths have been estimated at 5 million. Disease killed as much as one-third of the population in some areas and decimated the Roman army. The epidemic had drastic social and political effects throughout the Roman Empire.

- **Plague of Justinian 541–542 AD**

  The Plague of Justinian was a pandemic that afflicted the Byzantine Empire, including its capital Constantinople, in the years 541–542 AD. The most commonly accepted cause of the pandemic is bubonic plague, which later became infamous for either causing or contributing to the Black Death of the 14th century. Its social and cultural impact is comparable to that of the Black Death. In the views of 6th century Western historians, it was nearly worldwide in scope, striking central and south Asia, North Africa and Arabia, and Europe as far north as Denmark and as far west as Ireland. The plague would return with each generation throughout the Mediterranean basin until about 750. The plague would also have a major impact on the future course of European history. Modern historians named it after the Eastern Roman Emperor Justinian I, who was in power at the time and himself contracted the disease. Modern scholars believe that the plague killed up to 5,000 people per day in Constantinople at the peak of the pandemic. It ultimately killed perhaps 40% of the city's inhabitants. The initial plague went on to destroy up to a quarter of the human population of the eastern Mediterranean.

- **The Black Death 1347–1351**

  The Black Death (also known as The Black Plague or Bubonic Plague), was one of the deadliest pandemics in human history, widely thought to have been caused by a bacterium named Yersinia pestis (Plague), but recently attributed by some to other diseases. The origins of the plague are disputed among scholars. Some historians believe the pandemic began in China or Central

Asia in the late 1320s or 1330s, and during the next years merchants and soldiers carried it over the caravan routes until in 1346 it reached the Crimea in southern Russia. Other scholars believe the plague was endemic in southern Russia. In either case, from Crimea the plague spread to Western Europe and North Africa during the 1340s. The total number of deaths worldwide is estimated at 75 million people, approximately 25–50 million of which occurred in Europe. The plague is thought to have returned every generation with varying virulence and mortalities until the 1700s. During this period, more than 100 plague epidemics swept across Europe.

- **American Plagues 16th Century**

Before the European arrival, the Americas had been largely isolated from the Eurasian–African landmass. First large-scale contacts between Europeans and native people of the American continents brought overwhelming pandemics of measles and smallpox, as well as other Eurasian diseases. These diseases spread rapidly among native peoples, often ahead of actual contact with Europeans, and led to a drastic drop in population and the collapse of American cultures. Smallpox and other diseases invaded and crippled the Aztec and Inca civilizations in Central and South America in the 16th century. This disease, with loss of population and death of military and social leaders, contributed to the downfall of both American empires and the subjugation of American peoples to Europeans. Diseases, however, passed in both directions; syphilis was carried back from the Americas and swept through the European population, decimating large numbers.

- **Great Plague of London 1665–1666**

The Great Plague (1665-1666) was a massive outbreak of disease in England that killed 75,000 to 100,000 people, up to a fifth of London's population. The disease was historically identified as bubonic plague, an infection by the bacterium Yersinia pestis, transmitted through fleas. The 1665-1666 epidemic was on a far smaller scale than the earlier "Black Death" pandemic, a virulent outbreak of disease in Europe between 1347 and 1353. The Bubonic Plague was only remembered afterwards as the "great" plague because it was one of the last widespread outbreaks in England. Although the disease causing the epidemic has historically been identified as bubonic plague and its variants, no direct evidence of plague has ever been uncovered. Some modern scholars suggest that the symptoms and incubation period indicate that the causal agent may have been a disease similar to a viral hemorrhagic fever.

- **Great Plague of Milan 1629–1631**

The Italian Plague of 1629–1631 was a series of outbreaks of bubonic plague which occurred from 1629 through 1631 in northern Italy. This epidemic, often referred to as Great Plague of Milan, claimed the lives of approximately 280,000 people, with the cities of Lombardy and Venice experiencing particularly high death rates. This episode is considered one of the last outbreaks of the centuries-long pandemic of bubonic plague which began with the Black Death. German and French troops carried the plague to the city of Mantua in 1629, as a result of troop movements associated with the Thirty Years' War (1618–1648). Venetian troops, infected with the disease, retreated into northern and central Italy, spreading the infection. Overall, Milan suffered approximately 60,000 fatalities out of a total population of 130,000.

- **Great Plague of Marseille 1720–1722**

The Great Plague of Marseille was one of the most significant European outbreaks of bubonic plague in the early 18th century. Arriving in Marseille, France in 1720, the disease killed 100,000 people in the city and the surrounding provinces. This epidemic was not a recurrence of the European Black Death, the devastating episodes of bubonic plague which began in the fourteenth century. Attempts to stop the spread of plague included an Act of Parliament of Aix that levied the death penalty for any communication between Marseille and the rest of Provence. To enforce this separation, a plague wall, the Mur de la Peste, was erected across the countryside.

- **The Third Pandemic 1855–1950s**

"Third Pandemic" is the name given to a major plague pandemic that began in the Yunnan province in China in 1855. This episode of bubonic plague spread to all inhabited continents, and ultimately killed more than 12 million people in India and China alone. According to the World Health Organization, the pandemic was considered active until 1959, when worldwide casualties dropped to 200 per year. The bubonic plague was endemic in populations of infected ground rodents in central Asia and was a known cause of death among migrant and established human populations in that region for centuries; however, an influx of new people due to political conflicts and global trade led to the distribution of this disease throughout the world. New research suggests Black Death is lying dormant.[14]

And yet it very well could be brought out of dormancy by God during the first half of the 7-year Tribulation. Imagine the whole planet like this, truly so. Combine the Black Death with all these other types of *plagues* mentioned above, with their horrible accumulative effects, and you can see why God is warning us repeatedly to take heed now! This kind of existence is what awaits the planet on a massive scale! Not one country, not one area, not one group of people, but the whole planet all at the same time! And it won't even be just a few million deaths here and there, but literally nearly 2 billion! *One fourth of the earth* will be suffering under these kinds of *plague-ridden* conditions. Remember, this is after the war, after the famine-now this. Their house of cards, the false promises of the Antichrist, is crumbling all around them. In fact, speaking of wars, one of the worst plagues in history was spread globally due to war. See if you can guess which historical *plague* this one is:

"It was February and the tourist season was in full swing in this seemingly innocent town in Spain. The sun was shining, and by all appearances it seemed like a wonderful place to escape the horrors of WWI. But that was until the plague came to town. And the next thing you knew, it was everywhere.

The sickness preyed on the young and old alike with one day feeling fine but the next thing you know, you have a headache and your eyes start to burn. Then you start to shiver and go to bed, curling up in a ball but no number of blankets can keep you warm. Then you fall into a restless sleep, dreaming distorted nightmares as your fever begins to climb.

Then your face turns a dark brownish purple and you start to cough up blood whereupon your feet begin turning black. And finally, you start frantically gasping for breath as a bloody saliva bubbles out of your mouth and you actually start to drown because your lungs are filling up with it. It may take a few days, it may take a few hours, but there's nothing you can do to stop it, you're going to die!

And because of this plague, overnight, children were orphaned, families were destroyed, towns were decimated, and some populations were totally eliminated from the face of the earth. And those who lived through it said it was such a horrible time that they never ever want to talk about it again!

One-fifth of the world's population became infected with it, and thus it was described as the Biblical prophecy of the pale horse rider bringing death and hades behind it coming to pass. Why? Because when all was over, it killed more people in a few months' time than any other illness in the history of the world.

The year was 1918. The death toll was over 100 million people. The deadly plague was of course, the Great Influenza Outbreak."[15]

So, it will be again on an even bigger scale never before imagined in the first half of the 7-year Tribulation. Following *the second seal* judgment of global war will be *the third seal* famine and then *the fourth seal plague*. Just as the transfer of soldiers, people, food, supplies, etc., helped spread the Great Influenza and kill over 100 million people, so it will be again in the near future. Only this time it will be nearly *2 billion* people. We've seen *plagues* wipe out massive numbers of people in the past and we will see it again in the future, as these researchers share:

"Throughout human history, disease has killed people on a far more massive scale than war. More Union and Confederate soldiers died from disease during the Civil War than were killed in battle. Tens of millions of people died during the great influenza epidemic of 1918-19 – more than three times as many as the estimated soldiers who died in battle during World War I."

"Here is a pestilence that is going to take out one-fourth of the population of the earth. There will not be enough antibiotics and penicillin to go around in that day to stop it."[16]

Speaking of *stopping it*, what about *starting it*? Could it be that what makes this time period in the first half of the 7-year Tribulation so horrible and so *plague-ridden* like never before in the history of mankind is the possibility that not all of these *plagues* released upon the planet are *natural*? That is, could it be that some of them, maybe even many of them or most of them, will be *man-made,* as this researcher considers:

"The sword, famine, pestilence, and wild beasts will decimate this earth's population by one-fourth. This is something that, through His prophet Ezekiel, God had said would come: 'For thus saith the Lord GOD; How much more when I send my four sore judgments upon Jerusalem, the sword, and the famine, and the noisome beast, and the pestilence, to cut off from it man and beast?' (Ezek. 14:21).

The pale horse represents plague and pestilence that will stalk the earth. It also encompasses the possibility of germ warfare. Dr. Frank Holtman, head of the University of Tennessee's bacteriological department, said, 'While the greater part of a city's population could be destroyed by an atomic bomb, the bacteria method might easily wipe out the entire population within a week.'

We have seen the riding of the four horsemen, and this follows exactly the pattern that the Lord Jesus gave while He was on the earth. In Matthew 24:5-8, in the Olivet Discourse, He said: 'For many shall come in my name, saying, I am Christ; and shall deceive many [the white horse]. And ye shall hear of wars and rumors of wars [the red horse]: see that ye be not troubled: for all these must come to pass, but the end is not yet. For nation shall rise against nation, and kingdom against kingdom: and there shall be famines [the black horse], and pestilences [the pale horse], and earthquakes, in divers' places. All these are the beginning of sorrows.'"[17]

So, could that not logically be a part of the reasons why this is such a "sorrowful" time even as Jesus mentions? Could it be that just, as *plagues* or pestilences of the *pale horse* naturally follow the *wars and rumors of wars* of the red horse, so it is with the *cause* of these *plagues* in the first place? They too are a direct result of war? I say that because whether you realize it or not, *man-made plagues* or chemical weapons manufactured for germ warfare have not only been used in the past, but they're even still being used on people worldwide today. Let's take a look at that evidence:

"From pre-science alchemists to modern researchers, humans have always sought the chemistry of life. But the same can be said for the chemistry of death.

Four thousand years before mustard gas choked the trenches of World War I, Vedic kingdoms unleashed smoke screens and sleep-inducing toxins on the battlefields of India. Throughout antiquity, the Greeks, Romans and Spartans wielded chemical agents that burned the lungs, blinded the eyes, disrupted the bowels and scorched the skin.

Like murderous djinn unleashed from a lamp, these silent and often-invisible killers drifted across the battlefield in a wave of indiscriminate suffering and death.

But it wasn't till the 20th century that chemical warfare reached its full, terrifying potential. The following are some of the scariest chemical weapons ever developed. Breathe deep."

- ## BZ

  The chemistry of life and the chemistry of death frequently reflect one another. During the 1960s, free-thinking flower children took psychedelics and dreamed of a world without war. Meanwhile, U.S. Army researchers at Edgewood Arsenal studied some of the same hallucinogens in the name of psychochemical warfare. They also sought weapons in the form of rejected drugs from major pharmaceutical companies – some 400 a month, each commercially useless due to undesirable side effects. Out of this whirlwind of psychedelics, failed medicine and human experimentation, one chemical weapon emerged as the U.S. Military's standard incapacitating agent: 3-Quinuclidinyl benzilate or BZ. A rejected gastrointestinal medication, BZ proved highly useful in warfare due to its potent ability to depress the central nervous system. It dulls several crucial cognitive functions, including memory, problem solving, attention, and comprehension - and does so for upwards of three days. The United States deployed BZ against the Viet Cong during the Vietnam War, and allegedly explored its possible use as a contingency plan in the event of a civilian uprising. The U.S. ultimately abandoned the super-hallucinogen due to its unpredictability on the battlefield, but accusations of Iraqi BZ research, Syrian BZ use and even recreational use among insurgents continues to this day.

- ## Mustard Gas

  Mustard gas or sulfur mustard made its sinister name in World War I based on its power to incapacitate soldiers in the trenches. The mustardy-smelling, generally colorless gas might take anywhere from two to 24 hours to take effect, depending on concentration, but the resulting skin, eye and respiratory burns could put whole units out of commission. While most mustard gas victims recover in a matter of weeks, some experience permanent scarring, blindness and DNA damage as a result of exposure. Plus, mustard gas posed a danger to troops days or even weeks following its initial deployment. Especially in cold conditions, the dense gas can settle on the ground, only to be stirred up by a fresh set of boots.

- ## Ricin

Long before Walter White plotted to poison half the cast of 'Breaking Bad,' the U.S. military patented a method to purify ricin toxin for the Great War. Ah, but how to deploy it on a battlefield? The army couldn't very well go around sneaking it into everyone's chamomile tea. The Hague Convention of 1899 prohibited its use as a projectile coating, plus other dispersal methods proved ineffective. Ricin is derived from the castor bean plant (Ricinus communis), the same species responsible for all that castor oil in our medicine and food products. Grind the beans into oil and you're left with a mash byproduct – and that's where you'll find the toxin. While not a fast-acting toxin (symptoms take between 4-24 hours to set in), ricin is highly lethal to humans. A single milligram of the stuff is deadly if inhaled or ingested. As such, ricin remains most effective as an assassination poison. The most famous example of this occurred in 1969 when an assassin fired a ricin-laced pellet into the leg of defected Bulgarian writer Georgi Markov.

- **Phosgene Gas**

  Phosgene gas stands alone as the greatest killer of World War I. According to a 1987 Ministry of Defense report as many as 85 percent of all deaths in the Great War were due to phosgene. Either way, we're talking about a war that claimed 8.5 million military lives. Deployed extensively by both sides, this colorless, heavy gas would seep into the trenches with only a faint scent of fresh hay or corn to announce its presence – a true creeping death if there ever was one. Phosgene gas (COCl2) arises from the reaction of carbon monoxide and chlorine gas in the presence of activated charcoal. Outside of its extensive weaponized use in WWI, phosgene remains a major chemical ingredient in pesticides and plastics. First created in 1812, phosgene gas does not occur in the natural world and only exists as a product of human manufacturing.

- **Sarin**

  Nerve agents – the most nefarious of chemical weapons – are dreadfully specific in the way they attack the human body: They assault communication between organs and the brain. Specifically, nerve agents inhibit the enzyme acetylcholinesterase, which serves as the 'off switch' for glands and muscles. Except nerve agents don't turn anything off. Instead, they keep them running in overdrive. So, stimulation continues until the victim plummets into motionless, breathless unconsciousness. Sarin kills within seconds. The liquid has no color, no taste and no odor. Thankfully, it evaporates very quickly, making it a very potent but very immediate weapon. Sarin emerged in 1938 as a German pesticide, following tabun as the second in the G-series of nerve agents. While the Germans quickly realized the chemical's deadly potential, they never deployed it. Later, both the United States and the Soviet Union produced massive sarin stockpiles that also never saw military use. The same cannot be said for Iraq and Syria. In 1988, Saddam Hussein killed 5,000 Kurds in the northern Iraqi village of Halabja with sarin. More recently, Syrian forces reportedly killed between 500 and 1,300 men, women and children with sarin rockets.

- **Soman**

The third G-series nerve agent, soman, boasts improved lethality and persistence over its predecessors tabun and sarin. Volatile, corrosive and colorless, it also interferes with the enzyme responsible for 'turning off' glands and muscles, sending bodily functions into a sort of lethal overdrive. As with many of the substances on this list, the chemistry of life and death are again reflected in soman's origins. German biochemist Richard Kuhn discovered the deadly formula for soman in 1944, a mere six years after winning the Nobel Prize in Chemistry for his work on life-enhancing carotenoids and vitamins. The Germans stockpiled soman but, once more, never unleashed this or any other chemical weapon against armed combatants during the Second World War. Many historians credit this reluctance to a sort of chemical weapons trauma shared by Adolf Hitler and other high-ranking veterans of the First World War. Recently, however, biochemist Frank J. Dinan argued that Hitler's decision stemmed from the advice of chemist Otto Ambros, who misled Hitler into believing the allies also possessed an arsenal of nerve toxins. If Ambros' account is true, that one lie may have prevented the war in Europe from descending into another 'Chemist's war' of poison mists and invisible death.

- **Cyclosarin**

Poet William Butler Yeats observed that 'the best lack all conviction, while the worst are full of passionate intensity.' Study the evolution of man-made nerve toxins and you're bound to agree with him. Just consider cylosarin. Like its predecessors tabun, sarin and soman, this G-series nerve agent disrupts communication between organs and the brain - only it does so with deadlier finesse. Not only is cylosarin five times more lethal than sarin, it's also five times more durable. Cylosarin's physical characteristics at least make it easier to detect. While still a colorless liquid, it boasts a sweet, musty odor reminiscent of peaches. But it also evaporates at a far slower rate, increasing the likelihood of exposure. Fortunately, cylosarin's enhanced lethality comes at an enhanced price. Expensive chemical precursors largely prohibited its mass production. While Iraq reportedly used cylosarin in the Iran-Iraq war, they did so as part of a sarin/cylosarin mixture.

- **VX**

The victors of World War II wasted no time in plundering the secrets of their fallen adversaries. In Japan this meant Unit 731's heinously obtained medical findings on disease. In Germany, this meant rocketry, atomic science and the G-series nerve agents. These dark secrets soon gave birth to a new era of terrifying weaponry. By the early 1950s, the United Kingdom's Porton Down Laboratory had developed a new breed of nerve toxin: VX, the first of the dreaded V-series chemicals. In 1958 the British traded the formula for VX with the United States in exchange for the secrets of thermonuclear weaponry. By 1961 U.S. VX production was in full swing. The Soviet Union developed its own V-series nerve toxins, but, thankfully, saner heads seemed to prevail. As the Cold War between the U.S. and the U.S.S.R. thawed, both countries destroyed their chemical stockpiles. Like its fellow nerve agents, VX kills swiftly by assaulting the acetylchlolinesterase that serves as the off switch for glands and muscle. Its lethality is roughly 10 times that of sarin. Any skin contact with VX liquid is almost certainly fatal if not washed off immediately, and its high-durability allows it to remain in cold environments for months. As such, a VX-saturated area would be considered a long-term hazard – a no-man's land of invisible death.

- **Novichoks**

Before the Cold War ended and ink dried on the 1997 Chemical Weapons Convention, the Soviet Union developed the so-called 'novichoks.' Russian for 'new comers,' this series of fourth generation chemical weapons includes novichok 5, reportedly five times more toxic than VX and almost impossible to detect. Novichoks agents work much like other nerve agents, sending the body into lethal overdrive by attacking the enzyme that serves as an off switch for glands and muscles. Not much is known about these secretive chemicals, as most revelations about novichoks came via a 1992 disclosure in Moscow News by chemist Vil Mirzayanov, as well as his subsequent treason case. The Soviets began production of novichoks in the 1980s. Presumably those stockpiles are long destroyed, the factories in Uzbekistan that made them dismantled and cleansed. But the secrets of chemical warfare have a way of lingering, as does the inclination to summon them from the properties of the natural world.

• Chlorine Gas

Imagine a weapon so horrible that even those who deploy it are frozen in shock by its lethality. According to some historians, that's exactly what happened at the Second Battle of Ypres back in 1915. In an act that marked modern warfare's first major use of chemical weapons, the Germans deployed thousands of chlorine gas cylinders, wiping out two entire divisions of French and Algerian soldiers with this pungent, yellow-green killer. How awful was it? To quote British poet Wilfred Owen, the final doomed moments of a chlorine gas attack are characterized by 'guttering, choking, drowning' as the victim flounders around 'like a man in fire or lime.' See, when chlorine gas comes into contact with eyes, throat, and lungs, it reacts with moisture to form hydrochloric acid. So it burns. It chokes. It blinds – hence Owen's reference to lime or calcium oxide. Shocked by the gas's effectiveness, the Germans failed to take advantage. The allies held their position, but this was just the beginning of what some called 'The Chemist's War.' Other, more dangerous chemical agents quickly surpassed chlorine gas in the Great War, but chlorine remains an easily attained weapon due to the widespread use of chlorine in sanitation and manufacturing.[18]

What's interesting about this list, especially the last one mentioned, is that not only is "chlorine" used as a chemical warfare weapon, and is already in widespread various uses by mankind today and easy to obtain, but if you'll recall, it just so happens to be the exact same word used to describe the *Pale horse* in *the fourth seal*:

"The pale horse has a rider called 'Death,' and 'Hades was following close behind him' (6:8). The Greek word for 'pale,' chloros, elsewhere in Revelation describes the yellow-green of vegetation (8:7; 9:4). The word is the root for the English 'chlorine.' It is here used for the tell-tale and sickly look of death due to a virulent pestilence. The hue or tint in view here is probably to be understood as the color of a corpse – of death."[19]

Coincidence? Maybe, maybe not. But I do not see the usage of chemical warfare during this time frame, the first half of the 7-year Tribulation, as being totally out of the question. To me, it's plausible contextually as well as based on man's past warring behavior. But here's my point in all this. Imagine the whole planet like this. Imagine this is the daily existence of any person left alive at this time, no matter where they are, no matter where they look. This is all they see. Death everywhere! No wonder it's such a *plague-ridden* time! *Plagues* caused naturally from a planet littered with the death and decay of decomposing corpses everywhere from a butcherous *war* and a sickening *famine*, as well as *plagues* unleashed upon mankind from the usage of man's weapons of war, namely chemical weaponry. If you don't think it's a viable reality, then think again. We just saw that chemical weapons are still being used on people right up to today no matter how many warnings are thrown out there. Furthermore, consider the prophetic time frame of these events. This is during the 7-year Tribulation, specifically the first half. The Church is gone, we have been Raptured prior to the beginning of the 7-year tribulation. Therefore, that means we the Church, the "restraining influence," will be absent from the planet during these 7 years and thus mankind will no longer have any "moral restraint" to keep him from descending into this total dark destructive behavior upon each other. No, I think unfortunately, there will be a multitude of reasons for the multitude of *plagues* that will be unleashed on the planet during this time, causing nearly 2 billion people to be killed, as this man also agrees:

"What is pestilence? Actually, it's the same Greek word as the word for death, thanatos, but here it refers to the cause of death. Jesus said there will be earthquakes, following the famine it could be a word that encompasses natural disaster. I think that's right. If you have war at the level that's going to be happening in this particular time with the kind of weapons that we have today, there is going to be a cataclysm of earthquakes created by the bombs and the missiles and all of that devastating destruction.

It could also refer to natural disasters that God is going to set loose, such as earthquakes and floods. It could refer to biological weapons and chemical weapons which we have in vast abundance which could wipe out millions of people-one quart of nerve gas can kill a million people. It could refer to diseases.

Listen, when you have worldwide war and the devastation that's going to take place with that worldwide war, followed by the famine that's going to take place, you know as well as I do that there's going to be a problem with health, sanitation, all of those things.

I don't know if you remember this, but 20 million people died in flu epidemics in World War I because as nations moved around they brought viruses with them. Six million more died of Typhus in World War I. Mass death even by some pestilence disease like AIDS is possible. And there are more massive killing bacteria around. Typhus, you remember, killed 200 million people in four centuries.

We underestimate the power of disease to wipe out whole populations. "[20]

The **fourth cause** of this nearly 2 billion deaths on planet earth in *the fourth seal* is **Wild Beasts**.

Revelation 6:8b-i "Its rider was named Death, and Hades was following close behind him. They were given power over a fourth of the earth to kill by sword, famine and plague, *and by the wild beasts of the earth.*"

Basically, just when you thought it couldn't get any worse, now we are informed of the *fourth cause* of nearly 2 billion people dying in the first half of the 7-year Tribulation. Again, unlike the first two, and like just the third one, this cause has not been mentioned before, but it is certainly mentioned as part of the quadruple judgmental package that God unleashed in the past on wicked and rebellious people and will likewise do the same here in our text in the near future. He will be sending *the wild beasts of the earth* to attack man:

Jeremiah 15:2-3 "And if they ask you, 'Where shall we go?' tell them, 'This is what the LORD says: 'Those destined for death, to death; those for the *sword*, to the sword; those for *starvation*, to starvation; those for captivity, to captivity.' 'I will send four kinds of destroyers against them,' declares the LORD, 'the *sword* to kill and the *dogs* to drag away and the *birds of the air* and the *beasts of the earth* to devour and destroy.'"

Ezekiel 14:21 "For this is what the Sovereign LORD says: How much worse will it be when I send against Jerusalem my four dreadful judgments – *sword* and *famine* and *wild beasts* and *plague* – to kill its men and their animals!"

The general idea and picture here is, again, there will be no escape. You might make it through the butcherous war and sickening famine and even the *plague*-ridden existence, but just when you thought you were safe, just when you started to smile in relief, *the wild beasts* came and got you, and literally ate you

214

alive! Believe it or not, as wild as it sounds, this is not the first time in the Bible that God has used the animal kingdom that He created to do His will:

- God caused FROGS to invade Egypt: Exodus 8

- God caused GNATS to invade Egypt: Exodus 8

- God caused FLIES to invade Egypt: Exodus 8

- God caused the LIVESTOCK of Egypt only to die: Exodus 9

- God caused LOCUSTS to invade Egypt: Exodus 10

- God caused QUAIL to come for food: Numbers 11

- God caused poisonous SNAKES to bite people: Numbers 21

- God caused HORNETS to invade: Joshua 24

- God caused BEARS to maul youths: 2 Kings 2

- God caused a DONKEY talk and rebuke Balaam: Numbers 22

And so, it is that God will also cause *the wild beasts of the earth* to attack mankind again in the future during the first half of the7-year Tribulation for their wickedness and rebellion. God in essence reverses the roles of man and animals, and instead of man hunting animals for food, the animals will now seek man out for food, as these men share:

"God gave death and Hades authority to take one-fourth of the world's population. This evidently is the total number that will die as a result of all the catastrophes predicted so far. These catastrophes are war, the resulting famine, and disease. Attacks by wild animals will also contribute to the death rate."

"There is intentional irony in God's reversal of roles as men become the source of food for beasts (Gen.9:2-3 cf. Eze.29:5; Eke.39:17-20; Rev.19:17-18+). When man is disobedient to God, He reverses the original divine order where man was given dominion over the beasts (Gen.1:26-28; Gen.9:2-3) and gives man into the hand of beasts (Lev.26:22; Deu.32:24).

The beasts will be emboldened both because of the emaciated and sickly condition of men and the scarceness of their own food supply. Once food becomes scarce, wild animals which generally leave man alone will begin to attack man for food."[21]

In reality, what is going on here, as unbelievable as it seems, are scenes from the Alfred Hitchcock movie, "The Birds," the rabid dog movie, "Cujo" based on the Stephen King novel, the terrifying watery movie "Jaws" from Stephen Spielberg, or even the jungle movie, "The Ghost and the Darkness" featuring man-eating lions all wrapped into one, all going on simultaneously all around the world! No joke! This is what's coming to the planet! No wonder God said there's no safe place to hide, and no wonder He's been warning us repeatedly and encouraging us unceasingly to escape this horrific time frame through Jesus. In fact, let's again whet our appetite with what this terrible time frame will be like in the very near future for all who reject Jesus Christ and instead align themselves with the Antichrist. Imagine, wherever you go on the planet you run into one of these guys...or all of them:

- **The Lions of Njombe**

This is the worst case of man-eating lions in History. It was not a single man eater, but an entire pride that preferred human flesh over any other kind of food. It happened in 1932 in Tanzania near the town of Njombe. A large pride of lions went into a particularly brutal killing spree. Legend has it that the lions were being controlled by the witch doctor of a local tribe, named Matamula Mangera, who sent them into rampage as revenge against his own people after being deposed of his post. The tribesmen were so terrified of the man-eating lions that they wouldn't even dare speak of them, believing that a simple mention would cause them to appear. They begged the tribe chief to restore the witch doctor to his post, but he refused. The lions kept attacking and, eventually, took over 1,500 human lives (some say over 2000); the worst lion attack in History, and one of the worst cases of animal attacks ever recorded.

- **Two Toed Tom**

This huge male American alligator was said to roam the swamps in the border of Alabama and Florida during the 20s. He had lost all but two of the toes in his left 'hand', and left very recognizable tracks on the mud, so he was nicknamed 'Two Toed Tom' by the local people. He was said to have lost his toes in an iron trap. He measured four and a half meters long, and people claimed he was no normal gator, but a demon sent from Hell to terrorize them. Tom made himself infamous by devouring scores of cows, mules and, of course, humans, particularly women (snatched as they washed clothes in the water). Due to his frequent attacks, many farmers tried to kill Tom, but bullets were said to have little effect on him and all attempts on his life failed. One farmer even tried to kill him using dynamite; the farmer had been chasing Tom for twenty years, unsuccessfully, so he decided to throw fifteen dynamite-filled buckets into the pond were Tom was supposed to live, and finally get rid of the problem once and for all. The explosion killed everything in the pond, but not Tom. Moments after the explosion, the farmer and his son heard a horrible scream and splashing sounds coming from a nearby pond. They rushed to the place and saw Tom's bright eyes for a moment before he disappeared under the surface. The screams were later explained when the half-eaten remains of the farmer's young daughter appeared on the shore. Two Toed Tom was real, and he continued to roam the swamps of Florida for many years. People would constantly report seeing a huge male gator basking in lake shores and hearing his roars every morning. The most amazing part of the story is that, although he was most famous during the 20s, Tom was seemingly still alive during the 80s, when a huge gator lacking two of his toes was reported in the same swamps where he had roamed his entire life. Many hunts for the living legend were organized, but Two Toed Tom was never captured.

- **Kesagake**

The most dangerous wild animal in Japan is usually considered to be the Japanese Giant Hornet, which kills 40 people a year, on average. However, the largest, most powerful land predator in Japan is the Brown Bear, and, perhaps the most brutal bear attack in history took place in the village of Sankebetsu, Hokkaido, in 1915. At the time, Sankebetsu was a pioneer village, with very few people living in a largely wild area. The area was inhabited by brown bears, including a gigantic male known as Kesagake. Kesagake used to visit Sankebetsu to feed on harvested corn; having become a nuisance, he was shot by two villagers and fled to the mountains, injured. The villagers believed that, after being shot, the bear would learn to fear humans and stay away from the crops. They were wrong. On December 9 of 1915, Kesagake showed up again. He entered the house of the Ota family, where the farmer's wife was alone with a baby she was caring for. The bear attacked the baby, killing him, then went for the woman. She tried to defend herself by throwing firewood at the beast, but was eventually dragged to the forest by the bear. When people arrived to the, now empty, house, they found the floor and walls covered in blood. Thirty men went to the forest, determined to kill the bear and recover the unfortunate woman's remains. They found Kesagake and shot him again but failed to kill him. The animal fled, and they found the woman's partially eaten body buried under the snow, where the bear had stored it for later consumption. The bear later returned to the Ota family's farm, and armed guards were sent after him. But this left another village house unprotected, and Kesagake took advantage of this, attacking the Miyoke family's home and mauling everyone inside. Although some of the people managed to escape, two children were killed and so was a pregnant woman who, according to surviving witnesses, begged for her unborn baby's life as the huge bear advanced. Of course, it was all in vain; Kesagake killed her, too. When the guards realized their mistake and returned to the Miyoke house, they found the bodies of the two children, the woman and her unborn baby all laying in the blood-covered floor. In only two days, Kesagake had killed six people. The villagers were terrified and most of the guards abandoned their posts out of fear. The region was soon abandoned by villagers and became a ghost town. Even today, the Sankebetsu incident remains the worst animal attack in the history of Japan, and one of the most brutal of recorded history.

- **The New Jersey Shark**

These shark attacks took place in 1916, in a time where little was known about sharks of any kind, and some scientists even claimed that sharks were not dangerous at all. This is one of the very few cases of real 'man-eating sharks' known, with most shark attacks being isolated incidents. It all happened along the coast of New Jersey; the first victim was a young man named Charles Vansant who was attacked in very shallow water while swimming with a dog; several people, including his family, witnessed the attack, and a lifeguard rushed to rescue the young man. The shark was extremely tenacious and seemingly followed the lifeguard to the shore, disappearing shortly after. The shark's teeth had severed Vansant's femoral arteries and one of his legs had been stripped of its flesh; he bled to death before he could be taken to a hospital. Five days later another man, Charles Bruder, was attacked by the same shark while swimming away from the shore. At first it was reported by a witness that a red canoe had capsized; in reality, the 'red canoe' was a giant stain of Bruder's blood. The shark had bitten off his legs. He was dragged back to the shore, where the sight of his mangled body seemingly 'caused women to faint', but it was too late; he was dead by the time he got to the beach.

Although sharks had been seen in the area during those few days, scientists who were informed of the attacks claimed that sharks were unlikely to be responsible and said that the culprit had probably been a killer whale or a sea turtle! The next attacks took place not in the sea, but in a creek near the town of Matawan. Again, people reported seeing a shark in the creek, but they were ignored until, on July 12, an eleven-year-old boy was attacked while swimming and dragged underwater. Several townspeople rushed to the creek, and a man named Stanley Fisher dove into the water to find the boy's remains, but he too was attacked by the shark and died of his wounds. The final victim was another young boy barely 30 minutes after the attack on Stanley Fisher. Although he was severely injured, he was the only victim to survive. On July 14, a young female Great White Shark was captured in the Raritan Bay near the Matawan Creek. It is said that human remains were found in her stomach. Once confirmed that the Jersey attacks had been the work of a shark, there was media frenzy and a shark panic 'unrivaled in American history'. The incidents inspired Peter Benchley's most famous novel, Jaws, which would later be adapted into a movie by Steven Spielberg. Even today, lots of people who saw the movie are terrified of going into the water, and it all started in 1916.

- **The Bear of Mysore**

Sloth Bears maul many humans in India every year (one per week according to some). They rarely eat meat at all, and prefer to feed on termites and fruits, and are particularly fond of honey. However, there was a Sloth Bear that became infamous for being a man-killer. There are some very strange legends about the origins of the Mysore Killer Bear; some say that the bear was a male and that he had originally abducted a girl as his mate. The girl was rescued by villagers and the bear went into a killing spree as revenge. Another, more believable, version says the bear was a female whose cubs had been killed by humans, and that she became a man-killer to avenge them. However, most experts today believe that the bear was probably injured by humans and became abnormally aggressive as a result. The bear attacked three dozen people in the Indian state of Mysore. In typical Sloth Bear fashion, it would rip the victim's face off with its claws and teeth, and those who survived were often left completely disfigured. 12 of the victims died, and three of them were devoured, something extremely unusual.

- **The Beast of Gevauden**

One of the most infamous man-eaters, as well as the most mysterious of all, was the Beast of Gevauden. This beast (some claim there were actually two of them) terrorized the French province of Gevauden from 1764 to 1767. Although often claimed to have been an unusually large wolf, the truth is the Beast was never really identified. It was said to be larger than a wolf, with a reddish coloration and an unbearable smell, as well as teeth bigger than those of a normal wolf. The creature killed its first victim (a young girl) in June of 1764. This was the first of a series of very unusual attacks, where the beast would target humans, specifically, ignoring cattle and domestic animals. 210 humans were attacked; 113 victims died, and 98 were devoured. The attacks were so frequent and brutal that many believed the creature to be demonic, being sent by God as punishment; others thought it was a loup-garou, a werewolf. Although the mainstream view is that the 'Beast' was probably just a large wolf (or a couple of wolves, since some reports mention two beasts instead of one), the fact remains that the description of the creature doesn't seem to fit a normal European wolf, which was abundant and well known to people at the time. Some experts believe that the Beast may have been a hyena, possibly escaped from a menagerie. Although often seen as cowardly scavengers, hyenas are actually very powerful predators and they often prey on humans in Africa and some parts of Asia. (A man-eating hyena terrorized Malawi quite recently, forcing hundreds of people to leave their villages.) Just like the beast of Gevauden, hyenas are noted for their formidable teeth and strong odor, and they are also bigger and more powerful than average wolves.

- **The Ghost and the Darkness**

In 1898, the British started the construction of a railway bridge over the Tsavo river in Kenya. Over the next nine months, the unfortunate railway workers became the target of two man-eating lions (now known to have been brothers). These lions were huge, measuring over three meters long, and, as is usual among lions from the Tsavo region, they were maneless. At first, the two lions snatched the men from their tents, dragging them to the bush and devouring them at night. But soon they became so fearless, that they wouldn't even drag their victims away but would start feeding on their flesh just a few yards from the tents. Their size, ferocity and cunning were so extraordinary that many natives thought that they were not actually lions, but rather demons, or perhaps the reincarnation of ancient local kings trying to repel the British invaders (the belief of dead kings being reborn as lions was once very common in Eastern Africa). The two man-eaters were nicknamed The Ghost and The Darkness, and workers were so afraid of them that they fled by the hundreds out of Tsavo. The railway construction was halted; no one wanted to be the next victim of the 'devil lions'. The lions had killed 140 people. Like other man eaters, they were often said to kill even when not hungry.

- **The Panar Leopard**

The leopard is the smallest of the true 'big cats', but that doesn't make it any less deadly than its bigger relatives. As a matter of fact, the leopard is perhaps our oldest predator; leopard bite marks have been found in the fossil bones of our relatives, suggesting that the spotted cat was already dining on our ancestors long ago. The deadliest man-eating leopard of all times was the Panar leopard. This male leopard lived in the Kumaon area of India during the early 20th century. He was most active in the Panar province, where he killed over 400 people, being the second most prolific man eater in recorded history. It seems that the leopard had been injured by a hunter, and rendered unable to hunt wild animals, so it turned to man-eating to survive. Although the Panar leopard is the most infamous of all, there were others that were just as feared. The Kahani man-eater, for example, killed over 200 people, and the Rudraprayag man-eater, that stalked and killed pilgrims en route to a Hindu shrine, killed 125 people.

- **The Champawat Tigress**

During the late 19th century, a Nepalese region close to the Himalayas was terrorized by the most notorious and prolific man-eater of all times. Men, women and children were ambushed in the jungle by the dozens. The attacks were so frequent and so bloody that people started talking about demons, and even punishment from the gods. The one responsible was a Bengal tigress who had been shot by a hunter. She had escaped, but the bullet had broken two of her fangs. In constant pain, and rendered unable to hunt her usual prey, the tigress had become adam khor, a man eater. Soon, the victim count of the tigress reached 200. Hunters were sent to kill the beast, but she was too cunning and was seldom even seen by them. Eventually, the Nepalese government decided that the problem was big enough to send the National Army after the killer cat. Other than the case of the Gevauden beast, this was probably the only time in History when the army was deemed necessary to deal with a man eater. But they failed to capture the tigress. It is said that with every human she killed, she became bolder and more fearless, and eventually she started attacking in broad daylight and prowling around villages. Men wouldn't even dare leave their huts to work, for they could hear the roaring of the killer tigress in the forest, waiting for them. The tigress had killed 436 humans, and these were only the recorded victims, with probably many more who were never reported. She is still the most prolific individual man eater in History. Not only that; she killed more people than even the worst human serial killers (leaving genocide aside).

- **Gustave**

In the African, conflict-ridden country of Burundi lives the greatest man-eater of our time, a male Nile crocodile measuring six meters long and weighing around one ton. He is the largest Nile crocodile alive, as well as the largest individual predator in the entire African continent, and according to the natives, and to Patrice Faye (a French naturalist who has spent years trying to capture the man-eater), he has killed over 300 people by now! Although still alive and active, the crocodile (nicknamed 'Gustave' by Faye) has already become a legend. Natives say he kills for fun, not just for food; that he kills several people in every attack, and then disappears for months, or even years, only to reappear later in another, different location to kill again. No one can predict when or where he will appear next. He is also said to have a monstrous appetite, and rumor has it that he killed and devoured an adult male hippopotamus (an extremely dangerous and powerful animal that most crocodiles avoid). Gustave's body armor carries countless scars made by knives, spears and even firearms. A dark spot on the top of his head is the only remaining trace of a bullet wound that was supposed to put an end to his reign. But all hunters (and even, once, a group of armed soldiers) have failed to kill him. Faye himself tried to capture Gustave by building a huge underwater trap but, although the crocodile did show up, he never approached the cage. He just swam around it, 'as if mocking his would-be captors'. Said to be over 60 years old, Gustave is probably too experienced and smart to be fooled, so it seems likely that he will continue with his depredations and perhaps, soon, claim the title of the most prolific man eater for himself.[22]

Some would even add rats and rodents to this list of *wild beasts* that cause *one fourth of the earth to be killed.* That could also very well fit the context, especially when you take into account the combination of *plague* or pestilence, as this man shares:

"And then in Revelation 6 he adds not only pestilence, but he adds wild beasts. You say, 'What is that? We don't have any wild beasts in America? What's this talking about? We don't have wild beasts or anything, you've got to go to Africa to find lions or up in China somewhere to find Siberian tigers or whatever. What wild beasts?'

Let me ask you a question. Do you know the deadliest creature on the face of the earth? Not a snake, not a lion, not an alligator, a rat. Historically the deadliest creature on the face of the earth. Why?

Rats are annually responsible for the loss of billions of dollars of food in America alone, and death all over the world. Rats infested with Bubonic Plague killed one third of the population of Europe in the fourteenth century-that's Encyclopedia Americana's own figure. Rats can carry as many as thirty-five diseases at once and, amazingly, if ninety-five percent of the rat population is exterminated in a given area, it will replace itself in less than a year. It has killed more people than all the wars of history and it always makes its home where men dwell."[23]

So, take your pick of *wild beasts* and imagine this is your soon future reality, all because you laughed and mocked and scoffed like the Israelites of long ago who listened to lying prophets telling them everything was going to be fine when it wasn't. You may have somehow someway survived the bloodiest butchering in mankind's history. You may have managed to barely make it through the worst famine this planet has ever seen including getting eaten by other people. You may have even been one of the fortunate few who lived through plague after plague, man-made or natural. But now you turned the corner and Gustave was there. You ran away from him only to land in a pit of rats. You jumped out of that pit only to be chased down by a lion, tiger or leopard, or maybe all three. You jumped into the water to hide only to be surrounded by a band of sharks. You headed for higher ground only to have a pack of wolves running after you licking their chops. No sooner had you escaped them than a bunch of bears came out of the woods charging after you looking to maul you and eat you alive! This is no joke, this is your future, unless you accept Jesus Christ as your Lord and Savior *right now*! Please respond before it's too late!

In fact, to hopefully reach out to even the stubbornest diehard skeptic who states something like, "Well I don't have to worry about any of these so-called *wild beasts* attacking me because I live in the middle of America and these beasts only live in Africa or some other far off country or continent. I'm safe right here where I'm at." Really? You might want to think again. Look around. We have *zoos* that are full of *wild beasts* in virtually every major city of America and approximately *10,000 zoos worldwide.*[24] The point is, even today, during certain calamities, these *wild beasts in zoos* get loose and go hunting after humans, as this recent report reveals:

"Zoo Animals on the Loose After Deadly Flooding Hits Tbilisi, Georgia. The country of Georgia mobilized its special forces on Sunday and warned residents in the capital not to leave their homes after lions, tigers and bears – among other animals – escaped during floods that have claimed at least 12 human lives.

Heavy rains and wind hit Tbilisi overnight on Saturday, turning a normally small stream that runs through the hilly city into a surging river. Officials said 12 people were known to have died and about two dozen others were missing. The surging floodwater destroyed enclosures at the zoo, killing some animals and letting loose others.

Georgian Culture Minister Mikheil Giorgadze told NBC News: 'The special forces are doing everything to control the situation. We are all mobilized.'

It wasn't immediately clear if any of the people killed were attacked by animals. Three zoo workers were killed in the floods, the zoo said. One of them was Guliko Chitadze, a zookeeper who lost an arm in an attack by a tiger last month.

Helicopters were circling the city and residents were told to stay indoors except in case of an emergency.

A spokeswoman for the zoo told NBC News that many of the animals were killed in the flooding or by special forces, but it was not known how many remained at large.

'Not many animals are still on the loose, but it is difficult to say how many are still out there,' Mzia Sharashidze said.

Footage from Tbilisi showed a hippopotamus roaming the streets, while a bear could be seen climbing around an apartment window. The hippo was cornered in one of the city's main squares and subdued with a tranquilizer gun, the zoo said.

Six wolves were shot dead in a yard at an infectious diseases hospital, while NBC News viewed images of a dead lion, hyena, and a wolf – all presumably drowned in the floods.

The head of the Georgian Orthodox Church, Patriarch Ilia II, was quoted by the Interfax news agency as telling a Sunday Mass that Georgia's former Communist rulers bear responsibility for the disaster.

'When Communists came to us in this country, they ordered that all crosses and bells of the churches be melted down and the money used to build the zoo,' he said. 'The sin will not go without punishment. I am very sorry that Georgians fell because a zoo was built at the expense of destroyed churches.'"[25]

So, it is that another sin on a global scale will likewise not go unpunished, that of rejecting the love and mercy and forgiveness of Jesus Christ for the lies and false promises and false utopia of the Antichrist. Because of that, God gave *Death* and *Hades power over a fourth of the earth to kill by sword, famine and plague, and by the wild beasts of the earth.* Imagine this scenario in the 7-year Tribulation, when all kind of calamities hit on a global scale. Not just one but most likely 1000's of zoo animals from 1000's of zoos from around the world will escape. When calamities of this scope and size are unleashed, these *wild beasts* will not only get loose, but they too will become extra hungry in these global famine conditions, and thus will in turn hunt mankind down for food, aiding in this accumulation of nearly 2 billion people being *killed.* There was no escape in the past, there will be no escape in the future. Let us recall these passages of Scripture:

Ezekiel 33:27 "Thus shalt thou say unto them, 'Thus saith the Lord Jehovah: As I live, surely, they that are in the waste places shall fall by the sword; and him that is in the open field will I give to the beasts to be devoured; and they that are in the strongholds and in the caves shall die of the pestilence.'"

Amos 5:18-20 "Woe unto you that desire the day of Jehovah! Wherefore would ye have the day of Jehovah? It is darkness, and not light. As if a man did flee from a lion, and a bear met him; or went into the house and leaned his hand on the wall, and a serpent bit him. Shall not the day of Jehovah be darkness, and not light? Even very dark, and no brightness in it?"

How many different ways does God have to show us how horrible these judgments coming for wicked and rebellious mankind really are before we will listen? How many times does He have to warn us to repent and get saved *now* through Jesus before it's too late? How blunt does He have to be? *One fourth of the earth* will be *killed* in four different ways in *the fourth seal* judgment. By *sword, famine, plague,* and *the wild beasts of the earth*. There is only one way to escape this wretched reality (Jesus) and only one time to escape this horrible future (now). Turn to Him, I implore you. Jesus has provided the only way of escape, as this man shares:

"In Ezekiel chapter 14, starting in verse 13, listen to this, 'Son of man, if a country sins against Me by committing unfaithfulness and I stretch out My hand against it, destroy its supply of bread, send famine against it and cut off from it both man and beast, even though these three men, Noah, Daniel and Job, were in its midst, by their own righteousness they could deliver only themselves, declares the Lord God.

If I were to cause wild beasts to pass through the land and they depopulated it and it became desolate so that no one would pass through it because of the beasts, though these three men were in its midst as I live, declares the Lord God, they couldn't deliver either their sons or their daughters.'

In other words, the presence of righteous men ultimately won't stop the judgement.

'If I were to bring a sword on that country and say let the sword pass through the country and cut off man and beast from it, even though these three men were in its midst, Noah, Daniel and Jonah...or Job, rather, as I live they couldn't deliver their sons or their daughters.

'Or if I send a plague,' there are all four, 'against that country and pour out My wrath in blood on it to cut off man and beast even though Noah, Daniel and Job were in its midst, as I live they couldn't deliver it. For thus says the Lord God, how much more when I send My four severe judgments, sword, famine, wild beasts and plague to cut off man and beast from it.'

In other words, if they couldn't endure when one of them came, what are they going to do when all four hit at the same time? They're going to hit.

With war and famine and earthquakes, sanitation goes. No medicine, living conditions descend to a primitive level and the rats may be the wild beasts that run wild to kill. Awesome, divine judgment. And this is only the beginning...only the beginning, far more to come.

You would ask a question, 'Is there any hope for our world?' And the answer is no, there's no hope, this will come...this is inevitable. You ask another question, 'Is there any hope for me?' The answer is yes, yes, there's hope for you in Jesus Christ. Jesus has provided a way of escape.

Is it any wonder that the writer of Hebrews said, 'How shall we escape if we neglect so great a salvation?' And the answer is, we won't."[26]

So far, we've seen the increasingly horrible slaughter of *one fourth* of the unbelieving Antichrist followers, the inhabitants of the earth, in *the fourth seal.* Now we will see the slaughter of the people who actually do turn to God during the 7-year Tribulation. That is the topic of the next seal showing us the worst is yet to come:

"The four devilish forces, along with their four kinds of woe falling on a fourth of humanity, represent 'all the ways that death can come and which all result in death.' These first four seal judgments appear to be just 'a preliminary phase of the more terrible judgments to follow.'"[27]

Chapter Nine

The Breaking of the Martyrdom Seal

The **tenth thing** we see in the breaking of the planet is the **Ordering of the Fifth Seal**.

Revelation 6:9 *"When He opened the fifth seal*, I saw under the altar the souls of those who had been slain because of the word of God and the testimony they had maintained."

Now, before we get into just who these people are that are being *slain because of the word of God* in the 7-year Tribulation, we once again need to pay attention to just Who is in charge here and Who is *ordering the fifth seal*. It is *He.* So, the obvious question is, "Who is *He*." Well, based on the context, it's once again none other than *God Himself the Lamb.* Let us recall the context of how each seal begins:

Revelation 6:1a "I watched as the *Lamb* opened the first of the seven seals."

Revelation 6:3 "When the *Lamb* opened the second seal, I heard the second living creature say, 'Come!'"

Revelation 6:5 "When the *Lamb* opened the third seal, I heard the third living creature say, 'Come!'"

Revelation 6:7 "When the *Lamb* opened the fourth seal, I heard the voice of the fourth living creature say, 'Come!'"

Revelation 6:9 "When *He* opened the fifth seal, I saw under the altar the souls of those who had been slain because of the Word of God and the testimony they had maintained."

Revelation 6:12 "I watched as *He* opened the sixth seal. There was a great earthquake. The sun turned black like sackcloth made of goat hair, the whole moon turned blood red," ...

Revelation 8:1 "When *He* opened the seventh seal, there was silence in heaven for about half an hour."

Who is the One ordering and opening *the fifth seal*? As you can see, it is made absolutely clear in the beginning of each and every seal. It is *the Lamb, He, God*, who is doing all this. The first four times it's *the Lamb*, and the next three times it's *He*, obviously still speaking of *the Lamb* in the context. Therefore, once again, how anyone can say these events are the supposed wrath of man or satan is not only unbelievable, but it's downright unbiblical. God is the One in charge here, no one else! It is *He* that is at the helm, it is *He* that is ordering this, it is *He* that is calling the shots, make no mistake about it. How many times does *He* have to tell us before we get the message?

The **eleventh thing** we see in the breaking of the planet is the **Object of the Fifth Seal**.

As was stated at the end of the previous chapter, we are about to see events on planet earth get even worse if you can believe it. As we shall soon see, this *fifth seal* is the breaking of the Martyrdom Seal. *The murder of God's people* in the 7-year Tribulation is the *object* of discussion. Thus, the unbelieving world will now sink to a new low under the judgment of God in *the fifth seal*. Mankind does not reveal their so-called human potential greatness as they boast of even today. Rather they will instead demonstrate what God has known all along ever since the fall of man, their utter total depravity and their lust for murder and wickedness. It started with unrighteous Cain killing his righteous brother Abel for doing what is right and exposing Cain's wrong. It continued throughout history with the Jewish people, from whose loins would eventually come the Messiah, Jesus, being hunted down and suffering repeated attempts to remove them from the face of the earth, all the way from Haman to Hitler. So it will be again here in the 7-year tribulation. Once again wicked man rises up against God's righteous people and seeks to *murder* them. Only this time, it will be on a scale that will make even what Hitler did to the Jewish people during World War II look like child's play. This is the *object* of *the fifth seal*.

Revelation 6:9-11 "When he opened the fifth seal, I saw under the altar the souls of those who had been slain because of the word of God and the testimony they had maintained. They called out in a loud voice, 'How long, Sovereign Lord, holy and true, until You judge the inhabitants of the earth and avenge our blood?' Then each of them was given a white robe, and they were told to wait a little longer, until the number of their fellow servants and brothers who were to be killed as they had been was completed."

Matthew 24:9-13 "Then you will be handed over to be persecuted and put to death, and you will be hated by all nations because of Me. At that time many will turn away from the faith and will betray and hate each other, and many false prophets will appear and deceive many people. Because of the increase of wickedness, the love of most will grow cold, but he who stands firm to the end will be saved."

As we've already seen repeatedly, Revelation 6, and Matthew 24 are prophetically dealing with the same time-frame, the beginning portion of the 7-year Tribulation. Therefore, by observing these passages together, we can see that what the planet is in store for now is simply *the mass murder of God's people*. We know this *fifth seal* judgement is dealing with *the murder of God's people* on a global scale simply due to what the texts state. They were *slain because of the word of God*. They were *under the altar* located in heaven. They called out to God to *judge the inhabitants of the earth*, that is, the unbelieving Antichrist followers. They were *given a white robe* used for righteous people. They were *killed* along with *their fellow servants and brothers*. They were *persecuted* and *put to death*. They were *hated by all nations*. So, it is obvious that we are dealing with the *Global Martyrdom* and *the mass murder of God's people* in the 7-year Tribulation. Now, this shouldn't surprise us because Jesus told us this progression of wickedness in the 7-year Tribulation would happen. He likened these events in the 7-year Tribulation to *birth pains*.

Matthew 24:4-9 "Jesus answered: 'Watch out that no one deceives you. For many will come in My Name, claiming, 'I am the Christ,' and will deceive many. You will hear of wars and rumors of wars but see to it that you are not alarmed. Such things must happen, but the end is still to come. Nation will rise against nation, and kingdom against kingdom. There will be famines and earthquakes in various places. *All these are the beginning of birth pains.* Then you will be handed over to be persecuted and put to death, and you will be hated by all nations because of Me.'"

The word Jesus used there for *birth pain* is the Greek word "odin" pronounced "odeen" and it means, "the pain of childbirth, intolerable anguish." This is the reference He used to describe the dire horrible painful calamities that precede His Second Coming at the end of the 7-year Tribulation. Now any mother will tell you that the closer you get to the actual birth of a baby the *birth pains* increase in intensity. I recall when our first child, our daughter Rebecca, was born, that the hospital staff had my wife hooked up to some electronic digital device that measured the intensity of her *birth pains*. At first the numbers on the digital meter started out kind of low, but as time went on they soon got into the double digits and then even progressed high above the 100 mark. In fact, I did the "guy thing" and kept faithfully reporting to my wife each time she was "breaking a new high number" on the meter which, for some reason, she didn't seem to appreciate. Yet nonetheless, the numbers continued to escalate and even when I thought the numbers surely couldn't go any higher, they not only did, but they continued to do so right on up until the actual birth of our daughter. My point is, this is the exact same analogy that Jesus is likening to the events of the 7-year tribulation leading up to the *birth* or His Second Coming at the end of the 7-year Tribulation. It's going to gain in intensity as you go. Just when you thought it couldn't get any worse, it will. Just when you thought you couldn't hit an all new high, it gets even higher. And once this procedure begins, there's no stopping it!

Now let's go back to our passage. Once again, these events in Matthew 24 follow in perfect order to the events mentioned in Revelation Chapter 6. The *deceit* of the Antichrist and the *white horse rider*. The *global wars* and the slaughter of people in the *red horse rider*. The *famines* in various places from the *black horse rider*. The parallel passage of Luke 21 showed us the *global pestilence* and the *pale horse rider*. But now here's what I want you to note. Before we get to the events of *the fifth seal* in Revelation 6 we see this parallel phrase here in Matthew 24, *"all these are the beginning of birth pains."* What are *these*? It's the global deceit, global war, global famine, global death of people caused four different ways. Jesus is saying that *all these are the beginning of birth pains*. In other words, *you thought the first four seals were bad*? Wait until you see what happens next, including the murderous events of *the fifth seal*. This should not only get our attention, but it shows us that the planet is going to disintegrate even further, as this man shares:

"Like a woman has a child and the birth pains have a certain distance or a certain space between them as they begin, they get closer and closer and closer and closer together until they are coming rather rapidly just before the child is born, so it is in the time of the Great Tribulation. The beginning of sorrows has a certain distance between them and then they get closer and closer until they're coming almost concurrently in a holocaust of exploding trauma that occurs at the very end, when the kingdom comes.

If we read the other scriptures properly, they tell us that the time of the Tribulation, the time of the birth pains, will be a time when all the systems of man begin to disintegrate, a time when the Lord removes the restraining influence of the Holy Spirit, which holds back sin from reaching its maximum potential. All that will be removed, and sin will run wild.

And so, it is at that time, as the system begins to be destroyed by its own sinfulness, that there will arise a whole lot of false deliverers and false Messiahs trying to get people to follow them. The epitome of that group will be one called Antichrist. And he will be the ultimate false Messiah, the ultimate false savior that the world will ever see. And there may even be others competing for his power until he finally secures power worldwide.

That time period is going to be characterized by wars and rumors of wars. If you're not involved in one immediately, or even if you are, you'll hear about other wars. Hot war, cold war, every conceivable kind of war – global warfare, nation against nation, kingdom against kingdom. There will be worldwide warfare on a scale unknown prior to that time. In massive proportions, there will be an intensification of war across the earth.

In addition to the false Christs, in addition to the worldwide massacres and the wars, there will be disasters of staggering proportions over all the whole earth as the cursed earth itself begins to disintegrate. Famines, earthquakes, pestilences, fearful sights, and great signs from heaven. That's all going to mark that end time. The whole world begins to disintegrate.

Now, again, the world has had its share of famines. The world has had its share of plagues, its share of horrible events, holocausts. There have even been times when there have been unusual signs in the heavens. But nothing – nothing to even come close to this. Never to this extent and on this wide a scale in the history of the world. The whole world begins to self-destruct when sin runs rampant.

You see, the Lord has restrained sin. He is today restraining sin for the preservation of His people, for the preservation of His earth. But when He takes that restraining back, when He removes the restraint – and I believe that is concurrent with the Rapture of the Church – the Church is taken out so that we're not even here when all these things happen. We go out at the beginning – at the beginning of the 7-year Tribulation. We're taken out, then comes the Tribulation.

When the Church goes and all the redeemed are off the face of the earth, and as 2 Thessalonians says, 'God takes back the restraint,' then everything begins to disintegrate. And the created earth can't support the evil of the people in it when that evil is unrestrained. And everything in the universe begins to fly apart. The whole world begins to crumble. Sin runs rampant.

And the Lord says, 'All these are just the beginning of the end.' Just the beginning."[1]

Just the beginning of what? Of events that will be even worse than what you've already seen thus far with *the first four seals*, the global deceit, global war, global famine, and the global death of people caused by four different means. What makes this next turn of events even worse, or an increase in the *birth pain* scale, is that when *He*, God, *opens the fifth seal* we will now be moving from the slaughter and demise of the unbelieving Antichrist followers, *the inhabitants of the earth*, to the slaughter and martyrdom of the people who actually do turn to God during the 7-year Tribulation. Just when you thought things couldn't get any worse, they do. Just when you thought you've seen it all, here comes another wave of wickedness. Just when you thought mankind couldn't sink to a new low, he goes to an even deeper one. Apparently killing themselves wasn't enough. Now they will be seen butchering on a scale like never before, godly righteous people who were only trying to help them. It's senseless, ruthless, heartless, and wickedness unrestrained. There doesn't seem to be any sense of decency left at this point in the world. This will be the worst and most unprecedented time of global martyrdom and anti-Semitism this planet has ever seen or will ever see again. A whole new bloody holocaust on a scale never before is coming to the planet. Again, it will make what Hitler did look like chump change. The whole planet begins to unravel in its sinful demise and rejection of God, and things progressively get even worse from this point forward. This is what the *fifth seal* is all about. *He*, God, is abundantly clear and extremely graphic about it.

The **first question** about the object of the fifth seal is **The Identity of the Martyrs**.

Revelation 6:9-11 "When he opened the fifth seal, I saw under the altar *the souls of those who had been slain because of the word of God* and the testimony they had maintained. They called out in a loud voice, 'How long, Sovereign Lord, holy and true, until You judge the inhabitants of the earth and avenge our blood?' Then *each of them was given a white robe*, and they were told to wait a little longer, until the number of their fellow servants and brothers who were to be killed as they had been was completed."

Before we go any further in describing the events of *the fifth seal*, we need to take the time to clarify the identity of the ones who are being martyred here. I say that because some people unfortunately and erroneously say that these people being murdered here is the Church. They make this faulty assumption because of phrases in the text like, "they were slain because of the Word of God," "they maintained a testimony," "they cried out to God," and "they were given a white robe," and wrongly assume that since these are words and phrases used today as the Church, these people being slain here must be the Church. Not true. Rather, "context" is what determines the meaning of any given word in any given passage of the Bible.

For example, as we saw in our previous study, *The Rapture: Don't Be Deceived*, if you take the one English word, "cool" you can use it in many different ways. Even though it's spelled the exact same way, with the exact same letters, the "context" determines its meaning. For instance, what if I were to state the three following sentences:

- "Wow! That outfit you have on is cool!"
- "Hey, is everything okay? Your attitude towards me is kind of cool."
- "Brrrr. The weather outside is cool."

Now, notice how all three times, the word "cool" was spelled the exact same way but each one had a *totally different meaning*. What determined the *correct meaning* was the "context" in which it occurred. So it is with the martyred *souls of those who had been slain because of the word of God*. We know contextually that these *souls cannot be referring to the Church* because we've already seen a plethora of evidence that the Church is not even on planet earth during this time, let alone any time during the 7-year Tribulation. Rather, the Church escapes this time of God's wrath at the Rapture prior to the 7-year Tribulation as is indicated by the following evidence:

- The Jewish People and the Unbelieving Gentiles are the Audience of the 7-year Tribulation.

- The Church is not mentioned even once during the events of the 7-year Tribulation.

- The Church is promised not to experience God's wrath being poured out in the 7-year Tribulation.

- The Church is specifically promised to be kept from the 7-year Tribulation.

- The Church is seen up in heaven during the 7-year Tribulation.

- The Church comes back with Jesus at His Second Coming at the end of the 7-year Tribulation.

Furthermore, the context of the parallel passages of Revelation 6, that of Matthew 24 and Daniel 9, shows us that the audience has nothing to do with the Church.

- Matthew 24 deals with a rebuilt Jewish Temple with Jewish people apparently worshipping at it again. This has no significance for the Church because Jesus says the Church doesn't need a manmade Temple since we have become the Temple of God by the indwelling Holy Spirit.

- Matthew 24 tells the people during that time frame to "flee to the mountains." This cannot be the Church because only a small minute fraction of the Church lives in Israel. Also, if the place to "flee to" is the ancient rock city of Petra, as many scholars believe it is, there's no way that the whole Church could fit into it. But the Jewish people can.

- Matthew 24 also mentioned people "keeping the Sabbath." This cannot be referring to the Church to the Church doesn't observe a traditional Jewish Saturday Sabbath, but rather we worship on Sunday in honor of the Resurrection of our Lord Jesus Christ.

- The Church is never mentioned once in Daniel Chapter 9.

- The Church wasn't even in existence until 570 years after the Book of Daniel was written.

- The Old Testament writers, including Daniel, had no knowledge of the Church. The New Testament declares that it was a "mystery" to them.

- The Book of Daniel was written by a Jewish man with a Jewish name, for a Jewish people, for a Jewish time, not the Church.

- This time is also referred to in the Bible as Jacob's trouble, not the Church's trouble. It's not "Paul's Doom" or "Peter's Demise" or even "Ananias' Agony." It's Jacob's trouble, referring to the Jewish people.

Furthermore, if there is one thing the Bible is clear about, the Church is *saved from, rescued from,* and *not appointed unto God's wrath* in the 7-year Tribulation.

Romans 5:8-11 "But God demonstrates His own love for us in this: While we were still sinners, Christ died for us. Since we have now been justified by His blood, how much more shall we be *saved from God's wrath* through Him! For if, when we were God's enemies, we were reconciled to Him through the death of His Son, how much more, having been reconciled, shall we be saved through His life! Not only is this so, but we also rejoice in God through our Lord Jesus Christ, through whom we have now received reconciliation."

1 Thessalonians 1:10 "And to wait for His Son from heaven, whom He raised from the dead – Jesus, who *rescues us from the coming wrath.*"

1 Thessalonians 5:9-11 "For *God did not appoint us to suffer wrath* but to receive salvation through our Lord Jesus Christ. He died for us so that, whether we are awake or asleep, we may live together with Him. Therefore encourage one another and build each other up, just as in fact you are doing."

So, as you can see, the Bible clearly and emphatically declares that the Church is *saved from, rescued from*, and *not appointed unto* God's wrath, which includes His wrath being poured out during the 7-year Tribulation which begins with the opening of the seals. This is one of the most abundantly clear things we have been seeing in our study of Revelation 6. How many times has God stated that *He, the Lamb, God Himself,* is the One responsible for opening these seals and pouring out *His wrath* upon planet earth? Again, this is not man or satan's wrath, it is Almighty God's wrath, and He promised His beloved Bride, *the Church*, that *He will save, rescue,* and *not appoint them to His wrath*. Again, for an exhaustive detailed discussion of this Biblical truth of the Church being absent from the earth during the final week of Daniel's 70th week prophecy, the 7-year Tribulation, please check out our previous study, *The Rapture: Don't Be Deceived*.[2]

But as you can see, contextually, there is no way you can say that these *souls who had been slain because of the word of God* refer to the Church. So, the question is, "Who are they?" Well, they are simply identified as *the Tribulation saints*, or those who get saved *during the 7-year Tribulation*. First of all, we know that people can and will get saved during the 7-year Tribulation due to the powerful evangelism campaign going on in the world through the 144,000 male Jewish evangelists, the two witnesses, and the angel that flies through the sky declaring the eternal gospel.

Revelation 7:4,9 "Then I heard the number of those who were sealed: 144,000 from all the tribes of Israel. After this I looked and there before me was a great multitude that no one could count, from every nation, tribe, people and language, standing before the throne and in front of the Lamb. They were wearing white robes and were holding palm branches in their hands."

Revelation 11:3 "And I will give power to my two witnesses, and they will prophesy for 1,260 days, clothed in sackcloth."

Revelation 14:6 "Then I saw another angel flying in midair, and he had the eternal gospel to proclaim to those who live on the earth – to every nation, tribe, language and people."

Furthermore, we see the "fruit" of these efforts to share the Gospel in the 7-year Tribulation by looking at the "context" of what immediately follows after the mentioning of the identity and ministry of the 144,000 male Jewish evangelists. You see people all over the world getting saved.

Revelation 7:9-16 "After this I looked and there before me was *a great multitude that no one could count, from every nation, tribe, people and language*, standing before the throne and in front of the Lamb. They were wearing *white robes* and were holding palm branches in their hands. And they cried out in a loud voice: 'Salvation belongs to our God, who sits on the throne, and to the Lamb.' All the angels were standing around the throne and around the elders and the four living creatures. They fell down on their faces before the throne and worshiped God, saying: 'Amen! Praise and glory and wisdom and thanks and honor and power and strength be to our God for ever and ever. Amen!' Then one of the elders asked me, 'These in *white robes* – who are they, and where did they come from?' I answered, 'Sir, you know.' And he said, 'These are t*hey who have come out of the great tribulation*; they have washed their *robes* and made then *white* in the blood of the Lamb. Therefore, they are before the throne of God and serve him day and night in his temple; and he who sits on the throne will spread his tent over them. Never again will they hunger; never again will they thirst. The sun will not beat upon them, nor any scorching heat.'"

In other words, they will no longer have to experience the horrible atrocities of the 7-year Tribulation, the *hunger, thirst*, and *scorching heat*, mentioning just a few of the things that take place during that time frame. As you can see, it's not only clear that the Gospel goes forth even in the 7-year Tribulation, but it has a great effect. Many Tribulation saints are saved. A *great multitude that no one could count, from every nation, tribe, people and language* got saved. Therefore, that's how we are to rightly interpret the word "saint" and its usage throughout the horrible events of the 7-year Tribulation. Contextually, it cannot be referring to the Church. Rather, it has to be the *Tribulation saints*, the *multitude* that get saved during the 7-year Tribulation. This is the *identity* of the people *who are slain because of the word of God* as is mentioned in *the fifth seal* as well as other passages mentioning *saints* in the 7-year Tribulation:

Revelation 13:7 "He was given power to make war against the *saints* and to conquer them. And he was given authority over every tribe, people, language and nation."

Revelation 13:10 "If anyone is to go into captivity, into captivity he will go. If anyone is to be killed with the sword, with the sword he will be killed. This calls for patient endurance and faithfulness on the part of the *saints*."

Revelation 17:6 "I saw that the woman was drunk with the blood of the *saints*, the blood of those who bore testimony to Jesus."

Just because you see the word *saint* doesn't mean its referring to the Church. As it is with the identity of the martyrs of *the fifth seal,* so it is in these passages. Remember; context, context, context. We are talking about the *Tribulation saints*, the *multitude* who get saved *during the 7-year Tribulation.* The lesson is they should've gotten saved "before" the Rapture occurred prior to the 7-year Tribulation. Yes, they finally got saved; praise God for that, but now they're in a heap of trouble. This is because the Book of Revelation clearly states that most of the people who get saved during that horrible time frame will be horribly murdered and martyred, like we see in *the fifth seal*, and even have their heads chopped off.

Revelation 6:9-10 "When He opened the fifth seal, I saw under the altar the souls of those who had been *slain* because of the word of God and the testimony they had maintained. They called out in a loud voice, 'How long, Sovereign Lord, holy and true, until you judge the inhabitants of the earth and avenge our blood?'"

Revelation 20:4 "And I saw the souls of those who had been *beheaded* because of their testimony for Jesus and because of the word of God. They had not worshiped the beast or his image and had not received his mark on their foreheads or their hands."

Therefore, the point is this. Get saved now before it's too late! You don't want to be there! Once again, this is not a game. If you're reading this book and you're still not saved, what more does God have to do to get your attention? Only the Church age saints, *those who get saved now*, *today*, get to escape this horrible time frame!
But you might be thinking, "Now wait a minute. Some people bring up the fact that these martyrs in *the fifth seal* are wearing *white robes*? Isn't this referring to the Church since the Church also wear *white robes*?" Not at all. This is why the Bible draws a distinction between the *white robes* of the Church and the *white robes* of the Tribulation saints. Its two totally different words. The

martyrs or Tribulation Saints are clothed in *white robes* which are STOLE in Greek.

Revelation 6:11 "Then each of them was given a *white robe* (STOLE), and they were told to wait a little longer, until the number of their fellow servants and brothers who were to be killed as they had been was completed."

Revelation 7:9,13-14 "After this I looked and there before me was a great multitude that no one could count, from every nation, tribe, people and language, standing before the throne and in front of the Lamb. They were wearing *white robes* (STOLE) and were holding palm branches in their hands. Then one of the elders asked me, 'These in *white robes* (STOLE) – who are they, and where did they come from?' I answered, 'Sir, you know.' And he said, 'These are they who have come out of the great tribulation; they have washed their *robes* (STOLE) and made then *white* in the blood of the Lamb.'"

However, the Church is clothed in the white linen raiment of the priesthood which is HIMATION in Greek:

Revelation 3:4-5 "Yet you have a few people in Sardis who have not soiled their clothes (HIMATION). They will walk with me, dressed in white, for they are worthy. 5He who overcomes will, like them, be dressed in white (HIMATION). I will never blot out his name from the book of life but will acknowledge his name before my Father and his angels."

Revelation 3:18 "I counsel you to buy from me gold refined in the fire, so you can become rich; and white clothes (HIMATION) to wear, so you can cover your shameful nakedness; and salve to put on your eyes, so you can see."

Revelation 4:4 "Surrounding the throne were twenty-four other thrones and seated on them were twenty-four elders. They were dressed in white (HIMATION) and had crowns of gold on their heads."

Isn't it interesting that you see two totally different garments for two totally different groups of people? God is making an obvious distinction here. Those who get saved *now*, the Church, get a HIMATION *white robe* and avoid the 7-year tribulation, and those who unfortunately procrastinate too long and get saved after the Rapture, the Tribulation saints, receive a STOLE *white robe* and get martyred during the 7-year Tribulation.[3] Once again, I think the lesson is clear. Get saved *now*, get the HIMATION white robe on *today* through Jesus Christ and avoid the whole thing! You definitely don't want to be a part of the wrong group and get left behind to face this slaughter, as this researcher reveals:

"So, after you have false peace and war and famine and natural pestilence that results in widespread death of the quarter of the population of the world, you have persecution resulting in martyrdom. Now again this fit perfectly the teaching of our Lord in Matthew 24.

What follows the natural disasters and the pestilences that end life for a fourth of the earth is persecution. Jesus says, 'Then they'll deliver you to tribulation and kill you.' See how that parallels in Revelation chapter 6? The souls under the altar and the fifth seal are there because they were killed. It says you will be hated by all nations on account of My name.

Jesus says this is only the beginning of the pain, the real pain comes later. And you say if that's only the beginning...if that's only the beginning and it takes a fourth of the population of the world, boy, what is the rest going to be like? Persecution will be official, it will be government-led. You'll be hated by all nations on account of My name. All over the world, I believe, there will be government-led and religiously-inspired persecution. I think the courts will get involved in it. The governors will get involved in it. The synagogues and the liberal churches will get involved in it. It will be the kind of persecution that is handled officially.

The whole worldwide ecumenical religious system will get involved in it and religion will become the persecutor of the true believers. Read Revelation 17:6, the false harlot church will become drunk with the blood of martyrs. The persecution reflects worldwide hatred for God and Christ.

Remember now, the Church has been Raptured out before this begins. There will be conversions occurring early on in this period of time. People will be saved. But the persecution starts, the beginning of it in the first three and a half years, and it goes on all the way to the end.

The restrainer, according to 2 Thessalonians chapter 2 verse 7, who is the Holy Spirit, has been restraining sin. He's doing it now, holding it back, but during this period of time the restrainer let's go and sin runs amuck. The Holy Spirit pulls back His restraint and lets anti-god, Antichrist attitudes go unchecked. And as this begins, people are slain.

We see them, in our text of Revelation 6, already under the altar because they've been killed, they're already in heaven there. The slaying begins. It's coming from all over the world. For all intents and purposes, it is an effort to massacre any believer and every believer on the face of the earth. And their response is, 'Shut those people up. Kill them, we don't want to hear this.'

And many are going to be killed. Jews are going to be killed, as many as two thirds. Now it's just worldwide free-for-all kill Christians, kill Jews. And everybody becomes a murderer, as they're all under the power of satan. The slaughter is going to be massive. The multitudes that are going to come out of the time of Tribulation are going to be innumerable."[4]

In other words, it's going to be a bloodbath and you don't want to be there! Take the only way out *now*! Call upon the Name of Jesus Christ *today* and ask Him to forgive you of all your sins. These horrible events are coming, and it could happen much sooner than you think, maybe even while you're still reading this book. Don't be left behind! Heed God's warning before it's too late!

The **first detail** given about the object of the fifth seal is **The Location of the Martyrs**.

Revelation 6:9-a "When he opened the fifth seal, *I saw under the altar* the souls of those who had been *slain*."

Here we see an interesting *location* for these martyred Tribulation saints. Of all places for them to be residing at during *the fifth seal* announcement, it is *under the altar*. Therefore, the logical obvious question is, "Where is and what is this altar?" Well, contextually, scholars readily agree that the *location* of this *altar* is simply *in heaven*. The reason is twofold. One, these Tribulation saints are *slain* or killed and thus have to be in heaven since the Bible clearly teaches that when the redeemed die, they go directly to be with the Lord Jesus Who is in heaven.

2 Corinthians 5:8 "We are of good courage, I say, and prefer rather to be *absent from the body and to be at home with the Lord*."

When we the redeemed are *absent from our bodies*, that is, when we die, we go *home with the Lord*. Where is our Lord's home? We know without a shadow of a doubt that ever since the Ascension of our Lord Jesus following His Resurrection, He has been *in heaven* sitting at the right hand of the Father.

Mark 16:19 "After the Lord Jesus had spoken to them, *He was taken up into heaven* and He sat at the right hand of God."

Therefore, when we the redeemed die and are *absent from our bodies*, we go to our new *home in heaven* with our Lord Jesus. Now, since the Tribulation saints here in *the fifth seal* are also a part of the redeemed, when they die or are *slain* as seen here in this passage, they too likewise go to be at *home with the Lord* in heaven.

The second reason we know that the *location* of this *altar* mentioned in *the fifth seal* is *in heaven* is because the Book of Revelation repeatedly talks about an *altar already being in heaven*.

Revelation 6:9 "When He opened the fifth seal, I saw under the *altar* the souls of those who had been slain because of the word of God and the testimony they had maintained."

Revelation 8:3 "Another angel, who had a golden censer, came and stood at the *altar*. He was given much incense to offer, with the prayers of all the saints, on the golden *altar* before the throne."

Revelation 8:5 "Then the angel took the censer, filled it with fire from the *altar*, and hurled it on the earth; and there came peals of thunder, rumblings, flashes of lightning and an earthquake."

Revelation 9:13 "The sixth angel sounded his trumpet, and I heard a voice coming from the horns of the golden *altar* that is before God."

Revelation 14:18 "Still another angel, who had charge of the fire, came from the *altar* and called in a loud voice to him who had the sharp sickle, 'Take your sharp sickle and gather the clusters of grapes from the earth's vine, because its grapes are ripe.'"

Revelation 16:7 "And I heard the *altar* respond: 'Yes, Lord God Almighty, true and just are Your judgments.'"

So, we clearly see that the *altars* mentioned here in the Book of Revelation have their *location in heaven,* since they are in conjunction with the *slain* Tribulation saints who are *in heaven* after being *slain,* the angels of God doing God's bidding *from heaven,* and even bluntly stating that these *altars* are before God's throne and even before God Himself Who is obviously *in heaven.* Therefore, with these two factors, scholars readily agree that the *location* of this *altar* here in Revelation 6, and thus the *location* of these Tribulation saints who were martyred or *slain,* is *in heaven.*

Now here's where the real speculation begins. Scholars don't typically debate on the *location* of this *altar* and hence the *location* of the martyrs. The location is *in heaven* through and through. However, they do have differing opinions as to *which altar* is being spoken of *in heaven.* There seem to be two camps. The first opinion is that this is the *Altar of Sacrifice,* as these researchers declare:

"When Aaron and his sons were consecrated to the priesthood, after the blood of the bull was put on the horns of the altar of sacrifice (or burnt offering), the remaining blood was poured 'beside the base of the altar' (Ex. 29:12; Lev. 8:15). This pattern was also followed for the sin offering (Lev. 4:7).

The blood of the martyred saints is considered as an 'offering' before God as it accumulates at the base of the altar during this time of intense persecution of all who name the name of Christ (Matt.24:9). Like sacrifices, they had been slain for their testimony. Not sacrifices of atonement, but of devotion.

The picture of souls immediately in God's presence after death is in harmony with 2 Cor.5:8, and the fact that the martyrs are beneath the altar is consistent with the symbolism of Lev. 4:7, for the priest poured the blood of the sacrifice at the bottom of the altar, and the blood represented the life of the sacrifice (Lev.17:11-14). So, these martyrs will sacrifice their lives for God, and Heaven acknowledges this."

"The altar John saw was evidently in heaven (cf. Revelation 8:3; Revelation 8:5; Revelation 14:18). Earlier John had seen a throne-room in heaven (chs4-5), but now he saw a temple. Probably the concepts of palace and temple communicate aspects of God's magnificent dwelling-place in heaven (cf. Psalm 11:4; Psalm 18:6; Psalm 29:9-10; Isaiah 6:1: Habakkuk 2:20).

This altar was evidently an altar of sacrifice rather than an incense altar. Under this altar were the souls (Gr. psyche, lives) of people who had died for their faith in God and their faithfulness to Him during the period just described, i.e, in the Tribulation so far. That is to say, the life-blood of the martyrs has been poured out as an offering and a sacrifice to God [cf. Lev. 4:7; Phil. 2:17; 2 Tim. 4:6]."

"In the Old Testament sacrifices, most of the blood was poured out at the bottom or base of the altar (Leviticus 4:7). The life or soul of the animals – and of humans – was said to be in the blood (Leviticus 17:11). Paul used the idea of an offering to describe the persecution he suffered and his imminent martyrdom.

Both were, he said, 'like a drink offering' (Philippians 2:17; 2 Timothy 4:6). In that sense, Revelation sees Christians who suffer persecution or martyrdom as sweet sacrifices offered to God. The scene in Revelation 6 picturing souls under the altar is describing, in a graphic and meaningful way, that the faithful have been killed for their convictions."

"Well, who are then these martyrs whose souls, whose disembodied spirits, John was given the ability to see there in heaven? They are those saints who have been martyred under those first four seals. It is a picture of what happens to God's people, God's faithful witnesses down here in the earth in that awful period of tribulation.

Then there is an altar in heaven. The Book of the Hebrews very explicitly says this, and the Book of the Exodus presented the same thing. Moses made a material copy of the tabernacle of the temple that he saw in heaven. A pattern was given him from heaven of the material copy that Moses was to make down here in the earth. 'And Moses,' said the Lord in admonishing him, 'and Moses' was to make everything down here in this earth according to the pattern that he saw in heaven.' [Exodus 25:9,40].

Now this altar that he sees, 'And when He had opened the fifth seal, I saw under the altar,' that is the altar of sacrifice. And this word here, 'I saw those that were slain for the Word of God,' that's the Greek word sphazó, which is the Greek word for 'slain like a sacrifice' [Revelation 6:9]. Now isn't that an unusual thing? These who are martyred are looked upon as sacrifices offered unto God.

And that idea you will find all through the Bible, the idea of sacrifice unto God; that the pouring out of the life of the saints of God's people is a sacrifice unto

God. You'll find that idea for example in Romans 12:1, 'I beseech thee therefore, brethren, that you offer your bodies a living sacrifice unto God, a reasonable, a spiritual service.'

You'll find it again in the passage. 'For I am now ready to be offered up, and the time of my departure is at hand. I have fought a good fight, I have finished my course, I have kept the faith' [2 Timothy 4:6-7]. And as Paul faced his martyrdom, he looked upon that martyrdom as a sacrifice unto God, 'For I am now ready to be offered up, to be poured out as a libation unto God.'

The idea that our lives are to be given in sacrifice, to be offered on the altar of God a sacrifice unto Him, that idea is all through the Bible. And you find it here in the Book of the Revelation in the fifth seal."[5]

The second opinion concerning the identity of this *altar* mentioned in *the fifth seal* is that it is referring to the *Altar of Incense*. Here's the rationale for that belief from these men:

"If I were to choose, there were two altars in the tabernacle and two in the temple, one was the altar of burnt offering where sacrifices were made, that was in the outer part. The other was the altar of incense where prayers were offered, and it was right next to the sanctuary or the holy place. If I were to choose between the two I would lean toward choosing the altar of incense where incense pictured ascending prayer.

You read about that in Exodus chapter 40 and verse 5. But it's an altar in heaven and in this particular case it may well be emblematic of the altar of incense in the Old Testament because that's where prayer was symbolized in incense, and what you have here is people under this altar praying.

The altar...the burnt offering altar, people weren't under it, sacrifices didn't get under that altar, they got on top of it. So, it would seem to be that these people were under the altar praying. Their prayers could be symbolized in ancient times by the incense rising from the top of the altar.

It's important, at least, to recognize this altar because it's going to show up again. Back in Revelation chapter 5 verse 8 there were golden bowls full of incense which were the prayers of the saints. They may well have been coming off that same altar, incense, as I said before, symbolizing prayer.

Then in chapter 8 verse 3, 'Another angel came and stood at the altar holding a golden censure. Much incense was given to him that he might add it to the prayers of all the saints upon the golden altar which was before the throne, and the smoke of the incense with the prayers of the saints went up before God out of the angel's hand.'

I think that's kind of the clincher. It probably was like the altar of incense, very near the throne of God, very near the sanctuary where God dwelt. The burnt offering altar was out farther away and there would be no reason for any sacrifice in heaven but this particular indication that the prayers of the saints still have a place seems more reasonable to attach it to the altar of incense."

"John's attention is shifted back to Heaven where the souls of the martyrs are seen under the altar. There were two altars in the Temple on Earth – the Altar of Sacrifice, also called the altar of burnt offering or the table of the Lord, and the Altar of Incense. The Altar of Sacrifice was located outside the Temple in the Court of the Gentiles. The Altar of Incense, also called the golden altar (8:3), was in the Temple proper in front of the curtain into the Holy of Holies.

So, it is apparently under the Altar of Incense (because incense represents the prayers of the Saints [5:8] and it is at that altar where incense, with the prayers of the Saints, is offered to the Lord [8:3; 8:4]) that these souls are located."[6]

So which one is it? Is this *altar* mentioned here *in heaven* in *the fifth seal* the Altar of Sacrifice or the Altar of Incense? As one-man states profoundly yet bluntly:

"We don't know. I can read fifteen pages on people discussing what altar it is, and when I'm done I'm still saying I don't know what altar it is. If the Lord wanted us to know what altar it was He would have said what altar it was. But the fact is, there's an altar in heaven and this is where the souls who were martyrs of the Tribulation are."[7]

Boy, that's the whole point isn't it? We can debate until we're blue in the face over which altar this is and we still miss the point. You don't want to be here in this time frame! That's the point! You don't want to be a part of the slaughter. You want to be a part of the Rapture! It reminds me of the saying about the Church that oftentimes, "We major in the minors and minor in the majors." The major point is, these people died a horrible death and were a part of a satanic slaughter during the 7-year Tribulation. All because they procrastinated too long in getting saved, they didn't listen, they didn't respond, they entered the 7-year Tribulation and were hunted down and exterminated like spiritual vermin at the hands of the Antichrist and his wicked world system. They could have left at that Rapture of the Church prior to the 7-year Tribulation if only they would have received the Gospel *today*. Instead they ignored it and gave in to delay and found themselves *under the altar* as dead martyr murdered in *the fifth seal*. Why would you risk being in that time frame? That's the point! Therefore, the major issue isn't so much *which altar* as it is to *avoid this altar*! You don't want to be there as this man clearly reveals:

"So, our Lord says, 'Then they shall deliver you up to be afflicted and shall kill you and you shall be hated of all nations for My name's sake.' There will be a desecration. What do I mean by that? To desecrate means to treat a holy thing in an unholy way. And that's exactly what it says here. The holy people of God will be treated in an unholy way. There will be an outright and widespread persecution of the redeemed that exceeds all other persecutions. There is no other persecution to even compare with this.

So, He says to you who are believers in that day, you will be delivered up. True believers are going to be arrested. And they're going to be afflicted and they're going to be murdered. And they're going to be hated by all nations "for My name's sake." In other words, because they identify with the Lord Jesus Christ, they will pay with the hatred and animosity of the world.

You say, 'Well, where do the believers come from if the Church has been raptured?' When the Church has been Raptured, God sets loose in the world two witnesses listed in Revelation 11 and they go everywhere proclaiming the truth. They are murdered by the world, but they rise from the dead. And that will be a very convincing miracle because it says every eye in the world is going to see them. It will probably happen on national television, international television, satellite television. And they'll rise from the dead. And they'll have an impact in winning some people to Christ. And there will be people who come to the Savior during that period. But they will be the objects of persecution.

It will be a time of severe persecution and martyrdom. They will kill you. You will be murdered. You will be hated. You'll be hated by the whole world and all the nations; therefore, there will be no refuge, no place to hide, no place to escape.

Worldwide desecration of the saints. They will be martyred and massacred from one end of the globe to the other in that period of time."[8]

Wouldn't it just make sense to avoid it? That's the point. Let's not major in the minors. Please, I beg you, if you are reading this and if you haven't already done so, please, call upon the Name of Jesus Christ *now* and *avoid the altar of the fifth seal*! Ask Him to forgive you of all your sins *today*! If you delay, your worst, murderous, bloodiest nightmare awaits you. But if you would respond *now* you will leave at the Rapture of the Church before it all begins. The choice of how you arrive *in heaven*, if at all, is yours. Which saint will you be?

The **second detail** given about the object of the fifth seal is **The Reason for the Martyrs**.

Revelation 6:9 "When he opened the fifth seal, I saw under the altar the souls of those who had been slain *because of the word of God* and *the testimony they had maintained*."

If God didn't already get our attention with the major point of this passage-that is, *avoid the altar*, which is why He's sharing it with us *now* before it all occurs-this next section should get our attention even more. Now we see that God gives us the *reason why* these people were *slain* in the first place and made into these martyrs. First of all, it's *because of the word of God*. In other words, these people were killed simply because they shared the Bible and what God says. That's it. Not *because* they robbed a bank, they stole somebody else's car, they took a life of a friend, they burned somebody's house down, or they even purposely ran over somebody's pet, none of that stuff. It's simply *because of the word of God*. God's Word is so despised at this point that anybody who stands for it, preaches it, shares it, declares it, believes in it, promotes it, and reads it *will be killed*.

Now, as shocking as that is, that's only half of the reason why these people in *the fifth seal* were *slain* and turned into martyrs. The other reason is because of *the testimony they maintained*. What's interesting about the word *testimony* here is it's the Greek word "martyria" which is where we get the English word for "martyr" from. It means, "one who testifies, a witness before a judge, one who testifies of future events." The word *maintained* is the Greek word "echo" which means, "to hold on to, to be closely joined with." So, the next reason why these people were ruthlessly killed and martyred is because they testified about Jesus, that He's the real Messiah; they were His witnesses in a court of law, they held on tightly to Him, His way out, His truths, and what He said about the future, including the reason why these future events were occurring on planet earth in the 7-year Tribulation. These faithful godly people refused to budge from this and thus they were killed on the spot. They became "martyrs" for *maintaining* this "testimony." This is not a pleasant time for the faithful, to put it mildly.

In fact, I've often heard people today say something like this, "Well, if you Christians disappear at the Rapture before the 7-year Tribulation, I'll know then that what you were telling me about Jesus was true, so I'll just get saved then." Really? We already saw that most people who turn to God in the 7-year Tribulation will have their heads chopped off in Revelation Chapter 20, and now here we see that they will also be *slain* just for mentioning the Bible or even Jesus. So, you mean to tell me you won't turn to Jesus now when things are currently easy to be follower of God, at least here in the West, and yet you really think you'll turn to Him when these murderous planetary-wide events unfold, and your head is literally on the chopping block? Don't kid yourself! You're still missing the point. Get saved now! You don't want to be on the planet as this time and the only way to avoid this horrific scenario is to accept Jesus Christ as your Lord and Savior *today*! Take the way out, don't delay, this is a total nightmare as these men share:

"The revelation of the fifth seal makes clear that in the future time of Tribulation it will be most difficult to declare one's faith in the Lord Jesus. It may very well be that the majority of those who trust Christ as Saviour in that day will be put to death. This is confirmed in Revelation 7:1+ where another picture of the martyred dead of the tribulation is given, and in Revelation 13:1+ where death is inflicted on all who will not worship the beast.

Like the first martyr of the Church, Stephen (Acts 7:59), and Antipas of the Church at Pergamos (Rev. 2:13+), they will hold a consistent testimony up to and beyond the point of death (Rev.12:11+). They are faithful sheep whose blood is spilled for God's sake. 'Yet for Your sake we are killed all day long; we are accounted as sheep for the slaughter' (Ps. 44:22 cf. Rom. 8:36). Martyrdom in those days will be as common as it is uncommon today."

"The fifth seal describes the witnessing community, willing even to die for the truth of Jesus Christ. The synoptic Gospels carefully preserve Jesus' warning about persecution during this time frame (Mark 13:9-13; Luke 21:12-18). Matthew wrote: 'You will be handed over to be persecuted and put to death, and

you will be hated by all nations because of Me' (24:9). John remembered Jesus' words as well: 'A time is coming when anyone who kills you will think he is offering a service to God' (John 16:2). Thus, the fifth seal pictures tribulation on the true people of God because of their religious convictions."

"Why were they slain? First: wherever the Word of God is faithfully preached, there is always with it a concomitant. It cuts the consciences of men, and it brings reaction and violent opposition. And did you know, when we are at peace in Zion, you know why you're at peace? It's because you don't challenge the hosts of satan, and the world, and the devil. We have accommodated ourselves to it.

I could expatiate on that all day long, and I'm just like all the rest of us. I accept all of these things that debauch our children; that damn and ruin our homes and our families. I accept it. Why, I go up and down these streets and there's every kind of vile, and filthy, and salacious thing in this town that you could imagine. But I don't ever say anything about it.

We don't ever mention it. We are quiescent in our lives, and we have accommodated ourselves to these things. So, we live at perfect peace, and some of the finest and most respected of the citizens in our town are those who live by the debauchery and by the damnation of the souls of our people. But we accept it.

But these didn't; they stood up and they witnessed to the truth of Almighty God! And wherever that is done, you will find fierce reaction against it. Another thing: these men were testifying of the judgments that were coming upon this earth. Don't ever persuade yourself in your mind that things happen in the world just by accident. Whenever you live under the dark cloud of an ominous war, that's a judgment of Almighty God; always has been, is always depicted such in the Book. And when we live in troubles, and in fear, and in distress, and in anxiety about what may come, those things come from God.

The witness of the true minister of Christ and the prophet of the Lord is always that; that the judgment of God is going to fall upon this world and upon the house of iniquity and sin. Wherever there is a man of God who preaches the true message of God, he'll always have that in his message; that the wrath and judgment of God is going to fall upon the evil and upon the sin of this world.

Whenever you have a man and he preaches sugar and spice and everything nice, Chanel No. 5 perfume, rose water, whenever you have a man preaching that, he's no true man of God! For every true prophet of God that ever stood up to preach called the people to repentance because of the inevitable day of wrath and visitation and judgment of the Almighty. And if a man preaches the gospel today, that's what he'll be preaching. He'll be calling people to their knees in repentance for their sins and asking God's deliverance and forgiveness.

And that's what happened here. Now these martyrs witnessed to that, and of those awful and calamitous things that were happening, these men said, 'This is the judgment of God.' Well, in order to still them, it was just the same thing that happened in the days of the early Roman Empire. They were hated, and they were despised, and when anything bad happened – say they lost part in a battle or they lost a war – why, the cry was, 'The Christians to the lions!' or if they had a great flood or a great earthquake, 'The Christians to the lions!'

Just the same thing here; they were hated, and they were despised, and when these calamitous things came, why, they were charged with every evil thing that mind could imagine. And they were persecuted, and they gave their witness in blood and in fire."

"Why were they killed? Because of the Word of God. The world says we want them silent. We don't want to hear what they say. So, the killing starts. The world is not going to tolerate the preachers, not going to tolerate the Christian testimony.

What testimony? The testimony of Jesus. They were not only saying what's happening is in the Bible, they were also saying Jesus is the Christ, Jesus is the deliverer, Jesus is the Redeemer, Jesus is coming. They had maintained faithfully the testimony concerning Jesus Christ. They will be killed for proclaiming God's Word and proclaiming the gospel of Jesus Christ. They had maintained that as a part of their uncompromising commitment. And they will do it all the way to death, without compromising.

They were killed because they stuck faithfully to living and preaching the Word of God and the gospel of Jesus Christ. The cause of their martyrdom then is faithfulness, to live and speak God's Word and Christ's gospel. It seems to me in some parts of the world, and maybe even in our own country, we're moving fairly fast in that direction, aren't we?"[9]

In fact, I think it's even closer than people realize or even dare I say, want to admit. What you have going on in *the fifth seal is basically genocide.* Specifically, a genocide against the followers of God. Little do most people realize that the "birth pains" of this mass slaying of God's people has already begun. The following is a copy of the actual petition to former Secretary of State of the United States, John Kerry, appealing to him to put a stop to the *current-day genocide of Christians:*

The Honorable John F. Kerry
Secretary of State
U.S. Department of State
Washington, D.C. 20520

Dear Mr. Secretary:

We, the undersigned, believe America must end its silence about the ongoing genocide against Christians and other minority groups in Iraq and Syria.
The United Nations Convention on the Prevention and Punishment of the Crime of Genocide defines 'genocide' as killing and certain acts 'committed with intent to destroy, in whole or in part, a national, ethnical, racial or religious group.' Extensive and irrefutable evidence supports a finding that the so-called Islamic State's mistreatment of Iraqi and Syrian Christians, as well as Yazidis and other vulnerable minorities, meets this definition. This evidence includes:

- Assassinations of Church leaders

- Mass murders and deportations

- Torture

- Kidnapping for ransom

- Sexual enslavement and systematic rape of girls and women

- Forcible conversions to Islam

- Destruction of Christian churches, monasteries, cemeteries, and artifacts

ISIS's own public statements take 'credit' for the murder of Christians precisely because they are Christian and express its intent to wholly eradicate Christian and other minority communities from its 'Islamic State.' Whole families, villages and cities of our brothers and sisters in Christ are being completely exterminated. We implore you to speak up on behalf of these brutalized minority populations. We therefore urge you to declare that Christians, along with Yazidis and other minorities, are targets of ongoing genocide.[10]

As you can see, the wicked mindset to pull off this slaughter of God's people in the 7-year Tribulation, just *because of the word of God* and *the testimony they maintained* about Jesus, has already begun. That's the actual petition to stop this actual genocide. Now, it's bad enough that these people here in *the fifth seal* are killed in a genocidal fashion just *because of the word of God* and *the testimony they maintained*, but we need to back up a little bit and observe the *manner* in which they are killed. The word *slain* there is a very graphic term. This should *really* get our attention. It's the Greek word, "sphazo," and it literally means, "to slay, to slaughter, to butcher, to put to death by violence." This is not an average normal way of killing people. Not at all. This is a bloody butchering of people, a massive violent slaughter of people, putting people to death with a violent glee, being ecstatic about it, and this is being done specifically to people who turn to God during the 7-year Tribulation. When you take this gory detail into account, it gives us yet another amazing and shocking insight into the depths of depravity that mankind will sink into once the restraining influence of the Holy Spirit in the Church is removed at the Rapture prior to the 7-year Tribulation. Here we are in just the first half of this 7-year period, and mankind is so evil at this point that he literally begins to not only slaughter one another, but now he specifically slaughters godly people who only want to help them. It's reminiscent of the planet's celebratory attitude towards the death of God's Two Witnesses in Revelation Chapter 11 who preach God's righteousness during this same time frame.

Revelation 11:3,7-10 "And I will give power to my two witnesses, and they will prophesy for 1,260 days, clothed in sackcloth. Now when they have finished their testimony, the beast that comes up from the Abyss will attack them and overpower and kill them. Their bodies will lie in the street of the great city, which is figuratively called Sodom and Egypt, where also their Lord was crucified. For three and a half days men from every people, tribe, language and nation will gaze on their bodies and refuse them burial. The inhabitants of the earth will gloat over them and will celebrate by sending each other gifts, because these two prophets had tormented those who live on the earth."

Here we have, as was previously mentioned, one of the three ways that the Gospel goes forth in the 7-year Tribulation. God raises up Two Witnesses as prophets who preach *the word of God* and then *maintain* or *finish their testimony,* upon which they are *killed.* Now notice the attitude of the people who witness this evil deed. It's not just that the whole world is watching or *gazing on* their dead bodies (which by the way could only happen today with modern day satellite technology) and refusing them burial, which is an offense as we will see, but they are also *gloating over them* and even sending *celebratory gifts to each other* (which again could only happen today with modern day travel technology). Talk about evil behavior and an evil attitude!

Then we are even told *why.* The planet does this because their hearts have become so evil that they actually consider what these Two Witnesses were doing, that of preaching God's truth, encouraging them to turn to Him, as a form of *torment!* Can you believe that? Preaching *the word of God* and *maintaining a testimony* of Him is likened unto *torture?* Talk about descending into depravity! When the restraint of the Holy Spirit leaves at the Rapture of the Church prior to the 7-year Tribulation, mankind begins to go into a spiritual death spiral that descends into a horrible depravity that nose dives and never recovers. They crash all the way to the very end of the 7-year Tribulation. All moral decency and restraint disintegrates, even to the point where mankind will not only slaughter themselves, but they will even specifically hunt down and butcher godly people trying to help them and then even slay them in a violent glee. It's truly, as Jesus says, the worst time in the history of mankind. You definitely don't want to be there, as this man shares:

"They were killed there because that is the place where the great majority of their preaching goes on, because I believe they're the instruments that God uses to proclaim the saving gospel to Israel in the end that causes Israel's ultimate belief in their Messiah.

Please notice they're not buried. It says their dead bodies are in the streets. How will they do that? Television. That couldn't have been true before the invention of television. The whole world will look at their dead bodies 'for three and a half days' and will not permit their dead bodies to be laid in a tomb.' They'll watch them decay. Three days is enough to see some severe decay.

When Lazarus had been in the tomb only a few days, you remember the comment was, 'By this time he stinketh.' The unrepentant, unconverted masses will gloat with the Antichrist and give the Antichrist glory because He was able to kill these *two whom no one could kill, but by whom many died. The morbid ghoulish display of hatred shows how hardened they are as they let those bodies just lie in the street decaying.*

By the way, that was done in ancient times. When pagan people wanted to dishonor their enemies, they would leave their corpses lying in the street. That was the ultimate dishonoring, the ultimate denigration of someone.

In Deuteronomy 21:22 the Bible says, 'If a man has committed a sin worthy of death, he's to be put to death. You hang him on a tree; his corpse shall not hang all night on the tree, you shall surely bury him on the same day so that you do not defile your land.' God says you bury him the same day he dies.

But here is a celebration, a wild celebration. The beast has killed these two preachers. And the world has a party and will send gifts to one another. Hey, here's your present, Happy Dead Witnesses Day. I mean, this is the ultimate Christmas experience. There will be a wild party.

Now do you see how deep the world has plunged into hellishness? Cataclysms on the earth and in the heaven, the wrath of God, the Antichrist massacring any and all who oppose him. And in the midst of all these horrors, the world is really angry about two preachers of truth. And when they're dead, the party is on.

Those who dwell on the earth, by the way, is a technical term for the unconverted. It's used twelve times in the book of Revelation. It's a technical term referring to the unbelieving. So, the whole world by satellite TV joins the party and they make merry, the literal Greek word means to be of a jolly mind.

How can they be happy in that mess? They are happy because these men who confronted them about their sins and iniquities and the judgment of God are dead. Their emotional response certainly parallels their spiritual condition. Amazingly they start giving presents to each other because of the relief.

The ungodly rebels, the unrepentant sinners, followers of Antichrist are so sick and so weary of the power of these two that they put on a party like the world has never seen. This has got to be the biggest party the world has ever known. This has got to be the ultimate Mardi Gras. They don't hate Antichrist, they don't hate satan, they don't even hate the demons destroying them at the same time as much as they hate these two."[11]

What a sad, sad state of affairs. How low can you go? Just when you thought mankind couldn't get any more wicked, he goes even lower! How many times do we talk about the Rapture of the Church prior to the 7-year Tribulation even as Christians today, yet we fail to realize the effect our very departure will have on the planet. When the restraining influence of the Church is gone, the depravity for those who remain becomes unrestrained! What a nightmare scenario! There is nothing to hold them back from even the most heinous of crimes. Evil abounds, evil grows, evil spreads, evil escalates from day one of the Rapture all the way to the end of the 7-year Tribulation. No wonder God is telling us of these horrible events *now* before they occur. The message is loud and clear. You don't want to be there! Take the one and only way out *now* through Jesus Christ before it's too late. You don't want to be left behind. Your worst nightmare waits!

In fact, speaking of worst nightmare, we get yet another dark macabre insight into this horrendous genocidal behavior towards God's people in the 7-year Tribulation with this word *slain*. It turns out that it was also used as a "sacrificial term for slaughtering animals for sacrifice."[12] This means the emphasis again wasn't just that these people were "killed," but they were literally "slaughtered like sacrificial animals" in some sort of sick satanic glee. To be honest, this is very reminiscent of the Jewish Holocaust that happened during World War II. It just so happens that the word "holocaust" comes from a Greek word "holokaustos" that also means "animal sacrifice," one that was "completely or wholly burnt." Hence, "holo" "caust." This same Greek word was later Latinized as "holocaustum" and used to translate references to the Jewish "burnt offerings" mentioned in the Bible in the book of Exodus and Leviticus.[13] So in short, if you stir all this verbiage together, what you have is the unfortunate, unbelievable, horrific, mind-numbing news from God that, yes, believe it or not, another "holocaust" is coming to the planet. Even after all Adolf Hitler and the German leadership did to the Jewish people just a few decades ago, there really is coming a time, possibly very soon, much sooner than we may even want to admit, when "God's people will *again* be slaughtered like animals." In fact, let us remind ourselves of that horrendous genocidal event not that long ago, so as to prepare ourselves for what God is saying is coming to the planet again in our text here in *the fifth seal*:

"The holocaust was a genocide in which some six million European Jews were killed by Adolf Hitler's Nazi Germany, and the World War II collaborators with the Nazis. The victims included 1.5 million children and represented about two-thirds of the nine million Jews who had resided in Europe.

From 1941 to 1945, Jews were systematically murdered in the deadliest genocide in history, under the coordination of the SS, with directions from the highest leadership of the Nazi Party. Every arm of Germany's bureaucracy was involved in the logistics and the carrying out of the mass murder, turning the Third Reich into what one Holocaust scholar called 'a genocidal state.'

Every arm of the country's sophisticated bureaucracy was involved in the killing process. Parish churches and the Interior Ministry supplied birth records showing who was Jewish; the Post Office delivered the deportation and denaturalization orders; the Finance Ministry confiscated Jewish property; German firms fired Jewish workers and disenfranchised Jewish stockholders. The universities refused to admit Jews, denied degrees to those already studying, and fired Jewish academics; government transport offices arranged the trains for deportation to the camps; German pharmaceutical companies tested drugs on camp prisoners; companies bid for the contracts to build the crematoria; detailed lists of victims were drawn up by Dehomag (IBM Germany) using the company's punch card machines.

Not one social group, not one religious community, not one scholarly institution or professional association in Germany and throughout Europe declared its solidarity with the Jews. Just one of many instances included the 930 Jewish refugees aboard the MS St. Louis who were refused entry to Cuba, the United States and Canada, and the ship was forced to return to Europe.

The killings were systematically conducted in virtually all areas of German-occupied territory in what are now 35 separate European countries. Anyone with three or four Jewish grandparents was to be exterminated without exception. The Nazis envisioned the extermination of the Jews worldwide, not only in Germany proper.

The persecution was carried out in stages, culminating in the policy of extermination of European Jews termed the 'Final Solution to the Jewish Question.' Following Hitler's rise to power, the German government passed laws to exclude Jews from civil society and began to establish a network of concentration camps. As prisoners entered the death camps, they were made to surrender all personal property, which was catalogued and tagged before being sent to Germany to be reused or recycled. The German National Bank helped launder valuables stolen from the victims.

A distinctive feature of Nazi genocide was the extensive use of human subjects in 'medical' experiments. The most notorious of these physicians was Josef Mengele, who worked in Auschwitz. His experiments included placing subjects in pressure chambers, testing drugs on them, freezing them, attempting to change eye color by injecting chemicals into children's eyes, and amputations and other surgeries.

Subjects who survived Mengele's experiments were almost always killed and dissected shortly afterwards. Mengele worked extensively with Romani children. He would bring them sweets and toys and personally take them to the gas chamber. One historical account of his sickening behavior is as follows:

'I remember one set of twins in particular: Guido and Ina, aged about four. One day, Mengele took them away. When they returned, they were in a terrible state: they had been sewn together, back to back, like Siamese twins. Their wounds were infected and oozing pus. They screamed day and night. Then their parents – I remember the mother's name was Stella – managed to get some morphine and they killed the children in order to end their suffering.'

The Jews were later herded into ghettos where they were put to work. Here many thousands died from maltreatment, disease, starvation, and exhaustion. There is little doubt that the Nazis saw forced labor as a form of extermination. The expression Vernichtung durch Arbeit ('destruction through work') was frequently used.

A number of deadly pogroms (an organized massacre) occurred that the Nazis encouraged, while others were spontaneous. As many as 14,000 Jews were killed by Romanian residents and police. Some were murdered in the streets, there were mass shootings, Jewish women were chased by men and youth armed with clubs, and some were locked in barns and burned to death. One report is included below:

'The Germans came, the police, and they started banging houses: 'Raus, raus, raus, Juden raus.'...One baby started to cry...The other baby started crying. So, the mother urinated in her hand and gave the baby a drink to keep quiet... [When the police had gone], I told the mothers to come out. And one baby was dead...from fear, the mother [had] choked her own baby.'

Many of the mass killings were carried out in public. Mainly by shooting or with hand grenades at mass-killing sites outside the major towns. German witnesses to these killings emphasized the locals' participation. This person records the following:

'I saw them do the killing. At 5:00 pm they gave the command, 'Fill in the pits.' Screams and groans were coming from the pits. Suddenly I saw my neighbor Ruderman rise from under the soil...His eyes were bloody, and he was screaming: 'Finish me off!'...A murdered woman lay at my feet. A boy of five years crawled out from under her body and began to scream desperately. 'Mommy!' That was all I saw, since I fell unconscious.'

Jews gathered by the cemetery as ordered, expecting to be loaded onto trains. The crowd was large enough that most of the men, women, and children could not have known what was happening until it was too late; by the time they heard the machine gun fire, there was no chance to escape. All were driven down a corridor of soldiers, in groups of ten, and shot. A truck driver described the scene:

'One after the other, they had to remove their luggage, then their coats, shoes, and outer garments and also underwear. Once undressed, they were led into the ravine which was about 150 meters long and 30 meters wide and a good 15 meters deep. When they reached the bottom of the ravine they were seized by members of the Schutzpolizei and made to lie down on top of Jews who had already been shot...The corpses were literally in layers. A police marksman came along and shot each Jew in the neck with a submachine gun. I saw these marksmen stand on layers of corpses and shoot one after the other. The marksman would walk across the bodies of the executed Jews to the next Jew, who had meanwhile lain down, and shoot him.'

In August 1941 Himmler travelled to Minsk, where he personally witnessed 100 Jews being shot in a ditch outside the town. Karl Wolff described the event in his diary: 'Himmler's face was green. He took out his handkerchief and wiped his cheek where a piece of brain had squirted up onto it. Then he vomited. After recovering his composure, Himmler lectured the SS men on the need to follow the 'highest moral law of the Party' in carrying out their tasks.

The remaining Jews were either killed or deported to the death camps. The use of extermination camps (also called 'death camps'), equipped with gas chambers for the systematic mass extermination of peoples, was an unprecedented feature of the Holocaust. These were established and built for the systematic purpose of killing millions, primarily by gassing, but also by execution and extreme work under starvation conditions, i.e., being worked to death. Some camps tattooed prisoners with an identification number on arrival. Those fit for work were dispatched for 12 to 14-hour shifts. Roll calls before and after could sometimes last for hours; prisoners regularly died of exposure.

Experimental gas vans equipped with gas cylinders and a sealed trunk compartment, were used. In the Sachsenhausen concentration camp, larger vans holding up to 100 people were used, using the engine's exhaust rather than a cylinder. These gas vans were developed and run under supervision of the SS and were used to kill about 500,000 people. The vans were carefully monitored, and after a month of observation a report stated that 'ninety-seven thousand have been processed using three vans, without any defects showing up in the machines.'

A need for new mass murder techniques was also expressed by Hans Frank, governor of the General Government, who noted that this many people could not be simply shot. 'We shall have to take steps, however, designed in some way to eliminate them.' It was this problem which led the SS to experiment with large-scale killings using poison gas. Christian Wirth seems to have been the inventor of the gas chamber.

The Jews were then herded naked into the gas chambers. Usually they were told these were showers or delousing chambers, and there were signs outside saying 'baths' and 'sauna.' They were sometimes given a small piece of soap and a towel so as to avoid panic and were told to remember where they had put their belongings for the same reason. When they asked for water because they were thirsty after the long journey in the cattle trains, they were told to hurry up, because coffee was waiting for them in the camp, and it was getting cold.

Once the chamber was full, the doors were screwed shut and solid pellets of Zyklon-B were dropped into the chambers through vents in the side walls, releasing toxic HCN, or hydrogen cyanide. Those inside died within 20 minutes; the speed of death depended on how close the inmate was standing to a gas vent. Shouting and screaming of the victims could be heard through the opening and it was clear that they fought for their lives.

When they were removed, if the chamber had been very congested, as they often were, the victims were found half-squatting, their skin colored pink with red and green spots, some foaming at the mouth or bleeding from the ears. The gas was then pumped out, the bodies were removed (which would take up to four hours), gold fillings in their teeth were extracted with pliers by dentist prisoners, and women's hair was cut. The floor of the gas chamber was cleaned, and the walls whitewashed.

The work was done by the Sonderkommando, which were work units of Jewish prisoners. In crematoria 1 and 2, the Sonderkommando lived in an attic above the crematoria; in crematoria 3 and 4, they lived inside the gas chambers. When the Sonderkommando had finished with the bodies, the SS conducted spot checks to make sure all the gold had been removed from the victims' mouths. If a check revealed that gold had been missed, the Sonderkommando prisoner responsible was thrown into the furnace alive as punishment.

One account records that an inmate girl, 15 or younger, due to highly unusual circumstances, managed to survive the gas chamber and the SS commander replied, 'There's no way of getting around it, the child will have to die.' Half an hour later the young girl was led into the furnace room hallway and there received a bullet in the back of the neck.'

Prisoner transportation was often carried out under horrifying conditions in rail freight cars; many died before reaching their destination. There was a place called the ramp where the trains with the Jews were coming in. They were coming in day and night, sometimes one per day and sometimes five per day. Constantly, people from the heart of Europe were disappearing, and they were arriving to the same place with the same ignorance of the fate of the previous transport. Within a couple of hours, ninety percent would be gassed. Rudolf Hoss, Auschwitz camp commander stated:

'Children of tender years were invariably exterminated, since by reason of their youth they were unable to work. Very frequently women would hide their children under the clothes, but of course when we found them we would send the children in to be exterminated. We were required to carry out these exterminations in secrecy, but of course the foul and nauseating stench from the continuous burning of bodies permeated the entire area, and all of the people living in the surrounding communities knew that exterminations were going on at Auschwitz.'

By the spring of 1944, up to 6,000 people were being gassed every day at Auschwitz. Heinrich Himmler even stated, 'The hard decision had to be made that this people should be caused to disappear from earth.'

It is unlikely that the German population could avoid knowing about the persecution, considering such prevalence. Many argue that the German civilian population were, by and large, aware of what was happening. By at least 9 October 1942, British radio had broadcast news of gassing of Jews to the Netherlands. In 1942, Jan Karski reported to the Polish, British and US governments on the situation in Poland, especially the destruction of the Warsaw Ghetto and the Holocaust of the Jews. He met with Polish politicians in exile including the prime minister, as well as members of political parties.

He then traveled to the United States in July 1943, and personally reported to Roosevelt, telling him about the situation in Poland and becoming the first eyewitness to tell him about the Jewish Holocaust. During their meeting Roosevelt asked about the condition of horses in Poland but did not ask one question about the Jews. He also met with many other government and civic leaders in the United States, and also presented his report to the media, bishops of various denominations (including Cardinal Samuel Stritch) and members of the Hollywood film industry and artists, but without success.

Before and during World War II, the New York Times had maintained a strict policy in their news reporting and editorials to minimize reports on the Holocaust. They deliberately suppressed news of the Third Reich's persecution and murder of Jews, making it virtually impossible for American Jews to impress Congress, Church or government leaders with the importance of helping Europe's Jews.

Finally, liberation came. Colonel William W. Quinn of the US Seventh Army said of Dachau: 'There our troops found sights, sounds, and stenches horrible beyond belief, cruelties so enormous as to be incomprehensible to the normal mind.' One man recorded the following:

'Here over an acre of ground lay dead and dying people. You could not see which was which...The living lay with their heads against the corpses, and around them moved the awful, ghostly procession of emaciated, aimless people, with nothing to do and with no hope of life, unable to move out of your way, unable to look at the terrible sights around them...Babies had been born here,

tiny wizened things that could not live...A mother, driven mad, screamed at a British sentry to give her milk for her child, and thrust the tiny mite into his arms...He opened the bundle and found the baby had been dead for days. This day was the most horrible of my life.'"[14]

And yet, imagine this satanic dark reality coming again to the planet, only this time it's even worse and on an even grander scale with no human restraint and no liberation. It's a non-stop slaughter of God's people in any which way you can for seven years on the whole planet! In fact, the Bible even amazingly informs us that another *two-thirds* of the Jewish people will be killed in this soon coming *future holocaust* as we just read they were in the last one!

Zechariah 13:8 "In the whole land, declares the LORD, *two-thirds* will be struck down and perish; yet one-third will be left in it."

How sad it is to realize that, yet another horrible holocaust is coming to the planet, even after what Hitler did only just a few decades ago. You would think that recent history would restrain us from ever even contemplating let alone committing such an evil atrocity towards our fellow mankind, yet this is precisely what happens when all restraints are removed at the Rapture of the Church prior to the 7-year tribulation. All nations, not just Germany, will hunt down God's people and seek to exterminate them.

Matthew 24:9 "Then you will be handed over to be persecuted and put to death, and you will be hated by *all nations* because of Me."

Imagine the *whole planet* involved in another holocaust! *All nations* will haul God's people away and not just persecute them, but once again kill them, put them to death, just like in the Jewish Holocaust of not long ago. Speaking of which, if those horrible events we just read about, concerning the Holocaust of World War II, is how mankind behaved and treated each other with the restraining influence still being on planet earth, then can you imagine how sickening it will get when there is no restraint? Why, the next thing you know people will not only commit these horrible acts of inhumane slaughter of God's people who are only trying to help them, but they'll even go so far as to throw the world's biggest death party and send each other gifts like it's a birthday celebration or something.

Now, as horrific and unbelievable as that is, remember, this is what is really coming to the planet during the 7-year Tribulation, and this is precisely why God is *repeatedly* warning us in advance of these events in *the fifth seal*. The devil, the Antichrist, the false prophet, and even man's own depravity will institute yet another "Final Solution" to the "Followers of God problem." It really is coming, and you really don't want to be left behind! However, never forget, God not only has the last word, but if there's one thing He doesn't like, it's when people mess with His kids. If that's you being guilty of this behavior, you're going to be in big trouble! That's what we will now see in the next details concerning *the fifth seal*.

The **third detail** given about the object of the fifth seal is **The Shout of the Martyrs**.

Revelation 6:10 "*They called out in a loud voice*, 'How long, Sovereign Lord, holy and true, until You judge the inhabitants of the earth and avenge our blood?'"

So far, we've seen the location of the Tribulation Saints or Martyrs in heaven and the type of manner in which they were brutally murdered. Now we see the scene shift to the response of the Martyrs towards this horrible bloody treatment thrust upon them by the unredeemed back on earth. They simply make a request of Almighty God. They do not whisper this request to God, they do not make a soft reply, they don't even make a casual remark concerning their feelings toward how they were mistreated back on earth. No. These Tribulation Martyrs *called out in a loud voice*. The words *called out* is the Greek word, "krazo" and it means not just to "call out" but literally "to cry out, to shout, to scream." The words *loud voice* are the Greek words, "megas phone" which as you might have guessed is where we get the English word "megaphone" from. It means, "a massive, intense, great, mighty voice or speech." So, put these two together and you can see this is not a normal average everyday tone of voice here used by the Tribulation saints. It is a loud voice, a massive voice, an extremely loud scream. One that you not only would want to cover your ears for, but it's as if somebody prevented you from covering your ears and then they proceeded to place a megaphone right up to the side of your ear and then gave a big massive shout or scream into it. Ouch! This is an *intense voice*!

Therefore, it would appear that these Martyrs are matching intensity for intensity. Try to picture the timing here. Most likely, the last thing these Tribulation saints or martyrs heard on earth, before they were brutally murdered and slaughtered by *the inhabitants of the earth,* were the loud satanic glees and shouts of triumph from them as they methodically hunted these followers of God down and butchered them. Then instantly these Tribulation saints arrive *in heaven* (2 Corinthians 5:8 "Absent from the body is to at home with the Lord") whereupon they respond in kind with their own massive mega shout in heaven! Their loud declaration isn't in partnership with the Antichrist or even directed at satan. No, their *mega voice* is directed towards *Almighty God*! What we will see is that it's basically a super duper loud massive cry for a *timely vengeance* upon their murderers.

The first way we see this cry for a *timely vengeance* from the Tribulation saints is to *Whom* they cry out to. It's the *Sovereign Lord*. Not just God, not just Heavenly Father, but *Sovereign Lord*. This is the Greek word, "despotes" which means, "Lord or Master." These Tribulation saints acknowledge that God is not only their Heavenly Master but He's also the Lord of the Universe as well which means He not only rules over them, but all people. The *Sovereign Lord* is the One Who is in charge of everyone, everywhere, at all times through and through, even of the events that transpire during the 7-year Tribulation, including these martyrs' own death, by *the inhabitants of the earth*. God is the *Sovereign Lord*, the Author and finisher of life. He alone determines when we die and how long we live.

Job 14:5 "You have decided the length of our lives. You know how many months we will live, and we are not given a minute longer."

These *inhabitants of the earth* are not the ones in charge over the Tribulation saints' death, nor is satan or the Antichrist. Oh, they may have been the *instrument* which the *Sovereign Lord* chose to use to take His martyred saints into heaven and bless them with His presence and give them His Divine rest, but rest assured none of these events happened without God's Divine permission. Now, He is not the author of evil, but God is so powerful as the *Sovereign Lord* that He will use *all things* together for His Divine Holy purposes. Once again this shows us that even satan himself is not a loose cannon on deck, and the Antichrist is certainly not the one in charge during the 7-year Tribulation. The Bible clearly informs us that even satan himself has to report to the *Sovereign Lord* and only gets to do what God *allows* him to do.

Job 1:6,9-12 "One day the angels came to present themselves before the LORD, and satan also came with them. 'Does Job fear God for nothing?' satan replied. 'Have you not put a hedge around him and his household and everything he has? You have blessed the work of his hands, so that his flocks and herds are spread throughout the land. But stretch out Your hand and strike everything he has, and he will surely curse You to your face.' The LORD said to satan, 'Very well, then, everything he has is in your hands, but on the man, himself do not lay a finger.' Then satan went out from the presence of the LORD."

As you can see, the Bible very clearly teaches us that the devil only gets to do what God *allows* him to do. Again, satan is not a loose cannon on deck roaming around the earth doing whatever in the world he wants to do. No! God is the *Sovereign Lord*! God has put a limit on satan and thus he only gets to do what God allows him to do. Therefore, this shows us that these Tribulation saints are not messing around with their *mega shout* for a *timely vengeance.* They make their address to the *Sovereign Lord,* the One Who is the Master over them and over all people, all entities of all time, redeemed and unredeemed alike. They make their loud request to the One Who sees all and controls all, the One Who has power over all, even the Antichrist and satan himself. They don't go to man, they don't go to court system, they don't go to some small fry intervention scenario; no, they go straight to the top! To the One Who is in charge of *everything*! The *Sovereign Lord* Who has the Ultimate Authority over them and everyone else who ever existed. They skip over all other avenues and go straight to the Head over all! This tells us they are extremely *serious* about this request and they want it remedied in a *timely* fashion!

The second way we see this cry for a *timely vengeance* from the Tribulation saints is in the *question* posed to the *Sovereign Lord.* The phrase, "*How long...holy and true*" is basically an appeal for a *speedy retribution* for how they were mistreated. They don't ask, "Will you please," or "Would you consider," or even "Would you look into the possibility of;" no, they only ask, "*How long.*" They acknowledge that God is *holy and true;* therefore, they know that He *cannot* overlook their *unholy murders* by *the inhabitants of the earth,* and they also know that neither will God give into or fall for the *lying justifications* for these murderers and their false excuses for slaughtering these followers of God. They appeal to the fact that God is not only the *Sovereign Lord* overall and has the authority to do whatever He wants to do, but also to the fact that He's *holy and true* and thus He *has to do something* about this ungodly deed back on earth. It's not a matter of *will* God *judge* or *avenge their blood,* but a matter of *when,* hence the phrase, "*How long.*" They know it's coming. In fact, they know, *it has to come* because God is *holy and true.* Therefore, they just want to know, "*How long,*" until there will be a speedy retribution for the crimes committed against them back on earth.

The third way we see this cry for a *timely vengeance* from the Tribulation Martyrs, is in the *request* posed to the *Sovereign Lord...holy and true.*

The phrase, *how long...until You judge the inhabitants of the earth and avenge our blood,* is basically a desire for a *rapid vengeance* upon those who butchered them back on earth simply because they followed God. Now, granted, at first this might seem like an inappropriate request or even an ungodly desire for somebody who is a follower of God. Yet, these Tribulation saints not only acknowledge the *Sovereign Lord's holy and true* character, but now here they are simply acknowledging and following what God's Word says to do in these kinds of situations. He tells us in the Bible that *we* as His people are *not* to take *vengeance* upon our enemies, but rather we are to *leave that to Him.*

Deuteronomy 32:35 "It is Mine to avenge; I will repay. In due time their foot will slip; their day of disaster is near and their doom rushes upon them."

Romans 12:19 "Do not take revenge, my friends, but leave room for God's wrath, for it is written: 'It is Mine to avenge; I will repay,' says the Lord."

The Bible clearly tells us in both the Old and New Testaments that God promises *He will avenge His people, He will pour out His wrath* on their enemies, and He *will repay* the evildoers for what they have done *with doom and disaster.* This truth shows us that *nobody* gets away with anything and, therefore, I as a child of God don't have to dish out the so-called spanking myself. I don't have to resort to, "an eye for an eye and a tooth for a tooth." I don't need even to fall for the destructive behavior of returning "sin" for "sin." I just leave the situation, even other people's sinful behavior, in God's Holy Hand and know that justice *will be served.* It's just a matter of time. Oh, the unredeemed may slander us, harm us, abuse us, or even kill us, but God will *always* have the last word on their evil deeds. *He* will take vengeance, *He* will take care of it. It's *His* battle not ours. Be rest assured, *He will* fight for us; we just need to be still as *He* brings us swift justice.

Exodus 14:14 "The LORD will fight for you; you need only to be still."

2 Chronicles 20:15 "This is what the LORD says to you: 'Do not be afraid or discouraged because of this vast army. For the battle is not yours, but God's.'"

Luke 18:7-8 "And will not God bring about justice for His chosen ones, who cry out to Him day and night? Will He keep putting them off? I tell you, He will see that they get justice, and quickly."

God will take care of His own. We don't need to fret, we don't need to worry. Even if it seems like we're getting the short end of the stick, God will still have the last word. Nobody gets away with anything. Even if it seems like other people are getting away with their dirty deeds towards us as God's children, God will repay them sooner or later, you can bank on it. It's guaranteed; it's just a matter of time. Therefore, in essence, what these Tribulation saints are crying out in a loud *mega voice* to the *Sovereign Lord* is what's called an "imprecatory" prayer, or in other words, they are "asking for God's judgment." These are the same kind of requests we see King David and other prophets in the Bible making to God as well. They, along with the Tribulation saints, knew of God's promises to *avenge His people* of wrongdoings from others.

Psalm 10:14-15 "But you, O God, do see trouble and grief; You consider it to take it in hand. The victim commits himself to You; You are the helper of the fatherless. Break the arm of the wicked and evil man; call him to account for his wickedness that would not be found out."

Psalm 35:1-3 "Contend, O LORD, with those who contend with me; fight against those who fight against me. Take up shield and buckler; arise and come to my aid. Brandish spear and javelin against those who pursue me."

Psalm 58:6-8 "Break the teeth in their mouths, O God; tear out, O LORD, the fangs of the lions! Let them vanish like water that flows away; when they draw the bow, let their arrows be blunted. Like a slug melting away as it moves along, like a stillborn child, may they not see the sun."

Isaiah 6:11-12 "Then I said, 'For how long, O Lord?' And He answered: 'Until the cities lie ruined and without inhabitant, until the houses are left deserted and the fields ruined and ravaged, until the LORD has sent everyone far away and the land is utterly forsaken."

Jeremiah 47:6-7 "'Ah, sword of the LORD,' you cry, 'how long till you rest? Return to your scabbard; cease and be still.' But how can it rest when the LORD has commanded it, when he has ordered it to attack Ashkelon and the coast?'"

So, as you can see, even King David and the mighty prophets made similar requests to God as we see here in *the fifth seal* with the Tribulation saints, *"How long, Sovereign Lord, holy and true, until You judge the inhabitants of the earth and avenge our blood?"* In all these cases there is not any violation of

Scripture happening here. We all know we are to pray for our enemies and refrain from exhibiting an eye for an eye and a tooth for a tooth, but that is not what is going on here. Whether it's King David or even the Tribulation saints, no one is *avenging their own blood*, no one is committing an eye for an eye or a tooth for a tooth, and no one is returning sin for sin. Rather, they are just leaving *justice* in *God's Hands*, acknowledging His promises and His Word, and asking Him to do what He promised to do. *Vengeance is Mine saith the Lord; I will repay*. The *Sovereign Lord* will do what He has promised to do, and we are to simply rest in that, as these men share:

"Master implies divine might, majesty, power, and authority, and it stresses the absolute power of God. How much longer did they have to wait for God to avenge them? 'Holy and true' were attributes of Christ earlier (Revelation 3:7), but here the Father is probably in view since He is the ultimate source of the judgments.

John saw these martyrs calling out to their heavenly Master to punish their murderers. Contrast the prayers of Jesus (Luke 23:34) and Stephen (Acts 7:60) in which they asked God to be merciful to their murderers. The difference is that the time of God's longsuffering has now ended, and He has begun to pour out His wrath on sinners."

"Lord is despotēs which emphasizes His ownership of the saints. Let us always keep in mind that He can do whatever He desires with His sheep. In this case, He allows their slaughter as a testimony to their faith and the evil unfolding below which will finally be judged.

When God finally tramples the winepress of His wrath, it is described as 'the day of vengeance,' for 'the year of My redeemed has come' (Isa.63:3-4). This then, is the judgment associated with the fifth seal – that petition of God by the martyred saints seals the fate of those who put them to death. One of the duties of the Goel, the nearest of kin, was to avenge the blood of the family member who had been murdered (Num.35:19-21; Deu.19:6; Jos.20:3).

Their persecutors appear to be currently living on the earth, which argues for understanding these as recent martyrs from the times described by the seals. This phrase denotes the earth dwellers and has significance far beyond merely designating people who happen to be living upon the earth. In this book, it takes on a soteriological and eschatological sense as a technical phrase describing those in the end times who refuse salvation, persecute the saints, and continue to blaspheme God in the midst of judgment.

Revelation 3:10 "Since you have kept my command to endure patiently, I will also keep you from the hour of trial that is going to come upon the whole world to test *those who live on the earth*."

Revelation 6:10 "They called out in a loud voice, 'How long, Sovereign Lord, holy and true, until you judge *the inhabitants of the earth* and avenge our blood?'"

Revelation 8:13 "As I watched, I heard an eagle that was flying in midair call out in a loud voice: 'Woe! Woe! Woe to *the inhabitants of the earth*, because of the trumpet blasts about to be sounded by the other three angels!'"

Revelation 11:10 "*The inhabitants of the earth* will gloat over them and will celebrate by sending each other gifts, because these two prophets had tormented those who live on the earth."

Revelation 13:8 "*All inhabitants of the earth* will worship the beast – all whose names have not been written in the book of life belonging to the Lamb that was slain from the creation of the world."

Revelation 13:12 "He exercised all the authority of the first beast on his behalf and made *the earth and its inhabitants* worship the first beast, whose fatal wound had been healed."

Revelation 13:14 "Because of the signs he was given power to do on behalf of the first beast, he deceived *the inhabitants of the earth*. He ordered them to set up an image in honor of the beast who was wounded by the sword and yet lived.

Revelation 17:1-2 "One of the seven angels who had the seven bowls came and said to me, 'Come, I will show you the punishment of the great prostitute, who sits on many waters. With her the kings of the earth committed adultery and *the inhabitants of the earth* were intoxicated with the wine of her adulteries.'"

Revelation 17:8 "The beast, which you saw, once was, now is not, and will come up out of the Abyss and go to his destruction. *The inhabitants of the earth* whose names have not been written in the book of life from the creation of the world will be astonished when they see the beast, because he once was, now is not, and yet will come."

These are the ones being tested by this time of trial from God (Rev.3:10) and rejoice when God's two witnesses are killed (Rev.11:10). It is they who are subject to the wrath of God and who will be deceived into worshiping the beast (Rev.13:12,14). Even though an angel preaches the everlasting gospel to each one, they continue in their rejection of God to the end. Therefore, their names are not written in the Book of Life."

"There's coming a great day of God's vengeance which will bring about holocausts of destruction like the world has never known, a day when the just God and the righteous God and the holy God brings His long-awaited justice on sinful men and women. There is coming a day when grace is over with, and judgment falls. It is that very anticipation that is in view in the fifth seal.

This seal is all about vengeance. It is a cry, on the part of these souls identified here, for the Lord to avenge our blood, to bring about judgment. It is not inconsistent with God to make such a plea, although you would imagine in the world today that such a God does not exist. People have recast God in the form that pleases them, and, of course, have eliminated any thought of His being a vengeful God. But the God of Scripture is a God of vengeance.

The psalmist affirmed the same truth about God when he wrote, 'O Lord, God of vengeance, God of vengeance shine forth, rise up, O judge of the earth, render recompense to the proud.' That's from Psalm 94. And the psalm ends this way, 'The Lord our God will destroy.' There are a number of what are called imprecatory psalms where the inspired writer of the psalm is calling for God to destroy the wicked.

God is a God of vengeance, and vengeance displays God's glory. And vengeance displays God's justice. And vengeance displays God's holiness. And vengeance displays God's righteousness. And when all of that is put on display and God is fully vindicated, the righteous will be glad.

Proverbs 25:21 *says, 'If your enemy is hungry, give him food to eat, and if he's thirsty, give him water to drink.'*

That's the other side of it; we're to be compassionate, we're to demonstrate the love of God toward sinners, just as the love of God was demonstrated toward us while we were yet sinners. There is a balance. We are to seek mercy and compassion for those who are under the judgment of God, as well as seeking and longing for vengeance, which puts God on display and vindicates His holiness and His righteousness.

That doesn't mean we treat sinners with revenge or vengeful spirits or retributive attitudes. Yes, we long for the day when God's holiness and justice and righteousness is vindicated, but at the same time we know it's a fearful day for the ungodly, and in the meantime, we reach out in love and compassion and mercy to them.

In Revelation chapter 6, we come face to face with God's vengeance. The time of grace is really coming to its end. This is the seven-year period when Jesus Christ not only judges the ungodly but takes back the earth and the universe for His own possession. The 7-year tribulation is the time when God unleashes His vengeance, when God unleashes His judgment and His wrath on the earth like never before. "[15]

And boy does He ever! This is the life changing choice that people are making even today, whether they realize it or not. If they don't want to receive today the *Sovereign Lord's* love and grace and mercy and forgiveness through Jesus Christ for their sins that *have to be judged* because God is *holy and true,* including the sins of murdering His own people which God doesn't take kindly to, then *vengeance is theirs from the Lord.* The reason planet earth is so utterly destroyed in the 7-year Tribulation is not only the general wickedness and rebellion from *the inhabitants of the earth* but also the *murderous behavior* of *the inhabitants of the earth* towards God's people. They think they're making things better for planet earth and themselves by getting rid of the followers of God, but all they accomplish is making sure that they and planet earth experience even more of the *vengeance of God!* The message in *the fifth seal* is loud and clear! God sends His own "megaphone" back to the world: *"Don't mess with My kids! If you don't stop and repent right now, vengeance is mine saith the Lord! I will repay!"* And repay He does. It didn't have to be this way. It was their choice. The opportunity to be forgiven by God and enter into a beautiful relationship with Him through Jesus was there the whole time in God's Word, and even in the message that these Tribulation saints were trying to tell them via *the word of God and the testimony they had maintained. The inhabitants of the earth* could have received God's mercy just like the Tribulation saints themselves, but since they rejected it and *murdered the messengers,* here comes what God has promised throughout the ages to those who mistreat, abuse, use and even kill His own people, *justice.* They will get what they and anyone else justly deserve for that kind of ungodly unholy wicked murderous behavior. A big 'ol heaping pile of God's *vengeance.* You can bank on it! This is what we see in increasing measure throughout the 7-year Tribulation all the way to the end. The *Sovereign Lord* has it all under control, His people always come out on top, He always has the last word, and He always has a good plan even in the midst of others' evil behavior, even during the 7-year Tribulation. This is what we will now see in the final detail concerning *the fifth seal.*

The **fourth detail** given about the object of the fifth seal is **The Response to the Martyrs.**

Revelation 6:11 "Then each of them was given a white robe, and they were told to wait a little longer, until the number of their fellow servants and brothers who were to be killed as they had been was completed."

Here we see in a nutshell how the *Sovereign Lord*, God Almighty, is now *comforting* His people, the Tribulation Martyrs, by reassuring them that He's got all things under control and they don't have to worry about a thing. He's heard their intense, massive cry and, as their loving Heavenly Father, He *responds* immediately by giving them two things to help soothe their injured hearts from the treatment they received back on earth from *the inhabitants of the earth.*

The first comforting thing the *Sovereign Lord* gives the Tribulation martyrs, in response to their loud and intense cry, is a *new gift.* We see this in the phrase, "*Then each of them was given a white robe...*" Now, we already saw that this *white robe* is a totally different robe than the Church, who left at the Rapture prior to the 7-year Tribulation, receives these Tribulation Saints are clothed in *white robes,* which are STOLE in Greek, while the Church is clothed in the white linen raiment of the priesthood, which is HIMATION in Greek. Two totally different garments for two totally different groups of people. Again, the lesson was that the Tribulation saints should've gotten saved *today* through Jesus Christ and receive a HIMATION robe so as to avoid the whole 7-year Tribulation. Unfortunately, they procrastinated too long and got saved after the Rapture and received a STOLE robe instead. Nonetheless, even this STOLE *white robe* they received from God is still *a major comforting gift.* It reminds them of the wonderful truth that all their suffering and heartache, and all the evils they experienced back on earth in the 7-year Tribulation, are gone for good, and that they can now enjoy heaven instead, as this man shares:

"They got a gift. 'There was given to each of them a white robe.' Being clothed in white is a sign of purity. It's a sign of righteousness, a sign of blessedness, a sign of the beauty of holiness. The Greek term is a dazzling white robe of dignity and honor reaching to the ground, stole from which we get the word stole. What it tells us is the Lord gave them honor and dignity and righteousness and purity to clothe them. Their souls are pure and righteous. As soon as they arrived I believe they had that.

By the way, they're arriving all the time here. More of them are accumulating under the altar as more of them are being killed. And when they arrive, I believe they receive this honor and dignity and righteousness and purity and holiness...to each one of them is given upon their arrival a white robe, symbolizing the perfection that they have now entered into.

They were told they should rest for a little while longer. You might say, 'Well they're being impatient.' No, they're not being impatient because they're perfect and perfect people aren't impatient. They're in heaven. You say, 'Well they're bugging God.' No, no, they're not bugging God. Perfect people don't bug God either. He's just saying it's coming, but you rest a while. Rest has the idea of heavenly rest, bliss. You don't be concerned about it, it's not quite here yet, you just enjoy the bliss of heaven."[16]

So once again, the *Sovereign Lord* is reminding the Tribulation saints that *He's got it all under control*, whether the events in the 7-year tribulation, satan or the Antichrist, their own horrible murders and treatment by *the inhabitants of the earth*, or even the issue of the timing of His *vengeance*. He's *comforting* them by in essence saying, "You don't need to worry about that anymore. Don't even let it enter your brain. You just enjoy heaven now. Come, enter My rest. All you need to do is take this *white robe* and enjoy the eternal bliss I am giving to you and rest assured, as you rightly stated, I am *holy and true,* and *I will* take care of things back on earth, doing what is just and right."

The second comforting thing the *Sovereign Lord* gives the Tribulation Martyrs in response to their loud and intense cry is a *new reminder*. We see this in the phrase, *"Then each of them...were told to wait a little longer, until the number of their fellow servants and brothers who were to be killed as they had been was completed."* Here we see God the *Sovereign Lord* answering the

Tribulation Martyrs' specific cry from earlier of, "*How long?*" It's not an out-of-place question they asked. It's one that has been asked throughout the ages by God's people concerning the evil injustices of this wicked world system, as this man remarks:

"They cry to the Lord, 'How long?' And God hears them. He bends down His ear to hear them and He says to them first, 'Wait a while, wait a while.' There is an elective purpose of God in these days. There are certain ones that are going to be offered, and He has got their names written down. There are certain ones that are going to be martyred, and their names are written down. 'You wait until these things have come to the full.'

Isn't it unusual, and a startling and an impressive thing that up there in heaven, in a disembodied state, in the intermediate period, those saints cry for the same thing God's people have cried for through all of the millenniums? 'O Lord, when is this final day to come? When is Thy kingdom coming? When is Thy will to be done in this earth as it is in heaven? When is it, Lord, that the people of God are going to be vindicated? When is it, Lord, that Thy great power will cast out evil and sin and death? When is it, Lord, that these things are coming to pass?'

Like John the Baptist in Matthew 11, 'Lord, I can see,' he says, 'the goodness of the ministry to the sick, and the healing of the blind. But, Lord, when is the ax going to be laid at the root of the tree? Are we to look for another Messiah, another Christ, who is going to bring the judgment of Almighty God? When is this,' said John the Baptist, 'I do not understand?'

Isn't that an amazing thing? The cry and the prayer of all the saints of all ages is just the same kind of a cry that these disembodied spirits utter to the Lord in heaven. 'Lord, when is this going to be? How long is evil going to reign? How long is death going to destroy? How long, Lord, is it going to be until Jesus shall come and set up His righteous kingdom in the earth?'

And the longing and the hope of God's people through the ages have always been just that. 'Lord, Lord, when does Jesus come? Why does He tarry? Why does He delay?' And then the prayer, 'Thy kingdom come, and Thy will be done, in earth as it is in heaven.' [Matthew 6:10]. And we're to wait. And we're to tarry. And we're to be patient, for that day is coming which Paul calls 'the blessed hope, the appearing of our great God and Savior Jesus Christ.' [Titus 2:13]."[17]

No, this is not an out-of-place question, "*How long?*" It's a common theme throughout the ages for God's people. Therefore, God *reminds* these Tribulation saints and saints of all time that we are to simply trust Him and know that His *timing is perfect*. Granted, we may not understand, we may not have all the answers, and we may not even fully comprehend what He's up to at all times. But that's not our concern. He knows what He's doing. As the *Sovereign Lord* He has *all things under control* and His *timing* is *perfect* and *precise*. He makes no mistakes. This is reiterated in the phrase, "u*ntil the number of their fellow servants and brothers who were to be killed as they had been was completed.*" God already knows the *exact precise* number of people who are going to be killed during the 7-year Tribulation. Every minute detail of the 7-year Tribulation is under His full control as the *Sovereign Lord*. Everyone's deaths, including their own and *their fellow servants and brothers* in the 7-year Tribulation, are under God's timing as the Author and Finisher of life. Again, how anyone can say that satan or man is in charge of these events in the 7-year Tribulation is beyond me. How many times does God have to make this abundantly clear, that He is the One in control? Therefore, we, let alone the Tribulation saints don't need to worry about any of this. Let these *reminders* comfort you. God knows what He's doing and it's all marching according to His plan, and His timing. Furthermore, His timing is always right, it's always the best, it's never late, but it's always on time. It's just His time, not ours. But that's okay, that's not our concern. Just trust Him and enjoy what He's won for His people, eternal bliss in heaven, and He'll work out the details back on earth. This is the first of two comforting reminders to the Tribulation saints.

I also see not only God giving the Tribulation saints a comforting reminder in His *control* of the events of the 7-year Tribulation, including the *timing* of these events, but He also reminds them that He is in control of their *purpose* as well. The response of, "w*ait a little longer, until the number of their fellow servants and brothers who were to be killed as they had been was completed,*" is God reminding them that, "I have taken care of you. I pulled you out of the horrible nightmare of the 7-year Tribulation. Your needs are met. You have a *white robe*. You're in heaven. You're okay. You are safe. Enjoy heaven. Enjoy your reward, enjoy this eternal bliss. Don't worry about planet earth anymore. I'll take care of that." But if you think about it, He's also reminding them of His *purpose* in waiting. To me, the phrase, "w*ait a little longer,*" is also God's way of saying, in essence, "Your needs are taking care of. You're fine. You're safe. But now I'm going to go save some more. I have a *purpose* in this. Just wait a little bit." It's like when a boat capsizes in the ocean and a rescuer brings the first wave of people safely to shore, but then naturally goes back to see if they can save even more. In fact, they will continue to do so until the very end, until there is absolutely no sign or any possibility of anyone else being able to be rescued. He goes back again and again until all potential survivors have either been rescued or have unfortunately perished. He has to make sure. In fact, if he did not do this he would be looked upon as some sort of horrible ogre. So, it is with God in the 7-year Tribulation. The phrase, "*wait a little longer, until the number of their fellow servants and brothers who were to be killed as they had been was completed*," is God's way of saying, "I'm saving as many as I can." God's *purpose* in having the Tribulation saints *wait a little longer* is a reminder that He's going to save even more people, *just like them*. He is not condoning all the evil and sinful behavior of this wicked world system and being slow and callous about it, either today or in the 7-year Tribulation. Rather, we already saw that *He will avenge*. Judgment is coming. Justice *will be* served! Rather, He is simply going *back for more survivors* in the depths of the water grave of the 7-year Tribulation until there is no opportunity left. If He didn't do that, what kind of God would He be? One researcher puts it this way:

"Here again a most difficult reality presents itself. God, who has the power to step in and end this holocaust at any moment, instead chooses to allow it to play out in all its gruesome detail. Although we will never fully apprehend His divine patience, we know that it is explained, in part, by His great mercy toward those who have not yet turned, the glorious testimony being accrued by the martyred saints, and the filling up of the cup of injustice of the perpetrators. If He were to move immediately in vengeance at the time of their request, then some would be eternally lost that are yet to become their brethren. More millions will be saved under the preaching of God's witnesses in these seven years."[18]

God is in essence reminding the Tribulation saints that He is a patient and merciful God, and He is only allowing this period when they are to *wait a little longer* so as to give people time to repent and be saved just like they were.

2 Peter 3:9 "The Lord is not slow in keeping His promise, as some understand slowness. He is patient with you, not wanting anyone to perish, but everyone to come to repentance."

The *Sovereign Lord* is not slow in keeping His promises. He's not condoning or being lax towards the wickedness of others, including the evil murderous behavior of *the inhabitants of the earth* towards the Tribulation saints in the 7-year Tribulation. No, not at all. He will avenge and pour out His vengeance. He is *holy and true*. It will happen, *it has to happen*. You can bank on it. But He is also patient and merciful, just like He was with the Tribulation saints when He gave them a chance to be saved in the 7-year Tribulation, even though He didn't have to. He could have cut His mercy off right after the Rapture of the Church, before all this horror on planet earth began, but He didn't. In fact, think about it-the Tribulation saints may very well have been some of the people guilty of mocking and ridiculing *the Church* prior to the Rapture and then of course they found themselves left behind. Fortunately, they responded to God's call of salvation in the 7-year Tribulation, albeit late, and thus suffered the consequences, namely a brutal bloody murder by *the inhabitants of the earth*. But the point is, they, of all people, should appreciate God's patience and mercy in wanting more people to have a chance to be saved just like they were, even though it's going to involve even more deaths. God is reminding these Tribulation saints of His patience and mercy. He is not an ogre, or a slow indifferent Deity to pain and suffering. No. God is a loving God and He wants as many people to be saved as can be. He does not take pleasure in sending people to hell.

Ezekiel 18:23 "Do I take any pleasure in the death of the wicked? declares the Sovereign LORD. Rather, am I not pleased when they turn from their ways and live?"

Ezekiel 33:11 "Say to them, 'As surely as I live, declares the Sovereign LORD, I take no pleasure in the death of the wicked, but rather that they turn from their ways and live. Turn! Turn from your evil ways! Why will you die, O house of Israel?'"

So, in essence, in *the fifth seal* God is "crying out" with His own "megaphone" to Israel and the unbelieving Gentiles, *the inhabitants of the earth*, "Why must you perish! Please turn! Turn from your evil ways and repent! I'm not willing that any of you should perish but that everyone come to repentance. Why will you die, O house of Israel and inhabitants of the earth?" God's wonderful merciful loving patience is on display here in the phrase, "w*ait a little longer, until the number of their fellow servants and brothers who were to be killed as they had been was completed*." He's not condoning the wickedness and evil in the world today, and He's certainly not condoning the wickedness and evil in the 7-year Tribulation, including the murder of His own people. Rather, He is on a rescue mission. He sees the boat going down, and He's trying to reach out to as many people as He can and rescue them from His ongoing wrath and increasing vengeance, *due to the wickedness and evil* in the world that His *holy and true* character *must judge*. Turn! Turn! Turn! is the reminder in this final detail in *the fifth seal*. Why? Because, be assured, just like a sinking ship, time eventually runs out and thus the opportunity to be saved doesn't last forever. If the offer to be saved comes your way and God's Hand is extended towards you and you still reject it, then you yourself have sealed your utter doom. God gave you time, He gave you the opportunity, but you rejected it. This ship, planet earth, is going down the drain in the 7-year Tribulation. You better not reject it but accept God's Hand of salvation before it's too late! Things are about to get even worse, as this man shares:

"And they cry out, it says, with a loud voice. They're very impassioned, they're crying out. 'How long: You're holy, which means You've got to deal with sin; You're true; You have to be faithful to Your promise, You who are separate from evil, You who are faithful to Your Word. How long before You act against evil and keep Your word?'

These prayers are not personal vendettas, they're not thirst for personal revenge. Their wholly desire is for the end of iniquity. Their wholly desire is for the destruction of satan. Their wholly desire is for the devastation of Antichrist and the false prophet and all who followed him. Iniquity has reached its height in the slaughter. 'How long until You avenge our blood?'

Will not God judge when His elect cry out to Him? This intercession in the fifth seal activates the tortures to come in the sixth and seventh seals, which include the trumpet and bowl judgments. Grace is nearing its end. Man is a wicked wretched animal and it's only the restraining power of the Holy Spirit that holds him back.

The world is going to enter into atrocities that men haven't even conceived of, slaughter and massacre unheard of. Why? Because it will be turned over to satan unrestrained. And we will have a worldwide Manson family. The world is headed in this direction. You can't even think about this without a certain frightening feeling."[19]

　　Get *saved now* if you're not, is the merciful reminder in *the fifth seal*! God's wrath continues to be poured out and His vengeance is just getting cranked up over for the murder of His children. Things are about to sink to a whole new level of destruction on planet earth and you don't want to be there! This ratcheting up of God's vengeance is what we will now see in the next seal judgment.

Chapter Ten

The Breaking of the Doomsday Seal

The **twelfth thing** we see in the breaking of the planet is the **Ordering of the Sixth Seal**.

Revelation 6:12a "I watched as *He opened* the sixth seal."

Looking at this verse, being this far now into Revelation Chapter 6, one would almost be tempted to say something like this, "Alright already! How many times do we have to go through this? I get it! I get it! *He*, God *the Lamb* is opening this seal too! How many times do we have to do this?" Well again, not only does this obviously inform us of just how important the identity of the opener of the seals really is, because God is constantly reiterating it to us, revealing the One Who is responsible for the wrath being poured out in all these seals during the first half of the 7-year Tribulation, but believe it or not, it still won't be the last time. In fact, the next time God informs us of the identity of the One opening these seal judgments, He's even more emphatic about it. This shows us that He really, really wants us to get this truth into our heads that *He*, God *the Lamb*, is the One Who is responsible for this wrath in the 7-year Tribulation, not man or satan. Let's now take an advanced look at that next reminder.

Revelation 6:15-17 "Then the kings of the earth, the princes, the generals, the rich, the mighty, and every slave and every free man hid in caves and among the rocks of the mountains. They called to the mountains and the rocks, 'Fall on us and hide us from the face of Him who sits on the throne and *from the wrath of the Lamb*! For the great day of their wrath has come, and who can stand?'"

So here we basically see the shocking response from all levels of society, every type of position, all types of people, rich and poor, free and slave, elite and commoner alike, all saying the exact same thing, in complete agreement, in response to these seal judgments, *"Fall on us and hide us from the face of Him who sits on the throne and from the wrath of the Lamb*!" There it is, plain as day. You can't get any clearer than this. The horrific, earth shattering judgments that have been thrust upon planet earth in the 7-year Tribulation are coming *from the wrath of the Lamb*. Once again, how anyone can say that these seal judgments are the wrath of man, let alone the wrath of satan, is not only unbelievable, it's downright unbiblical just based on this single text alone. God has contextually repeatedly been making this truth abundantly clear from the very beginning of the seals, as we've been seeing, that *the Lamb* is the One *opening these seals* and thus is responsible for this wrath poured out on planet earth. Now He gets even more blunt about it in this verse, showing us that these events are all coming *from the wrath of the Lamb*. Make no mistake about it. If you didn't get this truth from the repeated statements over and over again from the very beginning of Chapter 6 that *the Lamb* is the One *opening each and every seal* and thus is responsible for this wrath, let it now be made known loud and clear, this really is *the wrath of the Lamb*. This must be an incredibly important truth for God to go to such great lengths to make sure we understand just Who the true author of this wrath is.

Yet, what's even more unbelievable is how these same people, who try to squeeze their preconceived ideas and false teachings into the Book of Revelation, that this wrath on planet earth in the seal judgments is not from *the Lamb* but rather man or satan, will also try to twist this exact same verse that clearly identifies this wrath as coming *from the Lam,b* and actually say that it only refers to the *sixth seal* and the events that follow forward. They try to justify their false teaching by saying the very next verse says, *"For the great day of their wrath has come"*, and since it says *has come,* then it only means this wrath mentioned here started right then and there, i.e. it *has come*, in other words it just arrived. Well, with all due respect, nice try, but once again this denies the Biblical text. First of all, God contextually repeated over and over again, in *all the seals*, including the *sixth seal*, that *the Lamb* is the One Who is opening them up and thus is the One Who is responsible for unleashing the wrath that followed each time. Secondly, the phrase *has come* will not allow for their faulty assumption that this wrath has just begun. Rather, as this researcher points out, the Greek verb tells us emphatically that this wrath has been going on all along:

"The controlling verb in verse 17, 'is come' (lthen), is aorist indicative, referring to a previous arrival of the wrath, not something that is about to take place."[1]

Once again, there it is, plain as day. There is no way of getting around this truth from God. You cannot deny the Greek verb. It is what it is. As interpreters of the Bible, we are to allow the Bible to speak out to us what it says, not try to squeeze into it what our preconceived ideas and false teachings want it to say. God is the author of the Bible, not us. Therefore, God is clearly here emphatically, telling us over and over again, and even in a blunt manner, that this wrath being poured out on planet earth in the 7-year tribulation is not only *the wrath of the Lamb*, but it's been going on from the very beginning of the *first seal* all the way up to the *sixth seal* and it will continue to the very end! It didn't just start in the *sixth seal* but has been going on the whole time! It's all God's wrath, the wrath of *the Lamb,* through and through. How ironic it is that this text plainly revels how all levels of society, every type of position, all types of people, rich and poor, free and slave, elite and commoner alike in the 7-year Tribulation know and get this obvious truth, *"Fall on us and hide us from the face of Him who sits on the throne and from the wrath of the Lamb,"* but people today still refuse to acknowledge it. The *sixth seal* causes *the inhabitants of the earth* under *the wrath of the Lamb* to be in complete unison as to where these judgments are coming from, because they are in the midst of the dreaded, prophesied Day of the Lord, the 7-year Tribulation, as this man points out:

"It would be difficult to paint any scene more moving or more terrible than that described at the opening of the sixth seal. Up to now, the effects of the first five seals, although unprecedented in their global impact, could still be explained away as an intensification of what history already records: conflict, war, death, famine, disease, and martyrdom.

With the opening of the sixth seal all such explanations vanish, for the signs which attend this seal are unmistakable in their uniqueness and scope. The magnitude of the earthquake and cosmic disturbances that will occur when Christ breaks the sixth seal (Rev.6:12-14+) forces the conclusion that this will be an awesome expression of the wrath of God, not the work of unregenerate mankind.

When the sixth seal is opened, there are unmistakable global signs of astronomical proportions, but the Lamb has yet to ride forth on His horse (Rev.19:11+) – He is still in heaven losing seals.

Paul declared that the broad Day of the Lord will come like a thief in the night – suddenly, unexpectedly, when the victims are unprepared (1 Th.5:2). A thief depends upon the element of surprise for success. He does not give his intended victims a forewarning of his coming. Paul's point – the unsaved will be given no forewarning of the coming of the broad Day of the Lord – rules out any of the seals of Revelation as being forewarnings of the beginning of the broad Day.

For example, it rules out the sixth seal (Rev.6:12-14+) which will cause great cosmic disturbances and a major earthquake causing the people of the world to flee to the mountains in terror (Rev.6:15-17+). If the disturbances of the sixth seal were a precursor to the Day of the Lord, the unsaved thereby would be given a graphic forewarning of its coming and would not be caught by surprise when it comes. Thus, the Day of the Lord would not come unexpectedly like a thief in the night.

By the time of the sixth seal, the Day of the Lord must be already underway. Having already come without warning, like a thief in the night, it is now made unmistakable to the earth dwellers in the cosmic signs which attend this seal. "[2]

In other words, just like the Greek verb states, these people in the *sixth seal* are simply acknowledging that *the wrath of the Lamb* has been going on from the very beginning of the *first seal,* when they were unfortunately caught by surprise like a thief in the night, with the Day of the Lord or the 7-year Tribulation. The *sixth seal* and its horrific events force them to cough up this truth that was there the whole time. Too bad people today wouldn't do the same.

The **thirteenth thing** we see in the breaking of the planet is the **Object of the Sixth Seal**.

As we shall soon see, the scene here in Revelation 6 is going to switch from heaven back to earth. God's people were martyred and seen in heaven in the previous seal, the *fifth seal*, crying out for Him to fulfil His promise to *avenge their blood*. Now what follows in the *sixth seal* is the immediate mind-blowing response from God to their request. This is why the *sixth seal* is aptly called the breaking of the Doomsday Seal. *Mankind's utter doom* for their sins in general, as well as their sin of murdering God's people, is the *object* of discussion. Here we will witness not just portions of the planet or even just portions of humanity being affected, but *the whole planet* literally is about to be rocked by God! This is the *object* of *the sixth seal*.

Revelation 6:12-17 "I watched as he opened the sixth seal. There was a great earthquake. The sun turned black like sackcloth made of goat hair, the whole moon turned blood red, and the stars in the sky fell to earth, as late figs drop from a fig tree when shaken by a strong wind. The sky receded like a scroll, rolling up, and every mountain and island was removed from its place. Then the kings of the earth, the princes, the generals, the rich, the mighty, and every slave and every free man hid in caves and among the rocks of the mountains. They called to the mountains and the rocks, 'Fall on us and hide us from the face of Him who sits on the throne and from the wrath of the Lamb! For the great day of their wrath has come, and who can stand?'"

Luke 21:11 "There will be great earthquakes, famines and pestilences in various places, and fearful events and great signs from heaven."

Again, we've already repeatedly seen how Revelation 6 and Matthew 24 are prophetically dealing with the same time-frame, the beginning portion of the 7-year Tribulation. Therefore, by observing these passages together, we can see that what the planet is in store for now is simply *a series of massive doomsday events,* one after another, non-stop, forcing the people on the planet to acknowledge where these global catastrophes are coming from, even since the beginning of the 7-year Tribulation. The global judgments have been coming *from the wrath of the Lamb* the whole time, but now things are ramping up even more. God doesn't mess around with sin, including the sin of murdering His people. Now He cranks things up, if you will, even more, in harmony with His birth pain analogy. This tells us that even after all we've seen thus far, it's about to get even worse, as this researcher agrees:

"Jesus will radically alter His creation in Revelation 6:12-17. The scene shifts back to earth as Jesus opens the sixth seal. John tells us that the earth will be affected by six cosmic catastrophes. In these three verses, God shakes the universe like a rag doll. As a result, the entire world will know that there is a God. They will also know that His divine wrath is unleashed against their rebellion."[3]

In other words, it's Doomsday time! In fact, the word "doomsday" is defined as, "The destruction of the world, a foreboding and impending calamity, a widespread total destruction, a day of reckoning." This is what is coming to planet earth in the *sixth seal.* This is the *object.* This is what it's all about. A systematic shocking foreboding destruction of planet earth. Impending calamity and total widespread destruction for all mankind. Great utter terror from all walks of life as God has His day of reckoning over the sins of mankind, including the sins of murdering His own people. I said it before, I'll say it again. Don't mess with God's kids! If you do, this is what you can expect. Not just the earth, but the universe itself will be shaken like a rag doll. Wow! How many times has it been stated before, but obviously needs to be stated again now here in this text, "You don't want to be here!" If you're reading this and you're still not saved, what more does God have to do to get your attention? You better cry out to Jesus and ask Him to forgive you of all your sins *now,* otherwise you too will be shaken with the rest of the planet like a rag doll by the wrath of God, literally, *the wrath of the Lamb.* You too will cry out in utter terror over the utter doomsday events that are going to be unleashed upon planet earth. There is only one way to escape this horrible end times scenario and that is to get saved *now, today,* before it's too late! Don't be left behind to face the Doomsday of God! It will be the greatest time of terror this planet has ever seen up until this time, as this researcher shares:

"Now remember, there is a seven-sealed book, or scroll, that contains the information about Christ taking over the universe. As each seal is broken, another scene develops. These seven seals unfold in a seven-year period yet to come in the future that we know as the time of tribulation, the time of Jacob's trouble, Daniel's seventieth week. And during this period of time, the Lamb, the Son of God, is unrolling the scroll because He has both the authority to do so as the heir of everything and the power to do so as God.

So, the Lamb of God, the Son, the Lord Jesus Christ here in this vision that John sees, is unrolling this scroll which describes the events as He takes over the universe from satan and the demons and sinners who occupy it. The first force was false peace. The second force we saw was war. The third force was famine. The fourth force was pestilence. The fifth force was vengeance. The force being exemplified and described in the sixth seal is fear.

Fear is a powerful emotion, powerful enough in this scene for people to begin the world's largest prayer meeting, only they don't pray to God, they pray to the mountains and the rocks. And they pray for the mountains and the rocks to fall on them. A prayer for suicide, a prayer for destruction. They're so afraid, they would rather die than face the wrath of God, the wrath of the Lamb.

If we were to title the sixth seal, we might title it 'Scared to death.'"[4]

Boy, isn't that the truth! Why is the planet "scared to death" at this time in the 7-year Tribulation? Because as we are to see, the Hand of God is about to beat to a pulp the planet He created, with His wrath!

The **first detail** given about the object of the sixth seal is **The Beating of the Planet**.

Revelation 6:12-14 "I watched as he opened the sixth seal. There was a great earthquake. The sun turned black like sackcloth made of goat hair, the whole moon turned blood red, and the stars in the sky fell to earth, as late figs drop from a fig tree when shaken by a strong wind. The sky receded like a scroll, rolling up, and every mountain and island was removed from its place."

The details we are given in these next three verses simply show the planet taking a beating from God. It's a series of events, a series of blows, one after the other in rapid fashion, delivering a shock and awe punch to *the inhabitants of the earth*. Picture if you will a boxing ring filled with people proud and arrogant boasting in themselves and their so-called utopian accomplishments. In the midst of this selfish, deceitful chatter God steps into the ring and starts swinging. Each blow is precise and each and every blow hits its intended target with a force that is unbelievable. One by one the boastful mouths are silenced, and the bodies begin to pile up with one knockout punch after another being delivered by the Hand of Almighty God. The fear that mankind experiences from being in this "ring" with Almighty God is beyond belief, as this man shares:

"As each of the seals has been broken we have seen what is to come. First there is a false peace, orchestrated by false prophets and false christs, led by the Antichrist, leading the world to an imaginary utopia which is immediately shattered by the second seal which is war, worldwide war, war all over the globe, followed by famine, the obvious result of war, the scarcity of food, followed by death through pestilence and disaster so that one fourth of the population of the whole world perish in a very brief time. And then we saw the fifth, the breaking out of persecution. And then we saw the martyrs praying for God's vengeance.

All of those first five, mark this, had an element of human agency. There were human agents in orchestrating the peace. There are human agents involved in the war, the famine, the death that comes through pestilence. There are human beings involved even in the vengeance as there are believers praying for this to come. They, of course, are men and women, even though glorified at that point.

Now when you come to the sixth seal, God acts without men. You've come to a level of intervention by God that is holy and solely His own. A more frightening scene and realization couldn't even be imagined. What hits is unavoidably attributable only to God. And the paralyzing, terrifying act is inconceivable and devastating."[5]

You arrogant, foolish, deceived people. You rejected God, you blasphemed God, you sinned against God, you even had the audacity to rejoice and throw a worldwide party in the face of God over the killing of His very own people, and now God steps into the ring called planet earth and begins to pummel His detractors. Unlike the movie character Rocky Balboa, the planet will not be getting back up off the mat when God gets through delivering His mighty blows. Let us now observe those beatings.

The **first beating** of the planet from the sixth seal is **The Great Earthquake**.

Revelation 6:12a-b "I watched as he opened the sixth seal. *There was a great earthquake.*"

If you're familiar with the massive influx of super hero movies being cranked out by Hollywood lately, you'll notice how many of the superhuman characters have a certain dramatic way of landing after dropping from a large height. They always seem to land on a bended knee with one of their fists hitting the ground. When they enter the scene in such fashion it results in a colossal shockwave that permeates the ground, causing destructive reverberations for many blocks around this epicenter. The streets, sidewalks, and pavement rumble and liquefy, forcing vehicles to flip over and buildings to collapse. Thanks to computer animation and graphics, Hollywood is able to make these depictions look life-like and spectacular. Well, believe it or not, what we are about to see in the opening of the *sixth seal* is Almighty God doing the same thing, only it's not a make-believe Hollywood movie, it's planet earth's soon coming reality. And neither does God need computer graphics to pull it off. He just uses His Holy fist, and the results make anything Hollywood could come up with look like a grade "B" black and white silent movie in comparison to the destruction God will cause at this stage of the 7-year Tribulation. When God turns from using man as His tool of judgment, and instead enters the scene Himself, if you will, in the sixth seal, not only will sidewalks flip, but whole cities will be crushed. Not only will vehicles spiral end to end, but whole populations will be blown away. Not only will pavement and buildings liquefy and crumble, but whole portions of the planet will be *removed from their places*. If anyone knows how to make a dramatic entrance, it's Almighty God! And the fear is quite understandable, as the Bible warns.

Psalm 90:7,11 "We are consumed by Your anger and terrified by Your indignation. Who knows the power of Your anger? For Your wrath is as great as the fear that is due You."

Hebrews 10:30,31 "For we know Him Who said, 'It is mine to avenge; I will repay.' It is a dreadful thing to fall into the hands of the living God."

      Dreadful is certainly the appropriate word. It's the Greek word, "phoberos", from which we get our English word "phobia". It means, "inspiring fear, something terrible, something formidable, literally a terrifying thing." When the wrathful Hand of God comes down in the *sixth seal*, a whole new phobia spreads across planet earth. Psychologists won't have time to write about it, let alone discuss it. It will erupt in a second and spread like a massive wave from one corner of the globe to the other. Mankind will instantly be inspired to fear, they will be filled with dread, they will shake, they will tremble at this approaching formidable Foe. It's the most terrifying thing they've ever encountered or will ever encounter again because, for most of them, they will be decimated and destroyed in this reverberating blow, this global shockwave that is released by the Hand of Almighty God.

      So how does this fearful time begin? It starts with *a great earthquake*. Notice it's not just an earthquake but *a great earthquake*. It's the Greek words, "megas seismos" which literally means, "a massive, large, or great shaking, commotion, or tempest." In short, this is not your average everyday earthquake that we hear about all the time on the news today erupting in various parts of the world. In fact, let's whet our appetite concerning the devastating effects of earthquakes in general that mankind has experienced in the past, in hopes to understand more fully what planet earth will be going through when this "megas seismos" hits the planet in the *sixth seal*. The following lists some of the worst earthquakes every recorded by man.

- **Ashgabat, Turkmenistan, Oct. 5, 1948**

7.3 magnitude, 110,000 deaths. This quake brought extreme damage in Ashgabat (Ashkhabad) and nearby villages, where almost all the brick buildings collapsed, concrete structures were heavily damaged and freight trains were derailed. Damage and casualties also occurred in the Darreh Gaz area in neighboring Iran. Surface rupture was observed both northwest and southeast of Ashgabat.

- **Kanto, Japan, Sept. 1, 1923**

7.9 magnitude, 142,800 deaths. This earthquake brought extreme destruction in the Tokyo-Yokohama area, both from the temblor and subsequent firestorms, which burned about 381,000 of the more than 694,000 houses that were partially or completely destroyed. Although often known as the Great Tokyo Earthquake (or the Great Tokyo Fire), the damage was most severe in Yokohama. Nearly 6 feet of permanent uplift was observed on the north shore of Sagami Bay, and horizontal displacements of as much as 15 feet were measured on the Boso Peninsula.

- **Ardabil, Iran, March. 23, 893**

Magnitude not known, about 150,000 deaths. The memories of the massive Damghan earthquake had barely faded when only 37 years later, Iran was again hit by a huge earthquake. This time it cost 150,000 lives and destroyed the largest city in the northwestern section of the country. The area was again hit by a fatal earthquake in 1997.

- **Haiyuan, Ningxia , China, Dec. 16, 1920**

7.8 magnitude, about 200,000 deaths. This earthquake brought total destruction to the Lijunbu-Haiyuan-Ganyanchi area. Over 73,000 people were killed in Haiyuan County. A landslide buried the village of Sujiahe in Xiji County. More than 30,000 people were killed in Guyuan County. Nearly all the houses collapsed in the cities of Longde and Huining. About 125 miles of surface faulting was seen from Lijunbu through Ganyanchi to Jingtai. There were large numbers of landslides and ground cracks throughout the epicentral area. Some rivers were dammed, others changed course.

- **Damghan, Iran, Dec. 22, 856**

Magnitude not known, about 200,000 deaths. This earthquake struck a 200-mile stretch of northeast Iran, with the epicenter directly below the city of

Demghan, which was at that point the capital city. Most of the city was destroyed as well as the neighboring areas. Approximately 200,000 people were killed.

- **Haiti, Jan 12, 2010**

Magnitude 7.0. According to official estimates, 222,570 people killed. According to official estimates, 300,000 were also injured, 1.3 million displaced, 97,294 houses destroyed and 188,383 damaged in the Port-au-Prince area and in much of southern Haiti. This includes at least 4 people killed by a local tsunami in the Petit Paradis area near Leogane. Tsunami waves were also reported at Jacmel, Les Cayes, Petit Goave, Leogane, Luly and Anse a Galets.

- **Sumatra, Indonesia, Dec. 26, 2004**

Magnitude 9.1, 227,898 deaths. This was the third largest earthquake in the world since 1900 and the largest since the 1964 Prince William Sound, Alaska temblor. In total, 227,898 people were killed or were missing and presumed dead and about 1.7 million people were displaced by the earthquake and subsequent tsunami in 14 countries in South Asia and East Africa. (In January 2005, the death toll was 286,000. In April 2005, Indonesia reduced its estimate for the number missing by over 50,000.)

- **Aleppo, Syria, Aug. 9, 1138**

Magnitude not known, about 230,000 deaths. Contemporary accounts said the walls of Syria's second-largest city crumbled and rocks cascaded into the streets. Aleppo's citadel collapsed, killing hundreds of residents. Although Aleppo was the largest community affected by the earthquake, it likely did not suffer the worst of the damage. European Crusaders had constructed a citadel at nearby Harim, which was leveled by the quake. A Muslim fort at Al-Atarib was destroyed as well, and several smaller towns and manned forts were reduced to rubble. The quake was said to have been felt as far away as Damascus, about 220 miles to the south. The Aleppo earthquake was the first of several occurring between 1138 and 1139 that devastated areas in northern Syria and western Turkey.

- **Tangshan, China, July 27, 1976**

Magnitude 7.5. Official casualty figure is 255,000 deaths. Estimated death toll as high as 655,000. Damage extended as far as Beijing. This is probably the greatest death toll from an earthquake in the last four centuries, and the second greatest in recorded history.

- **Shensi, China, Jan. 23, 1556**

Magnitude about 8, about 830,000 deaths. This earthquake occurred in the Shaanxi province (formerly Shensi), China, about 50 miles east-northeast of Xi'an, the capital of Shaanxi. More than 830,000 people are estimated to have been killed. Damage extended as far away as about 270 miles northeast of the epicenter, with reports as far as Liuyang in Hunan, more than 500 miles away. Geological effects reported with this earthquake included ground fissures, uplift, subsidence, liquefaction and landslides. Most towns in the damage area reported city walls collapsed, most all houses collapsed and many of the towns reported ground fissures with water gushing out.[6]

Wow! A quarter million people. Nearly one million people. As you can see, recorded earthquakes throughout history have had some horrible and devastating effects, let alone massive death toll numbers. Yet, as shocking and horrific as those recorded earthquakes were in the past, it still pales in comparison to the earthquake that is coming in the near future in the *sixth seal*! Mankind has never seen, let alone experienced, an earthquake like this one. Not even close! That's because the earthquake that takes place in the *sixth seal* is not just an earthquake like those we just read, about but rather *a great earthquake*, a "megas seismos." This means, modern-day historians do not have even a category to put this one in. Modern-day seismologists don't even have a reference point, let alone accurate recoding equipment, to size up this powerful "megas seismos" that's coming from God. As one researcher puts it:

"The first catastrophe that Jesus brings (in the sixth seal) is a 'great earthquake' that will rock the whole world."[7]

This is one rock concert you definitely don't want to be a part of! Yes, the planet will be "a rockin' and a rollin'" alright during this time. But it will not be from the beat of a pelvic gyrating tune; rather it will be "a rockin'" from the beating that it's taking from the earth-shattering mega quake sent by Almighty God! No smiles or bobbing of heads here. Only screams of terror and groans filled with sorrow as the planet begins to rip apart. The prophesied shaking of the planet has begun, as these researchers point out:

"Jesus said great earthquakes would be one of the signs of 'the beginning of sorrows' (Mtt.24:7-8). The OT prophets also predicted a time when God would intensely shake the earth. Haggai revealed that global earthquakes and the overthrow of the Gentile kingdoms would precede the return of God's glory to His (millennial) Temple:

For thus says the Lord of hosts: 'Once more (it is a little while) I will shake heaven and earth, the sea and dry land; and I will shake all nations, and they shall come to the Desire of All Nations, and I will fill this temple with glory,' says the Lord of hosts. I will overthrow the throne of kingdoms; I will destroy the strength of the Gentile kingdoms. I will overthrow the chariots and those who ride in them; the horses and their riders shall come down, everyone by the sword of his brother. (Hag 2:6-7,22)

Joel saw earthquakes associated with the mighty judgments of God poured out in the Day of the Lord, judgments which were intended to cause people to turn to God.

The earth quakes before them, the heavens tremble; the sun and moon grow dark, and the stars diminish their brightness. The LORD gives voice before His army, for His camp is very great; for strong is the One who executes His word. For the day of the LORD is great and very terrible; who can endure it? 'Now, therefore,' says the LORD, 'Turn to Me with all your heart, with fasting, with weeping, and with mourning.' (Joel 2:10-12)

In the Old Testament earthquakes were also regular features of divine visitation. When God descended on Mount Sinai, 'the whole mountain trembled violently' (Exodus 19:18). Isaiah prophesied of a time when the Lord would 'shake the earth' (Isaiah 2:19). In Haggai, the Lord says: 'In a little while I will once more shake the heavens and the earth, the sea and the dry land' (2:6).

This language had been picked up in Jewish writings of the intertestamental period and had become typical of apocalyptic tracts. In apocalyptic literature the 'end of the world' was described by cosmic disturbances of various kinds."[8]

Yes, it will literally be "the end of the world." The planet at this time in the 7-year Tribulation is literally in the beginning stages of being beaten to a pulp by the Hand of God, and this massive earthquake here that "rocks the whole world" is just the first blow. Speaking of just the beginning, another interesting and horrible side-effect of earthquakes is not only the massive devastation and huge death tolls caused by the shaking in general, but they also trigger two other types of disasters that lead to *even more* devastations and deaths. These killer side effects are Tsunamis and Landslides. So once again, let us whet our appetite concerning these two additional devastating effects caused by earthquakes so as to get a fuller picture of what happens when *the inhabitants of the earth* experience this "megas seismos" in the *sixth seal*:

TSUNAMIS

Tsunamis can be generated by any significant displacement of water in oceans or lakes, though are most commonly created by the movement of tectonic plates under the ocean floor, during an earthquake. But they can also be caused by volcanic eruptions, glacial carving, meteorite impacts or landslides.

- **Ise Bay, Japan - 18 January 1586**

  The earthquake that caused the Ise Bay tsunami is best estimated as being of magnitude 8.2. The waves rose to a height of nearly 20 feet, causing damage to a number of towns. The town of Nagahama experienced an outbreak of fire as the earthquake first occurred, destroying half the city. It is reported that the nearby Lake Biwa surged over the town, leaving no trace except for the castle. The Ise Bay tsunamis caused more than 8,000 deaths and a large amount ofdamage.

- **Ryuku Islands, Japan - 24 April 1771**

  A magnitude 7.4 earthquake is believed to have caused a tsunami that damaged a large number of islands in the region; however, the most serious damage was restricted to Ishigaki and Miyako Islands. It is commonly cited that the wave that struck Ishigaki Island was estimated to have been around 36 to 50 feet high. The tsunami destroyed a total of 3,137 homes, killing nearly 12,000 people in total.

- **North Pacific Coast, Japan - 11 March 2011**

  A powerful tsunami travelling 800km per hour with 33 feet high waves swept over the east coast of Japan, killing more than 18,000 people. The tsunami was spawned by a 9.0 magnitude earthquake that reached depths of 24.4km-making it the fourth-largest earthquake ever recorded. Approximately 452,000 people were relocated to shelters, and still remain displaced from their destroyed homes. The violent shaking resulted in a nuclear emergency, in which the Fukushima Daiichi nuclear power plant began leaking radioactive steam. The World Bank estimates that it could take Japan up to five years to financially overcome the $235 billion damages.

- **Sanriku, Japan - 15 June 1896**

This tsunami propagated after an estimated magnitude 7.6 earthquake occurred off the coast of Sanriku, Japan. The tsunami was reported at Shirahama to have reached a height of 125 feet, causing damage to more than 11,000 homes and killing some 22,000 people. Reports have also been found that chronicle a corresponding tsunami hitting the east coast of China, killing around 4,000 people and doing extensive damage to local crops.

- **Northern Chile - 13 August 1868**

This tsunami event was caused by a series of two significant earthquakes, estimated at a magnitude of 8.5, off the coast of Arica, Peru (now Chile). The ensuing waves affected the entire Pacific Rim, with waves reported to be up to 69 feet high, which lasted between two and three days. The Arica tsunami was registered by six tide gauges, as far off as Sydney, Australia. A total of 25,000 deaths and an estimated US$300 million in damages were caused by the tsunami and earthquakes combined along the Peru-Chile coast.

- **Nankaido, Japan - 28 October 1707**

A magnitude 8.4 earthquake caused sea waves as high as 82 feet to hammer into the Pacific coasts of Kyushyu, Shikoku and Honshu. Osaka was also damaged. A total of nearly 30,000 buildings were damaged in the affected regions and about 30,000 people were killed. It was reported that roughly a dozen large waves were counted between 3 pm and 4 pm, some of them extending several kilometres inland at Kochi.

- **Enshunada Sea, Japan - 20 September 1498**

An earthquake, estimated to have been at least magnitude 8.3, caused tsunami waves along the coasts of Kii, Mikawa, Surugu, Izu and Sagami. The waves were powerful enough to breach a spit, which had previously separated Lake Hamana from the sea. There were reports of homes flooding and being swept away throughout the region, with a total of at least 31,000 people killed.

- **Krakatau, Indonesia - 27 August 1883**

This tsunami event is actually linked to the explosion of the Krakatau caldera volcano. Multiple waves as high as 121 feet were propagated by the violent eruptions and demolished the towns of Anjer and Merak. The sea was reported to recede from the shore at Bombay, India and is said to have killed one person in Sri Lanka. This event killed around 40,000 people in total.

- **Lisbon, Portugal - 1 November 1755**

A magnitude 8.5 earthquake caused a series of three huge waves to strike various towns along the west coast of Portugal and southern Spain, up to 98 feet high, in some places. The tsunami affected waves as far away as Carlisle Bay, Barbados. The earthquake and ensuing tsunami killed 60,000 in the Portugal, Morocco and Spain.

- **Sumatra, Indonesia - 26 December 2004**

The 9.1 magnitude earthquake off the coast of Sumatra was estimated to occur at a depth of 30 km. The fault zone that caused the tsunami was roughly 1300 km long, vertically displacing the sea floor by several metres along that length. The ensuing tsunami was as tall as 164 feet, reaching 5 km inland near Meubolah, Sumatra. This tsunami is also the most widely recorded, with nearly one thousand combined tide gauge and eyewitness measurements from around the world reporting a rise in wave height, including places in the US, the UK and Antarctica. An estimated US$10b of damage is attributed to the disaster, with around 230,000 people reported dead.

LANDSLIDES

- Chungar, Peru: 1971. 200 people died.

- Nebukawa, Japan: 1923. 200 people died.

- Sichuan Province, China: 1981. Over 240 people died.

- Darjeeling, India: 1980. 250 people died.

- Hauncavelica Province, Peru: 1974. 200 to 300 people died.

- Goldau Valley, Switzerland: 1806. 500 people died.

- Rio De Janeiro, Brazil: 1966. 550 people died.

- Chiavenna Valley, Italy: 1618. 2,240 people died.

- Khait, Tadzhikistan USSR: 1949. 12,000 people died.

- Armero, Columbia: 1985. 23,000 people died. (Here's just one account):

It was just an average evening with an average family tucked into bed all nice and neat when, suddenly, 12-year-old Rosita was awakened by the sound of clattering jars. She got up to look around, and that's when she noticed that the clay pots weren't the only things shaking-so was the floor of the house!

So, she did what any 12-year-old would do and cried out to her mom who only replied, 'Oh, honey, don't worry. Go back to bed. It's only the volcano shaking.' So, with her mother's reassurance, Rosita simply lay back down in her bed in total peace and silence.

But that was about to change. All of a sudden Rosita heard a strange sound, like twigs snapping, so she ran to the front door of her home and what she saw made her freeze right there in her tracks.

Something like brown foam was coming out of the streets headed her way, ando she screamed in utter terror. Why? Because that brown foam was a massive wall of mud 132 feet high filled with trees traveling at 30 mph! First it started dragging beds along, then it started crushing walls, then it actually caused cars to run the people down.

But that was just the beginning. Soon entire buildings were completely destroyed, breaking into pieces, adding boulder-sized chunks of concrete to the mud, which now meant the wall of mud became like a wall of tractors that chopped and shredded everything in its path.

And when the screams and cries and the mud flow had finally silenced, the death toll rang out. In just a few minutes time, 23,000 people were drowned in a pool of mud.

- Kansu, China: 1920. Over 180,000 people died.[9]

Whoa! Tidal Waves approaching 200 feet high going inland for several miles drowning everything in their wake! Walls of mud over 130 feet high crushing everything in their path! As you can see, recorded tidal waves and landslides throughout history have had some horrible and devastating effects, let alone massive death toll numbers. Yet, as gut-wrenching and dreadful as those recorded tsunamis and landslides were in the past, they still pale in comparison to the tsunamis and landslides that are coming in the near future in the *sixth seal*! This is due to the fact that this future coming earthquake is not only the biggest and most terrifying the planet has ever seen, and thus will produce the biggest and most terrifying tsunamis and landslides the planet has ever seen, but this earthquake is literally a "side effect" itself of an even larger "shaking." This is because "megas seismos" really refers to "everything shaking" including the universe. It's not just speaking of planet earth. It's the difference between a person shaking a snow globe (planet earth) and the shaking of the whole house (the universe) that has the snow globe in it. Yes, the earth will be rockin' and a rollin' when *the Lamb* opens the *sixth seal,* but it's only because the whole universe is shaking around it, causing earth to shake as well. It's such an unbelievable scene to try to describe, what is coming here in the *sixth seal,* as this man shares:

"Now, this particular scene really cannot be described. We can make an attempt at it. And I believe that we should because the Scripture outlines frightening features, and the detail here is given by the Lord in order that we might understand something of the horror of this day.

Earthquakes frighten people. They create phobias, believe me. We constantly are being told about the big one out here in California. We've been told for years that one day we're going to shake right off into the ocean. And we have a sort of fear of that. Every time there's a little shake, all the appointments in the psychological, psychiatric offices go up as people run there to deal with their phobias and their fears. But whatever little shakings we experience are nothing to be compared with this, more erratic a shaking than anything imaginable.

There have always been earthquakes, they come now and then, here and there. But this isn't really talking about just an earthquake. I know that's the way the word is translated, and interestingly enough it's probably as close a translation as you can get because there isn't really an English equivalent. The cataclysm that comes here is more powerful and more intense and more destructive than all the earthquakes of all time put together. It is a single massive final event, God's wrath at full operation.

Now God at His own discretion likes to shake the world now and then. He shook it at Sinai when He gave the law. He shook it when Elijah called on Him. He shook it when Jesus, His Son, was murdered before Him. He shook it when He wanted to release Paul and Silas from jail. And He shakes it now and then through history for His own purposes.

But this is more than any earthquake; like any of those that God Himself did, this is something beyond that. You'll be interested to know that the Greek word is seismos from which we get the English word seismograph which is an instrument to measure shaking. Matthew 8 translates this same word, seismos, tempest, to describe what happened on the Sea of Galilee. It's a shaking, an agitation, a severe agitation.

It means a quaking, a shaking, an agitating.

But the word 'earth' is not here. It would have been better to translate it 'and there was a great shaking,' because frankly it isn't just the earth. The first thing he mentions is the sun and then the moon and then the stars careening out of the sky, and then the sky splitting apart like a scroll and only then does he say every mountain and island start to move. A shaking more than an earthquake, this is a seismos in the universe.

You have to understand, these people have already been through so much, this is really going to be a devastating thing. They've been dragged in the last few years through global wars, worldwide famine, worldwide plagues and pestilences, that have killed one fourth of the population of the world, and it all happened just at the time they thought they had reached world peace.

And the false prophets are still crying, 'Peace, peace, peace and safety; we're nearly at utopia. As soon as we get God's people massacred, utopia will come; they're the problem.' And also, through this time period, remember, 2 Thessalonians 2 says the restrainer is removed who holds back sin. And so, sin is unrestrained, immorality unrestrained, wickedness, vice, godlessness, Christlessness rampant.

Then in a moment, while some sleep and others are awake, while some are driving their car down the freeway and some are flying in an airplane, and some are walking, and some are jogging and some are at work and some are reading the paper in their dens and some are watching television and some are playing tennis and some are at home and others are in a hotel, some are in an auditorium, some are at a sporting event, some are at school, the whole universe starts to shake...a seismos from God that no seismograph could ever measure.

And, you see, this is such a frightening thing because man always counts on the stable universe. He always counts on dawn and darkness, on the cycle of the rotation of the earth and the seasons, as it moves in orbit. Man demands uniformity in his world. And that's what evolution tells him-It always goes on the same way. Remember Peter's words about the scoffers; all things continue as they have from the beginning, it all goes on the same way.

In a moment that theory is utterly exploded when the great seismos hits. "[10]

No wonder people are scared to death! No wonder mankind is instantly inspired to fear, filled with dread, shaking and trembling not only physically but in absolute utter terror! The most terrifying thing they've ever encountered or will ever encounter again has now been thrust upon them. The Hand of Almighty God has just pummeled His creation with one devastating blow that creates a rapid shockwave across the planet and universe itself, leaving behind a massive trail of destruction and decimation in its wake. And to think, that was just blow number one. The second punch, the second beating, is coming next!

The **second beating** of the planet from the sixth seal is **The Sun Turning Black**.

Revelation 6:12a-c "I watched as he opened the sixth seal. There was a great earthquake. *The sun turned black like sackcloth made of goat hair*."

Now immediately following this *great earthquake*, this "megas seismos," this great shaking from the Hand of God, we see the next side effect. We are simply told that *the sun turned black like sackcloth made of goat hair*. This second beating of course brings up some obvious questions. First, "What is sackcloth?" Well, as the text implies, it was simply a very coarse woven fabric made typically from black goat hair. We don't wear it today, yet it was a very common garment worn in Biblical times, especially at funerals, as this man shares:

"Sackcloth is what people wore to a funeral. Sackcloth was a rough garment that you wore when you wanted to mourn somebody. You put it over you like a robe

and it went all the way to the floor so that none of you was seen. You wouldn't want to draw attention to yourself while mourning the death of someone. It was very dark, very black. And that's how the sun will be, as black as a black mourner's robe woven out of black goat's hair."[11]

If you've ever wondered why we still have the tradition today of wearing "black" garments at funerals, here it is. Be thankful, though, that we no longer maintain the tradition of putting on the actual sackcloth garment of coarse black goat hair. It does not appear to be very comfortable. Also, be glad that as Christians we are not associated with this time frame in the 7-year Tribulation, when God uses *sackcloth* to describe *the sun* to send a strong message to *the inhabitants of the earth* in the *sixth seal*. It's not a good sign, which leads us to the next question.

The second question concerning this second beating of the planet from God is, "Why of all colors did the sun turn black?" We've already seen that sackcloth was a garment worn at funerals, so the message here from God to *the inhabitants of the earth* is not looking good. He didn't use party colors or celebratory hues like they did when they murdered His people. Rather God used black, the color worn at a funeral. But of all things to compare the "blackness" of the sun to, why *sackcloth*? God didn't say the sun turned black like velvet, black like coal, or even black like an inkwell. Why was it *black like sackcloth*? Well, when you observe the usage of *sackcloth* in the Bible, as well as *the sun* in the sky, the message one receives is a very dark, ominous, and yet another horrible one:

SIGNS IN SKY ARE ASSOCIATED WITH THE TIME OF THE END

Matthew 24:29 "Immediately after the distress of those days *the sun will be darkened*, and the moon will not give its light; the stars will fall from the sky, and the heavenly bodies will be shaken."

Mark 13:24-25 "But in those days, following that distress, *the sun will be darkened*, and the moon will not give its light; the stars will fall from the sky, and the heavenly bodies will be shaken."

Luke 21:11,25 "There will be great earthquakes, famines and pestilences in various places, and fearful events and great *signs from heaven*. There will be signs in *the sun*, moon and stars. On the earth, nations will be in anguish and perplexity at the roaring and tossing of the sea."

SUN IN SKY WILL BE DARKENED IN TIMES OF JUDGMENT

Isaiah 13:10 "The stars of heaven and their constellations will not show their light. The rising *sun will be darkened,* and the moon will not give its light."

Ezekiel 32:7-8 "When I snuff you out, I will cover the heavens and darken their stars; I will *cover the sun with a cloud*, and the moon will not give its light. All the shining lights in the heavens I will darken over you; I will bring darkness over your land, declares the Sovereign LORD."

Joel 2:10 "Before them the earth shakes, the sky trembles, *the sun and moon are darkened*, and the stars no longer shine."

Amos 8:9-10 "In that day, declares the Sovereign LORD, I will make *the sun go down at noon and darken the earth in broad daylight*. I will turn your religious feasts into mourning and all your singing into weeping. I will make all of you wear sackcloth and shave your heads. I will make that time like mourning for an only son and the end of it like a bitter day."

"Blackness and darkness is often associated with judgment. When God judged Egypt, He brought thick blackness. When God came to Mount Sinai to lay down the law, it was shrouded in black smoke. When God judged His Son, you remember, on the cross for our sins, from noon till three o'clock the world went black. And Isaiah looked at this judgment time and he saw this blackness. It was revealed to him in Isaiah 13; 9-11, 'Behold the day of the Lord is coming, cruel with fury and burning anger to make the land a desolation. He will exterminate its sinners from it. The stars of heaven and their constellations will not flash forth their light. The sun will be dark when it rises. The moon will not shed its light. Thus, I will punish the world for its evil and the wicked for their iniquity. I will put an end to the arrogance of the proud and abase the haughtiness of the ruthless.' Down in verse 13, 'I will make the heavens tremble, the earth will be shaken from its place, at the fury of the Lord of hosts in the day of His burning anger.' A blackness, a darkness comes over the universe."[12]

SACKCLOTH ASSOCIATED WITH
MOURNING, REPENTANCE & JUDGMENT

"Sackcloth and ashes were used in Old Testament times as a symbol of debasement, mourning, and/or repentance. Someone wanting to show his

repentant heart would often wear sackcloth, sit in ashes, and put ashes on top of his head. Sackcloth was a coarse material usually made of black goat's hair, making it quite uncomfortable to wear. The ashes signified desolation and ruin.

When someone died, the act of putting on sackcloth showed heartfelt sorrow for the loss of that person. We see an example of this when David mourned the death of Abner, the commander of Saul's army (2 Samuel 3:31). Jacob also demonstrated his grief by wearing sackcloth when he thought his son, Joseph, had been killed (Genesis 37:34). These instances of mourning for the dead mention sackcloth but not ashes.

Ashes accompanied sackcloth in times of national disaster or repenting from sin. Esther 4:1, for instance, describes Mordecai tearing his clothes, putting on sackcloth and ashes, and walking out into the city 'wailing loudly and bitterly.' This was Mordecai's reaction to King Xerxes' declaration giving the wicked Haman authority to destroy the Jews (Esther 3:8-15)). Mordecai was not the only one who grieved. 'In every province to which the edict and order of the king came, there was great mourning among the Jews, with fasting, weeping, and wailing. Many lay in sackcloth and ashes' (Esther 4:3). The Jews responded to the devastating news concerning their race with sackcloth and ashes, showing their intense grief and distress.

Sackcloth and ashes were also used as a public sign of repentance and humility before God. When Jonah declared to the people of Nineveh that God was going to destroy them for their wickedness, everyone from the king on down responded with repentance, fasting, and sackcloth and ashes (Jonah 3:5-7). They even put sackcloth on their animals (verse 8). Their reasoning was, 'Who knows? God may yet relent and with compassion turn from his fierce anger so that we will not perish.' (verse 9)."[13]

Okay, it's not looking good for *the inhabitants of the earth*! When God says here in the *sixth seal* that *the sun turned black like sackcloth,* He is sending an unmistakable, clear, ominous message to planet earth. "All you who have rebelled against Me, all of you who have sinned against Me, all you who killed My people, all you who had the audacity to then gloat and even celebrate over the death and murder of My people, what you now have in store for you is a global funeral! You needed to repent and mourn over your wicked deeds, but because you refuse to do so, blackness will now cover the earth. Doom and destruction will descend upon you as My fierce anger brings wrathful judgment upon you for what you have done. The time of the end is upon you! Weep, wail, mourn bitterly, and beat your breast for what is about to come! Dark days lie ahead and I'm just getting started!"

In fact, even if God didn't explicitly mention the word "ashes" the word "ashes", that are usually associated with sackcloth, in this verse, when one takes a look at the cause of why *the sun turned black like sackcloth* in the first place, those ashes may very well be provided by God in abundance, upon everyone's head, whether they want them there or not, which leads us to the next question.

The third question concerning this second beating of the planet from God is, "What caused the sun to turn black?" Well, when one observes the chronological context of this passage, it would appear this second beating, *the sun turning black like sackcloth,* is a side effect of the first beating, the *great earthquake.* When God shakes the universe which then in turn shakes the earth, all kinds of things are going to be triggered on the earth including earthquakes, which will then trigger off volcanoes, which will then trigger unbelievable massive amounts of ash and debris into the atmosphere, which will then trigger this response from *the sun*, as these men share:

"The upheaval, the shaking, shakes everything and the upheaval is so enormous that it blackens out the sun. What does blacken out the sun? Why does the sun go black? Dr. Henry Morris, a wonderful scientist, creationist, writes this.

'The seismos described here is worldwide in scope for the first time in history. Seismologists and geophysicists in recent years have learned a great deal about the structure of the earth and about the cause and nature of earthquakes. The earth's solid crust is traversed with a complex network of faults, with all resting on a plastic mantle whose structure is still largely unknown. Whether the crust consists of great moving plates is a current matter of controversy among geophysicists, so the ultimate cause of earthquakes is still not known.

In all likelihood, the entire complex of crustal instabilities is a remnant of the phenomena of the great Flood, especially the breakup of the fountains of the great deep. In any case, the vast network of unstable earthquake belts around the world suddenly begins to slip and fracture on a global basis, and a gigantic earthquake ensues. This is evidently naturally accompanied by tremendous volcanic eruptions, spewing vast quantities of dust and steam and gases into the upper atmosphere. It is probably these that will cause the sun to be darkened and the moon to appear blood red.'"

"Then the sun will become 'black as sackcloth made of hair.' 'Sackcloth' was a very rough cloth made from the hair of a black goat and worn in times of mourning and despair (Rev.11:3). The blackening or darkening of the sun, as a sign, speaks of God's judgment and the withdrawal of His longsuffering. It shows this will be a time of great despair for man.

What causes this darkening? We are not told; we can only speculate. Perhaps it is caused by the ash, dust, and debris which will fill the sky when the earth begins to quake (Rev.6:14). This will undoubtedly cause volcanic eruptions which will make Mount St. Helens look like a hiccup by comparison. When there is a large volcanic eruption, the sun becomes darkened by the substances in the air."[14]

Well, there are your ashes to go along with your *sackcloth*! One can only imagine what this shaking of the universe does to the earth when it begins to shake as well. Earthquakes, tsunamis, landslides, volcanoes, ash spewing everywhere, the lights go out with no place to hide anywhere on the planet-what a horrible, dark time! No wonder mankind is instantly inspired to fear, filled with dread, shaking and trembling not only physically but in absolute utter terror! Yet another terrifying thing that they've never encountered or will ever encounter again has been thrust upon them. The Hand of Almighty God has just pummeled His creation with another devastating blow that now creates a global mourning, weeping and wailing in total bitterness mixed with fear, leaving the planet in a foreboding, eerie, ominous darkness. And to think, that was just blow number two. The third punch, the third beating is coming next!

The **third beating** of the planet from the sixth seal is **The Moon Turning Red**.

Revelation 6:12a-d "I watched as he opened the sixth seal. There was a great earthquake. The sun turned black like sackcloth made of goat hair, *the whole moon turned blood red…*"

Now we see another side effect following this *great earthquake*, this "megas seismos", this great shaking from the Hand of God. First *the sun turned black like sackcloth,* and then we are simply told that *the whole moon turned blood red*. This third beating brings up some obvious questions as well. First, "Why of all colors does the moon turn blood red?" As we saw, the sun was already blackened, adorned with funeral clothes, if you will, depicting times of mourning and judgment. Now of all colors God uses to describe *the whole moon* at this time, it's not just *red* but *blood red*. It wasn't pink like a grapefruit, purple like party dress, or even plaid like a Scotsman's kilt. Why is it specifically *blood red*? Well, when you observe the usage of a *blood red moon* in the Bible, the message God is sending to *the inhabitants of the earth* is that, yet another bloody nightmare has fallen upon them:

BLOOD RED MOON ASSOCIATED WITH THE TIME OF THE END

Matthew 24:29 "Immediately after the distress of those days the sun will be darkened, and *the moon will not give its light*; the stars will fall from the sky, and the heavenly bodies will be shaken."

Mark 13:24-25 "But in those days, following that distress, the sun will be darkened, and *the moon will not give its light*; the stars will fall from the sky, and the heavenly bodies will be shaken."

Luke 21:11,25 "There will be great earthquakes, famines and pestilences in various places, and fearful events and great *signs from heaven*. There will be signs in the sun, *moon* and stars. On the earth, nations will be in anguish and perplexity at the roaring and tossing of the sea."

BLOOD RED MOON OCCURS IN TIMES OF JUDGMENT

Isaiah 13:10 "The stars of heaven and their constellations will not show their light. The rising sun will be darkened, and *the moon will not give its light*."

Ezekiel 32:7-8 "When I snuff you out, I will cover the heavens and darken their stars; I will cover the sun with a cloud, and *the moon will not give its light*. All the shining lights in the heavens I will darken over you; I will bring darkness over your land, declares the Sovereign LORD."

Joel 2:30-31 "I will show wonders in the heavens and on the earth, blood and fire and billows of smoke. The sun will be turned to darkness and *the moon to blood* before the coming of the great and dreadful day of the LORD."

By the way, as a side note, when it says here in the Book of Joel that, "The sun will be turned to darkness and the moon to blood before the coming of the great and dreadful day of the LORD," it's not talking about a timing issue but rather a placement issue. I say that because some would say that this verse indicates that the Day of the Lord hasn't happened yet here in the first half of the 7-year Tribulation, in the *sixth seal*. They rationalize that since the text says that the "sun will turn to darkness and the moon to blood" *before* the Day of the Lord, this must mean the timing of the Day of the Lord begins *after* these events, the sun and the moon turning their colors, occur. However, again, the usage of the word "before" here in the Book of Joel is not speaking of a timing issue, but rather a placement issue. The word "before" in Joel is the Hebrew word "paniym" which literally means, "in the face of, or in the presence of." It has nothing to do with timing of an event, like we would think of something happening "before" or "after." Rather it's speaking of the placement of an event. Like if I were to say, I sat at a table (which was there the whole time), and someone sat "before me" a jar of juice and a plate of food on the table. That wouldn't mean that the table wasn't there "before" the jar of juice and plate of food showed up. That would be ridiculous. It's not talking about the timing of the two items, but the placement of the items. It's just telling you "where" these two items were placed on the table that was there the whole time. The jar of juice and plate of food were placed not to the "left" of me or to the "right" of me but rather they were placed right there "before me" at the table. That's it. The table was there the whole time! Thus, all Joel is saying here concerning "the table of events" called the Day of the Lord or the 7-year Tribulation, is that you can expects these two items of the "sun turning to darkness" and "the moon to blood" to be there on that table. It will happen "in the presence" of that event. That's it.

This may seem like an exercise in semantics, but as we saw before, this is a serious issue. As we saw earlier, the Day of the Lord *begins* at the *beginning* of the 7-year Tribulation, because the Day of the Lord speaks of a time when God pours out His divine wrath, anger, and destruction which, as we've been seeing, obviously includes *all the seal judgments* which occur during the first half of the 7-year Tribulation. It doesn't start "after" the *sixth seal*, but the been going on the whole time since the seals started at the beginning of the 7-year Tribulation. This is precisely why the Apostle Paul promises the Thessalonians comfort and rejoicing because the Church cannot and will not be a part of this time frame. We will be Raptured out prior to the Day of the Lord, the 7-year Tribulation, because we are not appointed unto God's wrath that is being poured out during that time.

Now back to the issue at hand, *the whole moon turned blood red,* and answering the question, "Why of all colors does the moon turn blood red?" As we saw in the above verses, when the moon turns color, does not give off its light, and specifically turns blood red, it speaks of a terrible coming judgment and the time of the end for mankind. Clearly, it's not a good time frame and you definitely don't want to be around during that time! Then add to this description what we also saw earlier concerning the color red itself, and what it means in the Scripture back in the *second seal* and the red horse rider. There we saw red was symbolic of death and destruction, times of sorrow, an approaching storm or army, and signaling that a bloody violent danger is coming your way! Yikes! It's looking even worse for *the inhabitants of the earth!* When God says here in the *sixth seal* that *the sun turned black like sackcloth,* and now *the whole moon turned blood red,* He is sending a dark, foreboding, bloody message to planet earth. "All you who have rebelled against Me, all of you who have sinned against Me, all you who killed My people, all you who had the audacity to then gloat and even celebrate over the death and murder of My people, what you now have in store for you is a global bloody nightmare! You spilled the blood of my people all over the earth and even celebrated their death in what you called a dream come true. Now I will color your *whole moon blood red* bathing you in its frightful glow, signaling that the greatest danger you could ever imagine has now come upon you! Judgment lies ahead, death and destruction, times of sorrow, a dark, threatening storm is headed your way. Your party is over. My angelic army is coming, and your worst nightmare is just getting started!"

The second question concerning this third beating of the planet from God is, "What caused the moon to turn blood red?" Well, many experts believe that, thanks to the science of seismology, we now know this effect on the moon as well as the sun fits the perfect description of an after-effect of an earthquake. It's called a volcanic eruption. We now know that when a volcano erupts, it spews massive amounts, literally tons of volcanic ash into the air. This in turn darkens the sunlight, almost like something's covering it, like maybe sackcloth, and at night, the moon takes on a reddish color, like it's blood-colored, as these men share:

"Not only will the sun become black, John tells us 'the whole moon became like blood.' As a sign, this speaks of the loss of life. How eerie this all will be, to look up at night and see a blood-red moon. Evidently, through the atmospheric changes brought about by the shaking of the earth and the heavens, particles or substances will be in the air which will cause the moon to take on a red cast."

"The third thing that he notes is that the moon becomes like blood. Literally the text says, 'the whole moon.' You have a total eclipse. Whatever it is that causes it, it's vivid. Now you understand that when this begins to happen it affects everything. It effects daylight and darkness. There will be no daylight. It affects

plant life, it affects man, it affects the animal world. All the cycles by which animals' function, plants function, humans function thrown into total chaos. "[15]

That's the key word. Chaos. When the whole universe shakes in the opening of the *sixth seal*, chaos unleashes. It will in turn shake the whole planet, which will in turn trigger of the world's biggest earthquake up until that time, which will then trigger off massive volcanoes erupting all over the world spewing forth an unimaginable amount of ash beyond anyone's wildest dreams. What effect will this have on *the inhabitants of the earth*? There will be so much ash and debris in the sky during that timeframe that in the day *the sun turned black like sackcloth,* and at night *the whole moon turned blood red.* Thanks to modern seismology not only why these events occur, but we now know why they occur in the order they do. So, let us once again whet our appetites concerning the cause of these two devastating effects on planet earth, the darkened sun and bloody moon, that are caused by volcanic eruptions, so as to get a fuller picture of what *the inhabitants of the earth* will be experiencing when this "megas seismos" goes off in the *sixth seal*:

Volcanoes have been among the most devastating and dangerous natural forces in our past, but it is not just throughout history that they wreaked havoc on human life, but right up to the 21st century. Their volatility and unreliability have changed our world's landscape over time and also the lives of the people living in their shadows.

- **MT. GALUNGGUNG, JAVA INDONESIA:** Date: 1882 - Death toll: 4,011

  The Volcano erupted in October in 1882. As well as killing 4,011 people the eruption also destroyed 114 villages. Mt Galunggung is located on the Pacific Ring of Fire, a well-known collection of volcanoes along a horseshoe shape around the coasts of Asia and the west coasts of Central and South America. This particular eruption was a VEI (Volcanic Explosive Index) 5 volcanic eruption.

- **MT. KELUT, INDONESIA:** Date: 1919 - Death toll: 5,110

  When Mt. Kelut erupted in 1919, over 100 villages were destroyed due to lethal lahars that traveled a distance for 40 kilometers. During this eruption 38 million cubic meters of water were ejected from the crater lake. The volcano has erupted on a large scale several times since 1919, including once in 1966 and again in 1990.

- **MT, VESUVIUS, ITALY:** Date: 1631 - Death toll: 6,000

Since the famous eruption of 79 AD Mt. Vesuvius has erupted more than a dozen times. The Volcano unexpectedly erupted between the hours of 6 and 7am on 16th December 1631. During this eruption the surrounding area suffered from multiple earthquakes, large ash clouds, showers of rock and pumice and a river of lava flowing from the conical crater of the volcano. The eruption lasted several days, and it was not until 19th December that rescue efforts were able to commence.

- **THE LAKI VOLCANIC SYSTEM, ICELAND:** Date: 1783-1784 - Death toll: 9,350

This eruption lasted a whopping eight months, spewing a total of 14.7 cubic kilometers of lava and 27km of fissures. Despite the extremely high volume of volcanic material that was expelled from the volcano during this eruption, this was not the primary cause of the large death toll. It was in fact the deadly gas emission that was the killer. Large quantities of gas were released into the atmosphere consisting of water vapor, carbon dioxide, sulphur dioxide, hydrogen chloride and flouride. This ultimately created a cloud that remained over Iceland and proceeded to create acid rain, poisoning livestock and the soil.

- **MT.VESUVIUS, ITALY:** Date: AD 79 - Death toll: 10,000+

This is possibly one of the most famous volcanic eruptions in history and it is particularly infamous due to the burial of two Italian towns, Herculaneum and Pompeii. This eruption is so well documented due to the eyewitness account of Pliny the Younger. During this eruption Mt. Vesuvius expelled a deadly cloud of volcanic gas, stones, ash and fumes that rose to a tremendous height of 33km. The eruption lasted two days and was made even more tragic because of the fact that the unsuspecting residents of the Bay of Naples were unaware that they were living in the shadow of a deadly volcano.

- **MT.UNZEN, JAPAN:** Date: 1792 - Death toll: 12,000-15,000

The eruption of Mt. Unzen in 1792 is the most catastrophic and deadly in all of Japan's history. The initial eruption triggered a landslide and tsunami. Mt. Unzen consists of a group of composite volcanoes located east of Nagasaki. It is said that most of the death toll was as a result of the landslide and tsunami; evidence of the devastating landslide can still be seen today.

- **NEVADO DEL RUIZ, COLUMBIA:** Date: 1985 - Death toll: 23,000

Despite being considered a medium sized eruption, the volcanic event still had devastating consequences for the surrounding regions. The eruption commenced in the night and caused both cold and hot mudflows, which buried the town of Armero.

- **MT. KRAKATOA, INDONESIA:** Date: 1883 - Death toll: 36,000

Due to this eruption a massive two thirds of Krakatoa actually collapsed, destroying a large portion of the island. There were significant effects felt across the world; the sound of the explosion was so loud that it was heard in Australia, and spectacular sunsets were experienced around the globe for months following the eruption.

- **MT. PELEE, WEST INDIES:** Date: 1902 - Death toll: 40,000

At the time of the eruption the volcano was thought to be dormant, but a series of eruptions began on April 25th, 1902, resulting in the final eruption on May 8th 1902. This final eruption was so destructive that it destroyed the city of St. Pierre. There were only two survivors.

- **MT. TAMBORA, INDONESIA:** Date: 1816 - Death toll: 92,000

As a result of this eruption the once tall volcano that stood at 13,000 feet was reduced to 9,000 feet. Also due to the destructive eruption, 1816 became known as the "year without summer" because the ash in the atmosphere reduced the temperature; this was felt worldwide, not just in Indonesia. Interestingly, it is thought that an additional 100,000 people may have died from crop failures as far away as Europe and America due to the reduction in temperatures, a direct result of the eruption.[16]

No way! Tens of thousands of people dying all in one shot! Whole towns and communities totally wiped from existence. Global temperatures across the earth plummet into winter-like conditions! No wonder these people are scared to death! Yet, as mind-blowing and devastating as those recorded volcanic eruptions were in the past, they still pale in comparison to the severity and amount of volcanic eruptions that are coming in the near future in the *sixth seal*! This is due to the fact that, once again, thanks to modern science, we now know that there are not only volcanoes all over the planet, but we even have what the experts call *super volcanoes* on the planet. In fact, one of the big ones that's supposed to be going off anytime now in the United States, is the infamous Yellowstone Caldera or Super Volcano, that experts are saying, "Would explode with a force 1,000 times more powerful than Mount St. Helens, spewing forth lava and ash into the sky that would fan out and dump a layer of toxic air and ash 10 feet deep up to 1,000 miles away, turning 2/3rds of the U.S. into an uninhabitable wasteland, forcing millions to flee." Now, here's my point. That's just one Super Volcano going off taking two-thirds of the U.S. with it. What about all the other Super Volcanoes on the planet, let alone other volcanoes? What's going to happen when they all go off when this "megas seismos" occurs in the *sixth seal*? There's a ton of them! The stats are that, "There are about 1,500 potentially active volcanoes worldwide, aside from the continuous belt of volcanoes on the ocean floor. Many of these are located along the Pacific Rim in what is known as the Ring of Fire." When the whole universe shakes, the whole planet shakes. When the whole planet shakes, all the tectonic plates on the earth shake. This in turn triggers off all the volcanoes on the planet. How do I know? Well, the following is a global map of all the current active volcanoes that we know exist around the planet. Notice where the USGS has them positioned on the following page:

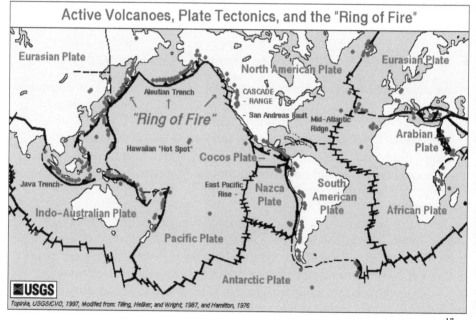

As you can see, all the dots, the volcanoes, are lined up right on top of all the fault lines around the earth. So now, for the first time in mankind's history, we can see that when this "megas seismos" in the *sixth seal* goes off, the one that *removes every mountain and island from its place*, all those fault lines are going to get adjusted, which will then proceed to trigger off not just one volcano, but most likely all those volcanoes are all going to go off at the same time all over the world! What would that do? I bet it would cause, *the sun to turn black like sackcloth* and *the moon to turn blood red* all over the planet! Think of the global devastation from this single event! If one volcano in the past killed nearly 100,000 people in one fell swoop, what's going to happen when all these volcanoes all over the earth go off, including all the super volcanoes? Will the United States even be in existence after this event? If one volcano in the past took out whole towns and communities all in one shot, how many thousands of towns and communities all over the world will we wiped out in the *sixth seal*? If one volcano in the past caused temperatures to drop and erased a whole summer, what will happen to the temperatures and seasons from this point forward on planet earth when all the volcanoes around the world erupt at the same time? No wonder mankind is instantly inspired to fear, filled with dread, shaking and trembling not only physically but in absolute utter terror! Yet another terrifying thing that they've never encountered or will ever encounter again has been thrust upon them. The Hand of Almighty God has just pummeled His creation with another devastating blow that now creates a global bloody nightmare that is signaled day and night in the sky reminding them each and every day that the greatest time of wrath-filled judgment they could ever imagine has now been thrust upon them, leaving the planet in a shocking, otherworldly, dreadful glow. And to think, that was just blow number three. The fourth punch, the fourth beating, is coming next!

The **fourth beating** of the planet from the sixth seal is **The Stars Falling**.

Revelation 6:13 "And *the stars in the sky fell to earth*, as late figs drop from a fig tree when shaken by a strong wind."

Just when you thought things couldn't get any worse for *the inhabitants of the earth* in the *sixth seal*, now we see yet another side effect following this *great earthquake*, this "megas seismos", this great shaking from the Hand of God. First *the sun turned black like sackcloth*, then *the whole moon turned blood red*, and then we are simply told on top of that *the stars in the sky fell to earth*. Thus, this fourth beating brings up some obvious questions as well. First, "What message is God sending with these stars falling from the sky?" As we saw, the sun being blackened depicted times of mourning and judgment and the moon being reddened revealed a bloody nightmare. Now of all things to happen next to planet earth, it's not just "things" that start falling from the sky, but *stars* fall from the sky! It wasn't birds, bombs, big ice chunks, or even blustery tornadoes falling from the sky. It was specifically *stars*. What does this mean? Well, as with the other events mentioned in the *sixth seal*, when you observe the usage of stars *falling from the sky* in the Bible, the message God is sending to *the inhabitants of the earth* is that an even worse bloody scenario is headed their way:

STARS FALLING FROM SKY
ASSOCIATED WITH THE TIME OF THE END

Matthew 24:29 "Immediately after the distress of those days the sun will be darkened, and the moon will not give its light; *the stars will fall from the sky*, and the heavenly bodies will be shaken."

Mark 13:24-25 "But in those days, following that distress, the sun will be darkened, and the moon will not give its light; *the stars will fall from the sky*, and the heavenly bodies will be shaken."

Luke 21:11,25 "There will be great earthquakes, famines and pestilences in various places, and fearful events and great *signs from heaven*. There will be signs in the sun, moon and *stars*. On the earth, nations will be in anguish and perplexity at the roaring and tossing of the sea."

STARS FALLING FROM SKY
OCCURS IN TIMES OF JUDGMENT

Isaiah 34:1-4 "Come near, you nations, and listen; pay attention, you peoples! Let the earth hear, and all that is in it, the world, and all that comes out of it! The LORD is angry with all nations; His wrath is upon all their armies. He will totally destroy them, He will give them over to slaughter. Their slain will be thrown out, their dead bodies will send up a stench; the mountains will be soaked with their blood. All the stars of the heavens will be dissolved, and the sky rolled up like a scroll; all *the starry host will fall like withered leaves from the vine, like shriveled figs from the fig tree.*"

Okay, just when you thought it couldn't get any worse for *the inhabitants of the earth,* it just did! What a horrific scene! When God says here in the *sixth seal* that *the sun turned black like sackcloth,* and *the whole moon turned blood red,* and now *the stars in the sky fell to earth,* He is sending yet another wrathful, angry, bloody message to planet earth. "All you who have rebelled against Me, all of you who have sinned against Me, all you who killed My people, all you who had the audacity to then gloat and even celebrate over the death and murder of My people, what you now have in store for you is a global bloody slaughter! You spilled the blood of my people all over the earth and killed them as if the sky were the limit. Now I will reign down upon you *stars falling from the sky* and I will crush you without limit! You will be squashed like bugs, soaking the earth with your blood! You will be slain and slaughtered right and left with no place to hide, until your dead bodies are piled up in a heap!" In short, the planet is in a "heap" of trouble with God! You definitely don't want to be here during this time! Take the only way out through Jesu Christ now before it's too late!

The second question concerning this fourth beating of the planet from God is, "Are these literal stars falling from the sky?" I say that because we now know, thanks to modern astronomy, that many stars are not just big, but they are so big that they would totally dwarf planet earth. For instance, some stars are estimated to be 1,500 times larger than our Sun, and yet the Sun itself is so big compared to Earth that 1.3 million Earth's would fit into our one Sun![18] So, obviously, just one of these stars 1,500 times bigger than the Sun would totally obliterate planet earth, and yet the text says *stars* plural. How could humanity, let alone the planet, continue to exist to finish out the rest of the 7-year Tribulation? Well, to answer that, we simply need to observe the original meaning of the word *star* that is used in our text. It's the Greek word, "aster" as in the English word, "asteroid." It's not necessarily referring to an actual giant star, as these researchers share:

"John also says that the stars will be affected. The word 'star' (aster) is used of any heavenly body seen at night (i.e., stars, planets, asteroids, meteors, etc.). These are not stars as we often use the word, which are huge and often dwarf the earth in size. These are likely meteorites, which are small by comparison to the earth. John compares them to unripe figs falling to earth from a fig tree when shaken by a great wind."

"Stars is [asteres] from which we get the word asteroid. The word is also used of the supernatural manifestation which led the magi to the babe (Mtt.2:2), Christ who is the 'morning star' (Rev.2:27+; Rev.22:16+), angels (Rev.1:16+;Rev.2:1+

Rev.3:1+; Rev.9:1+), and astronomical objects (Mtt.24:29; Mark 13:25; 1 Cor. 15:41; Rev.6:3+; Rev.8:10+). Here and in Rev.8:10+ stars are said to fall to the earth. It seems best to understand these as asteroids or meteors, for even the smallest sun would consume the entire planet should it ever fall to earth.

The stars proper are certainly still found in their places after the fulfilment of this vision. And remembering that the Scriptures often speak in the common language of men, without reference to the distinctions of science, and that even science itself still popularly speaks of 'falling stars,' when it means simply meteoric phenomena, it appears but reasonable that we should understand the apostle to be speaking of something of the same sort.

The most likely identification of these particular falling stars is that of a great swarm of asteroids that pummel the earth. Such an event has never occurred in historic times, but scientists have long speculated about the probability of either past or future earth catastrophes caused by encountering a swarm of asteroids." [19]

In other words, it's coming. Even the scientists today are saying we are "ripe" for this kind of apocalyptic event from the sky. Speaking of *ripe*, that's what this text also adds in reference to these *stars* or asteroids that *fell to the earth*. When they do, it will be *as late figs drop from a fig tree when shaken by a strong wind*. That is, they will be coming down in great quantity, as this man shares:

"This word properly denotes 'winter-figs,' or such as grow under the leaves, and do not ripen at the proper season, but hang upon the trees during the winter. This fruit seldom matures, and easily falls off in the spring of the year. A violent wind shaking a plantation of fig-trees would of course cast many such figs to the ground. The point of the comparison is, the ease with which the stars would seem to be shaken from their places, and hence, the ease with which they fall." [20]

In other words, when these *stars* or asteroids start falling, there will be a ton of them! These *late figs* fall off easily as it is, but when you add a *shaking from a strong wind*, they will be dropping en masse in one big giant cluster. Boom! Bang! So, it is when God literally shakes the universe with this "megas seimos" in the *sixth seal*. This not only shakes the planet and the sky, but even space itself is affected. It in turn causes asteroids/meteors en masse to drop from space headed for planet earth! Boom! Bang! One after another in quick succession slamming into the planet as *late figs drop from a tree when shaken by a strong wind*. This isn't just one asteroid or meteor hitting the planet, but a ton of them *all at the same time* in rapid order! You definitely don't want to be on the planet when this beating takes place! You better get saved now through Jesus Christ! In fact, once again, let us whet our appetite concerning the impact of meteors and asteroids on planet earth in general, so as to get a fuller picture of what *the inhabitants of the earth* will be experiencing at this stage when this "megas seismos" goes off in the *sixth seal*:

"When it comes to comet impacts, the denizens of Earth may be living on borrowed time. Of course, comets are only about half the problem – there are plenty of asteroids whizzing around the inner solar system too – so we decided to have a look and see just how close modern society has come to destruction since 1900, and how close we're going to come over the next 100 years. The answers aren't reassuring.

NASA's list of potentially hazardous asteroids (PHAs) currently numbers 959. That's 1,000 asteroids that astronomers pretty much know are going to get closer than 7.5 million kilometers to Earth, about 20 times the distance from here to the Moon. Five of those are expected to come between Earth and the Moon over the next century. So, we'll have a few close shaves but nothing to worry about, right? Not so fast. The total number of PHAs and comets astronomers think are out there being probably more like 20,000. That means we've mapped about 5% of the objects that stand a good chance of hitting us. So, take the future part of this chart as a best-case scenario. The past five close encounters, however, show just how vulnerable we are:

1) **The Comet of 1491**. This one must've scared the heck out of some folks. At a little less than four times the distance to the moon, this was the closest pass ever recorded at the time, and no one knows for sure how big it was. Little did our ancestors know how much more interesting things would get.

2) **Tunguska, 1908**. One of the most famous Earth close calls of all time, it was also a pipsqueak. For a long time, scientists believed a comet perhaps 60 meters in diameter exploded over Siberia with a force of as much at 30 megatons, or about 2,000 times more powerful than the atomic bomb dropped on Hiroshima, though nothing solid ever hit the planet. All those pictures of flattened forest certainly look impressive, but last year, scientists re-crunched the numbers and found that the comet could've been as small as 30 meters, and the blast just 5

megatons. In other words, much smaller objects can do way more damage than we ever thought before. Gulp.

3) **The Great Daylight Fireball of 1972**. The name says it all – it doesn't get much closer than this. Size estimates range from 3 to 14 meters in diameter, depending on whether it was ice or rock. Whatever it was, the object called US19720810 burned through the atmosphere from Utah to Canada for about a minute and a half. Luckily, the space rock struck a glancing blow – had it hit Earth directly, it could've blasted us with 1/2 a Hiroshima worth of energy.

4) **2004 FH and 2004 FU162**. At 30 meters in diameter and made of solid rock, 2004 FH would be a thumper of Tunguska proportions if it ever hit home. In the right (or wrong) place, it could destroy a city. As it was, it passed 43,000 kilometers above Earth on March 18, 2004. Three weeks later, FU 162 came whizzing along. Astronomers discovered it at basically the same time as the 6-meter in diameter rock soared just 6,400 kilometers above Earth's surface.

5) **Comet Hyakutake**. Now we're getting into civilization-threatening territory. At 2 kilometers in diameter, this comet only got within about 40 lunar distances to Earth in 1996. Compared to our other close calls, that's pretty comfortable, but consider this: it was discovered less than two months before its closest pass. Had it been on a collision course with Earth there's almost nothing we could've done other than brace for the million dead, massive climate disruption, crop failure, 500-foot high tsunami...you get the idea.

FUTURE:

6) **1999 AN10**. In a little less than 20 years, our usually quiet Earth-Moon system is going to have a lot of visitors. In August 2027, AN 10 is going to get about one lunar distance from Earth, and we'll get a chance to see just how big this bad boy is. Estimates range from 1/2 to 2 kilometers in diameter, plenty large to leave a dent in humanity if it ever gets closer.

7) **2001 WN5**. Just six months after AN10 comes a callin' WN5 will get even closer, just about splitting the difference between Earth and the Moon. At 700 meters in diameter, this asteroid has a got potential for major damage.

8) **99942 Apophis**. By far the most famous of the end-bringing objects we know about in our solar system, astronomers thought for a while that this 270-meter-

wide rock had an almost 3% chance of hitting us. Since then, odds have been lowered to 1 in 43,000 that it could slam into Earth in 2029. But if it passes through a gravitational keyhole – a tiny region in space that could tweak its orbit ever so slightly – an impact could still happen on April 13, 2036.

9) **2005 WY55**. Just 200 meters wide, astronomers think this asteroid could still pack a wallop. Right now, it's scheduled to get within about 75,000 km of Earth, but impact odds are big enough to keep in mind – currently they're rated at around 1 in 70,000. If our number comes up on that fateful day in May 2065, look out – blast yield estimates from this rock range to 1,100 megatons.

10) **2000 WO107**. Depending on how well humanity holds up under climate change, bird flu, and all the other things that could potentially kill us off, we might be able to look up and see WO107 zoom by in December 2140. The 400-meter-wide rock isn't scheduled to hit us – it should get about half way between Earth and the Moon – but if calculations are off by even a little bit (and all of the future examples here have some uncertainty) we could care a lot.[21]

So again, even scientists today admit we really should care a lot about this future coming catastrophic event. It's not just a matter of "if" but "when" we are going to be pummeled by a large-scale asteroid. In fact, there's been all kinds of warnings for many years. Even Hollywood's getting in on the act by making all kinds of movies about this looming danger. Scientists are saying "when" we get struck by an asteroid, the damage would be absolutely inconceivable. Quote, "If a space rock were to hit the earth, the damage would be devastating. The amount of destruction would depend if it hit land or ocean. Regardless of the impact location, loss of human, animal, and plant life on a grand scale would take place, particularly if it impacted a big population area." "The shockwaves from that would create huge tsunami waves, destroying both coastlines and inland areas."[22] In fact, speaking of shockwaves, let's now try to get an idea of how much of an "explosive impact" just one of these asteroids would have on planet earth by looking at some of the biggest explosions man has ever experienced on the planet thus far:

BIGGEST EXPLOSIONS

- **FOAB:** Largest explosion created by a non-nuclear weapon.

FOAB (Father of all Bombs) is a Russian tactical weapon, designed to detonate in mid-air and deliver an incinerating shockwave to the target area below it. The bomb yields the equivalent of 44 Tons of TNT, making it about as powerful as the smallest nuclear weapons in existence. However, FOAB does not generate the radioactive fallout that nuclear weapons do. FOAB is part of a "miniature arms race" between the United States and Russia. In 2003, the United States developed MOAB (Massive Ordinance Air Blast Bomb) which is a similar device with a yield of 11 tons of TNT. MOAB was quickly termed the "Mother of all Bombs" in accordance with its acronym. In an apparent response, Russia developed its "Father of all Bombs", in 2007, which it claims is four times as powerful and slightly lighter in weight.

- **Minor Scale:** Largest man-made conventional explosion.

Minor Scale was a test performed by the United States, on June 27, 1985. The United States Defense Nuclear agency detonated almost 5,000 tons of ammonium nitrate fuel oil, to simulate the effect of a nuclear weapon. The main purpose was to see how a small nuclear weapon would affect military hardware.

- **Tunguska Event:** Largest impact in recorded history.

On June 30, 1908, there was a large explosion above the Podkamennaya Tunguska River, in Russia. The explosion created an estimated yield of 10-15 megatons of TNT, or about 1,000 times the yield of the atomic bomb that destroyed Hiroshima, Japan. While there are a good number of conspiracy theories as to what caused the explosion, the majority of the scientific community agrees that it was caused by a meteoroid exploding in mid-air. Even though the meteoroid exploded in mid-air, the event is still considered an impact. The explosion is believed to have occurred in mid-air because, even though there have been several searches for it, no one has ever been able to find the crater. However, there was an area of about 2,150 square km where trees were bent away from the hypocenter of the blast.

- **Ivy Mike H-Bomb:** Man-made explosion.

The Ivy Mike hydrogen bomb was based on the thermonuclear device demonstrated during the Test George conducted by the US on 9 May 1951 as part of Operation Greenhouse series of four nuclear device detonation tests. The Ivy Mike test yielded an explosion of 10.4Mt, 700 times the explosive force of the weapon dropped on Hiroshima. The nuclear weapon employed an implosion device similar to that of "Fat Man" bomb, which exploded over Nagasaki.

- **MK 24/B-24 nuclear bomb:** Man-made explosion.

The Mk-24 thermonuclear bomb, which was one of the most powerful nuclear weapons built by the US, was designed based on the Yankee test device. Yankee was one of the six detonations in the Castle nuclear detonation test series. The Mk-24 was produced in a number of configurations with explosive force ranging from 10Mt to 15Mt.

- **Mk-17/EC-17 nuclear bomb:** Man-made explosion.

The Mk-17, weighing over 18t, was the heaviest thermonuclear nuclear weapon ever made by the US. It was also the first operational hydrogen bomb of the US Air Force. The Mk-17 had an estimated yield of 10Mt to 15Mt. About 200 Mk-17 bombs were produced by 1955.

- **TX-21 "Shrimp" nuclear bomb:** Man-made explosion.

The TX-21 "Shrimp" thermonuclear weapon was exploded by the US on 1 March 1954 during its biggest ever nuclear weapon test, Castle Bravo, at Bikini Atoll in the Marshall Islands. The detonation yielded an explosion force of 14.8Mt. The TX-21 was also a scaled down variant of the TX-17 thermonuclear weapon first tested during the Castle Romeo exercise in 1954. The TX-21 was exploded 7ft above the surface and radioactive fallout spread over more than 11,000km2. The explosion dispersed radioactive substance over some parts of Asia, Australia, the US and Europe.

- **B41 nuclear bomb:** Man-made explosion.

The B41 or Mk-41 with a yield of 25Mt is the most powerful thermonuclear weapon ever fielded by the United States. About 500 bombs were produced between 1960 and 1962, remaining in service, until July 1976. The development of Mk-41 commenced in 1955 to fulfil the US Air Force's requirements for a Class B (10,000lb), high yield thermonuclear weapon. The prototypes were test fired during Operation Hardtack Phase I in 1958.

- **Tsar Bomba:** Largest man-made explosion.

Tsar Bomba was a hydrogen bomb developed by the Soviet Union, and tested on October 30, 1961. With a yield of 57 megatons, it was the most powerful man-made explosion ever, detonated with the force of 3,800 Hiroshima explosions, The bomb was actually originally intended to be more around 100 megatons, but the fallout of such a device would have been too problematic. Even though Tsar Bomba was detonated in the very remote location of the Novaya Zemlya island chain, north of the Russian mainland, it still caused a great deal of collateral damage. A village 55 km from the test site was completely leveled. Damage to buildings occurred as far away as Norway and Finland. The explosion created a mushroom cloud 64 km high, and a shockwave that was still detectable on its third passage around the earth.

- **Mount Tambora Eruption:** Largest Earthbound explosion recorded by humans.

On April 5, 1815, Mt. Tambora erupted in Sambawa, Indonesia, creating the most powerful explosion ever witnessed by humans in historic times. The Tambora eruption is estimated to have unleashed the equivalent of 800 megatons of TNT, making it about 14 times more powerful than Tsar Bomba. The eruption was heard as far away as Sumatra, which is 2,600 km away. Before the eruption, Mt. Tambora was 4.3 km tall, but after it was only 2.85 km tall. The volcano created an ash column 43 km high, and dispersed ash into the stratosphere and around the globe. This ash blocked out the Sun and caused the year 1816 to be the second coldest year in recorded history. Crop failures and famines occurred all over Europe and North America.[23]

Simply unbelievable! Here we have the Tsar Bomb, the most powerful man-made bomb/explosion ever that was 3,800 times the size of the bomb dropped on Hiroshima, yet the Mount Tambora explosion was 14 times bigger than that! And that's just one explosion. Imagine thousands of those kinds of explosions going off all over the planet all at the same time when *the stars in the sky fall to earth.* Furthermore, what's going to happen when they strike not just a deserted island or some spot out in the middle of nowhere in the ocean, but rather in a populous area? What kind of devastation will that bring to the planet? Well, once again, let us see if we can imagine what that kind of horrific scenario would look like:

"Last week, an asteroid fell from the sky and struck the Lake Michigan area. What if it had been a city-killer instead? Early last Monday morning, a giant fireball was witnessed by thousands of people across multiple states, as it

plunged from outer space into Lake Michigan. Sonic booms could be heard for nearly 100 miles as houses shook. A brilliant but eerie green glow, created by the elements in the meteor heating up in the atmosphere, resulted in more than 200 calls to the American Meteor Society. And reports of people seeing it ranged as far east as New York and as far south as Kentucky.

Although no fragments have been recovered, it's estimated that this meteor was between 1 and 7 tons in mass: around the size of a minivan. Moving at a speed of tens of thousands of miles per hour, the energy of this asteroid strike was equal to about 500 tons of exploding TNT.

According to Philipp Heck, scientist at the Field Museum of Natural History in Chicago, impacts like this on Earth aren't rare at all. 'Such an event of this magnitude didn't occur over the Midwest/Chicagoland area since 2003 when the Park Forest meteorite produced a similar fireball. Globally such events are much more frequent, many times each year, but mostly happen over the ocean and are therefore not observed.'

Asteroids a few meters in size strike Earth a few times each year on average, and only rarely impact a populated area. But when they do, the world takes note. The 2013 impact in Chelyabinsk, Russia, was the most destructive such strike in modern times. It may have only been about ten meters across, but its impact in an urban area caused millions of dollars' worth of property damage and resulted in more than 1,500 documented injuries. A century earlier, the Tunguska event leveled over a thousand square kilometers of forest, exploding with an energy of between 5 and 10 MegaTons of TNT: similar to an atomic bomb.

There are nearly a billion objects in our Solar System capable of causing that level of devastation on Earth, and 300,000 of them are already in our neighborhood. These Near-Earth Objects (NEOs) pose the greatest threat to Earth's cities.

While the closest asteroids ever observed to swing by Earth are understandably small – under 10 meters – the danger of a 100 meter-sized asteroid striking Earth is catastrophic. We know that such asteroid strikes (Tunguska-level and up) are relatively common, occurring every few hundred years somewhere on Earth. While the ones striking the ocean or uninhabited land (like most of Russia or Canada) will have little-to-no impact on humanity, the destructive force from such an impact is undeniable.

Meteor (Barringer) crater, in the Arizona desert, is over 1.1 km (0.7 mi) in diameter and represents only a 3–10 MegaTon release of energy. A 300–400-meter asteroid strike would release 10–100 times the energy.

Thousands of years ago, cities were a minuscule fraction of Earth's surface; practically all asteroid strikes were guaranteed to occur over virtually uninhabited areas. Today, urban areas cover more than 3% of Earth's land area, meaning that out of every 100 asteroid strikes our planet receives, roughly one of them will strike a city. And if that asteroid is around 100 meters in size or larger, the effects would be catastrophic.

The consequences of a 100meter-sized asteroid striking New York.

The first thing to happen would be the fireball from the initial strike, which would span nearly four kilometers in diameter for an asteroid only 100 meters in size. (And that's its size in space, not when it reaches the ground!) Next is the catastrophic effects of radiation: thermal, not nuclear. This won't poison you, but will simply cook you, albeit more slowly than the fireball does, covering nearly double the area of the fireball. Buildings will be immediately leveled by the blast far beyond that. While extending more than twice as far out, structures will need to be demolished due to structural damage. And finally, extending out for approximately 40 kilometers in diameter, every human being will experience burns on their skin simply due to the heat emitted. All told, more than 2.5 million people would die if such an asteroid struck midtown Manhattan.

The consequences of a 500 meter-sized asteroid striking Chicago.

Increase the asteroid to about 500 meters in size, and the destruction goes on for hundreds of miles instead. A strike of this magnitude in the wrong location could result in the death of approximately 10 million people were it to strike an area like Chicago, or more than 30 million were it to strike one of the most populous regions in the world like Tokyo or Mexico City.

We're now finding more than 1,000 new such objects every year. A city being destroyed is quite likely."

"Small asteroids frequently whiz past Earth or enter our atmosphere and burn up. Even relatively small asteroids are capable of inflicting major damage should they penetrate our atmosphere and explode in a populated area. Then there's the big one. An extinction-level asteroid event that many scientists say could, one day, end us.

We also wondered what kind of devastation might be caused to iconic American cities if these objects were to hit. To find out, we combed NASA's database of past and future NEOs and then estimated the impact of a few of them. Here's what we found.

NEOs are comets or asteroids that orbit the sun and come close to – or even intersect with – the Earth's orbit. They can be just a few feet in size (whew!) or several miles in diameter (yikes!).

We analyzed NASA's database of more than 36,000 recent close encounters to find the five closest near-earth objects. All of these NEOs are estimated to be quite small, between 5 and 8 meters in diameter. But don't relax just yet. It's estimated that more than 300,000 NEOs exist that are more than 40 meters wide and could potentially cause damage by crashing into Earth or exploding in the sky. If that news isn't troubling enough, all of these 300,000 pesky NEOs have yet to be identified, according to the National Science and Technology Council.
In a New York Impact

The film "Deep Impact" (1998) imagines – in vivid detail – what New York City might look like where it was bombarded with comets from space. It isn't pretty. Buildings and people are obliterated as fireballs zoom overhead and sea levels rise. Hollywood is full of exaggeration, but if a NEO like 2013FK were to crash into Earth, the scenario presented in the film may not be so far afield.

If the island of Manhattan were ground zero to a substantial NEO, the results would be devastating. According to our calculations, there would be more than 2.5 million deaths, and people as far away as Yonkers, Queens, and Newark would likely sustain skin burns.

San 'Fried'cisco

With California's propensity for earthquakes, residents are somewhat accustomed to living under the threat of a natural disaster. San Francisco, in particular, has experienced a number of damaging and dangerous earthquakes. Since 1979, four earthquakes with a magnitude of 5 or greater on the Richter scale have struck the city. The good news is that if a near-Earth object were to *strike the Golden City, its residents would probably be somewhat prepared for a sudden environmental event. The bad news is that the force of the NEO could trigger earthquakes in an area that is already unstable.*

In our imagined scenario of 2015 BN509 hitting San Francisco, about half of the impact would, thankfully, occur over the Pacific Ocean. That in itself could cause powerful tsunamis to strike coastal areas all along the Pacific Ocean and beyond. The deadly impact in the continental United States would extend well to the west – easily affecting Reno and Lake Tahoe.

Windy City Wipeout

Our scenario of a major near-Earth object impact on Chicago is the deadliest of all. With a radius of searing heat extending beyond the Windy City to the populous cities of Grand Rapids, Cedar Rapids, Milwaukee, Indianapolis, Louisville and St. Louis – the death toll would well exceed 9 million. This illustrates that where an NEO strikes is significant in terms of its overall impact on human life.

Faster Than a Speeding Meteor

When we think of giant space rocks, we may imagine them as slow-moving behemoths, gradually lumbering through the solar system. In fact, these objects are whizzing through space at an alarming speed. Would Earth's best scientists move quickly enough to stop 'the big one' if it were discovered to be heading our way?"[24]

Once again, for the first time in mankind's history, we can now see that when this "megas seismos" in the *sixth seal* goes off and *the stars in the sky fall to earth*, the earth-shattering city-destroying people-annihilating effects will be utterly unbelievable! No Hollywood story can mimic this kind of scenario from God! It's not just one *star* or asteroid falling to the earth, its *stars* plural or asteroids falling to the earth. It's a multitude of them falling all at once, one after another, in rapid succession, boom, bang, all at the same time like *late figs dropping from a tree when shaken by a strong wind*! One explosion after another explosion! One city annihilated right after another one is annihilated! Millions of people vaporized here in a blink of an eye and then another mega populace is vaporized over there! No wonder mankind is instantly inspired to fear, filled with dread, shaking and trembling not only physically but in absolute utter terror! Yet another terrifying thing that they've never encountered or will ever encounter again has been thrust upon them. The Hand of Almighty God has just pummeled His creation with another devastating blow that now creates a wrathful atmospheric scenario where people all over the earth will be crushed like bugs, and whole populations will be wiped from existence with rapid fire precision from the sky! Chicken Little was right! Mankind's greatest fear has come upon them, as this researcher shares:

"And then a fourth feature, out of that blackness, verse 13, the stars of the sky fell to the earth. Fiery balls come careening out of the darkness, and I guess you might say if you remember the fairy tale, Chicken Little's fear comes true.

The word 'stars,' or 'asteraes' can refer to any celestial body, large or small, not limited to what we know as a star. It could be a star, but it could also refer to an asteroid, meteor. Perhaps that's the best understanding of it here. The earth is going to get showered by asteraes plummeting out of the sky.

Scientists, by the way, have speculated for years what a massive asteroid meteor shower hitting the earth would be like, the unbelievable destruction that it would create. Where are people going to go? Where are they going to go in the panic of this all over the globe? Where are they going to go? No way can they escape.

When you preach a message like this you assume people are going to say, 'Ah, that's ridiculous...that's absolutely ridiculous.' The scoffers have always said, 'Everything continues as it has from the beginning, nothing ever changes, the sky is always the same, the planets always move in the same orbit, everything is fine.'

Well if you've been thinking that, an issue of Newsweek magazine might rattle your cage a little bit. The cover story says, 'Doomsday science, new theories about comets, asteroids and how the world might end.' That's the title. And the cover has a rendering, a depiction of the earth and plummeting toward the earth is a flaming fireball, as we have just read being described. The article inside is absolutely amazing.

'On March 23, 1989 an asteroid a half mile across missed the earth by just seven hundred thousand miles. No one saw it coming. If it had arrived a mere six hours later, it might have wiped out civilization. Astronomers are scurrying to start a census of just what threats lurk in the solar system and as the pace of discovery picks up, so should the pace of any earthling's heart. Earth runs its course about

the sun in a swarm of asteroids...says astronomer Donald Yeomans of NASA's Jet Propulsion Laboratory in Pasadena...sooner or later our planet will be struck by one of them.'

If you turn to the article you'll find a copy under the picture that says this, 'A deadly collision could suck out the atmosphere, scorch the earth and shroud the planet in dust.' And then the article says this, 'It comes screaming out of the sky like a scud from hell, bigger than a mountain and packed with more energy than the world's entire nuclear arsenal. It hits the atmosphere at a hundred times the velocity of a speeding bullet, and less than a second later smack into the ground with an explosive force of 100 million megatons of TNT. The shock waves from the crash landing travelling 20 thousand miles an hour levels everything within a hundred and fifty miles. Simultaneously a plume of vaporized stone shoots up from the impact sight, blasting a hole through the atmosphere and venting hot debris. The vaporized rock cools, condensing back into hundreds of millions of tiny stones. As they streak back to the ground over the next hour, they heat up and soon the very air glows hot pink. Steam hisses from green leaves, buildings and even trees burst into flame. Nitrogen and oxygen in the atmosphere combined into nitric acid, any surviving life crawling out of a burrow or cave gets pelted with a rain as caustic as the acid in a car battery.

That's what astronomer Henry Mellosh of the University of Arizona calculates what would happen if something six miles across fell from space and smacked into earth. Six miles also happens to be the probable size of the Swift Tuttle comet. Swift Tuttle is the peripatetic frozen dirt ball that an astronomer declared has a one in ten thousand chances of hitting earth on August 14, 2126. So much for the friendly skies.'

It says in another part of the article, 'In the late 1980's they were finding fifteen asteroids a year of the size that could eliminate human society. Now they're up to thirty-five a year and gunning for one hundred a year. On just four summer nights in 1990 one scientist found three. One asteroid that crosses directly earth's orbit is twenty miles wide, large enough...large enough to do immeasurable, incalculable damage. There is a half dozen bigger than five miles across.'

The article goes on to describe these kinds of things that are floating around up there. Some are truck size, it says, that is smaller than thirty feet across. They pack a wallop of 50 thousand tons of TNT. Such an asteroid or comet may produce a meteoric fireball, a burst of light and heat, but is usually too high in the atmosphere to cause significant damage.

Then there are some the size of a building a diameter between thirty and three hundred feet. They come into our space and they explode five miles up with a force of twelve megatons. They annihilate reindeer thirty miles away, ignite the clothes of a man sixty miles away, and level more than 700 square miles of a Siberian forest.

If one the size of that rock hit the rural United States, calculates John Pike, director of Space Policy for the Federation of American Scientists, it could kill seventy thousand people, cause four billion in property damage, and could also flatten buildings twelve miles away, according to the NASA panel. If it hit an urban area, there would be upwards of three hundred thousand deaths. If it hit in a seismic zone, it could trigger earthquakes topping 7.5 on the Richter Scale.

Those aren't bad. The next one is the size of a mountain. If an asteroid six hundred feet across fell in the mid-Atlantic Ocean, calculates astrophysicist Jack Hills of Los Alamos National Laboratory, it would produce massive tidal wave six hundred feet high on both the European and North American coasts. Larger asteroids, half a mile across, would surely hit the earth and rank as the greatest catastrophe in human history. Thanks to the cloud of dust thrown up by this kind of million megaton explosion, there would be no crops anywhere for a year.

Then there are city size ones, they say, asteroids or comets larger than three miles across, like Swift Tuttle. If one of them hit the Gulf of Mexico, it would create waves three miles high. Nine hundred miles away the mammoth wall of water would still be fifteen hundred feet high. Such an asteroid landing in the Gulf of Mexico would flood Kansas City. The impact would make entire continents burst into flame, block sunlight, and make agriculture impossible. Humans would go the way of trilobites. And all God has to do is say the word and it all happens.

Isn't that amazing? Mankind knows that this is a threatening universe. They can't prevent it, it's going to come. If they read the book of Revelation, they can know it's going to come. The only thing they can't know is when it's going to come. But it's going to come. And when it comes, and the earth starts being pummeled by asteroids and meteorites and comets and whatever bits and fragments that God intends for them in the moment of His wrath, the world is going to know that it is God. So, there is reason for fear, plenty of reason for fear. And now the scientists from a non-biblical perspective are beginning to awaken to it. "[25]

In other words, even they know it's a real threat. It's really going to happen, *stars in the sky*, asteroids/meteors, *falling to earth*, really is coming to our planet in our near future you can bank on it; it's just a matter of time. When God gives the word, they're a going to start dropping like *late figs drop from a fig tree when shaken by a strong wind*, and every Hollywood disaster movie just got put on steroids. Only it's not a make-believe movie with 3-D special effects, but mankind's nightmarish reality as a result of God's wrathful effects. I'll say it again: There's only one way out of this mess, and that's though Jesus Christ. Call upon His Name, ask Him to forgive you of all of your sins, believe in your heart that God raised Him from the grave, and the Bible says you will be saved! Do it now before it's too late! Why? Because, believe it or not, that was just blow number four. The fifth punch, the fifth beating, is coming next!

The **fifth beating** of the planet from the sixth seal is **The Sky Receding**.

Revelation 6:14 *"The sky receded like a scroll, rolling up*, and every mountain and island was removed from its place."

As if *stars* or asteroids en masse careening out of the sky, slamming into the earth, blowing things up, vaporizing people wasn't bad enough to instill fear into *the inhabitants of the earth* in the *sixth seal*, now we see yet another terror inspiring event from the sky following this *great earthquake*, this "megas seismos" this great shaking from the Hand of God. First *the sun turned black like sackcloth*, then *the whole moon turned blood red*, then *the stars in the sky fell to earth*, and now we see that *the sky receded like a scroll rolling up*. Not so surprisingly, this fifth beating brings up some obvious questions as well. First, "What message is God sending with the sky receding like a scroll?" Well, I assume that by now you're starting to see a pattern here in the *sixth seal*. The message is not good no matter how you slice it! Not at all! It gets worse as you go! The sun being blackened depicted times of mourning and judgment, the moon being reddened revealed a bloody nightmare, the stars falling from the sky portrayed an explosive wrath-filled pummeling, and now of all things to happen next to planet earth, it's not just *stars* falling from the sky, but the *sky itself begins to crack and split apart*! It wasn't the sky turned a brilliant shade of blue pleasing to the eye or was decorated with another wonderful rainbow-filled promise from God and everybody was comforted, and neither did it say that the sky was dotted with white fluffy clouds shading everyone and providing them with a gentle refreshing breeze after all the things they've been through. No. It was *the sky receded like a scroll rolling up*. What's God saying to them? Once again, as with the other events mentioned in the *sixth seal*, when you observe the usage of the *heavenly bodies being shaken* and *the sky rolling up like a scroll* in the Bible, the message God is sending to *the inhabitants of the earth* is that, yet another heart-stopping judgment is headed their way:

SKY RECEDING ASSOCIATED WITH THE TIME OF THE END

Matthew 24:29 "Immediately after the distress of those days the sun will be darkened, and the moon will not give its light; the stars will fall from the sky, and *the heavenly bodies will be shaken*."

Mark 13:24-25 "But in those days, following that distress, the sun will be darkened, and the moon will not give its light; the stars will fall from the sky, and *the heavenly bodies will be shaken*."

SKY RECEDING OCCURS IN TIMES OF JUDGMENT

Isaiah 34:1-4 "Come near, you nations, and listen; pay attention, you peoples! Let the earth hear, and all that is in it, the world, and all that comes out of it! The LORD is angry with all nations; His wrath is upon all their armies. He will totally destroy them, He will give them over to slaughter. Their slain will be thrown out, their dead bodies will send up a stench; the mountains will be soaked with their blood. All the stars of the heavens will be dissolved, and *the sky rolled up like a scroll*; all the starry host will fall like withered leaves from the vine, like shriveled figs from the fig tree."

This has to be one of the freakiest moments in the history of mankind. What an unbelievable sight! *The inhabitants of the earth* don't even have time to catch their breath from one earth-shattering judgment before the next one arrives. One after another after another. It truly is the time of the end! When God says here in the *sixth seal* that *the sun turned black like sackcloth,* and *the whole moon turned blood red* and *the stars in the sky fell to earth,* and now *the sky receded like a scroll rolling up,* He is sending yet His next wrath-filled shocking message to planet earth. "All you who have rebelled against Me, all of you who have sinned against Me, all you who killed My people, all you who had the audacity to then gloat and even celebrate over the death and murder of My people, and even did it in the very presence of Me, what you now have in store for you is a global peek at Who is coming your way! You acted like I wasn't real, you mocked and scoffed at My existence, you assumed I was blind and could not see in the dark, let alone your evil deeds in the daylight. Now I will show you with Whom you have to deal, who is responsible for these constant global rapid-fire disasters that have been coming your way ever since the beginning of the 7-year Tribulation. I will split the sky in two, rolling it up like a scroll, and you will see clearly Who's been watching you the whole time, *and* Who is coming back to set up His reign on planet earth as the King of kings and Lord of lords. It's time, planet earth, to meet your Maker! Boom! Mike drop! What a scary, foreboding, ominous message for *the inhabitants of the earth*! You don't want to be here at this time! If you're not saved already and you're still reading this, you better get saved now before it's too late! You would much rather hear from God, "Come up here!" at the Rapture of the Church in the sky before the 7-year Tribulation begins, than during the 7-year Tribulation, "Planet earth, meet your Maker. Look up in the sky and see Who is headed your way!" One man puts it this way:

"Isaiah had been shown this fearsome time:

'Behold, the day of the LORD comes, cruel, with both wrath and fierce anger, to lay the land desolate; and He will destroy its sinners from it. For the stars of heaven and their constellations will not give their light; the sun will be darkened in its going forth, and the moon will not cause its light to shine. I will punish the world for its evil, and the wicked for their iniquity; I will halt the arrogance of the proud and will lay low the haughtiness of the terrible. I will make a mortal more rare than fine gold, a man more than the golden wedge of Ophir. Therefore, I will shake the heavens, and the earth will move out of her place, in the wrath of the LORD of hosts and in the day of His fierce anger.' (Isa.13:9-13) In these judgments, God is shattering the puny pillars of support which men trust in when they turn away from Him.

'See that you do not refuse Him who speaks. For if they did not escape who refused Him who spoke on earth, much more shall we not escape if we turn away from Him who speaks from heaven, whose voice then shook the earth; but now He has promised, saying, 'Yet once more I shake not only the earth, but also heaven.' Now this, 'Yet once more,' indicates the removal of those things that are being shaken, as of things that are made, that the things which cannot be shaken may remain. Therefore, since we are receiving a kingdom which cannot be

333

shaken, let us have grace, by which we may serve God acceptably with reverence and godly fear.' (Heb.12:25-28)

The increasingly severe judgments which fall during this period are specifically designed to remove hope in all else but God so that all creatures recognize their utter dependence upon the Creator. Hope placed anywhere else is idolatry. God now begins a systematic destruction of the natural order (sun, moon, stars, earth) which men have often deferred to in place of the Creator. In its failure to recognize the Creator, environmentalism eventually fails in its effort to preserve the creation."[26]

The second question concerning this fifth beating of the planet from God is, "Is this a literal splitting of the sky?" I say that because, even as Christians, we are sometimes quick to "downplay" or "naturalize" "supernatural" physical events from God. I don't know if this is due to the harmful spillover effects of living in such an anti-God evolutionary mindset of the world nowadays, or simply due to our own unbelief. But some believers are all too hasty to say that the "splitting of the sky" mentioned here in the *sixth seal* must surely be a "symbolic" event. The irony of this is that these same believers would not even hesitate to state rightfully that God created the whole universe and earth as well as the sky out of nothing in one literal day. Yet, somehow, He cannot split that which He Himself created in the first place? It doesn't make sense. Besides, the Greek word for "receding", as in "the sky receded", is "apochorizo", and it literally means "to split apart, to sever to separate." It's only used twice in the New Testament, once here in Revelation 6, and the other in the Book of Acts referring to the "splitting apart" of the Apostle Paul and Barnabas.

Acts 15:39 "They had such a sharp disagreement that they *parted* company. Barnabas took Mark and sailed for Cyprus."

The Apostle Paul and Barnabas had a literal "parting of the ways," they "split apart." One went one direction and the other went the opposite direction. So, it is here with the *sky* in the *sixth seal*. God is going to literally "separate it, part it, split it in two." It will go in two different directions. Also, based on the context, every event thus far has been literal in the *sixth seal*, a great shaking of the universe and earth, the sun turning dark like sackcloth, the moon taking on a blood red hue, stars or asteroids falling from the sky, so why wouldn't this "splitting of the sky" also be literal? God created it, He can do whatever He wants with it! Furthermore, this isn't the first time we see in the Scripture God "parting the sky" to see what's behind it, that is, into His dimension, the Spirit realm. This is the same supernatural event that took place when Stephen, the first martyr of the Church, looked up into the *sky*:

Acts 7:55-57 "But Stephen, full of the Holy Spirit, looked up to heaven and saw the glory of God, and Jesus standing at the right hand of God. 'Look,' he said, '*I see heaven open* and the Son of Man standing at the right hand of God.' At this they covered their ears and, yelling at the top of their voices, they all rushed at him, dragged him out of the city and began to stone him."

Just as God "split apart" and "opened the sky" or "heaven" to send a stern message of warning to the stubborn rebellious people on earth right after the birth of the Church, so now He will do it again after the Rapture of the Church which occurs prior to the 7-year Tribulation, to the stubborn rebellious people who are left behind on earth. The first time the "sky split" it occurred right before the people of earth murdered Stephen, one of God's people. The next time God does it, it will be in response to *the inhabitants of the earth* murdering millions of God's people. The first time God "split the sky", the people on earth got angry and mad and killed Stephen. The second time the people on earth will run and hide as God dishes out His anger upon them for killing His people. No, this is not a "symbolic" splitting of the sky. It is a *literal event* just like it was before. These researchers confirm it as well:

"The sky receded. Receded is [apechōristhē]. The term is used to describe the parting of Paul and Silas from Barnabas and Mark (Acts15:39). The sky receded causing it to be "split apart" (NASB). At the appearance of the Judge at the Great White Throne Judgment, 'the earth and heaven fled away and there was found no place for them' (Rev.20:11+). The psalmist predicted a time when the heavens would 'grow old like a garment; like a cloak You will change them" (Ps.102:25).

Passages such as this tempt the interpreter to jettison the literal approach and 'go symbolic.' Yet events which are so far removed from our daily experience as to be completely foreign need not be incredible when initiated by the hand of the Almighty. It is as if we were to try to explain the design of a nuclear plant to the ant! The construction of the starry realm is far beyond our grasp, and the description which meets us here is at best an approximation which only hints at the full dimensions of what transpires.

Clearly, it is an enormous and terrifying sight which could not even begin to be explained by modern physics. "This is the human perception of the magnitude of the disturbance, but is not the ultimate passage of the heavens, which does not come until Rev.20:11+. The impression of all these heavenly phenomena is that the universe is coming apart.'

In response to these events, men recognize the wrath of the Lamb (Rev.6:16+). Mills offers an unusual suggestion concerning the purpose for the splitting of the sky:

'In order to ensure that there is no misunderstanding on the source of these disasters, God will open the heavens for an instant, and the people on earth will be given a glimpse of God and the Lamb on their thrones (Rev.6:16+).

Revelation 6:16+ pictures an extended scroll suddenly being split; the two ends recoil, spring-like, around the end rod to which the scroll is attached. Suddenly, earth can peer into Heaven as Stephen did in Acts 7:56. Man sees Him who sits on the throne and the Lamb. Men will know they are experiencing the wrath of God, and this knowledge will be even more fearsome to them than the great natural catastrophes they will have endured.'"

"Evidently the sky will appear to split and roll back in two opposite directions (Isaiah 34:4). The universe will seem to be coming apart. Apparently, the opening of the sky will give earth-dwellers a glimpse into the throne-room of heaven (Revelation 6:16)."

"In Rev. 6:14, the sky will split and roll back in two opposite directions. The opening of the sky will give earth-dwellers a window-like look into heaven where they see the Lord God and the Lamb. Apparently, this lasts for at least one full revolution of the earth, so all the world sees this (Rev.6:15)."[27]

The third question concerning this fifth beating of the planet from God is, "What are the effects on planet earth from this splitting of the sky?" Well, let's just let God answer that, shall we? *And every mountain and island was removed from its place.* No way! Not one mountain or one island, but *every* mountain and *every* island was affected by this splitting of the sky. Can you imagine what *the inhabitants of the earth* must be going through at this point? What fear, what terror? One minute they are still trying to gather themselves, reeling from the whole universe and planet shaking, the sun going dark, the moon turning blood red, stars or asteroids slamming into the earth exploding and vaporizing everything in their path. Then all of a sudden they are forced to look back up into the sky after probably trying to hide from it (what with the asteroids plummeting their way and all), only to see the sky now literally splitting apart, revealing another dimension in space, God's dimension, His heavenly throne room, and as it dawns on them just Who it is they are gazing upon, BOOM, every single mountain and every single island is *removed from its place*. No wonder there is such great terror and people are freaking out the way they do, as we'll see in even greater detail shortly. This has got to be the most mind-numbing series of unfortunate events mankind has ever gone through. It just doesn't stop! There's no time to adjust, let alone catch your breath!

By the way, this passage in Revelation 6 is not talking about a total "removal" of every mountain and island. Rather it's simply referring to the total "moving" of every mountain and island. The total "removal" doesn't take place until the very end of the 7-year Tribulation:

Revelation 16:17-20 "The seventh angel poured out his bowl into the air, and out of the temple came a loud voice from the throne, saying, 'It is done!' Then there came flashes of lightning, rumblings, peals of thunder and a severe earthquake. No earthquake like it has ever occurred since man has been on earth, so tremendous was the quake. The great city split into three parts, and the cities of the nations collapsed. God remembered Babylon the Great and gave her the cup filled with the wine of the fury of His wrath. *Every island fled away, and the mountains could not be found.*"

These two occurrences of mountains and islands "moving" in the Book of Revelation are two totally different events at two totally different times. Revelation 6 is simply a "moving" or "jolting", not a total "removal" like Revelation 16 where the islands and mountains *could not be found*. In Revelation 6, *removed* is the Greek word "kineo" which literally means, "to cause to move, to go, to set in motion or excite, or to throw into commotion." In Revelation 16, *fled away* is the Greek word, "pheugo" which means, "to flee away as in to vanish or disappear." The first time the mountains and islands are affected in the first half of the 7-year tribulation in Revelation 6, they are jolted from their positions, which is bad enough. But the second time they are affected in Revelation 16, at the very end of the 7-year Tribulation, they totally disappear. What a horrible crazy time! Praise God He has provided a way of escape through both halves, all the 7-year Tribulation, through Jesus Christ at the Rapture of the

Church which takes place prior! One can only imagine what shape the earth will be in after God gets done with it, as these men share:

"The seismic disturbances will be of such magnitude that the entire geography of the earth is permanently altered. The extensive mapping of the earth, both by GPS and sonar, will eventually be for naught as in a moment every geophysical mapping database is rendered obsolete. As great as this earthquake is, it is but a precursor to an even greater one associated with the seventh bowl at which 'every island fled away, and the mountains were not found' (Rev.16:19+). It would appear that at that time the islands sink from sight and the mountains are leveled by God's final outpouring of wrath."

"Then in terms that John can't even describe, verse 14, it says the sky was split apart in John's vision, literally ripped apart. It pictures the whole of the sky, like a scroll held open at tension. And all of a sudden, it's just ripped down the middle and the whole sky disappears; it's all gone. The stars are flying all over the place, careening. The whole universe is shaking. No sun, no moon, and the earth is being blasted with asteroids, meteorites plummeting out of the sky, as the universe breaks up. The heaven that was so familiar to us is ripped to pieces. This is the scene.

'And every mountain and island were moved out of their places.' This is hard to conceive...every mountain and island. The whole unstable crust of the earth begins to move and shift, and the faults split, and the volcanic gases come out. Dr. Morris further says, 'The earth's crust, highly unstable ever since the great Flood, will be so disturbed by the impacting asteroids, the volcanic explosions and the earthquakes, that great segments of it will actually begin to slip and slide over the earth's deep plastic mantle. Some such phenomenon may actually be triggered under this judgment of the sixth seal, dwarfing the damage occasioned by all the mighty earthquakes of the past. Everything shaking.'

Can I stop here and give a word to the environmentalists? Can I give a word to the 'Save the Earth' group? If you think man has messed up this earth, wait till you see what God does to it. This is a disposable planet, my friend; it was made disposable by sin. You wait till you see what its Creator does to it. He made it, sin devastated it, and He'll destroy it. It's a throw-away world now, it's a throw-away universe. But there will come a new cosmos...the new heavens and the new earth. Peter wrote about that in 2 Peter Chapter 3.

Well Jesus summed all of this up that we've just seen in those verses when He said in Luke 21:11, 'And there will be terrors and great signs from heaven.' And when it happens, people will die of fright. They will be scared to death. Can you understand that?

People are afraid of a lot of things, aren't they? They're afraid of a lot of things they shouldn't be afraid of. And usually, commonly, normally, they're not afraid of the one person they should be afraid of. Romans 2:5 says that sinners are accumulating sin that someday is going to feel the wrath of God. And those who have never feared Him will fear Him then.

But you don't need to be afraid. We don't have fear, we who are Christians, do we? Because we have escaped the wrath of God. We have been delivered from the wrath to come through Jesus Christ. He has changed our future destiny from wrath to blessing, from hell to heaven, from terror to rejoicing. We're not looking for this wrath, we're going to be caught up to be with the Lord before it ever hits, amen? If you put your faith in the Lord Jesus Christ, you will escape the wrath to come. 'Fear Him who after He has killed has the authority to cast you into hell. Yes, I say, fear Him.'"[28]

Unfortunately, that's not what the bulk of *the inhabitants of the earth* are going to do, as we shall see here shortly. But talk about a total waste of time. What a losing effort. What a worthless use of resources. Today mankind is funneling all his time, energy, and effort into "saving the planet" when God says in essence, "Oh yeah? Wait until you see what I do to it because of your sin! There's going to be hardly anything left when I'm done!" Why? Because wicked and rebellious mankind had the audacity to worship "mother earth" instead of Father God. Then they had the gall to wonder why His wrath had fallen upon them, when He clearly warned them nearly 2,000 years ago that this kind of global idolatry would ultimately lead to this very wrath-filled time.

Romans 1:18-25 "The wrath of God is being revealed from heaven against all the godlessness and wickedness of men who suppress the truth by their wickedness, since what may be known about God is plain to them, because God has made it plain to them. For since the creation of the world God's invisible qualities – His eternal power and divine nature – have been clearly seen, being understood from what has been made, so that men are without excuse. For although they knew God, they neither glorified him as God nor gave thanks to Him, but their thinking became futile and their foolish hearts were darkened.

Although they claimed to be wise, they became fools and exchanged the glory of the immortal God for images made to look like mortal man and birds and animals and reptiles. Therefore, God gave them over in the sinful desires of their hearts to sexual impurity for the degrading of their bodies with one another. They exchanged the truth of God for a lie and worshiped and served created things rather than the Creator – Who is forever praised. Amen."

There's the sin of the environmental movement. You had the audacity to worship "created things" including the "earth" instead of the Creator, and you wonder why His wrath is being revealed? You reap what you sow. Now He will take that which you "worship," the earth, and pummel it with His "wrath" until all that is left is an unrecognizable blob of clay. Even to the point where *every mountain and island is removed from its place*. Now, as shocking and sad as that is, it's about to get even worse. You would think that this pummeling from God would get the attention of *the inhabitants of the earth*. You would think that they would, "Fear Him who after He has killed has the authority to cast you into hell." You would think that they would be humbled by now and repent and turn to God and receive His mercy in the midst of His judgment even after all they've done and are responsible for. Surely after the sky and earth and even the whole universe being shaken from top to bottom, they would respond appropriately, right? Nope. Believe it or not, even after five punches, five beatings from the very hand of God upon this wicked and rebellious planet, they still refuse to turn to Him and instead say, "We would rather *die* than turn to You! We would rather call upon mother earth to *kill* us than receive Your mercy." This unbelievable sinful wicked hard-hearted response is what we will see now in the next and final detail concerning the object of the *sixth seal*.

The **second detail** given about the object of the sixth seal is **The Terror of the Planet**.

Revelation 6:15-17 "Then the kings of the earth, the princes, the generals, the rich, the mighty, and every slave and every free man hid in caves and among the rocks of the mountains. They called to the mountains and the rocks, 'Fall on us and hide us from the face of Him who sits on the throne and from the wrath of the Lamb! For the great day of their wrath has come, and who can stand?'"

So how does the planet respond to five beatings from the Hand of God upon His creation? Terror! Absolute utter terror. There's no way around it. This is exactly what the text exposes in great detail. Everyone on the planet simply erupts in total fear and wants to die immediately! Now, before we begin to dissect this amazing, hard-hearted, sin-filled response from *the inhabitants of the earth*, let's first deal with another possible question arising in the minds of some at this point, certainly the skeptic, when it comes to observing such an outpouring of God's wrath upon His creation. You can almost hear them say, "Why? Why is God doing this? I thought He was a God of love, and here He is beating the planet and pouring our His wrath upon people. I thought He loved people. What kind of God is this?" The problem with their question is that it assumes that God's wrath is not necessary and that somehow it would negate Him being a loving God. Neither is true, as this researcher points out:

"These verses are truly tragic. In the midst of unbelievable suffering, mankind does not pray to God for protection from His wrath. Instead, they cry out to the rocks and the mountains. The inhabitants of the earth will recognize for the first time the source of their trouble, yet they still refuse to respond to God's wrath.

God's wrath is one of His eternal attributes, the perfect complement to His love. The wrath of God is His necessary and just response to evil (Ps. 7:11). God's wrath is presently being revealed against unbelievers by letting them go their way and face the consequences of their behavior (Rom. 1:18-32). However, when the great day of God's wrath occurs, He will be far more active in the execution of His anger.

At this point, the world poses this question: 'As a Christian, aren't you supposed to be teaching that God is a God of love rather than a God of condemnation?' The inference is that somehow you are being unloving by reminding people of God's holiness and intolerance of sin. Suppose I tell my daughter that if she sticks her finger into an electrical outlet she will die. Am I being judgmental or loving? Warning people of inevitable consequences of sin is the most loving thing we can do, especially if it leads them to make the right choice.

I acknowledge that it is not pleasant to read about the carrying out of God's judgment on the world. There are many questions surrounding God's activity and His purpose in all this. It all seems so terrible. Why would God do these things, which cause such misery and pain? There are several reasons but three should suffice:

(1) God wants to bring people to repentance.
(2) God wants to demonstrate His patience.

(3) God wants to establish His justice.

Some lessons and applications may be drawn from this study:

(1) Our passage teaches the absolute sovereignty of God. The four riders are given their authority from heaven. Everything they do is directed and limited by Almighty God and the Lamb. God's people have nothing to fear from Antichrist, for the Lamb is their Lord.

(2) The four seals demonstrate the self-defeating character of sin. Antichrist shows us in a graphic way the spirit of self-aggrandizement that is one of the fruits of sin. All God needs to do is let events take their course and sinners will inevitably be punished.

(3) Christ's work includes not only redemption but also judgment. Those who will not embrace the Lamb as redeemer and share with Him the inheritance of the kingdom of God, will themselves be embraced by death and hades and dwell in the kingdom of the dead.

(4) In this passage Almighty God reveals what this vain, proud, and guilty world is coming to.

Our civilization shall one day expire under the Antichrist. The immediate future, therefore, holds not peace, but judgment. "[29]

No, God's wrath does not negate Him being loving. In fact, as was mentioned above, it's "the perfect complement of His love." Sin must be judged. Would it be loving to let it go on unrestrained forever? Would it be loving to allow wickedness to have no consequences? Would it be loving to turn a so-called blind eye to all the evil atrocities man has committed to each other, even those that never make it to court, while God Who is omniscient knows about every single one of them? No! Of course not! That kind of a God would be an ogre! Therefore, because the One and Only true God *is love*, He does something about all this evil. He puts a limit on it and He then puts an end to it with His wrath. Yet, even in the midst of His wrath being poured out to judge this sin, He is still reaching out to those under this wrath that they heaped upon themselves, and pleads with them to repent and receive His mercy before it's too late. How is that not loving? Besides, they didn't have to even be in the 7-year Tribulation under God's wrath in the first place. He has been warning the planet ahead of time for the last 2,000 years to avoid this harsh reality. It's a fearful message *that's supposed to instill fear* so that people will take appropriate action and avoid this serious danger that lies ahead. Fear is not bad if it motivates you to do the right thing and be led to safety in your time of need, as this man shares:

"Fear is a powerful emotion. Sometimes it is an overpowering feeling that takes control of the mind and makes one desire what is irrational. It takes control sometimes of the will and makes people behave in ways that are inexplicable. Fear, frankly, can create all kinds of responses, everything from cowardice to heroism, from strength to weakness, aggression to passivity, reason to confusion, clear thinking to total panic. Fear can strengthen the heart and make it beat faster. Fear can stop it dead. Fear can lead a person to have a total change in what he thinks and feels and does.

Fear is certainly a part of the human factor. It's a part of life. There are normal fears that all of us have, and God has given us the capacity to fear certain things for the sake of self-preservation and the protection of others. Normal fears that everybody has like the fear of disease, the fear of injury, the fear of the loss of family or the loss of love, the loss of a job, the loss of money, fear of death. And then as some tests have indicated, the most dominant fear, the fear of public speaking. Such common fears are usually handled somewhat adequately by most people.

If a person can't handle normal fear, we say that person has a phobia. By phobia we basically mean an abnormal response to a normal fear, or the invention of an abnormal and bizarre fear. A phobia is fear exaggerated. It is fear that disables a person. It is fear that is uncontrollable and unconquerable, it is fear that totally takes control of a person so that they cannot function normally. Such phobia leads to paranoia, panic attacks, and various kinds of deviant and anti-social behavior.

When you look at people and examine what they're afraid of, it's quite amazing. Ann Landers, interestingly enough, through all the years accumulating her mail, has listed what people are afraid of. She's got a list of the things people fear most. She says, 'First of all, there are very bizarre fears about which people have written me, such as the fear of falling into the toilet, the fear of certain colors, the fear of being buried alive, or the fear of calling someone by his given name. But the most common fears, according to my mail...she said...are the following: animals, bees, being alone, being stared at, blood, blushing, cancer, cats, choking, corpses, crowds, darkness, death, deformity, demons, dirt, dogs, dreams, elevators, enclosed space, flying, germs, height, horses, illness, insanity, insects, lightning, mice, nakedness, noise, pain, poverty, pregnancy, robbers, school, sexual intercourse, sleep, smothering, snakes, spiders, strangers, surgical operations, syphilis, thunder, travel, vomiting, work and worms.'

Frankly, that list is a list of fairly normal things, just stuff that's part of life. But it is amazing how people have phobias about normal things as well as inventing bizarre things like fearing certain colors and so forth. People fear all kinds of things. They fear normal things abnormally and they fear abnormal things. But rarely are they afraid of what they really ought to be afraid of...rarely.

In Hebrews 10:31 it states, 'It is a terrifying thing to fall into the hands of the living God.' The prior verse says, 'God said vengeance is Mine, I will repay, the Lord will judge His people.' Now that is something people ought to be afraid of. Cats and dogs and mice and lightning and noise and pain and pregnancy, those are minimal, those are the normal issues of life. If people are going to have a phobia, if they're going to have an uncontrollable, debilitating, disabling, exaggerated, unconquerable fear, let it be the fear of falling into the hands of the living God.

In Luke chapter 12 there is a familiar statement that follows this same thought. Luke 12:5, 'I will warn you whom to fear.' Jesus is talking. I want to tell you who to fear. In the verse before, He said, 'Don't be afraid of those who kill the body; don't be afraid of anything that could harm you physically; let me tell you who to fear. Fear the One who after He has killed has authority to cast into hell. Yes, I tell you, fear Him.' Who's that? That's God. Fear God. With all of the phobias and all of the fears that people have, here's one they rarely have, but should have.

And, in fact, I sometimes wonder if the church isn't busy today trying to make sure they don't have it, trying to make them feel that God is a benign grandfather who is this all time, ultimate, cosmic good guy. Jesus knew His Father well, He said fear Him. Because after He's killed, He has the authority to cast you into hell. Yes, I tell you, fear Him.

Right now, man is having his day, but soon it will be the Lord's day. One of the central prophetic themes in Scripture is the coming of the great day of God's wrath, also known as the day of the Lord. It is a frightening, inevitable day in the future of the world. We are reading about it right here in this particular section of Revelation.

What really comes through here is fear like no fear the world has ever known. It will lead to the world's largest prayer meeting only they're not talking to God; they're praying to the mountains and the rocks, as verse 16 says, and asking them to crush them."[30]

In other words, unfortunately, they respond with the wrong kind of fear. A healthy fear would cause them to cry out to God and ask Him to forgive them of their sins and shower them with His mercy through Jesus Christ, but instead they cry out to the mountains and the rocks to hide them from the wrath of God, which means they will perish in their way. In fact, they ask to be *crushed* rather than be saved through Christ! They fear alright, but *they don't fear what they should be afraid of.* And it's this misplaced fear that leads to their utter doom, as we shall now see.

The **first evidence** of terror on the planet created from the sixth seal is **The Global Crowd**.

Revelation 6:15 "Then the kings of the earth, the princes, the generals, the rich, the mighty, and every slave and every free man hid in caves and among the rocks of the mountains."

What is so striking about this global terror induced by the *sixth seal* is the identity of this global crowd that responds with this unfortunate, misplaced fear. Notice, the text didn't say that only the really evil people responded with this misplaced fear. It didn't say only those who are high up in the rankings, working for the antichrist, had this misplaced fear. It didn't even say that only those backwoods people who didn't know better had displayed this misplaced fear. No. It was literally every single kind of person on planet earth you can think of, from all different walks of life top to bottom. It wasn't just the *kings*, it was the *slaves*. It wasn't just the *princes* or *generals* or *rich*, it was even the *free man*. All people from all sectors of life, all pedigrees, as positions, *every* kind of person you can think of responded in this unfortunate manner, as these men share:

"In 6:15, John provides seven classes of society to stress the universal scope of this judgment. He then tells us that they 'hid themselves in the caves and among the rocks of the mountains and they said to the mountains and to the rocks, fall

on us and hide us from the face of Him who sits on the throne and the wrath of the Lamb, for the great day of their wrath has come, and who is able to stand?'"

Kings of the earth: *These are the kings which fail to 'kiss the Son, lest He be angry, and you perish in the way, when His wrath is kindled but a little" (Ps.2:12). They are the 'kings of earth who committed fornication and lived luxuriously' with Babylon, who were ruled by her, but will mourn her fall (Rev.17:2+, Rev.17:18+; Rev.18:3+, Rev.18:9+). They are the kings who 'gather...to the battle of that great day of God Almighty' (Rev.16:14+; Rev.19:19+). Here, they are 'gathered together as prisoners are gathered in the pit and will be shut up in the prison' (Isa.24:20).*

The great men...the mighty men: *[megistanes] the great ones and [ischyroi] strong ones. These are men who do not occupy official positions of rulership or military command, but who nevertheless influence and control the affairs of men from behind the scenes: from board rooms, golf courses, and luxury yachts. They are the 'captains of industry.' As the globalization of our world continues, power will reside more and more in the hands of these leaders of multinational corporations.*

Commanders: *[chiliarchoi] from [chilias] one thousand. The leaders over a thousand troops. Roughly equivalent to a major or colonel.*

Every slave and every free man: *Several verses indicate that even at the supposed 'height' of humanism's achievements at the time of the end, slavery will not yet have been abolished worldwide (Rev.13:16+; Rev.19:18+). The emphasis is upon the comprehensive nature of the judgments. The magnitude of the disturbances coming upon the earth is such that every man is affected.*

Hide themselves in caves: *Here is the classic record of man's response to his own sin – a vain attempt to hide from the omnipresent, omniscient, almighty God (Gen.3:8; Rev.6:16+). In the irony of God, those who persecuted God's servants, who were 'destitute, afflicted, tormented – of whom the world was not worthy,' who 'wandered in deserts and mountains, in dens and caves of the earth' (Heb. 11:38) now experience firsthand a similar affliction from the very hand of God."[31]*

I'll say it again, so much for the "human potential" movement that would have us falsely believe that mankind is basically good and will always rise to do the right thing, especially in times of crisis. Are you kidding me? What we see here is the "human depravity" movement on display, which God has known all along and has chosen to step into in order to rescue mankind. The dilemma is that mankind is rotten to the core because of the entrance of sin, and unless God in His mercy intervened, man would keep on choosing that which is wrong. So it is here. The healthy fear of God and the fear of His wrath, that should motivate mankind from all walks of life to repent and be saved, is *totally absent*. What you have in *total abundance* instead is man's depravity on display by *the inhabitants of the earth* in choosing the wrong kind of fear that leads to death. In fact, this unhealthy fear is so intense upon this global crowd that they are literally *scared to death*! Many of them during this time will literally start dropping like flies from heart attacks over this unhealthy, misplaced, depraved fear, as this researcher points out:

"Isaiah writes in chapter 2, 'Enter the rock and hide in the dust from the terror of the Lord and from the splendor of His majesty. The proud look of man will be abased and the loftiness of man will be humbled, and the Lord alone will be exalted in that day.' In verse 19 he says, 'Men will go into caves of the rocks and holes of the ground before the terror of the Lord and before the splendor of His majesty when He arises to make the earth tremble. In that day men will cast away to the moles and the bats, their idols of silver and their idols of gold, which they made for themselves to worship in order to go into the caverns of the rocks and the clefts of the cliffs, before the terror of the Lord and the splendor of His majesty, when He arises to make the earth tremble.'

The King is coming, but the world, all of them, the range of it, everybody is going to be in fear. And some will be scared to death.

Let me tell you something. In Revelation 6, we read about a day when everybody will have that fear. They'll have it to the phobia category. It will be the ultimate paranoia, it will be the universal panic attack. There is coming a day when the world will all have the same debilitating, uncontrollable, disabling, unconquerable phobia, a fear so overpowering that they will be scared to death.

What do you mean by that? Jesus said of that coming day, in Luke 21:26, 'Men will faint from fear.' The word 'faint,' apopsucho in Greek, appears only in that verse. You know what it means? To die...to literally breathe out their last. When that day comes there will be such fear that people will be scared to death. Some will die on the spot. They will die from sheer terror because they will realize they have fallen into the hands of the living God. It is His day of wrath and that is so terrifying it will stop their hearts.

And those who survive the initial fear will cry for the rocks to crush them to death before they have to face God, as if that could be a means of escape. Absolutely unbelievable scenario."[32]

I would agree. It's bad enough that mankind demonstrates his utter depravity instead of his self-inflated greatness during this outpouring of God's wrath in the *sixth seal*. But now they get so worked up in this unhealthy fear that they literally start dying of heart attacks! In fact, it gets even more depraved. Now we will see that mankind is so stubborn, so wicked, and so rebellious towards God and His mercy, that they don't even wait for the heart attacks induced from their unhealthy fear to kill them. Now they cry out for the earth to kill them! Their depraved choice to be crushed instead of saved by Christ is not a means of escape, but a one-way ticket to hell. They would rather die and go to hell than receive God's mercy and go to heaven. Talk about depraved! Absolutely unbelievable is right! Let's now take a look at their death wish.

The **second evidence** of terror on the planet created from the sixth seal is **The Global Cry**.

Revelation 6:16-17 "They called to the mountains and the rocks, 'Fall on us and hide us from the face of Him who sits on the throne and from the wrath of the Lamb! For the great day of their wrath has come, and who can stand?'"

What a sad, depressing, regrettable statement here from this global crowd of humanity from all walks of life. How do they respond to God's loving warning and wakeup call? How do they welcome His mercy in the midst of His much-needed judgment? Amazingly, they acknowledge that this *really is* coming from God, it's *the wrath of the Lamb*. The text leaves no question that *the inhabitants of the earth* know beyond a shadow of a doubt where all these calamities have been coming from and to Whom is the source. It's Jesus, God, *the Lamb*. By the way, as was mentioned earlier, the verb here *has come* doesn't mean that *the wrath of the Lamb* has just now started here, nor is it saying it's just now anticipated in the future. Rather, the verb *has come* is in the Greek aorist tense which speaks of a *past event*. This means that *the wrath of the Lamb* has already been going on and these people here in this text are just now acknowledging it.

Once again, it's ridiculous to say these chains of events are a result of the so-called wrath of man let alone satan, at this man shares:

"The reaction of the unbelieving world to the terrors unleashed by the sixth seal will not be one of repentance (Rev.9:21+; Rev.16:11+), but of mindless panic. They will finally acknowledge what believers have been saying all along, that the disasters they have experienced are God's judgment.

In what way could the events of the sixth seal be said to be 'man's wrath; as pre-wrath rapture advocates hold? These events occur 'when He opened the sixth seal' (Rev.6:12+). Who is He? The Lamb of Revelation (Rev.6:1+)! It is Jesus Christ who directly initiates these judgments. And how could astronomical and seismic manifestations such as these reflect the wrath of puny men? For what man could cause asteroids to fall to the earth and the sky to recede as a scroll (Rev.6:13-14+)? "[33]

I agree. It's ridiculous for anyone to say that man, let alone satan, is responsible for this *wrath* when it would require them to have God-like attributes which neither of them have. But be that as it may, instead of crying out to God, this global crowd of humanity from all walks of life *call to the mountains and rocks*. Instead of asking to be rescued by God, they beg to be hidden from God! Instead of receiving His mercy, they make a death wish to the earth! "Kill us now! *Mountains and rocks fall on us*! Get it over with now! Hurry!" It's a sad, sad state of affairs as these men share:

"The reaction of every category of humanity all over the world is amazing. It indicates that people's perception of God and the Lamb in heaven will be far more terrifying to them than the physical consequences of this judgment. Whereas the martyrs cry, 'Avenge us' (Revelation 6:10), these unbelievers cry, 'Hide us.' What sinners dread most is not death but having to stand before a holy and righteous God."

"And the people on the earth (the 'earth dwellers') would rather be crushed by rocks or in the flattened caves of mountains than to face the wrath of God. The earth dwellers know that it is ultimately the Lord who is causing these events. Every person, even the most hardened 'atheist,' knows, somewhere deep in his soul, that there is a God and that if he is not saved, he is going to have to face the wrath of God someday."

"But the heavenly disruption merely presages a greater terror. It is God's 'wrath.' People cry out to the rocks and mountains. John described the human reaction to these terrifying cosmic distresses. People hid in caves and tried to seclude themselves from God and Christ (6:15). This language, too, is reflected in the Old Testament. Isaiah had written: 'Men will flee to caves in the rocks and to holes in the ground from dread of the Lord and the splendor of his majesty, when he rises to shake the earth' (2:19).

The 'wrath of the Lamb' is an unusual expression – used only once. But we should note that this is something the terrified people call the calamities they experience. They do not see the Lamb of God as the one who gave his life for human sin or God as the one who sent his Son to die (John 3:16-17). The inhabitants of the world still see God only as a vengeful being.

The wrath of God isn't spiteful hate or personal vindictiveness. It is God's holy response to unrepented sin that is the cause of the misery and suffering humans bring upon themselves."

"So intense is their fear of God's judgments that they temporarily seek even death – anything to flee from His manifest presence (Hos.10:8; Luke 23:30; Rev.9:6+). Attempting to hide from God illustrates how sin and fear warp the intellect, for it is impossible to hide from the Omnipresent One (Job 34:22). How different the motivation of the godly from the ungodly? Those with faith in Christ desire His presence and seek His face. (Ps.17:15; Pr.8:7; Isa.45:19; Isa.58:2; Isa.65:1; Jer.29:13; Amos 5:4). Those who reject God fear His presence and flee His face. This dichotomy is seen today in the reaction of people to the preaching of the gospel."[34]

In other words, those to whom we preach today God's loving message of salvation, who yet reject it prior to the 7-year Tribulation, will most likely be the same members of this global crowd in the *sixth seal* halfway into the 7-year Tribulation who are still rejecting it, that is, if they're still alive at this time. In fact, speaking of the activity, behavior, and the mindset of people prior to the 7-year Tribulation manifesting itself towards the middle of it, we not only see today people rejecting the Gospel, but we even see people *right now* preparing to *hide themselves in caves and among the rocks of the mountains*. They're called "bunkers" or "bug out shelters." Isaiah 2:19 mentions this same behavior as well, *"People will flee to caves in the rocks and to holes in the ground* from the fearful presence of the LORD." The point is, people today are not only "prepping" in this manner, leading up to the events of the *sixth seal*, but just like the text says, it's a growing trend from all walks of life! Everyone *right now* is scrambling to get their very own underground bunker to hide out in a time of calamity, from rulers, the militaries, the rich, even to the average Joe, preparing to *hide in holes in the ground*:

MILITARIES HAVE BUNKERS

They're called D.U.M. B's and yes, it's dumb to try to hide away from God's wrath, but that's not what it stands for. It's an acronym that stands for Deep Underground Military Bases and they're all over the world, just like the text says. D.U.M.B.'s or Deep Underground Military Bases are not only reported to be in various places throughout the United States, but literally all over the world by different countries. They are made possible thanks in part to massive high-powered tunnel boring machines.

In fact, some of them are reported to actually be 'nuclear powered'; and can not only literally 'melt' solid rock leaving behind glass-like walls, but they can also drill a tunnel seven-miles long in just one day. Due to these technological abilities, some of these underground facilities are reported to be 42 levels deep and are between 2.66 and 4.25 cubic miles in size. They are basically large whole cities underground. Other reports say that they are connected by high-speed magneto-leviton trains that have speeds up to Mach 2. As to why these bases are being built underground, there are many different explanations. One report says that most of them are being built away from geotectonic areas because they know that catastrophe is coming.

THE RICH HAVE BUNKERS

Doomsday Prep for the Super-Rich. Some of the wealthiest people in America – in Silicon Valley, New York, and beyond – are getting ready for the crackup of civilization.

An armed guard stands at the entrance of the Survival Condo Project, a former missile silo north of Wichita, Kansas, that has been converted into luxury apartments for people worried about the crackup of civilization.

Steve Huffman, the thirty-three-year-old co-founder and C.E.O. of Reddit, which is valued at six hundred million dollars, was nearsighted until November 2015, when he arranged to have laser eye surgery. He underwent the procedure not for the sake of convenience or appearance but, rather, for a reason he doesn't usually talk much about: he hopes that it will improve his odds of surviving a disaster, whether natural or man-made. 'If the world ends – and not even if the world ends, but if we have trouble – getting contacts or glasses is going to be a huge pain,' he told me recently. 'Without them, I'm messed up.'

Survivalism, the practice of preparing for a crackup of civilization, tends to evoke a certain picture: the woodsman in the tinfoil hat, the hysteric with the hoard of beans, the religious doomsayer. But in recent years survivalism has expanded to more affluent quarters, taking root in Silicon Valley and New York City, among technology executives, hedge-fund managers, and others in their economic cohort.

Last spring, as the Presidential campaign exposed increasingly toxic divisions in America, Antonio García Martínez, a forty-year-old former Facebook product manager living in San Francisco, bought five wooded acres on an island in the Pacific Northwest and brought in generators, solar panels, and thousands of rounds of ammunition. 'When society loses a healthy founding myth, it descends into chaos,' he told me. García Martínez wanted a refuge that would be far from cities but not entirely isolated. 'All these dudes think that one guy alone could somehow withstand the roving mob,' he said. 'No, you're going to need to form a local militia. You just need so many things to actually ride out the apocalypse.' Once he started telling peers in the Bay Area about his 'little island project,' they came 'out of the woodwork' to describe their own preparations, he said. 'I think people who are particularly attuned to the levers by which society actually works understand that we are skating on really thin cultural ice right now.'

In private Facebook groups, wealthy survivalists swap tips on gas masks, bunkers, and locations safe from the effects of climate change. One member, the head of an investment firm, told me, 'I keep a helicopter gassed up all the time, and I have an underground bunker with an air-filtration system.' He added, 'A lot of my friends do the guns and the motorcycles and the gold coins. That's not too rare anymore.'

Tim Chang, a forty-four-year-old managing director at Mayfield Fund, a venture-capital firm, told me, 'There's a bunch of us in the Valley. We meet up and have these financial-hacking dinners and talk about backup plans people are doing. It runs the gamut from a lot of people stocking up on Bitcoin and cryptocurrency, to figuring out how to get second passports if they need it, to having vacation homes in other countries that could be escape havens.' He said, 'I'll be candid: I'm stockpiling now on real estate to generate passive income but also to have havens to go to.' He and his wife, who is in technology, keep a set of bags packed for themselves and their four-year-old daughter. He told me, 'I kind of have this terror scenario: 'Oh, my God, if there is a civil war or a giant earthquake that cleaves off part of California, we want to be ready.''

When Marvin Liao, a former Yahoo executive who is now a partner at 500 Startups, a venture-capital firm, considered his preparations, he decided that his caches of water and food were not enough. 'What if someone comes and takes this?' he asked me. To protect his wife and daughter, he said, 'I don't have guns, but I have a lot of other weaponry. I took classes in archery.'

For some, like Huffman, it's been a concern for years. 'Ever since I saw the movie 'Deep Impact,'' he said. The film, released in 1998, depicts a comet striking the Atlantic, and a race to escape the tsunami. 'Everybody's trying to get out, and they're stuck in traffic. That scene happened to be filmed near my high school. Every time I drove through that stretch of road, I would think, I need to own a motorcycle because everybody else is toast.'

Huffman has been a frequent attendee at Burning Man, the annual, clothing-optional festival in the Nevada desert, where artists mingle with moguls. He fell in love with one of its core principles, 'radical self-reliance.' Among survivalists, or 'preppers,' as some call themselves, FEMA, the Federal Emergency Management Agency, stands for 'Foolishly Expecting Meaningful Aid.'

Huffman has calculated that, in the event of a disaster, he would seek out some form of community: 'Being around other people is a good thing. I also have this somewhat egotistical view that I'm a pretty good leader. I will probably be in charge, or at least not a slave, when push comes to shove.'

Around the same time that Huffman, on Reddit, was watching the advance of the financial crisis, Justin Kan heard the first inklings of survivalism among his peers. Kan co-founded Twitch, a gaming network that was later sold to Amazon for nearly a billion dollars. 'Some of my friends were, like, 'The breakdown of society is imminent. We should stockpile food,'' he said. I asked Kan what his prepping friends had in common. 'Lots of money and resources,' he said. "It's like insurance."

Yishan Wong, an early Facebook employee, was the C.E.O. of Reddit from 2012 to 2014. He, too, had eye surgery for survival purposes, eliminating his dependence, as he put it, 'on a nonsustainable external aid for perfect vision.' In an e-mail, Wong told me, 'Most people just assume improbable events don't happen, but technical people tend to view risk very mathematically.' He continued, "The tech preppers consider it an event with a very severe downside, so, given how much money they have, spending a fraction of their net worth to hedge against this....is a logical thing to do.'

How many wealthy Americans are really making preparations for a catastrophe? It's hard to know exactly; a lot of people don't like to talk about it. ('Anonymity is priceless,' one hedge-fund manager told me, declining an interview.)

Sometimes the topic emerges in unexpected ways. Reid Hoffman, the co-founder of LinkedIn and a prominent investor, recalls telling a friend that he was thinking of visiting New Zealand. 'Oh, are you going to get apocalypse insurance?' the friend asked. New Zealand, he discovered, is a favored refuge in the event of a cataclysm. Hoffman said, 'Saying you're 'buying a house in New Zealand' is kind of a wink, wink, say no more. Once you've done the Masonic handshake, they'll be, like, 'Oh, you know, I have a broker who sells old ICBM silos, and they're nuclear-hardened, and they kind of look like they would be interesting to live in."

I asked Hoffman to estimate what share of fellow Silicon Valley billionaires have acquired some level of 'apocalypse insurance,' in the form of a hideaway in the U.S. or abroad. 'I would guess fifty-plus per cent,' he said.

On a cool evening in early November, I rented a car in Wichita, Kansas, and drove north from the city through slanting sunlight, across the suburbs and out beyond the last shopping center, where the horizon settles into farmland. After a couple of hours, just before the town of Concordia, I headed west, down a dirt track flanked by corn and soybean fields, winding through darkness until my lights settled on a large steel gate. A guard, dressed in camouflage, held a semiautomatic rifle.

He ushered me through, and, in the darkness, I could see the outline of a vast concrete dome, with a metal blast door partly ajar. I was greeted by Larry Hall, the C.E.O. of the Survival Condo Project, a fifteen-story luxury apartment complex built in an underground Atlas missile silo. The facility housed a nuclear warhead from 1961 to 1965, when it was decommissioned. At a site conceived for the Soviet nuclear threat, Hall has erected a defense against the fears of a new era. 'It's true relaxation for the ultra-wealthy,' he said. 'They can come out here, they know there are armed guards outside. The kids can run around.'

Hall got the idea for the project about a decade ago, when he read that the federal government was reinvesting in catastrophe planning, which had languished after the Cold War. During the September 11th attacks, the Bush Administration activated a 'continuity of government' plan, transporting selected federal workers by helicopter and bus to fortified locations, but, after years of disuse, computers and other equipment in the bunkers were out of date.

'I started saying, 'Well, wait a minute, what does the government know that we don't know?'' Hall said. In 2008, he paid three hundred thousand dollars for the silo and finished construction in December 2012, at a cost of nearly twenty million dollars. He created twelve private apartments: full-floor units were advertised at three million dollars; a half-floor was half the price. He has sold every unit, except one for himself, he said.

Most preppers don't actually have bunkers; hardened shelters are expensive and complicated to build. The original silo of Hall's complex was built by the Army Corps of Engineers to withstand a nuclear strike. The interior can support a total of seventy-five people. It has enough food and fuel for five years off the grid; by raising tilapia in fish tanks, and hydroponic vegetables under grow lamps, with renewable power, it could function indefinitely, Hall said. In a crisis, his SWAT-team-style trucks ('the Pit-Bull VX, armored up to fifty-calibre') will pick up any owner within four hundred miles. Residents with private planes can land in Salina, about thirty miles away. In his view, the Army Corps did the hardest work by choosing the location. 'They looked at height above sea level, the seismology of an area, how close it is to large population centers,' he said.

Hall led me through the garage, down a ramp, and into a lounge, with a stone fireplace, a dining area, and a kitchen to one side. It had the feel of a ski condo without windows: pool table, stainless-steel appliances, leather couches. To maximize space, Hall took ideas from cruise-ship design. We were accompanied by Mark Menosky, an engineer who manages day-to-day operations. While they fixed dinner – steak, baked potatoes, and salad – Hall said that the hardest part of the project was sustaining life underground. He studied how to avoid depression (add more lights), prevent cliques (rotate chores), and simulate life aboveground.

The condo walls are fitted with L.E.D. 'windows' that show a live video of the prairie above the silo. Owners can opt instead for pine forests or other vistas. One prospective resident from New York City wanted video of Central Park. 'All four seasons, day and night,' Menosky said. 'She wanted the sounds, the taxis and the honking horns.'

Some survivalists disparage Hall for creating an exclusive refuge for the wealthy and have threatened to seize his bunker in a crisis. Hall waved away this possibility when I raised it with him over dinner. 'You can send all the bullets you want into this place.' If necessary, his guards would return fire, he said. 'We've got a sniper post.'

These days, when North Korea tests a bomb, Hall can expect an uptick of phone inquiries about space in the Survival Condo Project. But he points to a deeper source of demand. 'Seventy per cent of the country doesn't like the direction that things are going,' he said.

After dinner, Hall and Menosky gave me a tour. The complex is a tall cylinder that resembles a corncob. Some levels are dedicated to private apartments and others offer shared amenities: a seventy-five-foot-long pool, a rock-climbing wall, an Astro-Turf 'pet park,' a classroom with a line of Mac desktops, a gym, a movie theatre, and a library. It felt compact but not claustrophobic. We visited an armory packed with guns and ammo in case of an attack by non-members, and then a bare-walled room with a toilet. 'We can lock people up and give them an adult time-out,' he said. In general, the rules are set by a condo association, which can vote to amend them. During a crisis, a 'life-or-death situation,' Hall said, each adult would be required to work for four hours a day and would not be allowed to leave without permission. 'There's controlled access in and out, and it's governed by the board,' he said.

The 'medical wing' contains a hospital bed, a procedure table, and a dentist's chair. Among the residents, Hall said, 'we've got two doctors and a dentist.' One floor up, we visited the food-storage area, still unfinished. He hopes that, once it's fully stocked, it will feel like a 'miniature Whole Foods,' but for now it holds mostly cans of food.

We stopped in a condo. Nine-foot ceilings, Wolf range, gas fireplace. 'This guy wanted to have a fireplace from his home state' – Connecticut – 'so he shipped me the granite,' Hall said. Another owner, with a home in Bermuda, ordered the walls of his bunker-condo painted in island pastels – orange, green, yellow – but, in close quarters, he found it oppressive. His decorator had to come fix it. That night, I slept in a guest room appointed with a wet bar and handsome wood cabinets, but no video windows. It was eerily silent and felt like sleeping in a well-furnished submarine.

I emerged around eight the next morning to find Hall and Menosky in the common area, drinking coffee and watching a news brief on 'Fox & Friends.' Before I headed back to Wichita, we stopped at Hall's latest project – a second underground complex, in a silo twenty-five mile away. As we pulled up, a crane loomed overhead, hoisting debris from deep below the surface. The complex will contain three times the living space of the original, in part because the garage will be moved to a separate structure. Among other additions, it will have a bowling alley and L.E.D. windows as large as French doors, to create a feeling of openness.

Hall said that he was working on private bunkers for clients in Idaho and Texas, and that two technology companies had asked him to design 'a secure facility for their data center and a safe haven for their key personnel, if something were to happen.' To accommodate demand, he has paid for the possibility to buy four more silos. Survival of the Richest.

AVERAGE PEOPLE HAVE BUNKERS

In recent years, survivalism has been edging deeper into mainstream culture. In 2012, National Geographic Channel launched 'Doomsday Preppers,' a reality show featuring a series of Americans bracing for the end of civilization. The première drew more than four million viewers, and, by the end of the first season, it was the most popular show in the channel's history. A survey commissioned by National Geographic found that forty per cent of Americans believed that stocking up on supplies or building a bomb shelter was a wiser investment than a 401(k). Online, the prepper discussions run from folksy ('A Mom's Guide to Preparing for Civil Unrest') to grim ('How to Eat a Pine Tree to Survive').

The reelection of Barack Obama was a boon for the prepping industry. Conservative devotees, who accused Obama of stoking racial tensions, restricting gun rights, and expanding the national debt, loaded up on the types of freeze-dried cottage cheese and beef stroganoff promoted by commentators like Glenn Beck and Sean Hannity. A network of 'readiness' trade shows attracted conventioneers with classes on suturing (practiced on a pig trotter) and photo opportunities with survivalist stars from the TV show 'Naked and Afraid.'

SURVIVALIST GUIDE TO BUILDING AN UNDERGROUND SHELTER

Building a bunker could be a great choice as there are at least a dozen scenarios where your life can be saved by having an underground bunker to hide and spend some time in. So, the idea of making a bunker is great for every survivalist enthusiast and a definite must have for every experienced survivalist. You will come to know that building a bunker isn't as easy as it might sound, but after you are all settled, and everything is done, you will be at peace knowing that no matter what happens, you and your family will be safe.

HOW TO GET STARTED?

Regardless of what you are building, you need a permit; that means that the entire construction process must be legally allowed and in accordance with your state's law. Otherwise, you might be facing unwanted law regulations and law suits – and that is the last thing you need.

One of those things is making sure that you are legally allowed to dig a big hole in your backyard; maybe there are gas or water pipes buried in your backyard and that is also why you need to check everything up legally. Once you are set with that and allowed to dig the hole, you can start digging.

MAKE A PLAN

No matter what you are up to, as a survivalist, you know you first need to make a plan – the things are not any different with building a bunker – it's quite the opposite as you will need to work out every detail before even starting with digging.

There are numerous factors to consider: you need to determine what kind of soil you have in your backyard or find out if you will need to dig through the concrete in order to build an underground bunker.

Some houses have concrete foundation that is deeply dug into the ground, so making a bunker in that case would require much more work and planning.

When all factors are considered, including mold, type of soil, ventilation, radiation and natural gas pockets that may or may not exist in your backyard, you can then determine whether you want to build a bunker under your home, or you might consider building a shack under which you will then build an underground bunker.

ADVANTAGES OF HAVING A BUNKER BUILT UNDER YOUR HOME

So, you've heard of some disadvantages of building an underground bunker under your home, but what are the advantages? There are many, in fact. If it is determined that building a bunker under your home is perfectly safe and doable, then you will have less troubles in providing electrical energy for your bunker, and the fact is that you will need electricity.

However, you can always turn to portable generators designed for home usage and pick one that runs on batteries or fuel. That way you won't need to worry about not having electrical energy in your bunker.

So, even if you don't build the bunker just under your house, you could still have sources of electric energy. But what about the entrance? You are not spending much time in the shack, are you?

So, building a bunker under a shack could be potentially useless unless you decide to build a tunnel leading from your home to the underground bunker, which requires more planning and more work although it is a fairly good idea and an interesting project.

The best is that the entrance to your bunker is easily accessible to you so in case you are not able to exit your house in order to safely enter the bunker, you can access your bunker through your house; preferably through your basement, covering it up from curious eyes.

SURVIVAL FEATURES

There is no surviving without water, so another thing to consider alongside building a bunker is to build your own water supply system. If you were lucky to find the underground water, you can use that and build a water supply system leading to your bunker for safe and easy accessibility once the bad scenario occurs. You can also use the rain water and install the rain water barrel system that will collect the rain water for you to use it later. Having water purifiers and life straws is a great back up option to have around the bunker.

Ventilation is another important aspect for having a fully functional bunker on long tracks, so do your research and find the most suitable ventilation system that will meet all your needs, so that your underground bunker could work perfectly. As a survivalist you are surely aware of how important preparation is, so prepare yourself, get ready and start digging!"[35]

But you can dig all you want, even until you're blue in the face, or even buy one that's ready-made, filled with all the latest luxuries and amenities, yet you'll never be able to *hide* yourself from *the wrath of the Lamb*! Even with all those different kinds of man-made underground bunkers, homemade, luxury, or even full-blown military accommodations, God's got a bunker buster that'll blow them *all* away. It's called His *wrath*! One breath from His nostrils and you're toast no matter how far you try to hide underground! There's only one way to escape it and that's through Jesus Christ. Only He can save you from the wrath to come. Yet this is precisely what these people, *the inhabitants of the earth*, don't do! It's an unbelievable response! You had the way out of your mess right in front of you the whole time, yet you chose to *hide out in a hole in the ground*! Then you even have the audacity to ask the question, *"Who can stand?"* Really? As if you didn't know the answer?

"In the phrase 'who can stand' or 'who is able to stand, 'able' is present tense. The phrase could be rendered: who is presently able to stand. Their exclamation does not concern a potential future situation, as if the wrath were to begin after the seventh seal. They are presently experiencing the wrath and recognize it by the events which have just transpired which have driven them to hide in caves and in the rocks. When the sky splits and rolls up like a scroll, mountains and islands move out of their place, and asteroids fall to earth, there is little doubt concerning the power involved – it is the judgment of God! These events are not a precursor to God's wrath, they are the result of His wrath. "[36]

There's no doubt that *the inhabitants of the earth* know where these events are and were coming from. They've known all along. They already admitted it was due to *the wrath of the Lamb*, and most likely they had even been repeatedly told as well by the very martyrs they killed in the *fifth seal* that how to escape the mess they were in is also *through the Lamb*. But now they have the audacity to act like they don't know *how to stand*? Seriously? You really want us to believe that you don't know what to do, or where to turn, or how to be saved? Really? No, you know. This is simply yet another indicator of the hardness of man's heart. This question they pose exposes their sinfully depraved hearts that are responsible for leading them to their utter doom, as these men share:

"Now, the amazing thing: they correctly interpret it. They are alarmed, and they look up to God who is visiting in judgment, and they call together the greatest prayer meeting the earth has ever seen. The kings are there, and the emperors; the great men are there, and the captains of the hosts; the rich men are there and the poor; all are in that prayer meeting, and they pray to – even John is amazed – they don't pray to God, they pray to the rocks and to the mountains. They seek a savior in the strata of the earth.

And they're crying to the deaf and inert mountains [Revelation 6:15-17]. There's no repentance, there's no turning to God, there's no confession of sin. Oh! Why do men not turn to the Lord in the face of death, and in the face of judgment, and in the face of the certain fury and wrath of God upon wrong? Why don't men turn to God? That is the amazement of John that he will express time and again in this Revelation.

For example, in the ninth chapter, after he describes those horrible things in the visitation of God whereby one-third of the earth is destroyed, John says, 'And yet they repented not of the works of their hands.' Then in the next verse, 'Neither repented they of their murders, their sorceries, their fornications, nor their thefts' [Revelation 9:20-21]. And that same thing you'll find John standing in amazement before in the sixteenth chapter of the Book of the Revelation, 'And men were scorched with great heat, and they blasphemed the name of God, and they repented not' [Revelation 16:9]. And in then in the eleventh verse, 'And they blasphemed God because of their pains and their sores and repented not of their evil deeds' [Revelation 16:11]. Isn't that an amazing thing?

All of you who are of my generation remember John Dillinger, public enemy number one, the most sought-after criminal in the history of the United States. The suffering of that man was beyond anything we could ever experience. Cut off the ends of his fingers in order to destroy the prints. With surgery, changed his whole face in order to hide himself. And with every footfall, and with every touch of the door, is a retreat into terror lest it be the judgment of a righteous and indignant lawful order. But he doesn't turn, and he doesn't repent, and he doesn't get right with God. Pain never changes human life, and never saves a soul. Even in the penitentiary when men are locked up behind bars and walls of stone, if a man is saved he's saved by the gracious gospel of the Son of God. The pen doesn't save him, it won't change his heart. That's a work of the grace of God. And you see it here in this sixth seal: curse God, blaspheme God.

They're like Pharaoh: they thought it was the end, but it wasn't the end. And their hearts became increasingly harder, just like Pharaoh. With the first plague and the second, the third plague and the fourth, until finally Pharaoh was as hard as iron! [Exodus 7:14-8:32]. Same way with these people in the earth: when they first saw these terrible phenomena, representative of the visitation and judgment of God, they are alarmed; but the end didn't come, and in those succeeding judgments, in their terrible visitations as we read them in the Book of the Revelation, they get harder, and they get harder, and they get harder until finally when the Lord comes in the nineteenth chapter of the book, these men are bold as lions and are there fighting against the Son of God and the Lamb of our hope [Revelation 19:11-19].

That's the human story. Every day when you say 'no' to Jesus, something happens to your soul. And every time you reject the overtures of grace, something happens to your heart, until finally you turn into an abysmal negation. Oh, it is hard for a man to repent, to turn, when his conscience is seared, and his heart is like a rock. And in this moment, if God appeals to your heart, 'Today, if you will hear His voice,' said the eloquent author of the Hebrews, 'Today if you will hear His voice, harden not you heart.' [Hebrews 3:15]."

"Those who don't die from fear are noted in verse 16 and 17 in the reaction. We saw the reason for their fear, the range of fear, now finally the reaction. It says they hid themselves in the caves and among the rocks of the mountains, just as Isaiah said. We wish we could have read, 'they repented', don't we? We wish we had read that they saw their sins and they cried out to God for mercy. They certainly have been warned over and over and over again. They have heard the gospel. They have tried to stamp out its preachers. We wish they had cried for mercy. But if you read their reaction in chapter 9, verse 21, they didn't repent of their murders, of their sorceries, of their immorality, of their thefts, they didn't repent, even though the trumpet judgments were on them. And in chapter 16 in line with the bowl judgments, verse 11, they blasphemed the God of heaven because of their pains and their sores and they didn't repent of their deeds. They *should cry for mercy, but like the demons of which James wrote, they believe and tremble, but they don't repent.*

Why don't they repent? Because they have followed the path of satan and they are deceived. They believed the lie. They identified with the Antichrist. And God has left them in that delusion. He has left them in that deception. He has turned them over to wrath. Verse 11 of 2 Thessalonians 2, 'God will send upon them a deluding influence so that they might believe what is false, in order that they all may be judged who didn't believe the truth but took pleasure in wickedness.' Like Pharaoh who hardened his heart and had his heart hardened by God, finally, they who harden their hearts will have their hearts hardened by God. And in that moment, they will not believe.

You say, 'Are you saying that nobody is going to repent?' No, during this period of time there will be innumerable Gentiles converted, as chapter 7 verse 9 says, so many they can't even be numbered, no man could even count them from every nation and tribe and people and tongue. Also, the Jews will be converted. Romans says, 'All Israel will be saved.' Zechariah says, 'The Jews will look up and they will look on the One whom they have pierced, and they will mourn for Him as an only son, and a fountain of blessing and salvation will be opened to Israel.' There will be salvation during this period of time among Gentiles and among the Jews as the Jews finally see their Messiah, believe in Him and receive the Kingdom.

But the vast people of the world will be crushed, their own death wish coming true, but they won't escape for they'll meet their Maker after death to be sent forever into eternal hell. They think if the mountains will crush them and if the rocks will crush their lives, they won't have to face God. Boy, are they wrong.

What is the importance of all of this for us? It should be obvious. If you're an unbeliever, be warned, you are, according to Romans 2:5, treasuring up wrath against the day of wrath. You're accumulating a debt which God will pay you back for with His wrath in the day of wrath. You need to be warned. If you know the truth of the saving gospel and you go on sinning willfully and reject it, the only thing you can look forward to is a terrifying expectation of judgment."[37]

In other words, don't harden your heart like these people here in the *sixth seal*, like Pharaoh, and thus *seal* your own utter doom forever in hell. Call upon the Name of Jesus Christ right now and ask Him to forgive you of all your sins and believe in your heart that God raised Him from the grave, and the Bible says you will be saved, not only from an eternity in hell, but also the 7 years of hell on earth in the 7-year Tribulation. Don't feign ignorance. You know better. If you're reading this and you're still not saved, how many times have you already been told the way out of this mess, the way *to be able to stand* through Jesus Christ? And now I'm telling you yet again. How many more chances do you think you have before its' too late? This might be your final one! The Rapture could happen at any moment! Don't be like *the inhabitants of the earth* here in the *sixth seal*. You know what you need to do. They knew what they needed to do. They just refused to act on it. How about you reading this book? Will you suffer the same fate as those in the *sixth seal*? The answer is right smack dab in front of your face the whole time as well! It's *the Lamb*! You've read about Him how many times now? Only He and He alone can give you *the ability to stand* in your time of need. If you would just repent and stop this depraved rebellion, then you too could be rescued before it's too late! Don't make the same mistake!

Unfortunately, speaking of mistakes, as we're about to see, for those who remain in their stubborn sinful rebellion against God, they just made things infinitely worse for themselves. Oh, they may have made it out of that *hole* they dug for themselves, they might still be alive on earth at this time, but now they will emerge into the greatest nightmare they have yet to experience to date. This is what we will now see in the opening of the *seventh* and *final seal*. Please, take the way out before it's too late! You don't want to be there!

Part III

The Final Warning of the Seals

Chapter Eleven

The Breaking of the Final Seal

The **fourteenth thing** we see in the breaking of the planet is the **Ordering of the Seventh Seal**.

Revelation 8:1a "When *He opened the seventh seal…*"

Well, there you have it. A perfect seven out of seven! As if it wasn't already abundantly enough clear just Who's the One responsible for all these wrathful judgments falling upon mankind and planet earth in the first half of the 7-year Tribulation, here we have it declared yet again. It is *He, God, the Lamb*, Who *opened the seventh seal* as well. Just like all the other *openings* of all the other *seals*, so it is here. God is making it plain as day to any and the identity of the One Who is behind all this wrath being poured out in a heaping abundance throughout *all* of the 7-year Tribulation. It's not man, it's not satan, it's *He*, God, Who is the One doing this. This adds yet even more guilt to the feigned ignorance of *the inhabitants of the earth*, let alone *people today* as to *how to be able to stand*, how to be able to escape this horrible time frame. God has already told you seven times in a row now with each and every one of the seven *seals* where all this was coming from, and He has repeatedly informed you multiple times to turn to *the Lamb* and be saved before it's too late. Don't feign ignorance. Don't act like you don't know. You know exactly where this is all coming from and you also know how to avoid it. Don't be like the hard-hearted people in the *sixth seal* who, by the way, may very well be *the same people today* who, reading this book, at this point yet refuse to respond, who will make up *the inhabitants of* the earth. No amount of information is good enough for them. No amount of reminders gets through their hard heart or stubborn mind. They just simply won't respond. They won't repent so as to be rescued from this horrible time frame! It's not only sad, it's scary because what we are about to see in the *opening of the seventh seal* is that *He*, God is about to cause everything on earth to get *even worse*! Thus, once again, you better get saved now if you're not! Don't be like *the inhabitants of the earth* in the *sixth seal*! Don't ask for the rocks to fall on you and crush you. Cry out to *the Lamb*! Don't try to hide out in the rocks in the ground and seek to cover yourself up. Call upon *He*, God, Jesus, the Only One Who can save you and cover up your sins! Run to the One and only *Rock* that can save you before it's too late! This is the final message of warning when *He*, God, *opened the seventh seal*, as these researchers share:

"We must ever bear in mind that it is the Lamb who opens each of the seals initiating the judgments which befall the earth and its citizens.

The seventh seal contains the seven trumpet judgments, and the seventh trumpet contains the seven bowl judgments. The full effects of opening all seven seals include all seven trumpet judgments and the seven bowl judgments: 6 seal judgments + 6 trumpet judgments + 7 bowl judgments = 19 specific judgments in all. At the opening of the seventh seal, 6 judgments (the six seals) have passed and 13 remain (six trumpets and seven bowls within the seventh trumpet)."

"As Joel said, 'For the day of the Lord is great and very terrible; Who can endure it?' (Joel 2:11b). It will be a time of unprecedented bloodshed and death. However, in the midst of these things, there are some who are able to stand because they are afforded special protection from God. The 144,000 from the twelve tribes of Israel, Jewish believers in Messiah Jesus, are protected so that their gospel mission (Rev.7:9+) can be accomplished during this time of unprecedented upheaval.

As for the earth dwellers, they will remain in denial. But then, amazingly, even this would pass. After these few terrifying days, the stars stopped falling and the terrible shakings ceased. The survivors emerged from their shelters and began again to rationalize their resistance to God. After all, these calamities could be explained scientifically, so perhaps they had been too quick to attribute them to God's wrath. They quickly set about rebuilding their damaged structures and became more resolute in their opposition to the gospel of Christ.

The book of Revelation discredits those who hold that God is so loving and kind that He will never judge people who have not received His Son. Though the modern mind is reluctant to accept the fact that God will judge the wicked, the Bible clearly teaches that He will. The Scriptures reveal a God of love as clearly as they reveal a God of wrath who will deal with those who spurn the grace proffered in the Lord Jesus Christ. The passage before us is a solemn word that there is inevitable judgment ahead for those who will not receive Christ by faith.

Dear reader, is your citizenship in heaven? Or do you remain an earth dweller yet? That day is not yet upon us! There is a Rock to which we still may fly and pray, with hope of security in its wide-open clefts. It is the Rock of Ages. There are mountains to which we may yet betake ourselves, and be forever safe from all the dread convulsions which await the world. They are the mountains of salvation in Christ Jesus.

I believe I am addressing some who have betaken themselves to them. Brethren, 'hold fast the profession of your faith without wavering; for He is faithful that promised.' (Heb.10:23.) But others are still lingering in the plains of Sodom, who need to take this warning to heart as they never yet have done. O ye travelers of the judgment, seek ye the Lord while He may be found, and call upon Him while He is near! And may God in His mercy hide us all from the condemnation that awaits an unbelieving world!"[1]

That is the warning when *He*, God, *opened of the seventh seal*. If you're not saved, you better get saved now! Run to the Rock that is higher than us, the Rock of Ages, Jesus *the Lamb*, Who alone can rescue you from this terrible fate! The order has been given, it will not be reversed, *He* has declared it to be, and things are about to get even worse than you could ever imagine for and on planet earth! This is what we will now see in the foreboding response to the *seventh seal*.

The **fifteenth thing** we see in the breaking of the planet is the **Response to the Seventh Seal**.

Revelation 8:1 "When He opened the seventh seal, *there was silence in heaven for about half an hour*."

Believe it or not, some would say that this is a proof positive as to why women won't be in heaven. That is because it says here that *there was silence in heaven for about half an hour*. Now, as tempting as it might be to believe, it's not only patently false, but with all humor aside, this *silence in heaven* sends an even more important truth than that one to the whole planet. As we will see, in a nutshell, its God's way of saying, "You haven't seen anything yet, planet earth! It's about to get far far worse for you than you could ever imagine! The worst is yet to come!" Why? Well, let's go back to the context we've seen so far. Here we have the wicked, stubborn and rebellious *inhabitants of the earth*, those that survived the pummeling of the *sixth seal*, coming out of their bunkers, assessing the damage, probably even nervously joking about how crazy that was to go through all that and how childish it was for them to think in their moment of despair that this really was caused by *the wrath of the Lamb*. "Why, surely," they rationalize, "this had to be simply yet another occurrence of mother earth cleansing herself from man's divisive harmful behavior, and now we need more than ever to work together as mankind and bond even tighter to the leadership of the Antichrist so as to quickly rebuild our soon coming utopia."

Now, if you think that's a wild assumption on my part, simply observe virtually every single global catastrophe movie that's been coming out of Hollywood for many years now. What's the plot? After the planet has been totally decimated by an asteroid, earthquake, tsunami, alien invasion, take your pick, what's always the final scene? Mankind "rises from the ashes" and sets to "unify himself" even more with each other and some "special leader" and become determined more than ever to rebuild society. It's almost like mankind is once again being prepared by Hollywood to fall for this terrible lie and behavior of those who manage to survive the effects of God's wrath in the *sixth seal*. Thus, with Hollywood's help, you can easily imagine this unfortunate response from *the inhabitants of the earth,* as well as God's response to them and their non-stop continued rebellion, when *He opened the seventh seal.* "All you who have rebelled against Me, all of you who have sinned against Me, all you who killed My people, all you who had the audacity to then gloat and even celebrate over the death and murder of My people, and did it in the very presence of Me, what you now have in store for you is worse than anything you could ever imagine! I warned you with all the shaking of the universe and earth itself. I darkened the sun and reddened the moon to get your attention. I sent asteroids careening from the sky and even split the sky in two to show you beyond a shadow of a doubt Who and what is headed your way and Who is responsible for this outpouring of wrath. In fact, you even admitted that these events were caused by Me, *the wrath of the Lamb*, yet instead of receiving My mercy that I extended to you, even though you clearly deserve My wrath, you still had the audacity to say you'd rather die than be rescued! You called out to mother earth to kill you instead of

Father God to save you! Now here you are crawling out of your *holes in the ground* and you're *already* starting to rationalize these events as something 'natural' instead of 'Supernatural.' You're *already*, in such a short amount of time, hard on the heels of surviving the *sixth seal*, back to your evil, rebellious, laughing, mocking, and scoffing ways. You know what? Now you're *really* going to get it! The worst is yet to come!" In other words, your non-stop continued rebellion has earned you your worst nightmare to date, as this man shares:

"The Lord Jesus Christ is still in command. Do not lose sight of the fact that Revelation presents Him in His glory as the Judge of all the earth. It may deceive you to have Him presented as the gentle Jesus who went about doing good – which He did, but we are also going to see the wrath of the Lamb someday. Men are not lost because they are sinners; they are lost because they have rejected Jesus who died for them. Even if you go into a lost eternity and have not accepted Christ, He died for you, and you simply made His sacrifice for you of no avail. You have trodden underfoot the blood of Christ when you take that kind of attitude and position toward Him.

This is a very solemn scene. The Lord Jesus Christ orders a halt on all fronts: heaven, hell, and earth. Nothing can move without his permission. He had already ordered the cessation of natural forces on the earth when He ordered the sealing and saving of two definite groups. Now, for a brief moment, there is a lull in judgment activity; there is a heavenly hush. Godet defined it: 'This silence is a pause of action.' It is the lull before the storm. Why is there this strange silence? God's patience is not exhausted.

When the sixth seal was opened, and nature responded with a mighty convulsion, brave men weakened for a moment. Christ gave them opportunity to repent. But like the Pharaoh of old who, when the heat was taken off, let his willful heart return to its original intention, many men will go back to their blasphemous conduct when there is a calm. They probably will even rebuke themselves for showing a yellow streak. They will say, 'It was only nature reacting. It wasn't God, after all. Everything can be explained by natural causes.'

This, my friend, is the lull before the storm. As someone has said, 'The steps of God from mercy to judgment are always slow, reluctant, and measured.' This silence marks the transition from grace to judgment. God is waiting. By the way,

He is waiting for you today if you have not come to Him. You can come to Him, for He is a gracious Savior."²

But no, you wouldn't have it. Instead you, maybe even you today reading this, immediately went right back to your stubborn, wicked, rebellious attitudes even after all God's warnings, and you still even now spurn, laugh, and mock His gracious offer to be saved. You know what? You made your bed. Now it's time to lie in it. The worst is yet to come!

The **first way** we see the worst is yet to come in the opening of the seventh seal is the **Meaning of the Silence**.

Revelation 8:1 "When He opened the seventh seal, *there was silence* in heaven for about half an hour."

The word there for *silence* in the Greek is, "sige" which simply means, "a hush, a total silence." It's only used one other time in the New Testament referring to the "hush" or "silence" of the murderous crowd when the Apostle Paul was getting ready to talk to them.

Acts 21:39-40 "Paul answered, 'I am a Jew, from Tarsus in Cilicia, a citizen of no ordinary city. Please let me speak to the people.' Having received the commander's permission, Paul stood on the steps and motioned to the crowd. When they were all *silent*, he said to them in Aramaic....'"

So just as a total "silence" or "hush" came across the violent mob that wanted to kill the Apostle Paul right before he spoke, so it is here that we have a total *silence in heaven* right before God speaks if you will with even worse judgments. Why? Because once again, not just a single crowd, but all *the inhabitants of the earth* have been guilty of seeking to kill and murder not just one of God's people, the Apostle Paul, but now millions of them, as many as they can find, so once again God creates another hush or *silence* just before *He* Himself acts upon their evil deeds. So, the obvious question is, "What's the meaning of this *silence*?" Well I think it represents several things all in one package and none of them are good for planet earth:

SILENCE GETS YOUR ATTENTION

Hitler became the main speaker at German Workers Party public meetings. It was during this period that he developed the techniques that made him into such a persuasive orator. Hitler always arrived late which helped to develop tension and a sense of expectation. He took the stage, stood to attention and waited until there was complete silence before he started his speech.

SILENCE BUILDS ANTICIPATION

Let me ask you a painful question: How many of you remember being spanked? If your parent was an effective disciplinarian, he/she made you wait for it. Good parents understand the art of psychological warfare. You probably remember when your dad said, 'Go into the bathroom, go downstairs, or upstairs. I'll be there in a few minutes.' I could almost feel the pain. Seriously, I don't know which was worse: the emotional anguish of waiting or the physical pain of discipline. I concluded, with Tom Petty & the Heartbreakers, that 'The Waiting is The Hardest Part.' In a similar way, God unleashes His power with an expression of silence and delay to ensure that He has the full attention of everyone in the universe.

As soon as each of the first six seals was opened, John either 'saw' something or 'heard' something, or both. When the seventh seal was opened, however, he saw nothing and heard nothing for about half an hour (v.1). Half an hour is not a long time, but half an hour of silence can seem like an eternity, whether it is 'dead air' on radio or television or a silent dinner for two after a quarrel between a husband and a wife. To get some idea of the effect, imagine that a Church youth group is doing a dramatic reading of the book of Revelation. When it comes to Revelation 8:1, it takes the verse literally so that all speech and all action stops – for thirty minutes – while the congregation fidgets and squirms. The silence is total.

A half-hour silence is not long, but things seem long or short in their context. If a preacher were to stop his sermon and remain silent for ten minutes, it would seem like an eternity. Since heaven is a place of constant praise and worship to God (Revelation 4:8-11), silence for about half an hour is a long time.

SILENCE PRECEDES A STORM

Why was there 'silence' in heaven for approximately 30 minutes? The silence intensifies a sense of anticipation and awe for God's awesome judgments to follow:

Habakkuk 2:20 "But the LORD is in His holy temple; let all the earth be *silent* before Him."

Psalm 46:8,10 "Come and see the works of the LORD, the desolations He has brought on the earth. Be *still* and know that I am God; I will be exalted among the nations, I will be exalted in the earth."

Zephaniah 1:7,15,17-18 "Be *silent* before the Sovereign LORD, for the day of the LORD is near. That day will be a day of wrath, a day of distress and anguish, a day of trouble and ruin, a day of darkness and gloom, a day of clouds and blackness. I will bring distress on the people and they will walk like blind men, because they have sinned against the LORD. Their blood will be poured out like dust and their entrails like filth. Neither their silver nor their gold will be able to save them on the day of the LORD's wrath. In the fire of His jealousy the whole world will be consumed, for He will make a sudden end of all who live in the earth.

Zechariah 2:13 "Be *still* before the LORD, all mankind, because He has roused himself from His holy dwelling."

Silence is the calm before the storm of judgment to come, as a few moments of calm precede the most devastating destruction of a tornado or hurricane. More likely, this silence in heaven demonstrates a sober, awestruck silence at the judgments to come, now that the seals are off and the scroll can be opened.

When the seventh seal is opened revealing the contents of the scroll, there is an ominous, awesome calm in Heaven (the only such silence in heaven mentioned in Scripture) before the greatest, most destructive 'storm' in history – the plagues of the judgments and the Wrath of God. After the 144,000 are sealed and the redeemed followers of Jesus are safe in Heaven, the four angels (7:1) will now release the winds of destruction on Earth. Judgment is getting ready to come upon the earth. This is the lull before the storm of judgment which is coming on the earth during this particular period. When I was a boy, my dad built a storm cellar wherever we moved. I spent half of my boyhood, during the spring and early summer, sleeping in the storm cellar.

Late one evening my dad and I were standing in the storm cellar doorway. He was watching a storm come up, and he saw that it was not going to hit our little town in southern Oklahoma. It hit one just about ten miles away. We could see the funnel as it let down near that little town. But before that storm hit, there was a certain stillness. The wind had been blowing, the rain had been coming down, there had been a great deal of thunder and lightning, but suddenly all of that stopped, and for a few moments there was a deathlike silence. Then the wind began to blow like I've never seen it blow. It was not a funnel-shaped hurricane or a tornado, but just a straight wind. It was all my dad could do to get that storm cellar door down, and I helped him hold onto the chain. The storm broke in all its fury. This is the way the second half of the 7-year tribulation will break upon the earth, and it is presented to us in this way in the blowing of the trumpets, which is the subject of chapter 8, verse 2, through chapter 11.

The silence in heaven is a silence of ominous foreboding. Even the Lord God Almighty pauses before the onward rush of this great and final judicial administration. In the first, the second, the third, and the fourth and the fifth and the sixth seals, by war and by famine, by pestilence and by bloodshed, by violence and by storm, one-fourth of all of the inhabitants of the earth have been swept away [Revelation 6:1-8]. And now, as they come to that great last and final seal, what does it mean for all of the inhabitants of this earth? [Revelation 8:1]. It's a calm before a storm. Haven't you seen the clouds gather and lower and the heavens turn black and sheets of lightning fall to this fearful and trembling earth? Then there's a hush and a quiet and a calm and a leaf hardly moves, and there's no breeze or wind for a moment. Then the crash of a resounding lightning flash and a thunderous roar and the deluge falls.

That's exactly the silence here. Before the awful sounding of the final judgment trumpets of God, there's a pause in heaven by the space of about half an hour: interminable, unbearable, though so short. Same kind of a thing as if you saw a drowning child and one minute and a half a minute are an eternity, so it is here, the silence and the stillness in heaven, a pause you could ever forget. You can feel, you can touch, its very intensity.[3]

Yes, this will be a *very intense* time for planet earth during this time. Even after all *the inhabitants of the earth* have been through, due to their own stubbornness, wickedness and rebellion, they still haven't seen anything yet! The biggest spanking, the most severe storm they've ever seen, is now on its way! God makes sure they get this ominous meaning by producing a *silence in heaven* when *He opened the seventh seal*. It gets their attention, it builds an uncomfortable anticipation in them, they squirm nervously as it dawns on them what they have now reaped for all the evil they have sown, that is, an even worse storm coming for them. This attention getting, nerve racking, stunning *silence* that God produces *in heaven,* right before He pours out even more of His wrath and judgment upon *the inhabitants of the earth,* sends home the frightening message to their hard hearts that all that they've been through thus far is mere child's play compared to what's coming next. No wonder Revelation Chapter 8 ends with the words:

Revelation 8:13 "Woe! Woe! Woe to *the inhabitants of the earth.*"

You definitely don't want to be on planet earth during this time when this *silence* is manifested by God! *Woeful* times lie ahead! That means, great sorrow, distress, misery, sadness, heartache, despondency, despair, agony, depression, regret, misfortune, disaster, adversity, hardship suffering, gloom and doom is headed their way! Woe! Woe! Woe! If you're not saved, you better get saved now through Jesus and avoid the whole thing! This is your *woeful* future when *He,* God, *opens the seventh seal* unless you repent now! The *silence* reveals this harsh reality.

The **second way** we see the worst is yet to come in the opening of the seventh seal is the **Place of the Silence**.

Revelation 8:1 "When He opened the seventh seal, there was silence *in heaven* for about half an hour."

As if the meaning of the *silence* wasn't enough to get the attention, build anticipation, make squirm, and illuminate that an even worse storm is coming for *the inhabitants of the earth,* now you have to consider the *place* in which this *silence* occurred. It's *in heaven.* When one takes into account all the constant activity of heaven up until this point, that of constant praise, constant shouts of glory, constant singing and worshipping God, and now you have a total *silence in heaven,* a total ceasing of the normal activity from on high, the feeling one gets is definitely *not a good one.* Something odd and ominous is about to take place. Something out of the ordinary is about to happen. Something otherworldly is going to occur if all of the normal activity of heaven literally comes to a screeching halt. It can't be good, whatever it is, and sure enough, it's not, as these researchers agree:

"In 8:1, John writes, 'When the Lamb broke the seventh seal, there was silence in heaven for about half an hour.' This is what's called a 'dramatic pause.'

Considering the catastrophic events of chapters 4-7, the sudden and deafening silence in heaven is startling (cf. 7:10). The impact of such silence must have

*been impressive, for until now, everything that has been done has been done
loudly. The word 'loud' (megas) has occurred six times already in the book:*

Revelation 1:10 "On the Lord's Day I was in the Spirit, and I heard behind me a
loud voice like a trumpet."

Revelation 5:2 "And I saw a mighty angel proclaiming in a *loud* voice, 'Who is
worthy to break the seals and open the scroll?'"

Revelation 5:12 "In a *loud* voice they sang: 'Worthy is the Lamb, who was slain,
to receive power and wealth and wisdom and strength and honor and glory and
praise!'"

Revelation 6:10 "They called out in a *loud* voice, 'How long, Sovereign Lord,
holy and true, until You judge the inhabitants of the earth and avenge our
blood?'"

Revelation 7:2 "Then I saw another angel coming up from the east, having the
seal of the living God. He called out in a *loud* voice to the four angels who had
been given power to harm the land and the sea."

Revelation 7:10 "And they cried out in a *loud* voice: 'Salvation belongs to our
God, Who sits on the throne, and to the Lamb.'"

*And will be found 15 times in Rev.8 and beyond: (8:13; 10:3; 11:12, 15; 12:10;
14:2, 7, 9, 15, 18; 16:1, 17; 19:1, 17; 21:3)." (But now there's only a silence and
one that lasts for a whole half hour. What a contrast to the rest of the activity in
the Book of Revelation. Surely something ominous is coming.)*

*In the Jewish temple, musical instruments and singing resounded during the
whole time of the offering of the sacrifices, which formed the first part of the
service. But at the offering of incense, solemn silence was kept. Zephaniah
revealed that silence would attend the Day of the Lord in response to the solemn
occasion where He will prepare a sacrifice and invite His guests (Zep.1:7). The
sacrifice will consist of the men who oppose God and the guests are the birds of
heaven who will feast upon them (Rev.19:17-18+). This silence precedes the Day
of the Lord in its narrow sense – the actual day when Christ returns and
physically defeats the armies gathered against him. The Day of the Lord, in its
broadest sense, is already in progress.*

The implication is that when the judgment about to happen becomes visible as the seventh seal is broken and the scroll unrolled, both the redeemed and the angels are reduced to silence in anticipation of the grim reality of the destruction they see written on the scroll. The half an hour of silence is the calm before the storm. It is the silence of foreboding, of intense expectation, of awe at what God is about to do.

When Heaven falls silent for half an hour, when all the singing, glorifying, and praising ceases, there will be a deep sense of foreboding. The judgments, every righteous soul knows, must be formidable in the extreme, yet they will shudder in awe at the prospect of having to witness their administration."

"When the Lamb broke the seventh seal of the scroll, silence fell on the heavenly scene. For 'half an hour' awesome silence continued as all of those assembled around the throne waited expectantly to see what God would do next. This is probably a literal 30 minutes since there are no clues in Revelation that we should interpret time references non-literally. The purpose of the silence is apparently to prepare for what is about to happen by heightening expectation of God's awesome judgments to follow."

"The first thing noticed, and the first thing written, when the Lamb of God opened the last and seventh seal, is a silence in heaven [Revelation 8:1]. That is unusual because heaven is never silent. It is filled by day and by night and through all of the unending ages, world without end, with the worship and the praise and the adoration of the heavenly hosts offered unto God our Father and unto God our Savior and unto God our Holy Comforter and Keeper. But, at the opening of the seventh seal, all heaven is mute and silent and intense.

You see, when the Lamb opened the first seal, there was heard a voice as of thunder saying: 'Come' [Revelation 6:1]. When the Lamb of God opened the second and the third and the fourth seals, that same thunderous voice was heard [Revelation 6:3-8]. When the Lamb opened the fifth seal He heard the cry of those who were martyred for Christ, saw them under the altar beseeching God for vengeance upon their blood shed in the earth [Revelation 6:9-10]. And when the Lamb of God opened the sixth seal, there was a great tremor throughout all the framework of nature and vast illimitable, indescribable consternation on the earth [Revelation 6:12-17]. But when the Lamb of God opens the seventh and last seal, there is a silence that could be felt. One dared hardly breathe. All motion in heaven stops. All praise and adoration ceases. There is silence, stillness, a vast indescribable calm [Revelation 8:1].

Why this silence in heaven? It is first, the silence of awe and of intense expectancy. This is the last and formal drama of the great and ultimate mystery of Almighty God. This is the last and ultimate seal. And we can just hear the unspoken intensity and expectancy of the hosts of heaven as they say to themselves, 'What now will God do? And what will be the final disposition of His judicial administration in this rebellious and blaspheming world?' It is an intense silence of expectancy."

"When the Lamb opens the scroll's seventh and final seal, there is dead silence in heaven for about half an hour. You talk about dramatic! This emphasizes the significance and awesomeness of the coming judgment that culminates in the eternal state. All in heaven are in breathless anticipation as they await God's final actions in bringing history to a close."

"It's kind of an interesting turn of events, when you think about it. Mankind has often complained about the silence of God, sometimes even expressing the complaint of the psalmist who said, 'May our God come and not keep silence.' Up till then in some ways angels and men have been noisy, but God has been silent. And now God is about to speak in the full fury of judgment, and angels and redeemed men in heaven are silent. The tables are turned.

The prophet Zechariah called for such silence in the light of God's glorious judgment, chapter 2 verse 13, 'Be silent, all flesh, before the Lord, for He has aroused from His holy habitation,' Zechariah 2:13. So when the Lamb opens the last seal, all of those in heaven know what it means. It means the end has come. The final judgment is about to be unleashed.

There are no more seals. The scene in heaven has been very noisy. We all know God loves noise, a joyful noise, loud singing. And He's been having all of that: four living beings have been praising Him, twenty-four elders have been singing of the praise not only of God the Father but of the Lamb, innumerable angels, there have been harps, there has been thunder, angels saying...Come...praying martyrs under the altar, singing Tribulation saints. There's been an awful lot of noise in heaven, the noise of praise.

But when the seventh seal is broken and what is to happen becomes visible as the scroll is unrolled, and the implication is they can all see what it says, they are reduced to utter silence. And all the triumphant ringing hallelujahs, all the exaltation halts. And I think it is the silence of awe, it is the silence of the anticipation of the grim reality of what is coming, as well as the joyous reality of the exaltation of Christ and the devastation of satan and sin. This half hour of silence is the calm before the storm, the silence of foreboding, the silence of expectation, the silence of awe.

It's interesting that John measures the time in his vision experience as about half an hour. Absolute silence in that large crowd of innumerable angels running into the millions, absolute dead silence for half an hour would seem like an eternity. The margin of suspenseful expectancy seems to us brief, but it must have seemed to him very long.

The hour has finally come. The saints are to be vindicated. Satan is to be conquered. Sin is to be punished. And Christ is to be exalted."[4]

It's a bitter sweet time, this *silence in heaven*. Sweet because it means that very soon Jesus Christ will come down and put an end to sin, satan, the Antichrist, the false prophet, all the evil and suffering and pain and all the injustice in the world. He will then establish His glorious and righteous Millennial Reign throughout the whole earth for 1,000 years whereupon He will be exalted. The great promise of the ages is about to be manifest. Sweet victory is at hand! Yet, this *silence in heaven* is also a bitter time, for it means even more doom, even more disaster, and even more destruction is in store for *the inhabitants of the earth* because they still refuse to receive God's mercy in the midst of His judgement and so will now perish in their way. It's sad because it didn't have to be this way. Again, the way out was there the whole time through Jesus Christ, but in their stubborn persistent wicked rebellion, they refused to receive and worship Jesus Christ the One and Only true Messiah, and instead chose to continually accept and follow the world's biggest false messiah, the Antichrist. They worship satan's man instead of the One and Only *Lamb*, Jesus Christ. So now, here in the *opening of the seventh seal*, they will reap an even bigger harvest of pain from all this evil and sinful behavior they have sown. If this seems harsh, then let us quickly recap their constant, wicked, non-stop, rebellious journey up until this point.

It started with the *first seal* and the *white* horse rider. The antichrist will feign righteousness and purity, but just like the Roman conquerors of old, he will be riding forth *victorious* in his *conquest* to *enslave* the world. They think he will usher in a time of global *law*, *governance*, and *strength*, but it is actually the beginning of a long *procession* of evil events leading to global domination and tyranny. They are at fault because they have chosen to reject the True Victor, Jesus, the Lamb of God, and so they will now receive His evil counterfeit, the imposter, the deceiver, the Antichrist. And so it is, just like the choosing of Barabbas over Jesus in His first coming, so the world will once again choose a *criminal* over *Christ* prior to His Second Coming. The world thinks they are getting great peace, unheralded peace, peace unthinkable, global peace and a fantastic global ruler, but they are soon to discover that it's really hell's man who unleashes a literal hell on earth. Mankind rejects God's truth, they reject His warnings, mock the Bible, and receive the prophesied coming future antichrist, thus sealing their fate. There is no excuse.

Then we saw the *second seal* and the false utopia come crashing down. The short-lived global party is now over. Sudden destruction has burst upon the planet. Global war counteracts the emptiness of the antichrist's false peace and false utopia. *Men slay each other*, peace is taken from *planet earth,* and *nations* will rise against *nations* and *kingdoms* against *kingdoms*. It is the most gruesome, bloody mess the world has ever seen, and the planet will become bathed in it. The antichrist promises the world a false peace and phony prosperity, yet no sooner than the world lets out a global sigh of relief, the fiery red war paint on his body unveils his bloody, murderous, motives. People all over the earth begin "to slaughter, to butcher, to murder with violence." They don't just die, they are literally butchered violently! Take all your Freddy Kruegers, take all your Jasons, take all your Chainsaw Massacre horrible shows, and unleash that same sick murderous behavior depicted in those wicked rotten movies, and now make it the attitude of everyone on the planet *for real*! What a gruesome, bloody, nightmarish scene! People are against people, neighbor against neighbor, family against family, friend against friend, countrymen against countrymen, all people, *all over the earth,* will start to *slay,* butcher, and murder one another, chopping one another to pieces. The whole world has in effect gone mad.

Then came the *third seal* and the global *famine* conditions with people en masse *starving* to death all over the world. *Food* on a global basis will be *measured* and doled out only to those who work for a whole day but it is only *barely enough to survive*. This global famine pulls the rug out from underneath the wicked and rebellious and even murderous behavior of planet earth. They spent their energy slaying and slaughtering one another and must be *famished* after all that. So as an act of judgement from God, planet earth's food supply will be totally decimated. He declares, '*Famine*!' Where there was once restaurants galore, now there is nothing but food lines! Nobody even asks you if you'd like fries with that because there are no fries! Everything was destroyed in your blind fury to murder, murder, murder! Now the only option you ever get is, "Would you like a quart of wheat for a day's wages, or three quarts of barley?" Thus death, decay, corpses, crying mourning, anguish, atrocities, heartache, tears, loss, and unspeakable behavior will be the daily existence of those who remain. The earth is turned into a planet full of Jobs scraping themselves on heaps of rubbish. Children begging for bread with no response. Young and old alike destitute in the streets lying in heaps. Their bodies blackened, not even recognizable. Their skin shriveled to the bones racked with hunger. They waste away dry as a stick. The famine conditions were so bad that even the *women cooked their own children* all across the planet all at the same time!

Then arrived the *fourth seal* and the *mass wave of death* across the planet, with *Death* and *Hades* scooping people up and sending them straight into hell as fast as they *died. One fourth of the earth* was *killed* in four different ways, *sword, famine, plague,* and *wild beasts.* There will be no escape from this, *global death* that is thrust upon the planet! They tried to hide out in their homes, but the *sword* came and got them. They tried to scurry into the open field, but *wild beasts* devoured them. They even went into a secure location to ensure their safety, but a *pestilence* floated right in and took them out. *No one* could escape. It's the most deadly, macabre, corpse ridden existence that human history will ever see. Here comes the morgue! *Death* descends upon humanity on an unimaginable scale, never before seen. Just like a decaying corpse, it's all downhill from here and the process of decay cannot be reversed. It's too late! The *death chill* has arrived! All because they rejected Holy Blessed One Jesus Christ for the lying deceitful Antichrist. They chose to dance with the devil and so they have simply reaped what they have sown. The *pale horse rider* is now bringing you your wages! Death, murder, destruction, corpses littered everywhere! *Death is coming for you*!

Then we saw the *fifth seal* where the scene shifts from earth to heaven to expose another wave of wickedness from wicked and rebellious mankind. Just when you thought they couldn't sink to a new low, they go even deeper. Apparently, killing themselves wasn't enough. Now they will be seen butchering on a scale like never before, godly righteous people who were only trying to help them. It's senseless, ruthless, heartless, and wickedness unrestrained. There doesn't seem to be any sense of decency left at this point in the world. This will be the worst and most unprecedented time of global martyrdom and anti-Semitism this planet has ever seen or will ever see again. A whole new bloody holocaust is coming that makes what Hitler did look like chump change, a *global genocide* of God's people. Mankind goes berserk and begins a systematic bloody execution, a massive violent slaughter, a butcherous extermination of God's people with a violent glee. *All nations* will haul God's people away and not just persecute them, but once again kill them, put them to death, just like in the Jewish Holocaust of not long ago. They think they're making things better for planet earth and themselves by getting rid of the followers of God, but all they accomplished was making sure that they and planet earth experience even more of the *vengeance of God*! They will get what they and anyone else justly deserve for that kind of ungodly, unholy, wicked, murderous behavior, a big 'ol heaping pile of God's *vengeance* and justice! Justice *will be* served!

Then that justice began in the *sixth seal* with *avenging the blood* of His people. God begins His own systematic destruction of the world, a foreboding and impending calamity, a widespread day of reckoning and doom for all mankind for the sins of murdering His own people. Don't mess with His kids! If you do, this is what you can expect. Not just the earth, but the universe itself will be shaken like a rag doll. The Hand of Almighty God pummels His creation with one devastating blow after another that creates a rapid shockwave across the planet, with a *great earthquake, the sun turned black, the moon turned red, the stars fell from the sky, the sky split apart,* and *every mountain and island was moved from their place*! God is sending an unmistakable, clear, ominous message to planet earth. "All you who have rebelled against Me, all of you who have sinned against Me, all you who killed My people, all you who had the audacity to then gloat and even celebrate over the death and murder of My people, what you now have in store for you is a global shaking, a global funeral, a global bloody nightmare, a global bloody slaughter, and a global fear that will rock you to the core!" *The inhabitants of the earth* don't even have time to catch their breath from one earth-shattering judgment before the next one arrives. One after another after another. It truly is the time of the end! "It's time, planet earth, to meet your Maker! Look up in the sky and see Who is headed your way!" Yet, even after all that, even though the planet is literally *scared to death* and they know this is from God, they would rather die and commit suicide than receive God's mercy. They *call to the mountains and rocks* to crush them instead of receiving Christ as their Savior!

Then on top of that, we see here in the *opening of the seventh seal* the mind-blowing, sin-filled even worse response from *the inhabitants of the earth.* You make it out of that *hole* you dug for yourself, you're one of the few still alive on planet earth, but now you shake it all off as if these catastrophes weren't really coming from *the wrath of the Lamb* as you even admitted yourself. Rather, nervously, half-jokingly, you now begin to excuse it all away as something natural instead of Supernatural and are more determined than ever to continue to forsake God and instead follow and listen to the Antichrist's lies. Even after all these warnings and pleading from God in the first half of the 7-year Tribulation, you're already back to your evil, rebellious, laughing, mocking and scoffing ways. This God says in a nutshell in the *opening of the seventh seal* with *silence in heaven for about half an hour*, "That's it! Now you're really going to get it! The worst is yet to come!"

No, God is not being unfair or unduly harsh, not when you look at this rebellious journey of *the inhabitants of the earth*. They had their chances over and over and over and over again, yet they persistently refused to take the way out, and instead continued in their wicked, stubborn, rebellion towards Almighty God, and consistently thumbed their noses at His amazing mercy, refusing to repent and be saved. Now they will experience the trumpet and the bowl judgments from God in the second half of the 7-year Tribulation, whereupon they will have to endure even worse things such as:

- 1st Trumpet – Hail/Fire - 1/3rd of Earth/Trees & All Green Grass Burned Up

- 2nd Trumpet – Huge Asteroid – 1/3rd of Sea Dies & 1/3rd Ships Destroyed

- 3rd Trumpet – Blazing Comet – 1/3rd of Rivers & Fresh Water Bitter – Many People Die

- 4th Trumpet – Solar Smiting - 1/3rd of Sun, Moon & Stars Struck – 1/3rd Day & Night without Light

- 5th Trumpet – Horde of Demon Locusts are Released – People with Mark Tortured 5 Months

- 6th Trumpet – Four Angels Loosed from Euphrates – 1/3rd Mankind Killed

- 7th Trumpet – Unleashes Bowl Judgments

- 1st Bowl – Ugly Painful Sores on Receivers of the Mark

- 2nd Bowl – All the Sea Turns to Blood – All Sea Creatures Die

- 3rd Bowl – All the Rivers & Fresh Water to Blood

- 4th Bowl – Sun Scorches People with Fire – People Curse God

- 5th Bowl – Kingdom of Antichrist Plunged into Darkness

- 6th Bowl – Euphrates River Dries Up Which Prepares Way for Kings of East for the Battle of Armageddon and three Evil Frog-Like Spirits Deceive the World for Armageddon, Out of Mouth of Satan, Out of Mouth of Antichrist, Out of Mouth of False Prophet

- 7th Bowl – Final Pronouncement – IT IS DONE! Greatest of all Earthquakes, A New Look for Jerusalem - Split in Three, All Cities Collapse, A Cup of Wrath for Babylon, All Islands and Mountains Gone, A Massive Hailstorm – 100 lbs. each, Angel Harvest of the Righteous, Angel Harvest of the Unrighteous where they are thrown into Hell, the Blood of those who die will be as High as Horses Bridle (4 feet deep) for 1,600 Stadia (200 Miles)

As you can see, once again, this is simply a sad, sad state of affairs. No wonder there is *silence in heaven for about a half an hour*. The calm before the storm. What you just read with the coming trumpet and bowl judgments, is about to be unleashed upon *the inhabitants of the earth*. It didn't have to be this way, if only they would have received God's salvation through Jesus Christ. And that's the point of *The Seals* for we the Christian. The logical response, knowing what's coming, it to get out there and warn as many people as we can, as this man shares:

"If you're a Christian, first of all you can be thankful for what you're going to escape. Amen? And we're going to be caught up together to meet the Lord in the air and we're going to be with Him, coming back with Him in glory to reign. Secondly, as a believer I'm not only to be thankful but I need to be faithful to evangelize, right? When I understand what is coming, I have to warn men. On the one hand I'm thankful that I'm going to be rescued from wrath, that I am not destined for the wrath to come. But on the other hand, there's a world of people that are and I have the saving message of Jesus Christ to bring to them that they might be delivered from that."[5]

But if you're reading this and you're not a Christian, the point for you with *The Seals* is this. The fate of *the inhabitants of the earth* in the near future might be *sealed* for some, but what about you today? You still have time. Maybe only a little, very little. In fact, why do you think God has you reading this book right now? What will it take before you yourself, not just these people in the future, stop in your own persistent rebellion of God's wonderful and merciful gracious offer to be saved from His wrath though Jesus Christ? Has not this description of the first half of the 7-year Tribulation, in *The Seals* that God has written down as a warning for the last 2,000 years, been enough for you? This is not a Hollywood movie, this is planet earth's soon coming reality. What more will it take to get *your attention* before it's too late, as these men share:

"The Book of Revelation ought not to terrify you, that is, if you're a true Christian. Actually, it ought to be a comfort to you. I thank God that He is going to judge this world that is running wild today. The way that mankind has blundered and gotten this world into a mess makes it look like it is filled with madmen. I thank God He is going to judge it, and He is going to judge it rightly.

It is very comforting to recognize that. People often urge me to speak out on my radio broadcast against certain things that are taking place. It is not my business to get on radio and denounce every wrong. My business is to give out just the Word of God, and that is what I am going to do. He is going to straighten this world out someday. I wouldn't have that job for anything in the world. I am glad it is His job. He is going to straighten out this world, and He is going to move in judgment.

Maybe you don't like the fact that the gentle Jesus is going to judge. We have already seen that the wrath of the Lamb will be terrifying to those on earth. My friend, when you talk about the gentle Jesus, you had better get acquainted with Him. He died for you, He loves you, and He wants to save you, but if you will not have Him, I tell you, there is waiting ahead of you a terrifying judgment.

Someone will say to me, 'You are trying to frighten people.' I would like to scare you into heaven if I could, but I know you are too sophisticated and cynical for that. But, my beloved, judgment is coming on this earth. I say, Hallelujah! I am glad that it is coming, and that God is not going to let the world go on like it is now. It has gone on long enough."

"Why, in the midst of all the holocaust and disasters and judgment, why don't people believe? Why will people still be in unbelief? Why, when salvation has been offered and judgment has been tasted? Why? And the answer is the same answer that Jesus gave in John 3, 'For God so loved the world that He gave His only begotten Son, that whosoever believes in Him should not perish but have eternal life; for God did not send the Son into the world to judge the world, but that the world should be saved through Him. He who believes in Him is not

judged; he who does not believe has been judged already because he's not believed in the name of the only begotten Son of God.'

Why? 'And this is the judgment: that light has come into the world, and men loved darkness rather than light, for their deeds were evil.' They love sin. They love it. Even through the Tribulation they love it. They love it. The prophet of old asked, 'Why will you die?' Ezekiel 33, 'Why will you die? Turn ye, turn ye; why will you die?' 'I have no pleasure'...He writes... 'in the death of the wicked.' 'Why will you die?' But they will. And they do.

God's provision in Jesus Christ is so that we need not die in our sins, right? And we don't need to suffer this horrible fate and a worst fate, eternal hell. Why will you die? Why, Jesus said, will you not come to Me that you might have life? The answer...Men love darkness because their deeds are evil, they love their sin, but their sin damns them.

We're here at this very table because by God's grace we've turned from sin. We will not die, will we? I don't want to die and go to hell, I don't want to die in my sins and never be able to go where Jesus is; I don't want to suffer a fate like that described in the seventh seal. And there's no need to. God offers in the grace of Christ deliverance, salvation, rescue, hope for all who receive His Son. And here we are as Christians who know and love the Lord Jesus Christ, and we read all of this, we have no fear, do we? We have no fear; this isn't for us. This isn't for us because we have been redeemed by God's grace. We take no credit for that. We put out the humble hand of a beggar and received a gift.

It is tragic beyond all description that the world will die in its sins and reject and reject...they rejected Jesus when He came, they reject His gospel now, they'll reject when they taste the furies of final judgment, because they love their sin. And I'm so thankful, aren't you, for the grace of God that reached out to you and to me and called us away from our sin. Because of that we have no fear of these things. Because of that our hearts grieve for the lost, but rejoice for what shall belong to Christ, and in Him to us."

"Harry Randall Truman was the caretaker of a recreation lodge on Spirit Lake, five miles north of Mt. St. Helens' smoke-enshrouded peak, in Washington. Harry had been warned by rangers and neighbors that the mountain was going to blow up. Geologists had been watching their seismographs for some time, and the *evidence predicted that the volcano would soon explode with such a fury that it would flatten the surrounding forest.*

Warnings blared from loudspeakers on patrol cars and helicopters and blinked from battery-powered signs at every major crossroad. Radio and television announcers pled with their audiences to flee to safety. Harry Truman ignored them all. He grinned on national television and said, 'Nobody knows more about this mountain than Harry, and it don't dare blow up on him.'

On May 18, 1980, at 8:31 A.M., the mountain exploded. I cannot help wondering if Harry regretted his decision, in the millisecond he had before the concussive waves, traveling faster than the speed of sound, flattened him and everything else for 150 square miles. Did he have time to mourn his stubbornness as millions of tons of rock disintegrated and disappeared into a cloud reaching ten miles into the sky? Did he have second thoughts as the wall of mud and ash 50 feet high buried his cabin, his cats, and his freshly mowed lawn, or had he been vaporized when the mountain erupted with a force 500 times greater than the nuclear bomb that had leveled Hiroshima, Japan, in 1945? There is even a song about old Harry, the stubborn man who put his ear to the mountain but would not heed the warnings.

The question that faces you the reader today is this: 'How do you stand in relation to the Lamb who breaks the seals?' Are you a Christian? Then you will be kept from 'the hour' of tribulation (Rev.3:10). Our Lord's counsel to you is, 'Be on the alert' (Matt.25:13) and 'Abide in Me' (John 15:4). Keep yourself in fellowship with Him. Be thankful that judgment for you is passed. No divine wrath remains for you.

Are you not a Christian? There is only one way to escape the judgment of the Lamb who breaks the seals. Trust in His death."[6]

In other words, get saved, and get saved now before it's too late! If you're honest, this book, *The Seals*, has been sad, not to mention shocking, to read. But the good news is, it doesn't have to end that way *for you*. Don't be like Harry. Don't scoff and mock, and in your prideful bravado *seal your own utter doom*. Take to heart the things written in this book, *The Seals*, and let it *seal another fate for you*. Receive Jesus Christ as your Lord and Savior *right now*. Call upon His Name and ask Him to forgive of all your sins and believe in your heart that God raised Him from the grave, and the Bible says you will be saved.

Not only from the 7-year Tribulation, but even hell itself. Please, I beg you, *seal it in your heart now* before it's too late! The Rapture could happen at any moment. You don't want to be left behind to face the worst time in the history of mankind. Listen to Jesus! An explosion way worse than any Mount St. Helens eruption really is coming to the whole planet earth and you really don't want to be here! Take the way out *now* through Jesus *the Lamb*. This is the timely message of *The Seals*.

How to Receive Jesus Christ:

1. Admit your need (I am a sinner).

2. Be willing to turn from your sins (repent).

3. Believe that Jesus Christ died for you on the Cross and rose from the grave.

4. Through prayer, invite Jesus Christ to come in and control your life through the Holy Spirit. (Receive Him as Lord and Savior.)

What to pray:

Dear Lord Jesus,

I know that I am a sinner and need Your forgiveness. I believe that You died for my sins. I want to turn from my sins. I now invite You to come into my heart and life. I want to trust and follow You as Lord and Savior.

In Jesus' name. Amen.

Notes

Chapter One *After the Rapture*

1. *Depiction of the Planet After the Rapture*
   (http://raptureready.com/soap2/cameron46.html)
2. *Quote The 7-year Tribulation is not for the Church*
   (http://www.gty.org/resources/print/sermons/66-24)
3. *Reasons Why the Church is not in the 7-year Tribulation*
   Billy Crone, *The Rapture: Don't Be Deceived*,
   (Las Vegas: Get A Life Ministries Publications, 2016)
4. *The Reaction of Church-Goers Left Behind After the Rapture*
   (http://www.studylight.org/commentaries/isn/revelation-6.html?print=yes)

Chapter Two *The Blessing of the Seals*

1. *Quote Revelation is an Early Edition of Future Events*
   (https://bible.org/seriespage/15-buckle-your-seatbelts-revelation-61-17)
2. *Quote Track Record of Psychics & Mediums*
   (http://www.sjrdesign.net/2012_PsychicPredictions.pdf)
3. *Quote Statistics of People Who Go to Psychics & Mediums*
   (http://www.americanfederationofcertifiedpsychicsandmediums.org/statistics.htm)
4. *Quote The Benefits of Studying the 7-year Tribulation*
   (https://bible.org/seriespage/15-buckle-your-seatbelts-revelation-61-17)

Chapter Three *The Prelude to the Seals*

1. *Biblical Proof of the Identity of the 24 Elders*
   Billy Crone, *The Rapture: Don't Be Deceived*,
   (Las Vegas: Get A Life Ministries Publications, Pgs.74-80, 2016)

2. *Quote God Going to War with the Planet*
   (http://www.gty.org/resources/print/sermons/80-202)
   (http://www.gty.org/resources/print/sermons/66-21)
3. *Biblical Proof of God's Wrath During Entire 7-year Tribulation*
   Billy Crone, *The Rapture: Don't Be Deceived,*
   (Las Vegas: Get A Life Ministries Publications, 2016)
4. *Quote The Purpose and Ownership of the Scroll*
   (http://www.gty.org/resources/print/sermons/80-202)
5. *Quote Only Jesus is Worthy to Open the Scroll*
   (http://www.gty.org/resources/print/sermons/80-202)
6. *Tears are Out of Place Over the Scroll*
   (http://www.gty.org/resources/print/sermons/66-20)
   (http://www.gty.org/resources/print/sermons/66-22)

Chapter Four *The Timing of the Seals*

1. *Comparison Chart of Matthew 24 & Revelation Chapter Six*
   Billy Crone, *The Rapture: Don't Be Deceived,*
   (Las Vegas: Get A Life Ministries Publications, Pg.64, 2016)
2. *Quote The Synoptic Gospels & the Day of the Lord*
   (http://www.biblestudytools.com/commentaries/revelation/revelation-6/revelation-6-1.html)
3. *Quote The Separation of the Church from Revelation Chapter Six*
   (http://threemagination.com/oyb/?d=12/15)
   (http://www.biblestudytools.com/commentaries/revelation/revelation-6/revelation-6-1.html)

Chapter Five *The Breaking of the Antichrist Seal*

1. *Quote The Meaning of the Word Revelation*
   (http://www.gty.org/resources/sermons/66-1/back-to-the-future-part-1)
2. *Quote The Lamb Institutes the Seals*
   (http://threemagination.com/oyb/?d=12/15#new)
3. *Quote The Purpose of the 7-year Tribulation*
   (https://bible.org/book/export/html/3734)
4. *Quote Why Are There Seven Seals?*

(http://www.gty.org/resources/print/sermons/66-23)

5. *Quote The Action Begins in Revelation 6*
   (http://www.wacriswell.org/PrintTranscript.cfm/SID/1654.cfm)
6. *Quote The Identity of the Living Creatures*
   (http://www.gty.org/resources/sermons/66-18/a-trip-to-heaven-part-3)
7. *Quote the Old Testament Usage of Thunder*
   (http://www.biblestudytools.com/concordances/naves-topical-bible/thunder.html)
8. *Quote God's Voice in the Thunder*
   (https://the-end-time.blogspot.com/2011/03/language-of-god-thunder.html)
9. *Quote Mankind Should Be Afraid of God's Judgments*
   (http://www.gty.org/resources/sermons/66-18/a-trip-to-heaven-part-3)
10. *Quote Jesus is Sovereign Over the Judgments in the 7-year Tribulation*
    (https://bible.org/seriespage/15-buckle-your-seatbelts-revelation-61-17)
    (http://www.biblestudytools.com/commentaries/revelation/revelation-6/revelation-6-1.html)
    (http://www.wacriswell.org/PrintTranscript.cfm/SID/1654.cfm)
11. *Quote The Object of the First Seal is the Antichrist*
    (https://www.studylight.org/commentaries/dcc/revelation-6.html)
    (http://www.wacriswell.org/PrintTranscript.cfm/SID/1654.cfm)
12. *Quote The Antichrist Feigns Righteousness & Purity*
    (http://www.gty.org/resources/sermons/53-7/the-coming-man-of-sin-part-1)
    (https://bible.org/seriespage/15-buckle-your-seatbelts-revelation-61-17)
13. *Quote The Roman Triumphal Procession*
    (https://en.wikipedia.org/wiki/Roman_triumph)
    (http://www.ancient.eu/Roman_Triumph/)
    (https://en.wikipedia.org/wiki/List_of_Roman_deities)
    (https://www.google.com/search?q=fasces&ie=&oe=)
14. *Quote The Antichrist is the White Horse Rider*
    (http://www.wacriswell.org/PrintTranscript.cfm/SID/1654.cfm)
    (https://bible.org/seriespage/15-buckle-your-seatbelts-revelation-61-17)
15. *Quote The Historic Purposes of Horses in War*
    (https://en.wikipedia.org/wiki/Horses_in_warfare)
    (https://en.wikipedia.org/wiki/Military_animal)
    (https://en.wikipedia.org/wiki/Destrier)
    (https://en.wikipedia.org/wiki/Horses_in_the_Middle_Ages#Horses_in_warfare)
16. *Quote Why the Rider on the White Horse is the Antichrist*
    (http://www.soniclight.com/constable/notes/htm/NT/Revelation/Revelation

.htm)
(https://bible.org/seriespage/15-buckle-your-seatbelts-revelation-61-17)
(http://www.revelationunderstoodcommentary.com/beginning-of-
sorrows.html)
(https://www.raptureready.com/featured/gillette/revsix.html)
(http://www.wacriswell.org/PrintTranscript.cfm/SID/1654.cfm)
(http://www.biblestudytools.com/commentaries/revelation/revelation-
6/revelation-6-2.html)
(https://www.gci.org/bible/rev/sixseals)
17. *Quote The Antichrist Riding Upon the World Scene*
(http://www.wacriswell.org/PrintTranscript.cfm/SID/1654.cfm)
18. *Quote People Saying the Bow Represents a Peaceful Coup*
(http://www.gty.org/resources/sermons/66-23/the-coming-of-world-peace)
(https://www.gty.org/resources/sermons/66-24/The-Beginning-of-the-End)
(http://www.revelationunderstoodcommentary.com/beginning-of-sorrows
.html)
19. *Quote People Saying the Bow Represents War & Conquest*
(https://bible.org/seriespage/15-buckle-your-seatbelts-revelation-61-17)
(https://www.gci.org/bible/rev/sixseals)
20. *Quote The Antichrist Ushering in a False Peace*
(https://bible.org/seriespage/15-buckle-your-seatbelts-revelation-61-17)
(http://www.gty.org/resources/sermons/66-23/the-coming-of-world-peace)
(https://www.raptureready.com/featured/gillette/revsix.html)
21. *Quote The Different Meanings of the Word Crown*
(http://www.gty.org/resources/sermons/66-23/the-coming-of-world-peace)
22. *Quote Permission to be Given for Roman Triumphal Processions*
(https://en.wikipedia.org/wiki/Roman_triumph)
23. *Quote The World Crowns the Antichrist*
(http://www.gty.org/resources/sermons/66-23/the-coming-of-world-peace)
24. *Quote Jesus Does Not Get His Authority from satan*
(http://www.revelationunderstoodcommentary.com/beginning-of-
sorrows.html)
25. *Quote God is in Total Control of 7-year Tribulation Judgments*
(https://www.studylight.org/commentaries/dcc/revelation-6.html?print=yes)
http://www.biblestudytools.com/commentaries/revelation/revelation-
6/revelation-6-2.html)
26. *Quote The Parthians Conquered Rome*
(http://www.soniclight.com/constable/notes/htm/NT/Revelation/Revelation
.htm)

27. *Quote The World has No Excuse Concerning Antichrist Deception*
(http://www.biblestudytools.com/commentaries/revelation/revelation-6/revelation-6-2.html)
(http://www.wacriswell.org/PrintTranscript.cfm/SID/1654.cfm)
28. *Quote The Reminder During the Roman Triumphal Procession*
(https://www.ancient.eu/Roman_Triumph/)
29. *Quote God is Still in Control of the Antichrist's Behavior*
(http://www.biblestudytools.com/commentaries/revelation/revelation-6/revelation-6-2.html)
30. *Quote Mankind Getting Ready to Receive Antichrist's Deception*
(https://archive.org/stream/66-Revelation/66-REVELATION_djvu.txt)

Chapter Six   *The Breaking of the War Seal*

1. *Quote False Prophets Preaching False Peace & Safety*
(https://www.gty.org/library/sermons-library/52-20/the-day-of-the-lord-part-2)
2. *Quote The Unending Wars of the Antichrist in the 7-year Tribulation*
(https://www.gty.org/library/sermons-library/66-24/the-beginning-of-the-end)
3. *The Various Meanings of the Color Red*
(http://www.itsaboutworship.com/symbolism-of-colors/)
(http://www.ucl.ac.uk/museums-static/objectretrieval/node/277)
4. *The Roman Meanings of the Color Red*
(https://en.wikipedia.org/wiki/Red)
5. *Quotes The Global Slaughter Coming from the Red Horse Rider*
(http://www.plymouthbrethren.org/article/5715)
(http://www.revelationunderstoodcommentary.com/beginning-of-sorrows.html)
(http://www.calvarybible.com/notes/Revelation/Rev%206.3-8.pdf)
6. *Quote World Leaders Promising Peace When War is Looming on Horizon*
(http://www.biblestudytools.com/commentaries/revelation/revelation-6/revelation-6-4.html)
7. *Quotes How Bloody it Will Be When Men Slay Each Other*
(http://www.plymouthbrethren.org/article/5715)
(https://soundfaith.com/sermons/37170-16-opening-of-the-seals)
(http://www.biblestudytools.com/commentaries/revelation/revelation-6/revelation-6-4.html)

(https://www.gty.org/library/print/sermons/66-24)
(https://www.wacriswell.com/PrintTranscript.cfm/SID/1654.cfm)
8. *Quote The World Has Gone Mad in the Second Seal*
(http://www.biblestudytools.com/commentaries/revelation/revelation-6/revelation-6-4.html)
9. *Quote The Differences Between Roman Swords*
(https://www.wacriswell.com/index.cfm/FuseAction/Search.Transcripts/sermon/1654.cfm)
(https://www.gty.org/library/print/sermons/66-24)
10. *Quote God Gives the Planet Over to War*
(https://bible.org/seriespage/15-buckle-your-seatbelts-revelation-61-17)

Chapter Seven *The Breaking of the Famine Seal*

1. *Quote Global War Produces Global Famine*
(https://www.gty.org/library/print/sermons/66-24)
2. *Quote The Different Secular & Historic Uses of the Color Black*
(https://en.wikipedia.org/wiki/Black)
3. *Quote What the Weighing of the Scales Mean in the Third Seal*
(https://bible.org/seriespage/15-buckle-your-seatbelts-revelation-61-17)
(https://www.gci.org/bible/rev/sixseals)
4. *Various Pictures Depicting Famines in Recent History*
(https://en.wikipedia.org/wiki/Famine)
(https://en.wikipedia.org/wiki/List_of_famines)
(http://www.dhakatribune.com/world/africa/2017/02/20/south-sudan-suffering-man-made-famine/)
5. *Quote The Voice in the Third Seal is from God*
(https://www.gty.org/library/print/sermons/66-24)
6. *List of Famines Mentioned in the Bible*
(http://www.believersweb.org/view.cfm?ID=1068)
7. *Quote How Wrong We are to Think that God Won't Judge*
(https://bible.org/book/export/html/3734)
8. *Quote Actual Accounts of the Leningrad Famine*
(http://www.dailymail.co.uk/home/books/article-2032706/BEYOND-HORROR-They-ate-cats-sawdust-wallpaper-paste--babies-Leningrads-agony-Nazis-tried-starve-submission-LENINGRAD-TRAGEDY-OF-A-CITY-UNDER-SIEGE-1941-44-BY-ANNA-REID.html)
9. *Quotes What Does the Wheat & Barley & Quarts Mean in the Third Seal*

(https://www.gci.org/bible/rev/sixseals)
(http://www.biblestudytools.com/commentaries/revelation/revelation-6/revelation-6-6.html)
(http://www.soniclight.com/constable/notes/htm/NT/Revelation/Revelation.htm?viewType=Print&viewClass=Print)
(http://www.raptureready.us/featured/gillette/paving.html)
(https://www.gty.org/library/print/sermons/66-24)

10. *Quotes What Does a Days Wages Mean in the Third Seal*
(https://soundfaith.com/sermons/37170-16-opening-of-the-seals)
(https://www.gci.org/bible/rev/sixseals)
(http://www.biblestudytools.com/commentaries/revelation/revelation-6/revelation-6-6.html)
(https://www.raystedman.org/new-testament/revelation/four-terrible-horsemen)

11. *Quote People Working for Food During the Leningrad Famine*
(https://en.wikipedia.org/wiki/Siege_of_Leningrad#Cannibalism)

12. *Quotes What Does the Oil & Wine Mean in the Third Seal*
(http://www.soniclight.com/constable/notes/htm/NT/Revelation/Revelation.htm?viewType=Print&viewClass=Print)
(http://www.studylight.org/commentaries/dcc/revelation-6.html5?print=yes)
(http://www.biblestudytools.com/commentaries/revelation/revelation-6/revelation-6-6.html)
(https://bible.org/seriespage/12-six-seals-61-17)
(http://www.bibletools.org/index.cfm/fuseaction/Bible.show/sVerseID/30800/eVerseID/30800/)

13. *Quote Riches Become a Curse in the 7-year Tribulation*
(http://www.revelationunderstoodcommentary.com/beginning-of-sorrows.html)

14. *Quote the Rotten Future for the Wealthy in the Third Seal*
(http://threemagination.com/oyb/?d=12/15)
(https://bible.org/book/export/html/3734)

15. *Quote The Effects of The Great China Famine*
(https://www.theguardian.com/world/2013/jan/01/china-great-famine-book-tombstone)

Chapter Eight *The Breaking of the Death Seal*

1. *Quote No One Will Escape the Effects of the Fourth Seal*
   (http://www.biblestudytools.com/commentaries/revelation/revelation-6/revelation-6-8.html)
2. *Quote What the Color of the Pale Horse Means*
   (https://bible.org/seriespage/15-buckle-your-seatbelts-revelation-61-17)
3. *Quote The Stages of Death*
   (https://en.wikipedia.org/wiki/Pallor_mortis)
4. *Quote The Historical Usage of Thanatos*
   (https://en.wikipedia.org/wiki/Thanatos)
   (https://en.wikipedia.org/wiki/Mors_(mythology))
5. *Quote What the Hebrew Idiom to Kill with Death Means*
   (http://www.revelationunderstoodcommentary.com/beginning-of-sorrows.html)
6. *Quote The Grave Digger is Coming*
   (https://www.gty.org/library/print/sermons/66-24)
7. *Quote The Historical Usage of Hades*
   (https://en.wikipedia.org/wiki/Hades)
   (https://en.wikipedia.org/wiki/Greek_underworld#Hades)
8. *Quote The Meaning of Hades Riding with Death*
   (https://www.gci.org/bible/rev/sixseals)
   (http://www.studylight.org/commentaries/dcc/revelation-6.html5?print=yes)
   (http://www.biblestudytools.com/commentaries/revelation/revelation-6/revelation-6-8.html)
   (https://bible.org/seriespage/15-buckle-your-seatbelts-revelation-61-17)
9. *Quote God is the One Who Give Death & Hades Their Power*
   (https://www.gty.org/library/print/sermons/66-24)
   (https://www.gci.org/bible/rev/sixseals)
10. *Quote Only Jesus Can Save You from Death & Hades*
    (https://www.gci.org/bible/rev/sixseals)
    (http://www.biblestudytools.com/commentaries/revelation/revelation-6/revelation-6-8.html)
11. *Quote the Total Deaths Caused by Political Wars Over the Last 100 Years*
    (http://www.forcingchange.org/under_war's_bloody_banner)
12. *Quote The Staggering Death Toll of the Fourth Seal*
    (http://www.biblestudytools.com/commentaries/revelation/revelation-6/revelation-6-8.html)
    (https://bible.org/seriespage/15-buckle-your-seatbelts-revelation-61-17)
    (http://www.revelationunderstoodcommentary.com/beginning-of-sorrows.html)

13. *Quote Death by Plague is Frightening*
    (http://www.biblestudytools.com/commentaries/revelation/revelation-6/revelation-6-7.html)
    (http://www.biblestudytools.com/commentaries/revelation/revelation-6/revelation-6-8.html)
14. *Quote Ten of the Worst Plagues in History*
    (http://listverse.com/2009/01/18/top-10-worst-plagues-in-history/)
    (https://www.ncbi.nlm.nih.gov/pubmed/19787658)
15. *Quote The Great Influenza Outbreak*
    (http://www.cnn.com/books/beginnings/9911/flu/)
16. *Quote Plagues Cause More Deaths than Wars*
    (http://www.biblestudytools.com/commentaries/revelation/revelation-6/revelation-6-8.html)
    (https://soundfaith.com/sermons/37170-16-opening-of-the-seals)
17. *Quote Plagues Could Also Come from Germ Warfare*
    (https://soundfaith.com/sermons/37170-16-opening-of-the-seals)
18. *Quote Different Chemical Weapons Used in Warfare*
    (http://www.stufftoblowyourmind.com/blogs/10-scariest-chemical-weapons.htm/printable)
19. *Quote The Pale Horse Color Comes from Chlorine*
    (https://www.gci.org/bible/rev/sixseals)
20. *Quote The Use of Chemical Weapons in the Fourth Seal*
    (https://www.gty.org/library/sermons-library/66-24/The-Beginning-of-the-End)
21. *Quote God Reverses the Roles of Man & Animals in the Fourth Seal*
    (https://bible.org/seriespage/15-buckle-your-seatbelts-revelation-61-17)
    (http://www.biblestudytools.com/commentaries/revelation/revelation-6/revelation-6-8.html)
22. *Quote Various Historical Examples of Man-Eating Animals*
    (http://listverse.com/2010/10/16/top-10-worst-man-eaters-in-history/)
23. *Quote Rats Could Be the Wild Beasts in the Fourth Seal*
    (https://www.gty.org/library/sermons-library/66-24/The-Beginning-of-the-End)
24. *Quote The Number of Zoos Worldwide*
    (http://news.nationalgeographic.com/news/2003/11/1113_031113_zoorole.html)
25. *Quote Current Article of Animals Escaping from Zoo*
    (http://www.nbcnews.com/news/world/lions-tigers-loose-tbilisi-georgia-after-flooding-destroys-zoo-enclosures-n375066)

26. *Quote Final Plea to Escape the 7-year Tribulation Through Jesus*
(https://www.gty.org/library/sermons-library/66-24/The-Beginning-of-the-End)
27. *Quote The Worst is Yet to Come*
(http://www.soniclight.com/constable/notes/htm/NT/Revelation/Revelation.htm?viewType=Print&viewClass=Print)

Chapter Nine   *The Breaking of the Martyrdom Seal*

1. *Quote The Planet Begins to Disintegrate as the Fifth Seal is Opened*
(https://www.gty.org/library/sermons-library/2368/the-signs-of-christs-coming-part-3
2. *Quote Why the Church is Absent During the 7-year Tribulation*
Billy Crone, *The Rapture: Don't Be Deceived,*
(Las Vegas: Get A Life Ministries Publications, 2016)
3. *Quote The Difference Between the White Robes*
Billy Crone, *The Rapture: Don't Be Deceived,*
(Las Vegas: Get A Life Ministries Publications, Pgs. 79-80, 2016)
4. *Quote The Fifth Seal is Going to be a Global Slaughter*
(https://www.gty.org/library/sermons-library/66-25)
5. *Quote The Altar in the Fifth Seal is the Altar of Sacrifice*
(http://www.biblestudytools.com/commentaries/revelation/revelation-6/revelation-6-9.html)
(http://www.studylight.org/commentaries/dcc/revelation-6.html?print=yes)
(https://www.gci.org/bible/rev/sixseals)
(https://www.wacriswell.com/sermons/1962/the-martyr-s-seal/)
6. *Quote The Altar in the Fifth Seal is the Altar of Incense*
(https://www.gty.org/library/sermons-library/66-25)
(http://www.revelationunderstoodcommentary.com/beginning-of-sorrows.html)
7. *Quote We Don't Know Which Altar is the Fifth Seal Altar*
(https://www.gty.org/library/sermons-library/66-25)
8. *Quote You Don't Want to Be in the Fifth Seal*
(https://www.gty.org/library/sermons-library/2368/the-signs-of-christs-coming-part-3)
9. *Quote Why People Were Killed in the Fifth Seal*

(http://www.biblestudytools.com/commentaries/revelation/revelation-6/revelation-6-9.html)
(https://www.gci.org/bible/rev/sixseals)
(https://www.wacriswell.com/sermons/1962/the-martyr-s-seal/)
(https://www.gty.org/library/sermons-library/66-25)

10. *Quote Petition to John Kerry to Stop Christian Genocide*
(http://stopthechristiangenocide.org/en/index.html)
11. *Quote The Death of the Two Witnesses*
(https://www.gty.org/library/sermons-library/66-38/two-witnesses-part-3)
12. *Quote The Word Slain Refers to Animal Sacrifice*
(https://bible.org/seriespage/15-buckle-your-seatbelts-revelation-61-17)
13. *Quote The Definition of the Word Holocaust*
(https://en.wikipedia.org/wiki/The_Holocaust)
14. *Quote The Murderous Events of the Jewish Holocaust*
(https://en.wikipedia.org/wiki/The_Holocaust)
15. *Quote God's Vengeance in the Fifth Seal*
(http://www.studylight.org/commentaries/dcc/revelation-6.html?print=yes)
(http://www.biblestudytools.com/commentaries/revelation/revelation-6/revelation-6-10.html)
(https://www.gty.org/library/sermons-library/66-25/gods-great-day-of-wrath?term=Father)
16. *Quote God Give the Tribulation Martyrs a White Robe*
(https://www.gty.org/library/sermons-library/66-25/Gods-Great-Day-of-Wrath)
17. *Quote The Question How Long from the Tribulation Martyrs*
(https://www.wacriswell.com/sermons/1962/the-martyr-s-seal/)
18. *Quote God Patiently Rescues People in the 7-year Tribulation*
(http://www.biblestudytools.com/commentaries/revelation/revelation-6/revelation-6-11.html)
19. *Quote Things Are About to Get Even Worse After the Fifth Seal*
(https://www.gty.org/library/sermons-library/66-25/Gods-Great-Day-of-Wrath)

Chapter Ten   *The Breaking of the Doomsday Seal*

1. *Quote The Greek Verb Has Come in the Sixth Seal*
(http://www.raptureready.com/robert-van-kampen/)

2. *Quote The Sixth Seal & the Day of the Lord*
   (http://www.biblestudytools.com/commentaries/revelation/revelation-6/revelation-6-12.html)
3. *Quote Jesus Radically Alters Creation in the Sixth Seal*
   (https://bible.org/seriespage/15-buckle-your-seatbelts-revelation-61-17)
4. *Quote The Sixth Seal Being Called Scared to Death*
   (https://www.gty.org/library/print/sermons-library/66-26)
5. *Quote God Beats Planet Earth in the Sixth Seal*
   (https://www.gty.org/library/print/sermons-library/66-26)
6. *Quote List of Worst Earthquakes*
   (http://www.nbcnews.com/id/42029974/ns/world_news-asia_pacific/t/top-deadliest-earthquakes-history/#.WScwwGjytPY)
7. *Quote Jesus Rocks the World in the Sixth Seal*
   (https://bible.org/seriespage/15-buckle-your-seatbelts-revelation-61-17)
8. *Quote The Prophesied Earthquakes in the Bible*
   (http://www.biblestudytools.com/commentaries/revelation/revelation-6/revelation-6-12.html)
   (https://www.gci.org/bible/rev/sixseals)
9. *Quote List of Worst Tsunamis & Land Slides*
   (http://www.australiangeographic.com.au/topics/science-environment/2011/03/the-10-most-destructive-tsunamis-in-history/)
   (http://landslides4791.weebly.com/top-10-worst-landslides-ever.html)
   (http://www.ngdc.noaa.gov/seg/hazard/stratoguide/nevadostory.html)
   (http://www.geology.sdsu.edu/how_volcanoes_work/Nevado.html)
10. *Quote The Whole Universe Shakes in the Sixth Seal*
    (https://www.gty.org/library/print/sermons-library/66-26)
11. *Quote What is Sackcloth*
    (https://www.gty.org/library/print/sermons-library/66-26)
12. *Quote Blackness Speaks of God's Judgment*
    (https://www.gty.org/library/print/sermons-library/66-26)
13. *Quote Sackcloth Speaks of Mourning Repentance & Judgment*
    (https://www.gotquestions.org/sackcloth-and-ashes.html)
14. *Quote What Causes the Sun to Turn Black*
    (https://www.gty.org/library/print/sermons-library/66-26)
    (https://bible.org/seriespage/15-buckle-your-seatbelts-revelation-61-17)
15. *Quote What Causes the Moon to Turn Blood Red*
    (https://bible.org/book/export/html/3734)
    (https://www.gty.org/library/sermons-library/66-26)
16. *Quote List of Worst Volcanic Eruptions*

(http://www.heritagedaily.com/2014/08/top-10-deadliest-volcanic-eruptions/104313)
17. *Quote Super Volcanoes & the Sixth Seal*
Billy Crone, The Final Countdown Vol.1,
(Las Vegas: Get A Life Ministries Publications, Pgs.130-136, 2016)
(https://www2.usgs.gov/faq/categories/9819/2693%20)
18. *Quote the Size of Stars*
(http://www.schoolsobservatory.org.uk/learn/astro/stars/class/starsize)
(http://www.suntrek.org/sun-as-a-star/sun-and-earth/comparing-size-sun-and-earth.shtml)
19. *Quote What Does the Word Star Mean in the Sixth Seal*
(https://bible.org/book/export/html/3734)
(http://www.biblestudytools.com/commentaries/revelation/revelation-6/revelation-6-13.html)
20. *Quote The Properties of Late Figs*
(http://biblehub.com/commentaries/revelation/6-13.htm)
21. *Quote List of Past & Possible Future Asteroid Impacts*
(http://io9.gizmodo.com/5018346/10-scariest-asteroid-attacks-on-earth-the-near-hits-and-approaching-terrors)
22. *Quote The Effects of an Asteroid Impact on Planet Earth*
Billy Crone, The Final Countdown Vol.1,
(Las Vegas: Get A Life Ministries Publications, Pgs.128-130, 2016)
23. *Quote List of Biggest Explosions*
(http://listverse.com/2011/11/28/top-10-biggest-explosions/)
(http://www.army-technology.com/features/featurethe-biggest-and-most-powerful-nuclear-weapons-ever-built-4206787/)
24. *Quote The Effects of an Asteroid Impact on a Populous Area*
(https://medium.com/starts-with-a-bang/this-is-what-would-happen-if-an-asteroid-hit-new-york-4b804f2bbc11)
(http://www.insurancequotes.com/home/near-earth-close-calls-cosmos)
25. *Quote Chicken Little's Fear is Manifested in the Sixth Seal*
(https://www.gty.org/library/print/sermons-library/66-26)
26. *Quote The Message of the Sky Splitting Apart in the Sixth Seal*
(http://www.biblestudytools.com/commentaries/revelation/revelation-6/revelation-6-13.html)
27. *Quote The Meaning of the Sky Splitting Apart in the Sixth Seal*
(http://www.biblestudytools.com/commentaries/revelation/revelation-6/revelation-6-14.html)
(http://www.studylight.org/commentaries/dcc/revelation-6.html?print=yes)

(https://bible.org/book/export/html/3734)
28. *Quote What Shape the Earth Will Be in After the Sixth Seal*
(http://www.biblestudytools.com/commentaries/revelation/revelation-6/revelation-6-14.html)
(https://www.gty.org/library/sermons-library/66-26)
29. *Quote Why God's Wrath is Necessary*
(https://bible.org/seriespage/15-buckle-your-seatbelts-revelation-61-17)
30. *Quote Having a Healthy Fear of God*
(https://www.gty.org/library/print/sermons-library/66-26)
(https://www.gty.org/library/sermons-library/66-27/Fear-of-the-Wrath-to-Come-Part-2)
31. *Quote The Global Crowd in the Sixth Seal*
(https://www.gty.org/library/sermons-library/66-27/Fear-of-the-Wrath-to-Come-Part-2)
(https://bible.org/seriespage/15-buckle-your-seatbelts-revelation-61-17)
(http://www.biblestudytools.com/commentaries/revelation/revelation-6/revelation-6-15.html)
32. *Quote People Die from Heart Attacks in the Sixth Seal*
(https://www.gty.org/library/sermons-library/66-27/Fear-of-the-Wrath-to-Come-Part-2)
(https://www.gty.org/library/print/sermons-library/66-26)
33. *Quote The Wrath of the Lamb is Not from Man*
(http://www.biblestudytools.com/commentaries/revelation/revelation-6/revelation-6-17.html)
34. *Quote The Sad Response to the Wrath of the Lamb*
(http://www.studylight.org/commentaries/dcc/revelation-6.html?print=yes)
(http://www.revelationunderstoodcommentary.com/beginning-of-sorrows.html)
(https://www.gci.org/bible/rev/sixseals)
(http://www.biblestudytools.com/commentaries/revelation/revelation-6/revelation-6-16.html)
35. *Quote Everyone Wants an Underground Bunker Today*
Billy Crone, The Final Countdown Vol.1,
(Las Vegas: Get A Life Ministries Publications, Pgs.125-126, 2016)
(http://www.newyorker.com/magazine/2017/01/30/doomsday-prep-for-the-super-rich)
(http://survival-mastery.com/diy/construct/how-to-build-a-bunker.html)
36. *Quote The Question Who Can Stand*

(http://www.biblestudytools.com/commentaries/revelation/revelation-6/revelation-6-17.html)
37. *Quote The Hardness of Man's Heart in the Sixth Seal*
(https://www.wacriswell.com/sermons/1962/in-the-day-of-his-wrath/)
(https://www.gty.org/library/sermons-library/66-27/fear-of-the-wrath-to-come-part-2)

Chapter Eleven *The Breaking of the Final Seal*

1. *Quote The Final Warning When God Orders the Seventh Seal*
(http://www.biblestudytools.com/commentaries/revelation/revelation-8/revelation-8-1.html)
(http://www.biblestudytools.com/commentaries/revelation/revelation-6/revelation-6-17.html)
2. *Quote Mankind Earns the Nightmare Coming in the Seventh Seal*
(https://archive.org/stream/66-Revelation/66-REVELATION_djvu.txt)
3. *Quote The Meaning of the Silence in Heaven*
(http://spartacus-educational.com/GERgwp.htm)
(https://bible.org/seriespage/17-worst-yet-come-revelation-81-13)
(https://www.biblegateway.com/resources/commentaries/IVP-NT/Rev/Opening-Seventh-Seal)
(https://www.blueletterbible.org/Comm/guzik_david/StudyGuide_Rev/Rev_8.cfm)
(https://bible.org/seriespage/17-worst-yet-come-revelation-81-13)
(https://www.blueletterbible.org/Comm/guzik_david/StudyGuide_Rev/Rev_8.cfm)
(http://www.revelationunderstoodcommentary.com/trumpet-judgments.html)
(https://archive.org/stream/66-Revelation/66-REVELATION_djvu.txt)
(https://www.wacriswell.com/sermons/1962/when-he-opened-the-seventh-seal1/)
4. *Quote The Message of the Place of Silence*
(https://bible.org/seriespage/17-worst-yet-come-revelation-81-13)
(http://www.biblestudytools.com/commentaries/revelation/revelation-8/revelation-8-1.html)
(http://www.studylight.org/commentaries/dcc/revelation-8.html?print=yes)
(https://www.wacriswell.com/sermons/1962/when-he-opened-the-seventh-seal1/)

(http://www.theoutlet.us/Rev.8.1-11.19.pdf)
(https://www.gty.org/library/sermons-library/66-31)
5. *Quote The Final Plea in the Seals for the Christian*
(https://www.gty.org/library/sermons-library/66-27/fear-of-the-wrath-to-come-part-2)
6. *Quote The Final Plea in the Seals for the Non-Christian*
(https://archive.org/stream/66-Revelation/66-REVELATION_djvu.txt)
(https://www.gty.org/library/sermons-library/66-31/the-seventh-seal?term=War%20and%20peaceWar%20and%20peace)
(https://bible.org/book/export/html/3734)